DRAGON DRIVE
VOLUME 1

The SHONEN JUMP Manga Edition

STORY AND ART BY
KEN-ICHI SAKURA

Translation/Lucy Craft, Corinne and Kohei Takada, Honyaku Center Inc.
English Adaptation/Ian Reid, Honyaku Center Inc.
Touch-up Art & Lettering/Jim Keefe
Design/Sam Elzway
Editor/Urian Brown

Editor in Chief, Books/Alvin Lu
Editor in Chief, Magazines/Marc Weidenbaum
VP of Publishing Licensing/Rika Inouye
VP of Sales/Gonzalo Ferreyra
Sr. VP of Marketing/Liza Coppola
Publisher/Hyoe Narita

Printed in the U.S.A.

Published by VIZ Media, LLC
P.O. Box 77010
San Francisco, CA 94107

SHONEN JUMP Manga Edition
10 9 8 7 6 5 4 3
First printing, April 2007
Third printing, August 2007

Th-

This is my first time!

Ken-ichi Sakura

I decided to write this card-game manga *Dragon Drive* in the year of the Dragon. I won't hide it; I was born in the year of the Dragon, too. It seems I am linked by fate with dragons so I will continue on the path of the soaring dragon and do my best!

Ken-ichi Sakura's manga debut was *Fabre Tanteiki*, which was published in a special edition of *Monthly Shonen Jump* in 2000. Serialization of *Dragon Drive* began in the March 2001 issue of *Monthly Shonen Jump* and the hugely successful series has inspired video games and an animated TV show. Sakura's latest title, *Kotokuri*, began running in the March 2006 issue of *Monthly Shonen Jump*. *Dragon Drive* and *Kotokuri* have both become tremendously popular in Japan because of Sakura's unique sense of humor and dynamic portrayal of feisty teen characters.

DRAGON DRIVE™

SHONEN JUMP MANGA EDITION

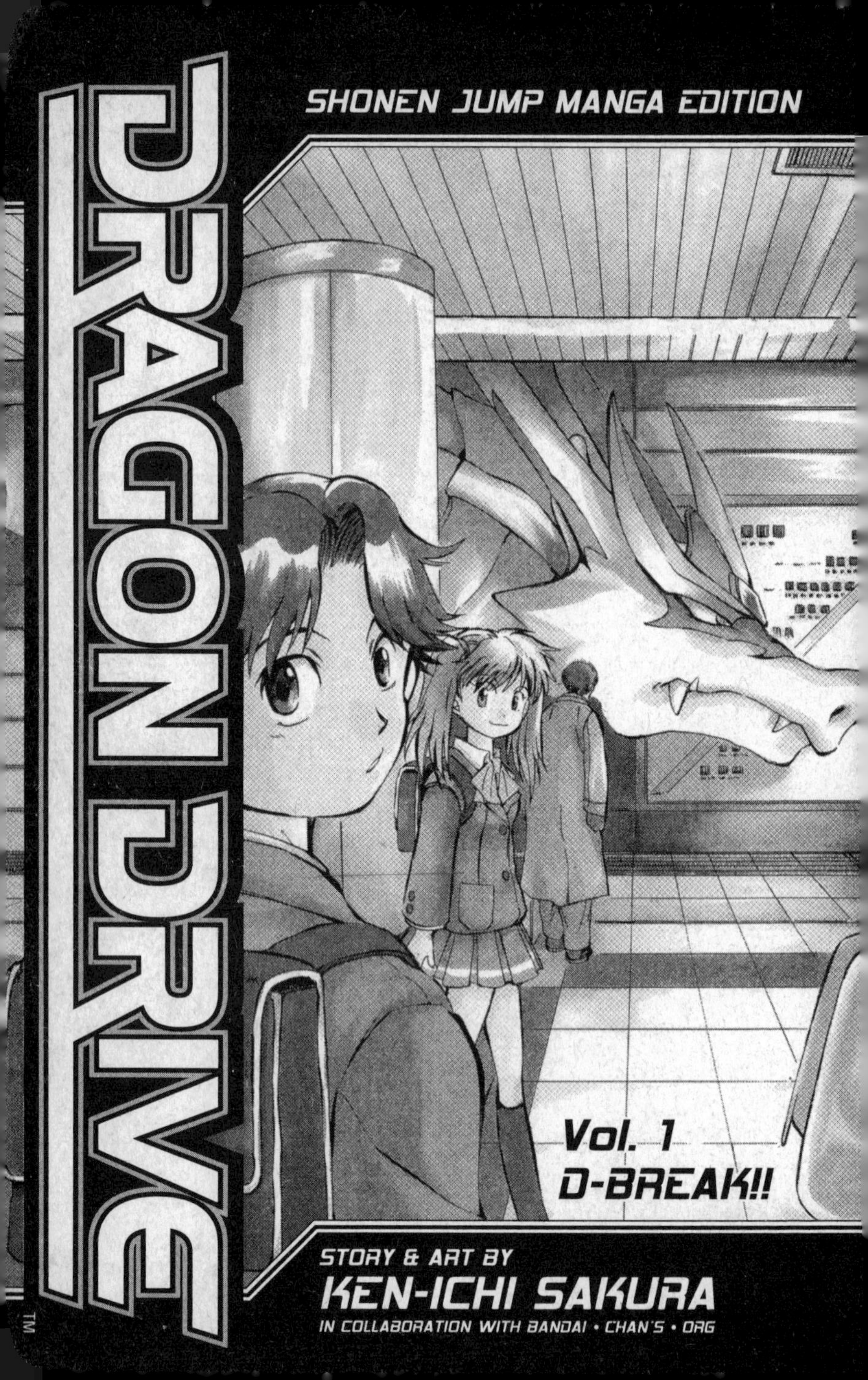

Vol. 1

D-BREAK!!

STORY & ART BY

KEN-ICHI SAKURA

IN COLLABORATION WITH BANDAI • CHAN'S • ORG

DRAGON DRIVE™

Vol. 1 D-BREAK!!

CONTENTS

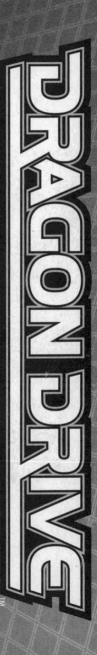

STAGE1 D–BREAK!!

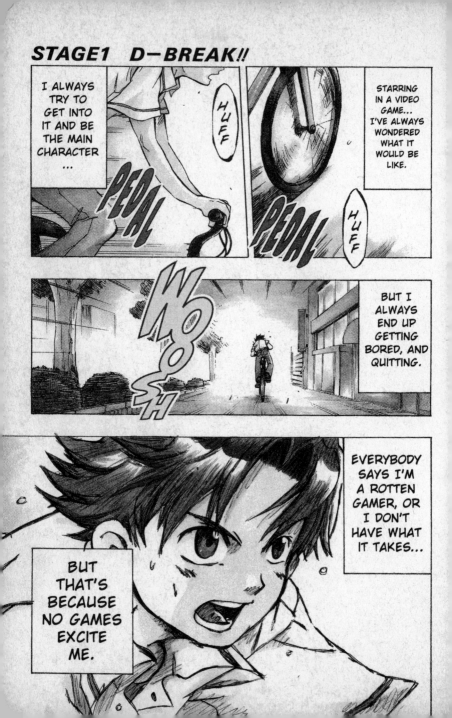

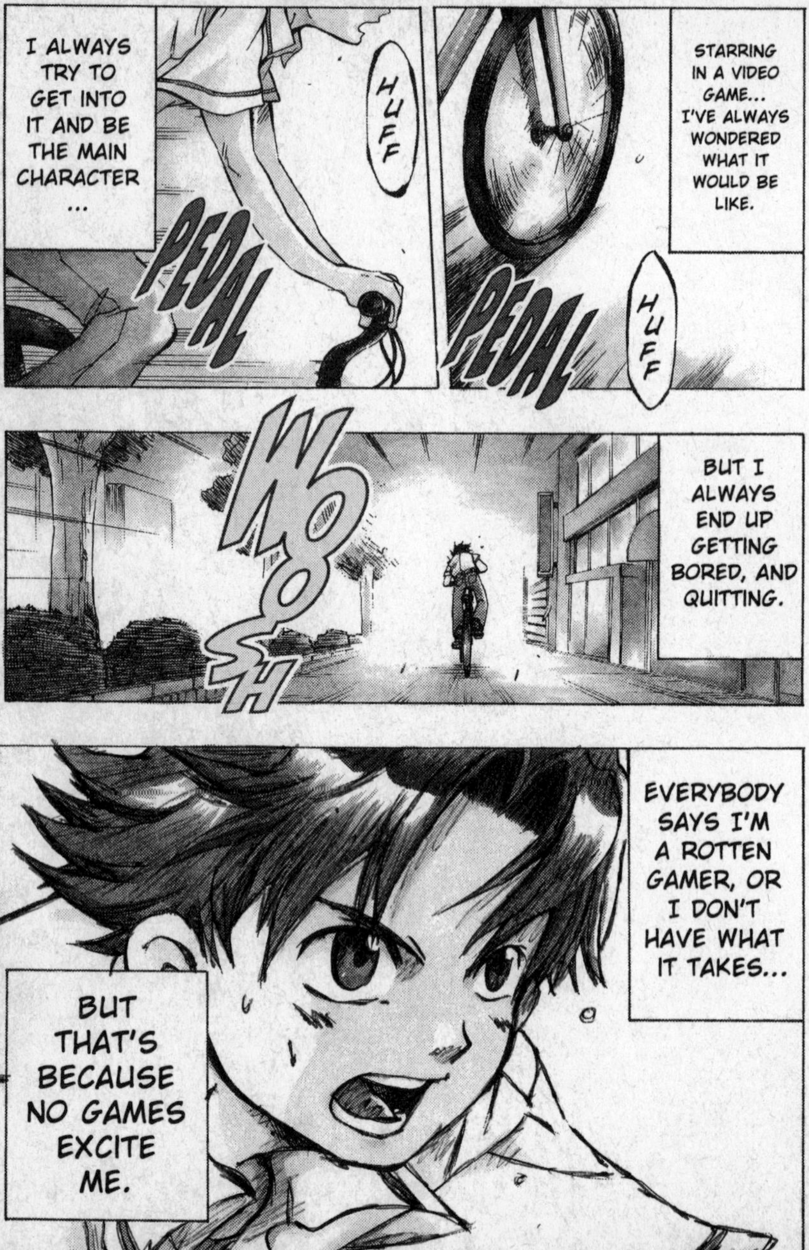
STARRING IN A VIDEO GAME... I'VE ALWAYS WONDERED WHAT IT WOULD BE LIKE.
HUFF
PEDAL
HUFF
I ALWAYS TRY TO GET INTO IT AND BE THE MAIN CHARACTER ...
PEDAL
BUT I ALWAYS END UP GETTING BORED, AND QUITTING.
WOOSH
EVERYBODY SAYS I'M A ROTTEN GAMER, OR I DON'T HAVE WHAT IT TAKES...
BUT THAT'S BECAUSE NO GAMES EXCITE ME.

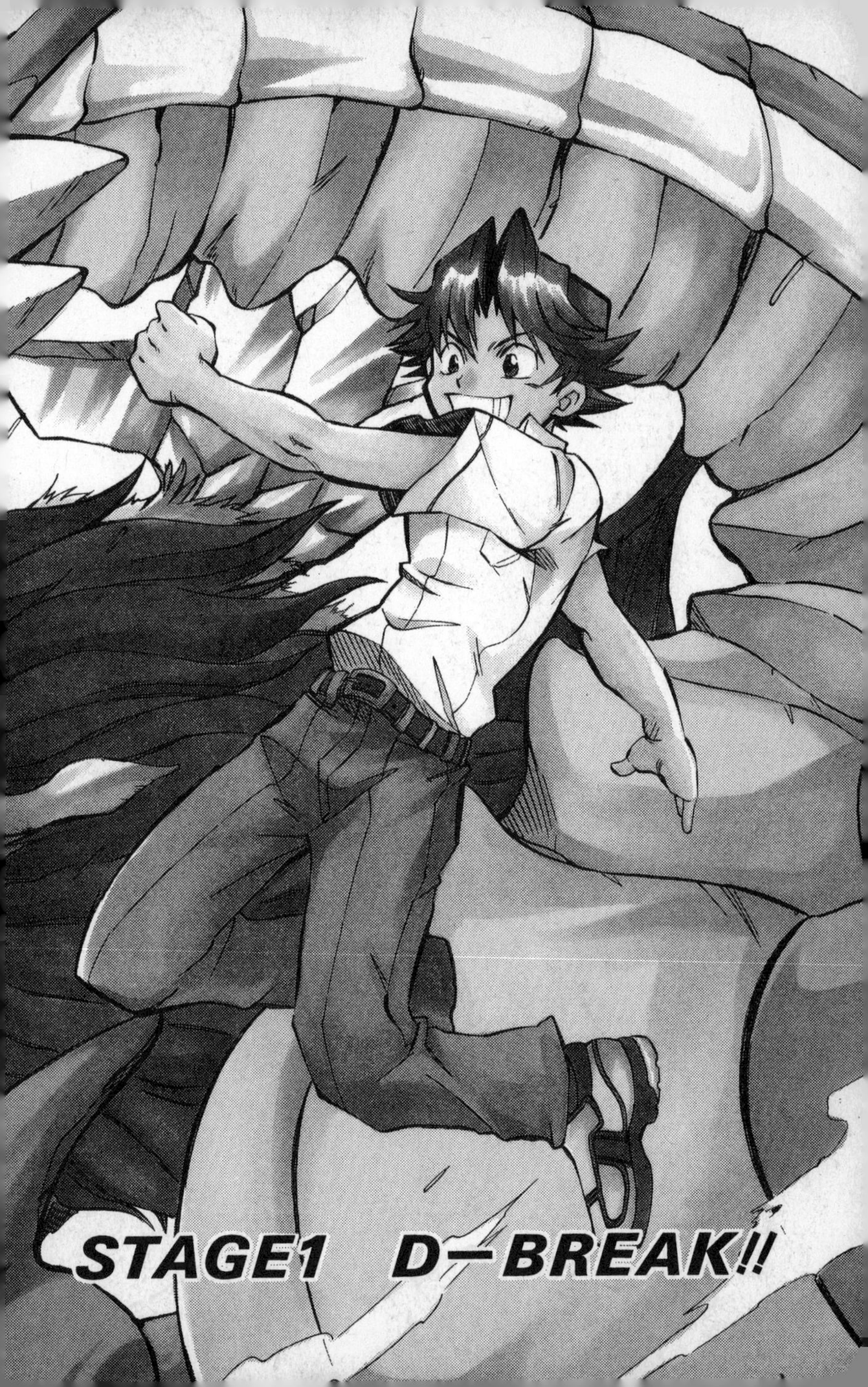
STAGE1 D—BREAK!!

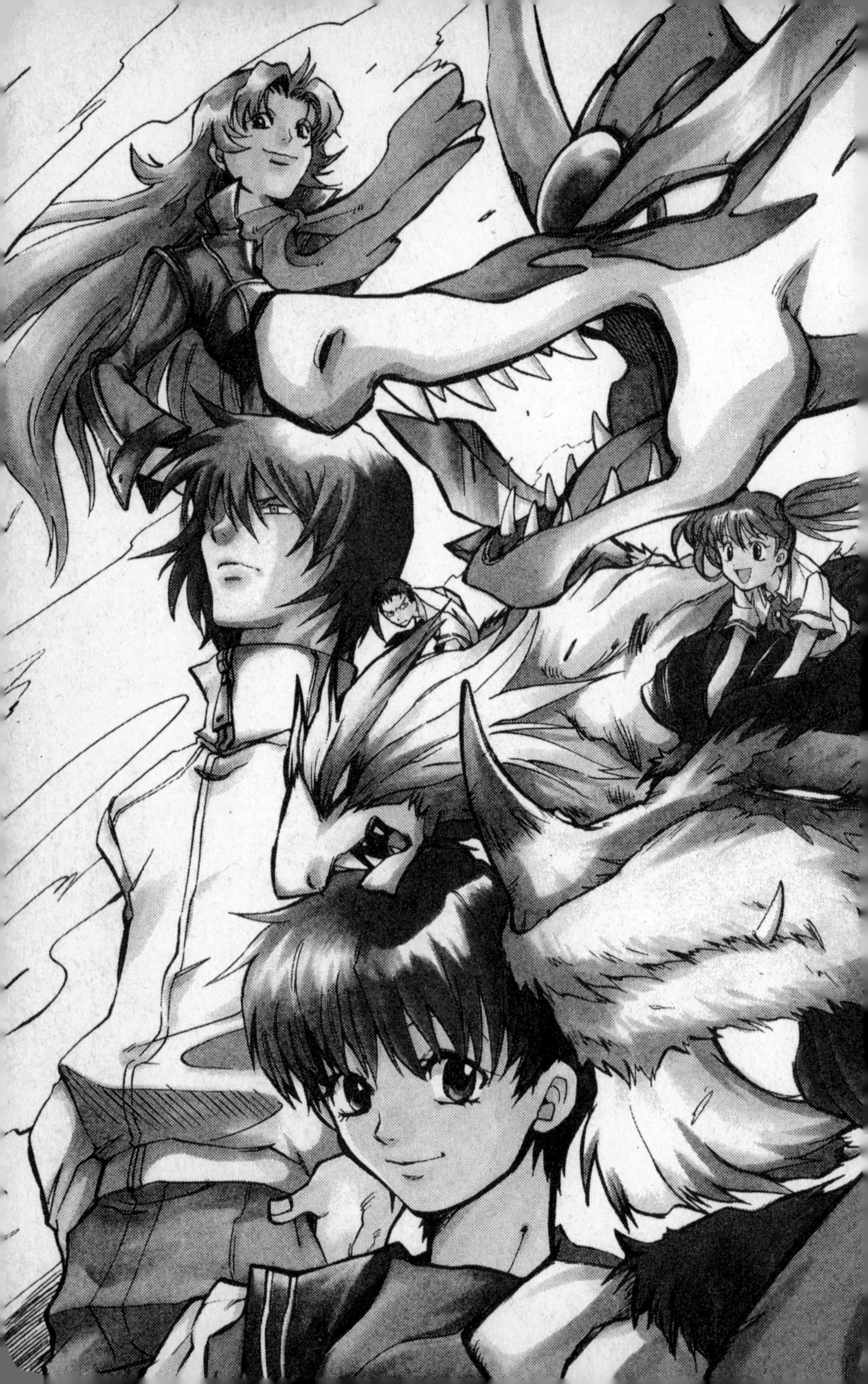

C H I B I
(?)

?

PLAYER: REIJI OZORA
TYPE: ?

A dragon surrounded by mysteries.
Default setting is a fighting ability of zero.

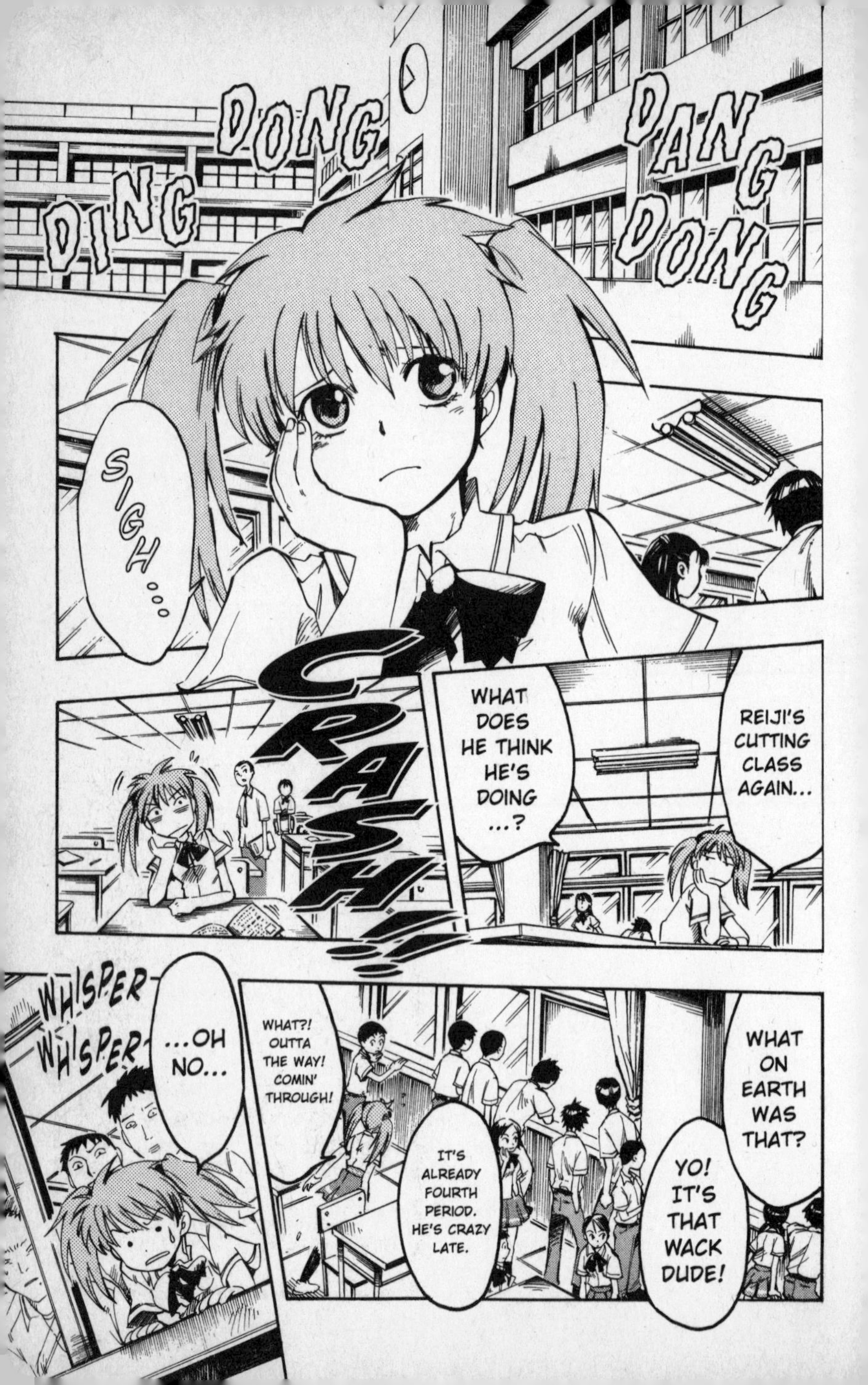
DANG DONG
DING DONG
SIGH...
REIJI'S CUTTING CLASS AGAIN...
WHAT DOES HE THINK HE'S DOING ...?
CRASH!!
WHAT ON EARTH WAS THAT?
YO! IT'S THAT WACK DUDE!
IT'S ALREADY FOURTH PERIOD. HE'S CRAZY LATE.
WHAT?! OUTTA THE WAY! COMIN' THROUGH!
...OH NO...
WHISPER WHISPER

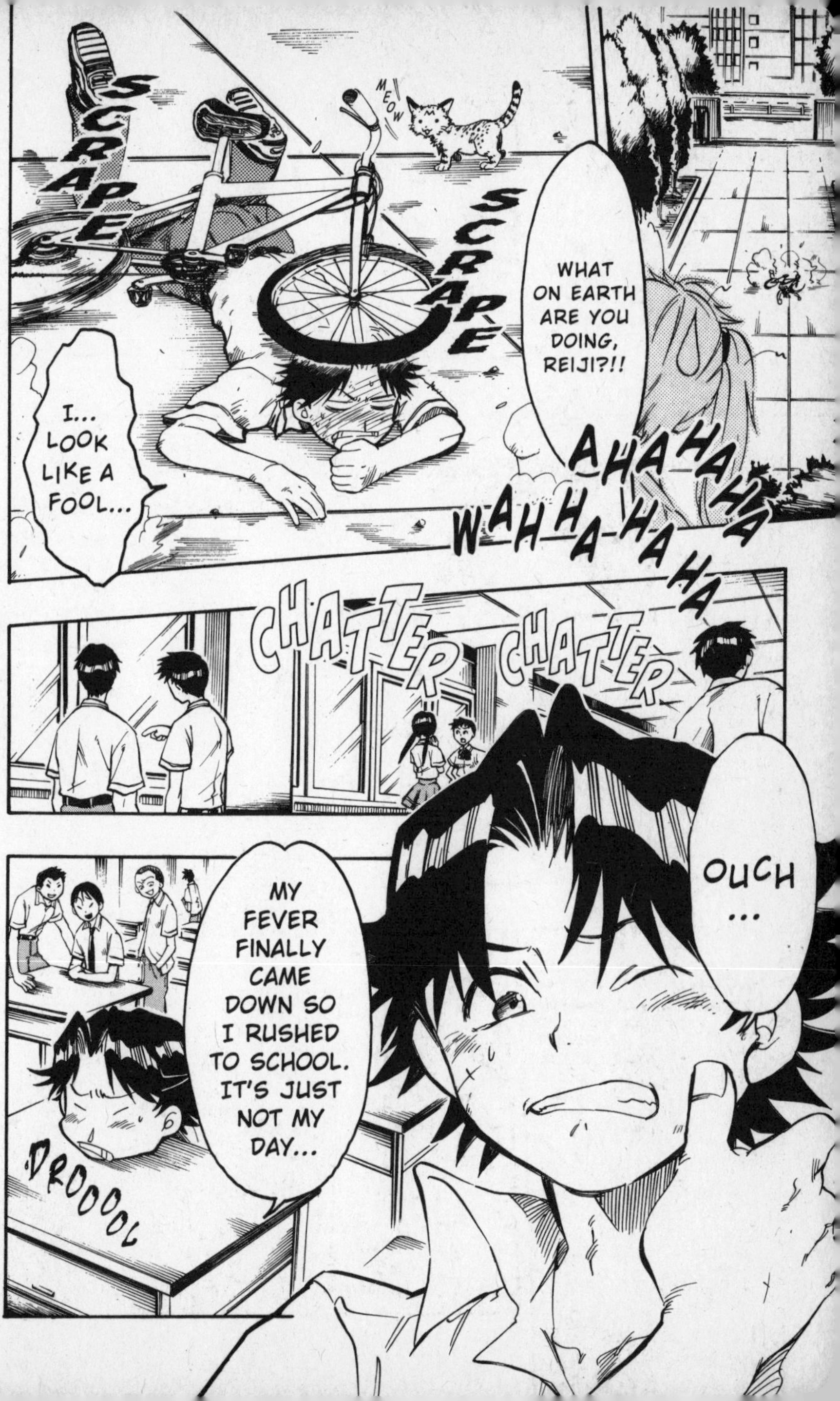
WHAT ON EARTH ARE YOU DOING, REIJI?!!
AHAHAHA
WAHAHAHAHA
SCRAPE
MEOW
SCRAPE
I... LOOK LIKE A FOOL...
CHATTER CHATTER
OUCH...
MY FEVER FINALLY CAME DOWN SO I RUSHED TO SCHOOL. IT'S JUST NOT MY DAY...
DROOOOL

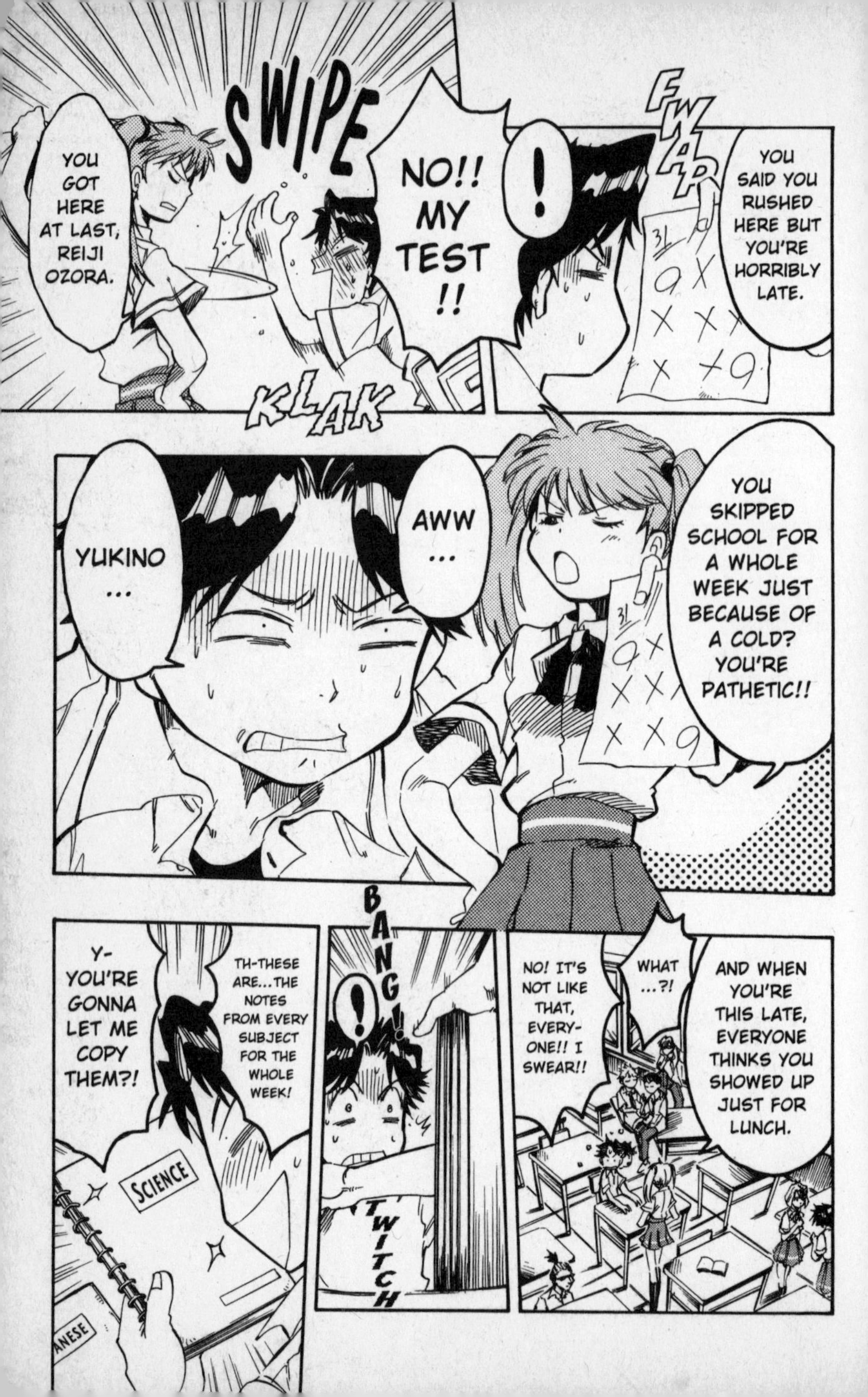

FWAP
!
YOU SAID YOU RUSHED HERE BUT YOU'RE HORRIBLY LATE.
NO!! MY TEST!!
SWIPE
YOU GOT HERE AT LAST, REIJI OZORA.
KLAK
YOU SKIPPED SCHOOL FOR A WHOLE WEEK JUST BECAUSE OF A COLD? YOU'RE PATHETIC!!
AWW ...
YUKINO ...
AND WHEN YOU'RE THIS LATE, EVERYONE THINKS YOU SHOWED UP JUST FOR LUNCH.
WHAT ...?!
NO! IT'S NOT LIKE THAT, EVERYONE!! I SWEAR!!
BANG!
!
TWITCH
TH-THESE ARE...THE NOTES FROM EVERY SUBJECT FOR THE WHOLE WEEK!
Y-YOU'RE GONNA LET ME COPY THEM?!
SCIENCE

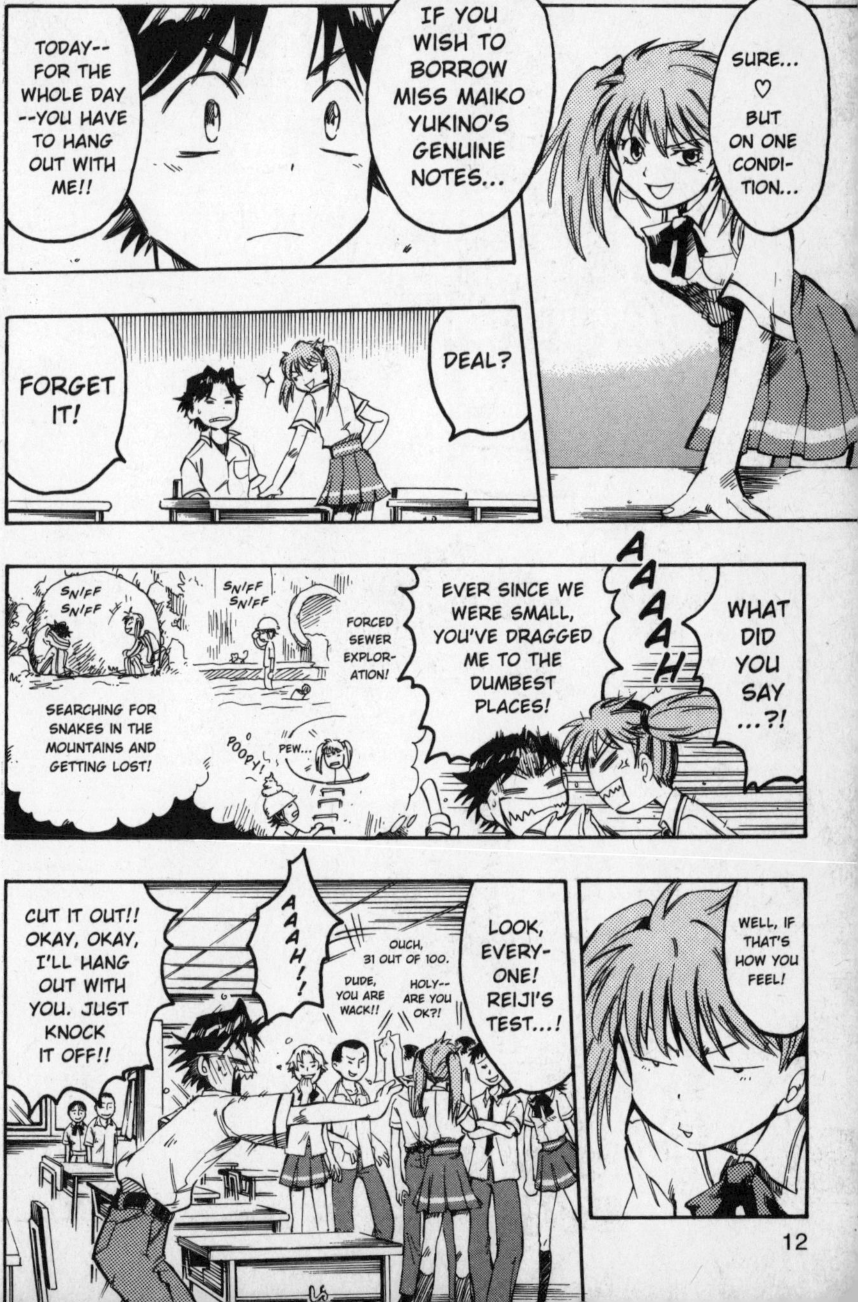
SURE... ♡ BUT ON ONE CONDITION...
IF YOU WISH TO BORROW MISS MAIKO YUKINO'S GENUINE NOTES...
TODAY-- FOR THE WHOLE DAY --YOU HAVE TO HANG OUT WITH ME!!
DEAL?
FORGET IT!
WHAT DID YOU SAY ...?!
AAAAH
EVER SINCE WE WERE SMALL, YOU'VE DRAGGED ME TO THE DUMBEST PLACES!
FORCED SEWER EXPLORATION!
SNIFF SNIFF
SNIFF SNIFF
SEARCHING FOR SNAKES IN THE MOUNTAINS AND GETTING LOST!
PEW...
POOPY!!
WELL, IF THAT'S HOW YOU FEEL!
LOOK, EVERYONE! REIJI'S TEST...!
AAAH!!
OUCH, 31 OUT OF 100.
HOLY-- ARE YOU OK?!
DUDE, YOU ARE WACK!!
CUT IT OUT!! OKAY, OKAY, I'LL HANG OUT WITH YOU. JUST KNOCK IT OFF!!

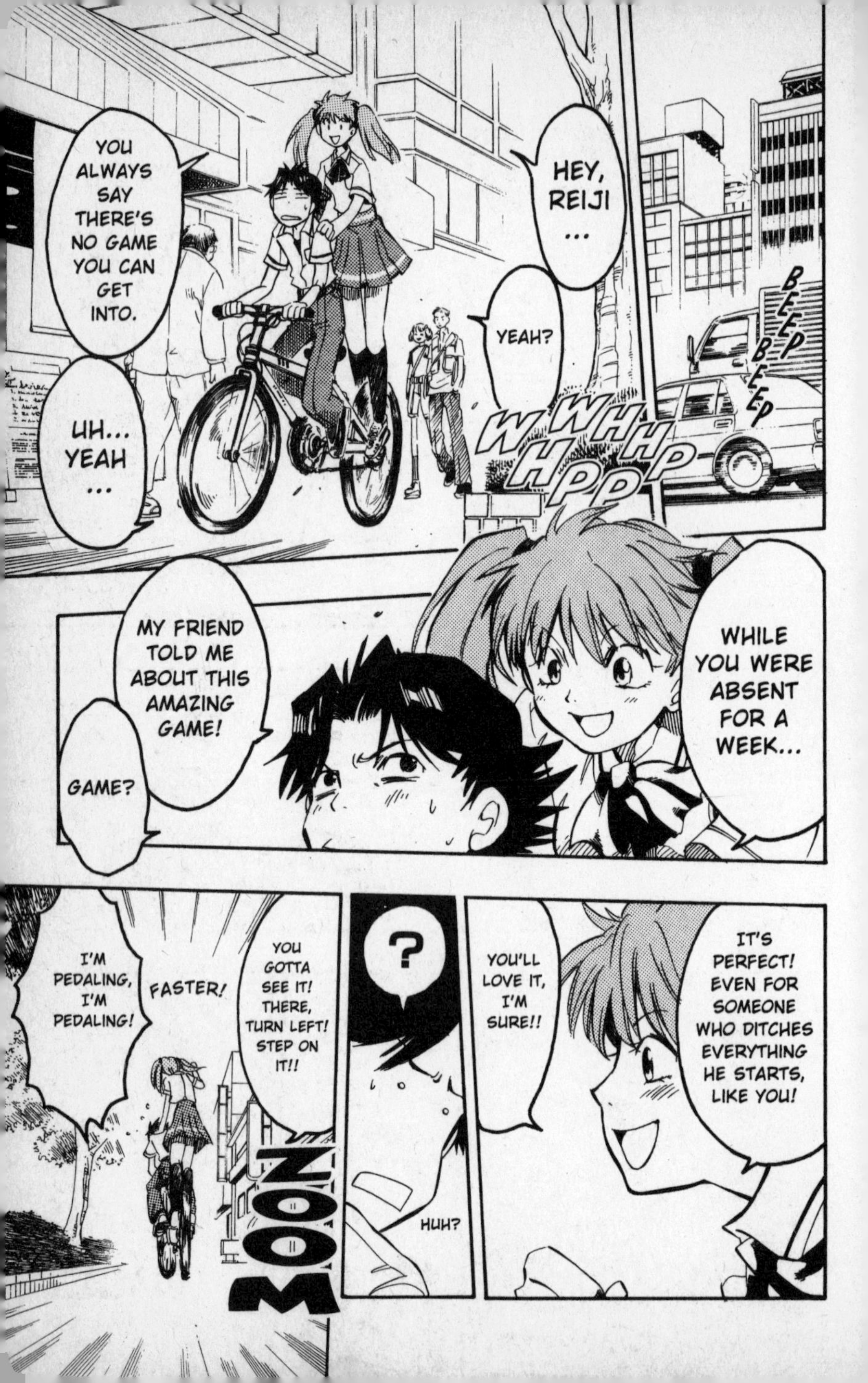
HEY, REIJI ...
YEAH?
BEEP BEEP
WHHHP WHHHP
YOU ALWAYS SAY THERE'S NO GAME YOU CAN GET INTO.
UH... YEAH ...
WHILE YOU WERE ABSENT FOR A WEEK...
MY FRIEND TOLD ME ABOUT THIS AMAZING GAME!
GAME?
IT'S PERFECT! EVEN FOR SOMEONE WHO DITCHES EVERYTHING HE STARTS, LIKE YOU!
YOU'LL LOVE IT, I'M SURE!!
?
HUH?
YOU GOTTA SEE IT! THERE, TURN LEFT! STEP ON IT!!
FASTER!
I'M PEDALING, I'M PEDALING!
ZOOOM

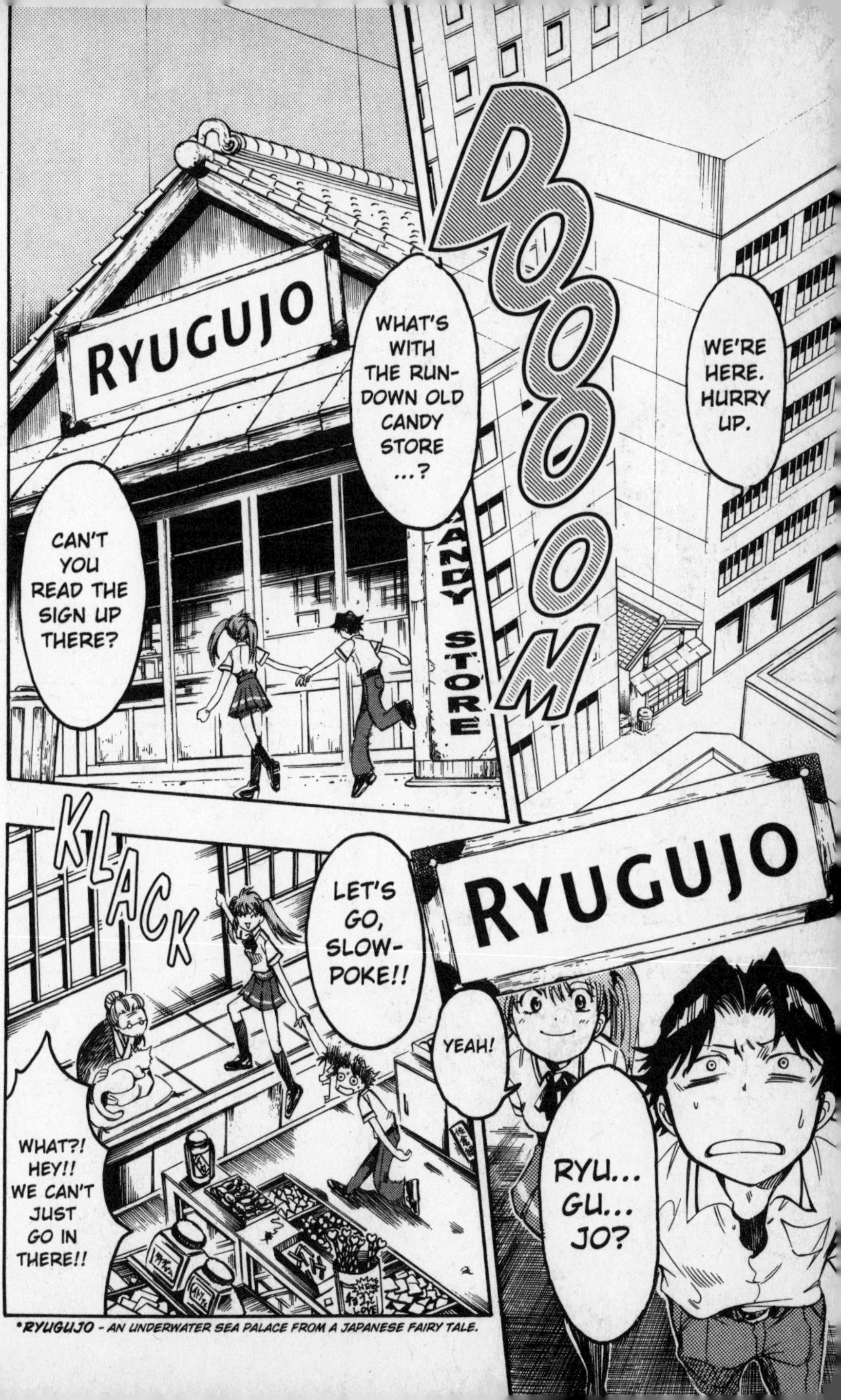
WE'RE HERE. HURRY UP.
BOOOOM
CANDY STORE
RYUGUJO
WHAT'S WITH THE RUN-DOWN OLD CANDY STORE ...?
CAN'T YOU READ THE SIGN UP THERE?
RYUGUJO
YEAH!
RYU... GU... JO?
KLACK
LET'S GO, SLOW-POKE!!
WHAT?! HEY!! WE CAN'T JUST GO IN THERE!!

*RYUGUJO - AN UNDERWATER SEA PALACE FROM A JAPANESE FAIRY TALE.

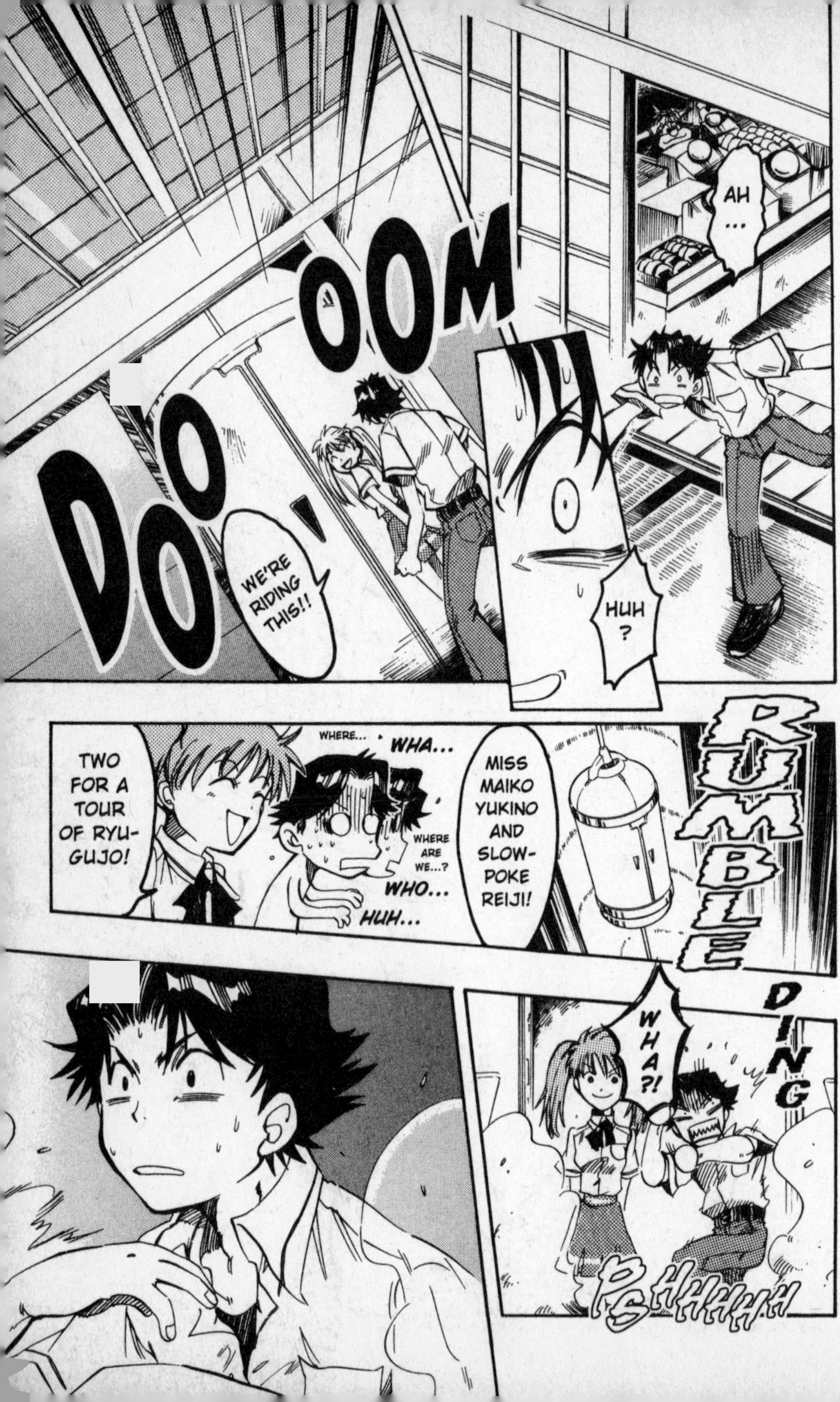

AH...
HUH?
DOOOOM
WE'RE RIDING THIS!!
RUMBLE
MISS MAIKO YUKINO AND SLOW-POKE REIJI!
WHA...
WHERE...
WHERE ARE WE...?
WHO...
HUH...
TWO FOR A TOUR OF RYU-GUJO!
DING
WHA?!
PSHHHHHH

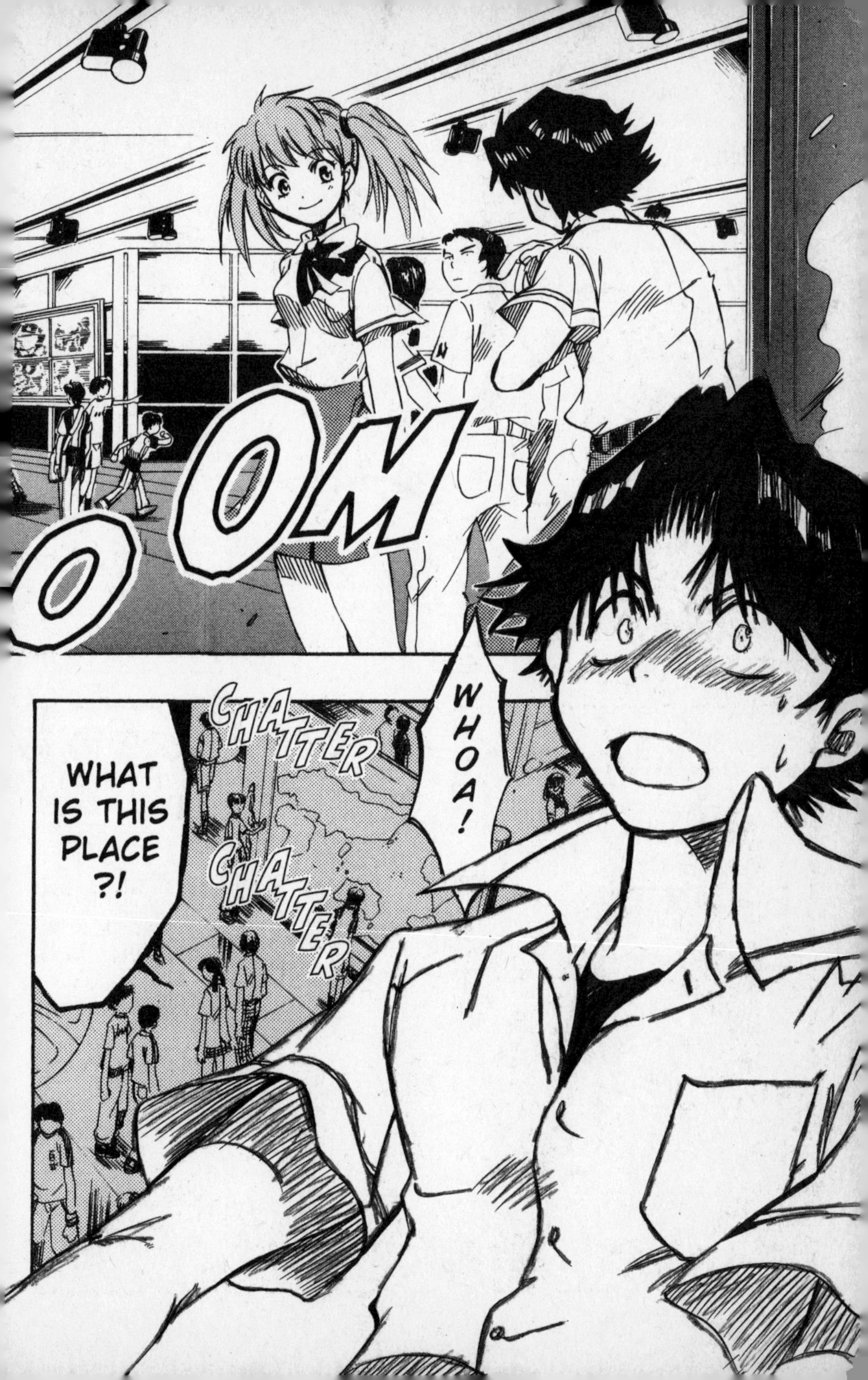
OOM
WHOA!
CHATTER
CHATTER
WHAT IS THIS PLACE ?!

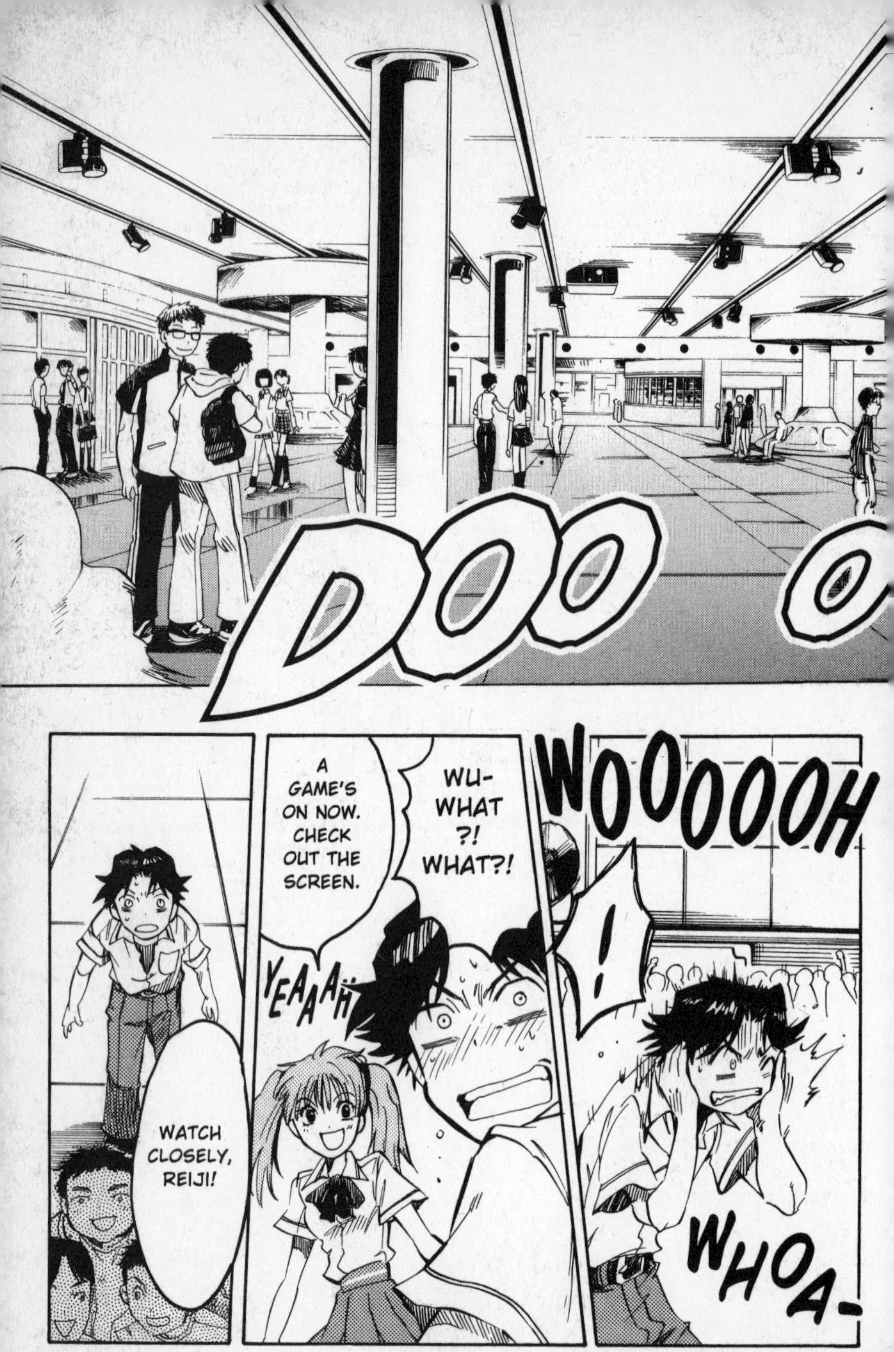
DOO O
WOOOOOH
!
WHOA-
WU-WHAT?! WHAT?!
A GAME'S ON NOW. CHECK OUT THE SCREEN.
YEAAAH
WATCH CLOSELY, REIJI!

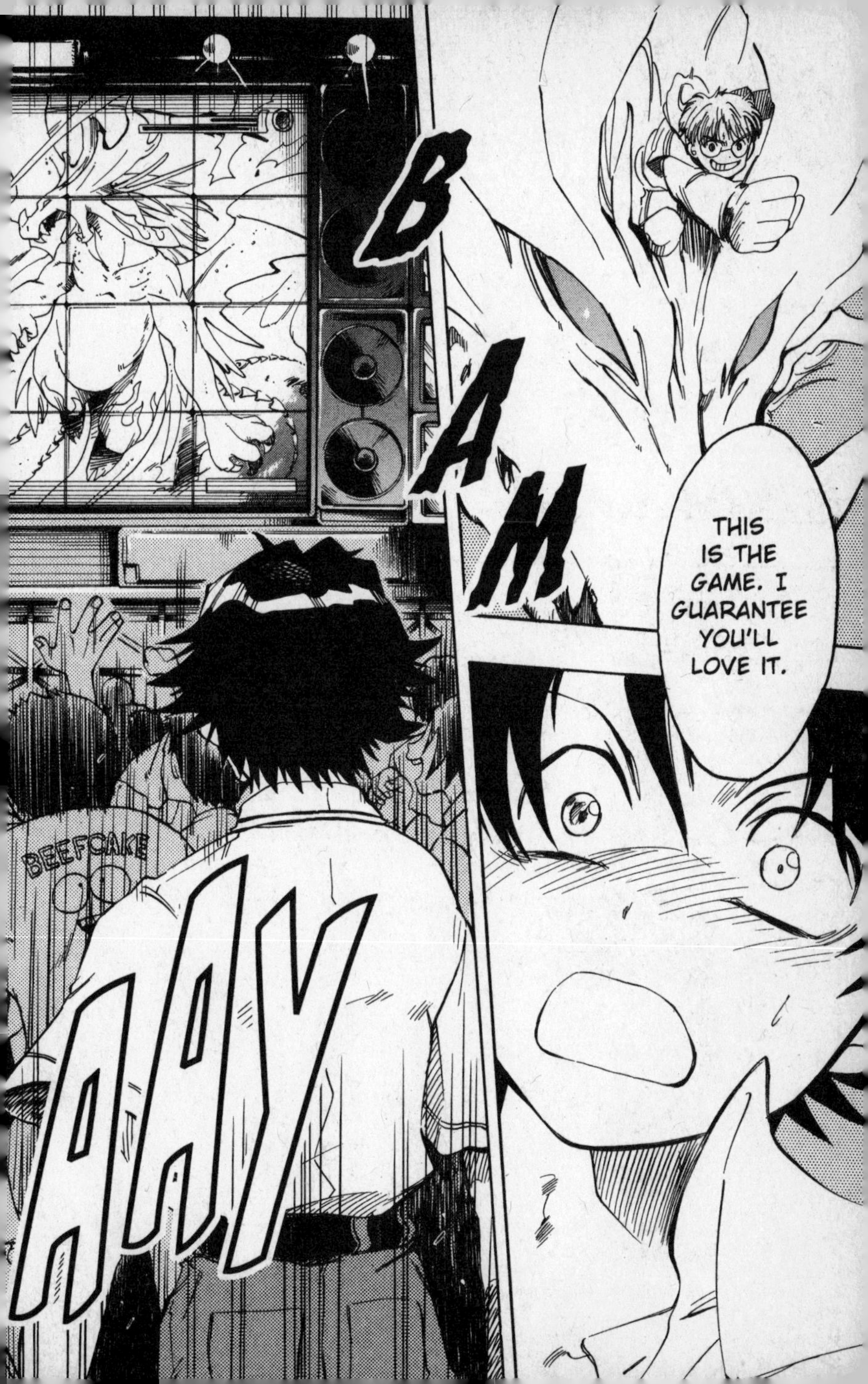
BAM
THIS IS THE GAME. I GUARANTEE YOU'LL LOVE IT.
BEEFCAKE
AAY

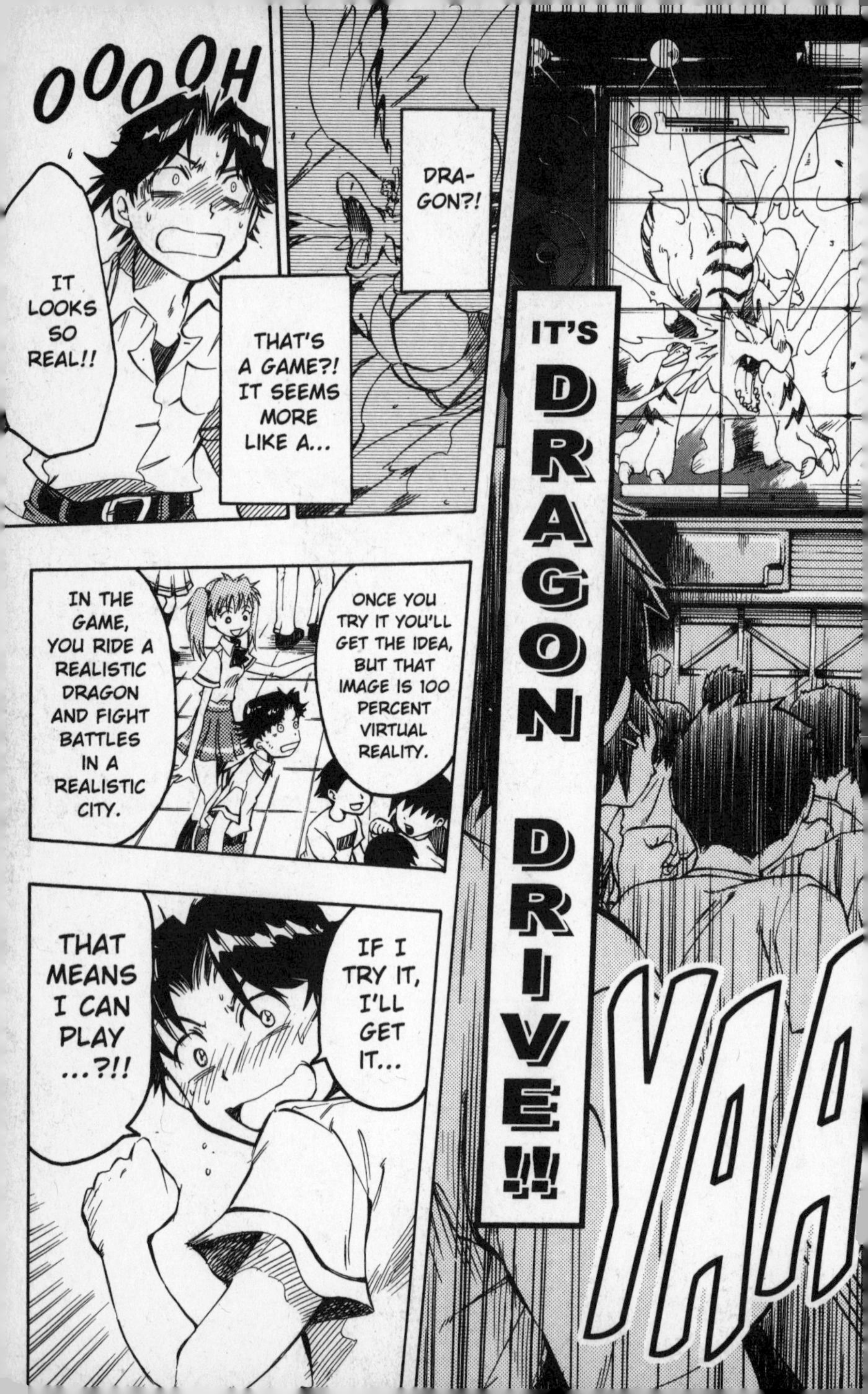
IT'S DRAGON DRIVE!!
YAA
DRA-GON?!
OOOOH
THAT'S A GAME?! IT SEEMS MORE LIKE A...
IT LOOKS SO REAL!!
ONCE YOU TRY IT YOU'LL GET THE IDEA, BUT THAT IMAGE IS 100 PERCENT VIRTUAL REALITY.
IN THE GAME, YOU RIDE A REALISTIC DRAGON AND FIGHT BATTLES IN A REALISTIC CITY.
IF I TRY IT, I'LL GET IT...
THAT MEANS I CAN PLAY ...?!!

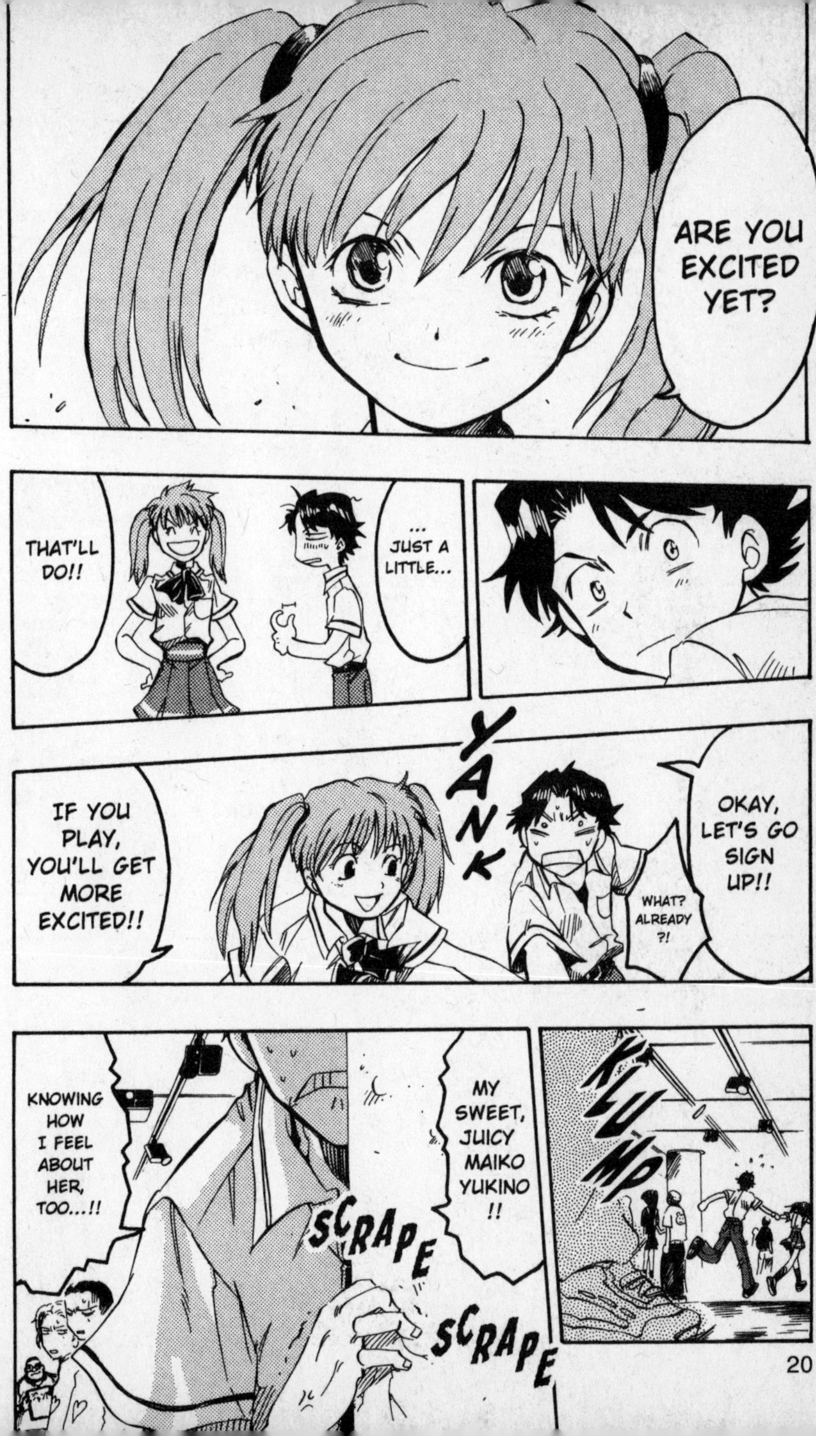
ARE YOU EXCITED YET?
... JUST A LITTLE...
THAT'LL DO!!
OKAY, LET'S GO SIGN UP!!
WHAT? ALREADY ?!
YANK
IF YOU PLAY, YOU'LL GET MORE EXCITED!!
KLUMP
MY SWEET, JUICY MAIKO YUKINO !!
KNOWING HOW I FEEL ABOUT HER, TOO...!!
SCRAPE
SCRAPE

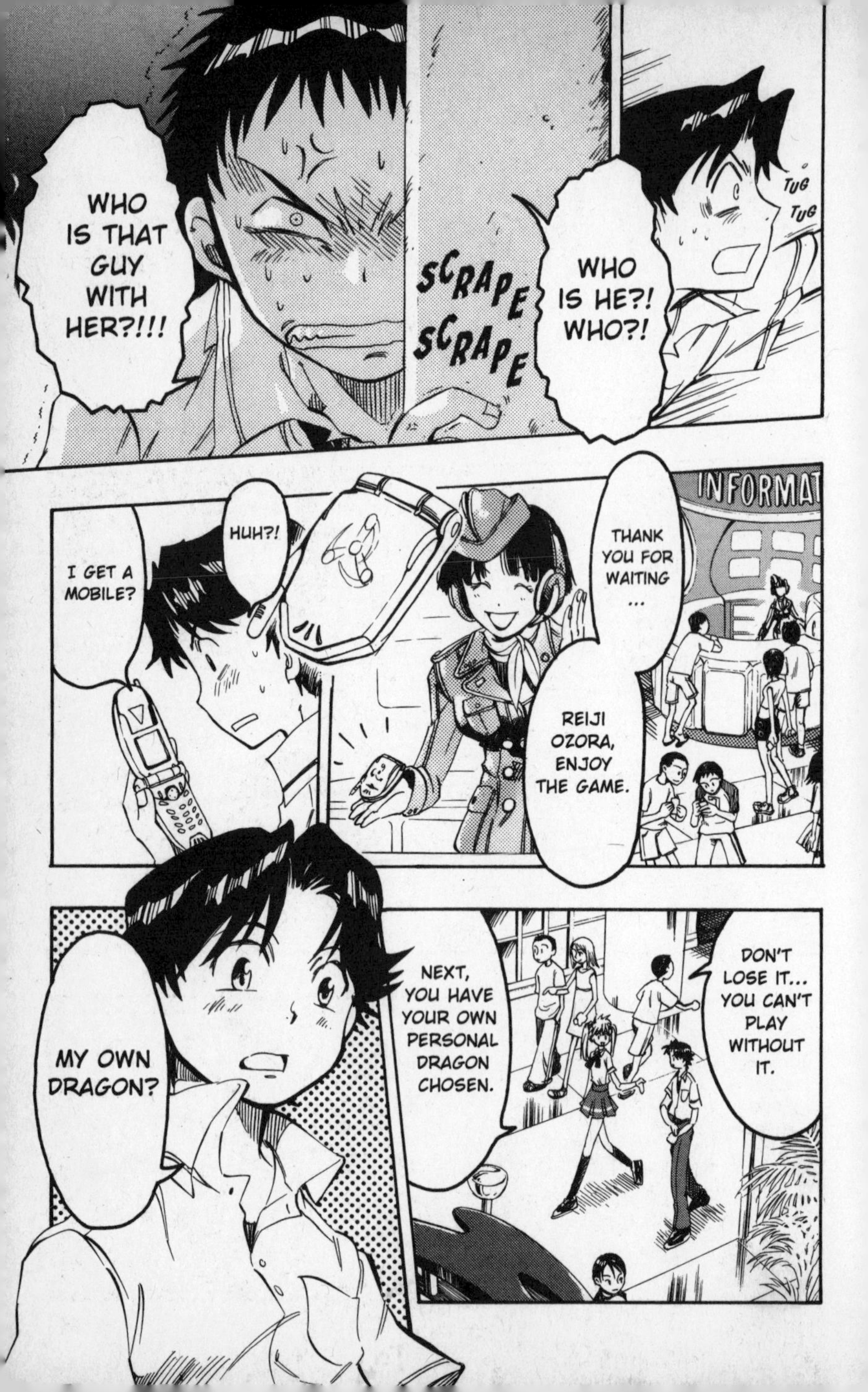
TUG
TUG
WHO IS HE?! WHO?!
SCRAPE
SCRAPE
WHO IS THAT GUY WITH HER?!!!
INFORMAT
THANK YOU FOR WAITING ...
REIJI OZORA, ENJOY THE GAME.
HUH?!
I GET A MOBILE?
DON'T LOSE IT... YOU CAN'T PLAY WITHOUT IT.
NEXT, YOU HAVE YOUR OWN PERSONAL DRAGON CHOSEN.
MY OWN DRAGON?

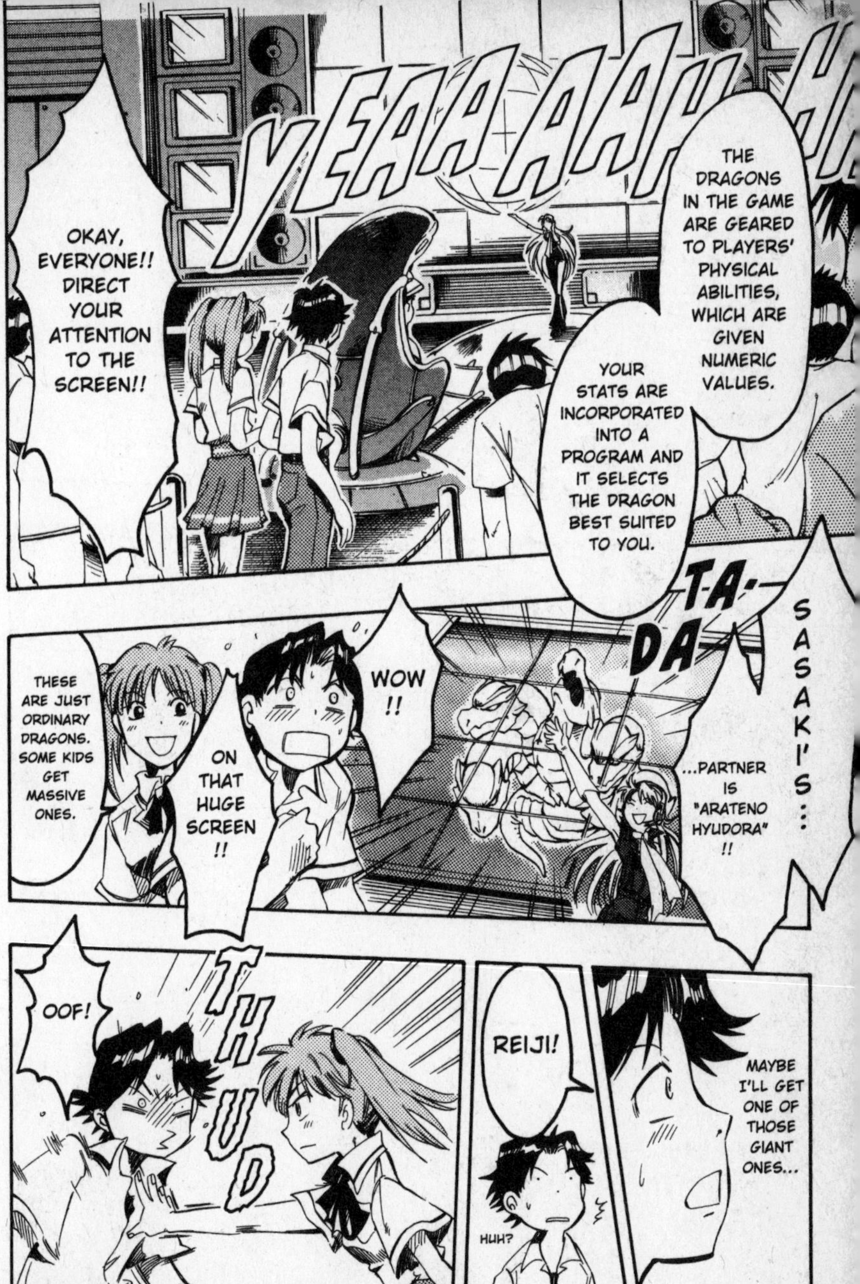
YEAAAAAH
THE DRAGONS IN THE GAME ARE GEARED TO PLAYERS' PHYSICAL ABILITIES, WHICH ARE GIVEN NUMERIC VALUES.
YOUR STATS ARE INCORPORATED INTO A PROGRAM AND IT SELECTS THE DRAGON BEST SUITED TO YOU.
OKAY, EVERYONE!! DIRECT YOUR ATTENTION TO THE SCREEN!!
T-A-DA
SASAKI'S...
...PARTNER IS "ARATENO HYUDORA"!!
WOW!!
ON THAT HUGE SCREEN!!
THESE ARE JUST ORDINARY DRAGONS. SOME KIDS GET MASSIVE ONES.
MAYBE I'LL GET ONE OF THOSE GIANT ONES...
REIJI!
HUH?
THUD
OOF!

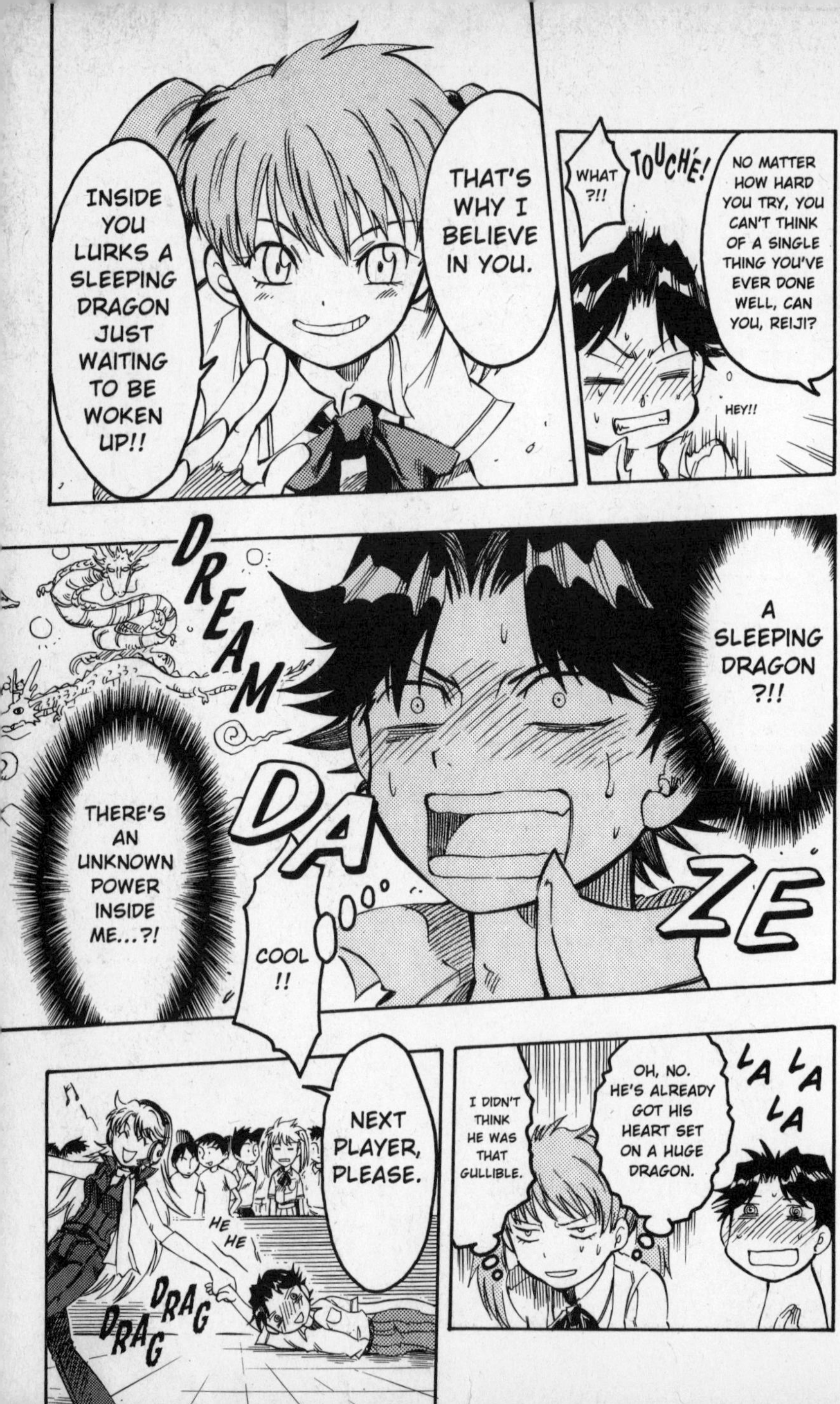
NO MATTER HOW HARD YOU TRY, YOU CAN'T THINK OF A SINGLE THING YOU'VE EVER DONE WELL, CAN YOU, REIJI?
TOUCHÉ!
WHAT ?!!
HEY!!
THAT'S WHY I BELIEVE IN YOU.
INSIDE YOU LURKS A SLEEPING DRAGON JUST WAITING TO BE WOKEN UP!!
A SLEEPING DRAGON ?!!
DREAM DAZE
THERE'S AN UNKNOWN POWER INSIDE ME...?!
COOL !!
LA LA LA
OH, NO. HE'S ALREADY GOT HIS HEART SET ON A HUGE DRAGON.
I DIDN'T THINK HE WAS THAT GULLIBLE.
NEXT PLAYER, PLEASE.
HE HE
DRAG DRAG

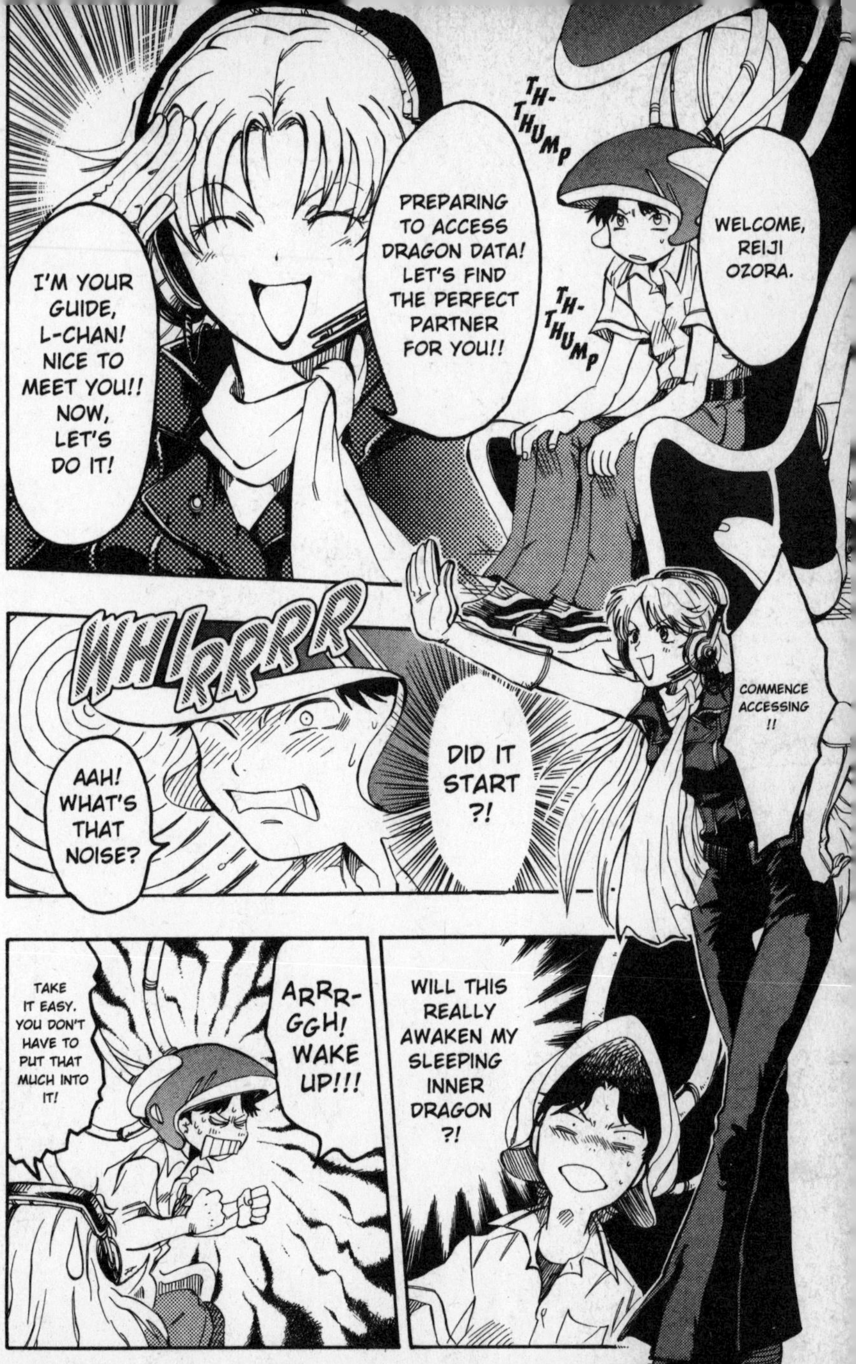
TH-THUMP
WELCOME, REIJI OZORA.
TH-THUMP
PREPARING TO ACCESS DRAGON DATA! LET'S FIND THE PERFECT PARTNER FOR YOU!!
I'M YOUR GUIDE, L-CHAN! NICE TO MEET YOU!! NOW, LET'S DO IT!
COMMENCE ACCESSING !!
DID IT START ?!
WHIRRRR
AAH! WHAT'S THAT NOISE?
WILL THIS REALLY AWAKEN MY SLEEPING INNER DRAGON ?!
ARRR-GGH! WAKE UP!!!
TAKE IT EASY. YOU DON'T HAVE TO PUT THAT MUCH INTO IT!

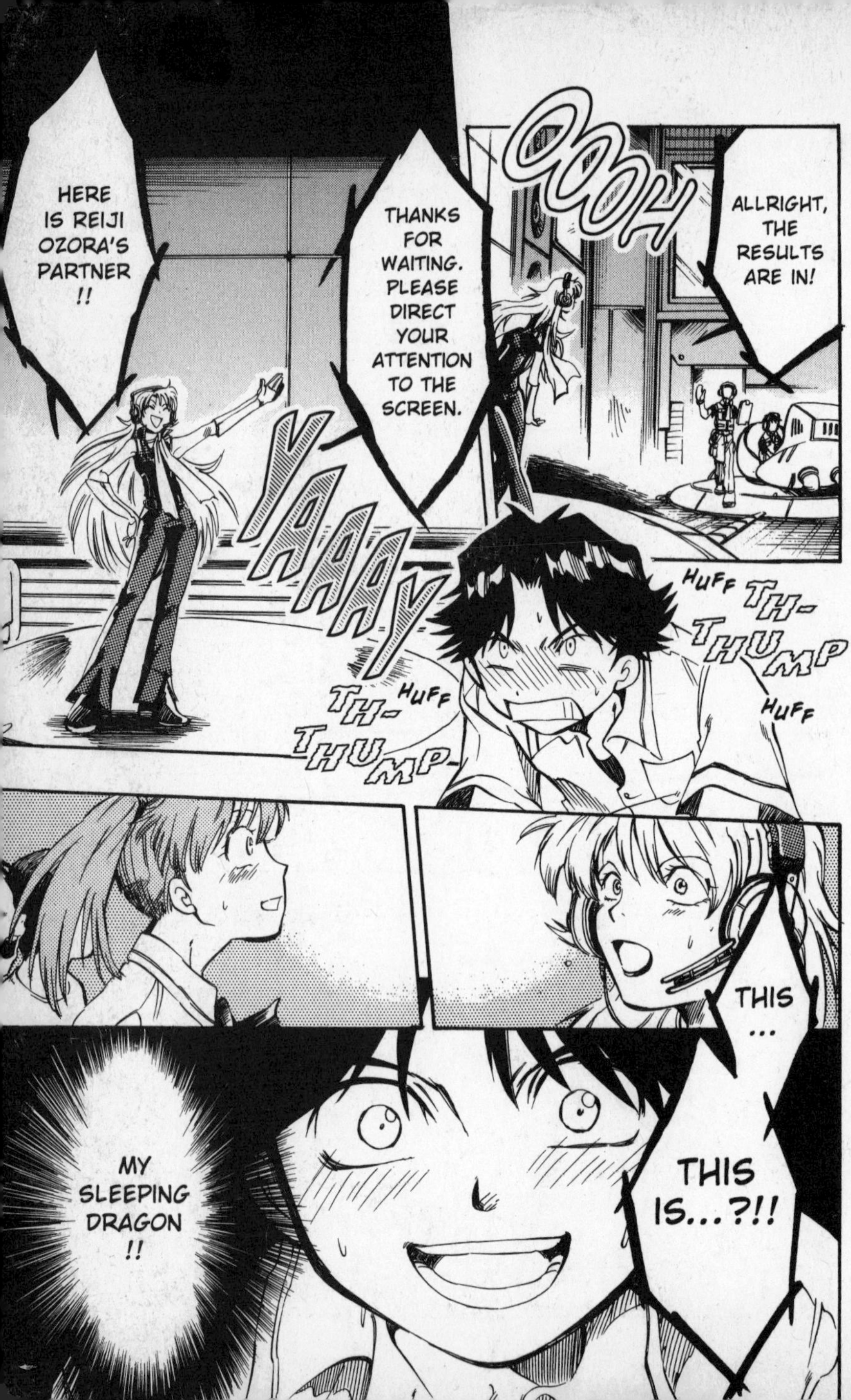
ALLRIGHT, THE RESULTS ARE IN!
OOOH
THANKS FOR WAITING. PLEASE DIRECT YOUR ATTENTION TO THE SCREEN.
HERE IS REIJI OZORA'S PARTNER!!
YAAAAY
HUFF TH-THUMP HUFF
TH- HUFF THUMP-
THIS...
THIS IS...?!!
MY SLEEPING DRAGON!!

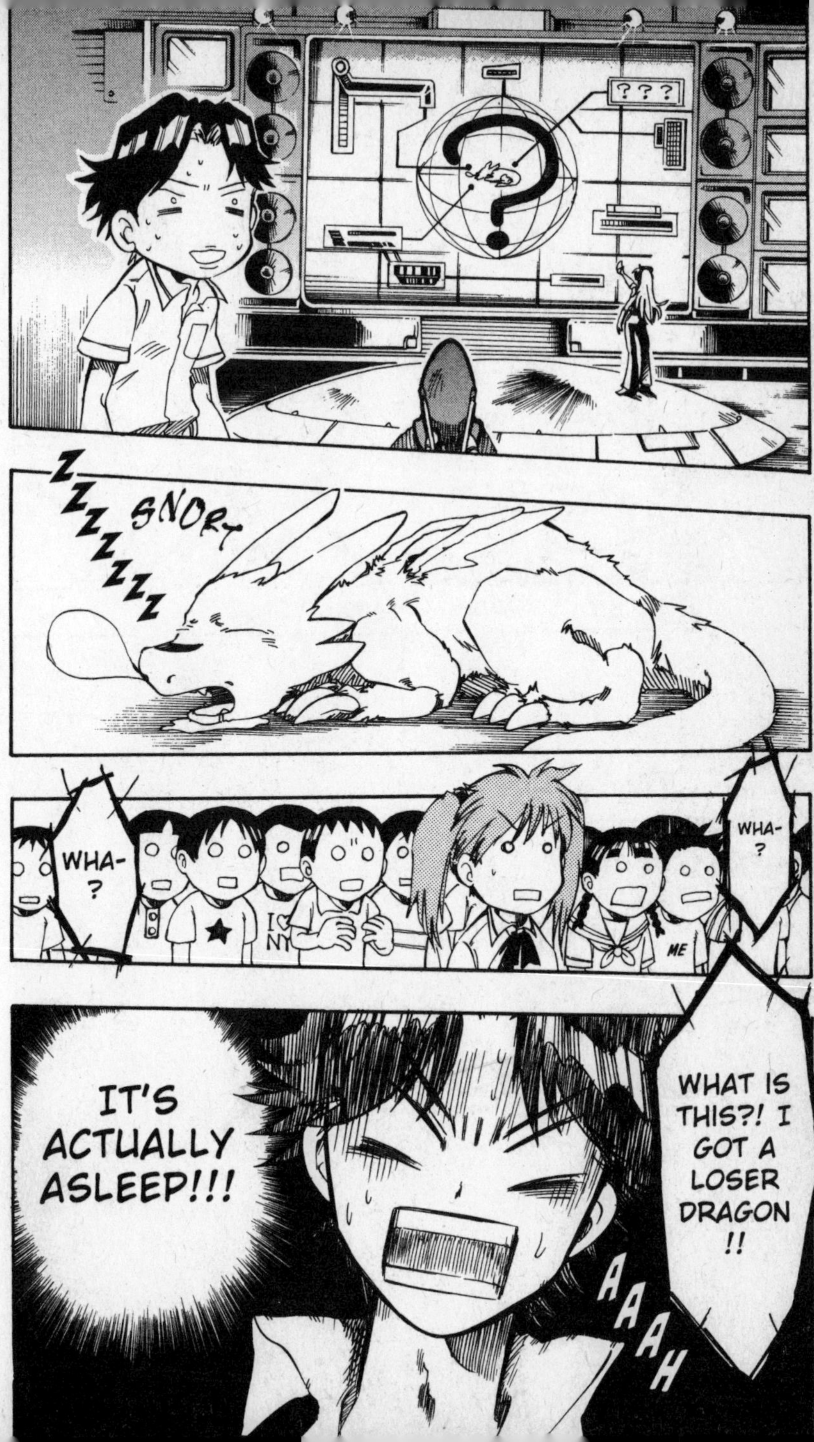
???
ZZZZZZZZ
SNORT
WHA-?
WHA-?
I ♡ NY
ME
WHAT IS THIS?! I GOT A LOSER DRAGON!!
IT'S ACTUALLY ASLEEP!!!
AAAAH

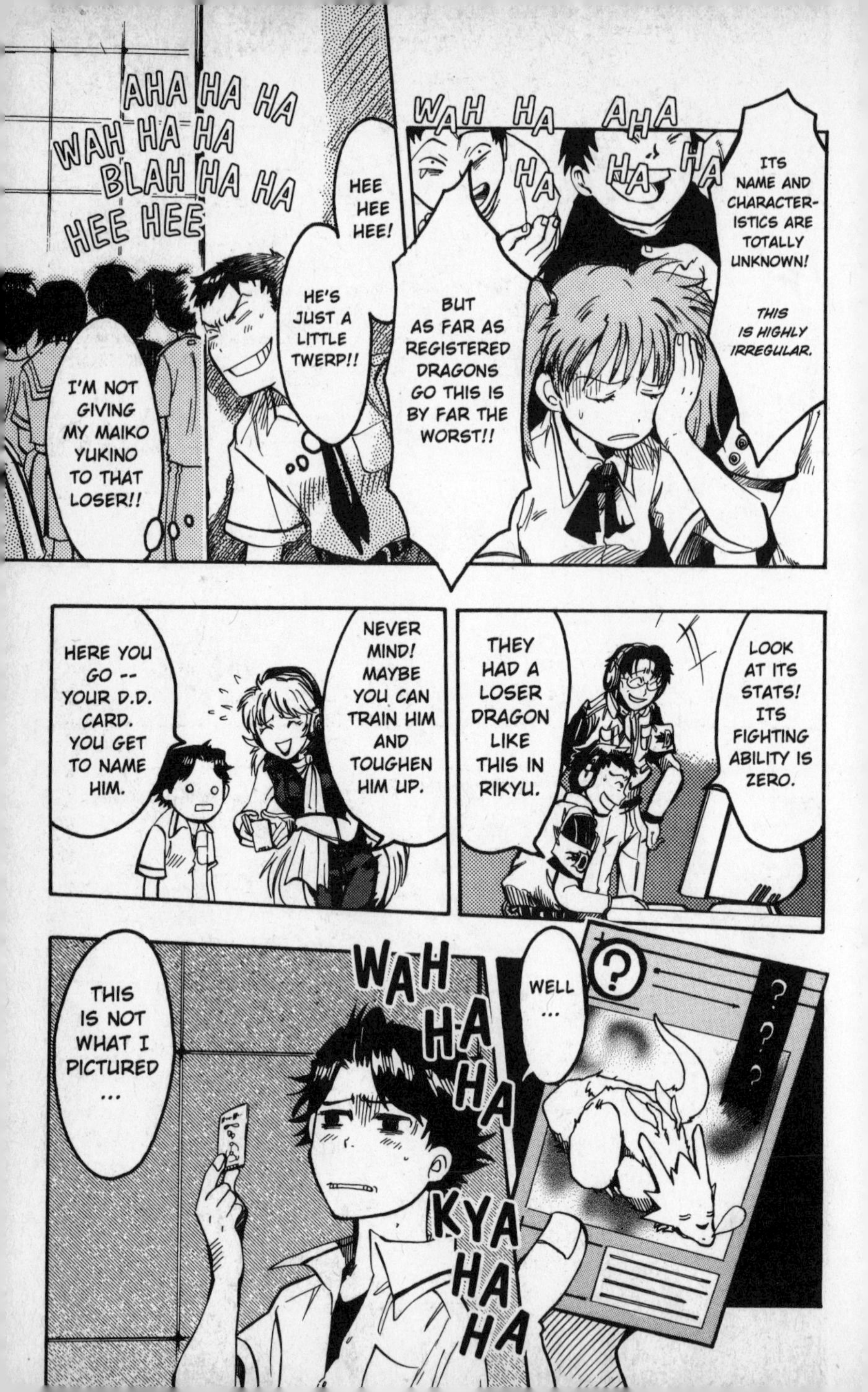
ITS NAME AND CHARACTERISTICS ARE TOTALLY UNKNOWN!
THIS IS HIGHLY IRREGULAR.
AHA HA HA
WAH HA HA
BUT AS FAR AS REGISTERED DRAGONS GO THIS IS BY FAR THE WORST!!
HEE HEE HEE!
HE'S JUST A LITTLE TWERP!!
AHA HA HA
WAH HA HA
BLAH HA HA
HEE HEE
I'M NOT GIVING MY MAIKO YUKINO TO THAT LOSER!!
LOOK AT ITS STATS! ITS FIGHTING ABILITY IS ZERO.
THEY HAD A LOSER DRAGON LIKE THIS IN RIKYU.
NEVER MIND! MAYBE YOU CAN TRAIN HIM AND TOUGHEN HIM UP.
HERE YOU GO -- YOUR D.D. CARD. YOU GET TO NAME HIM.
???
?
WELL ...
WAH HA HA HA
KYA HA HA HA
THIS IS NOT WHAT I PICTURED ...

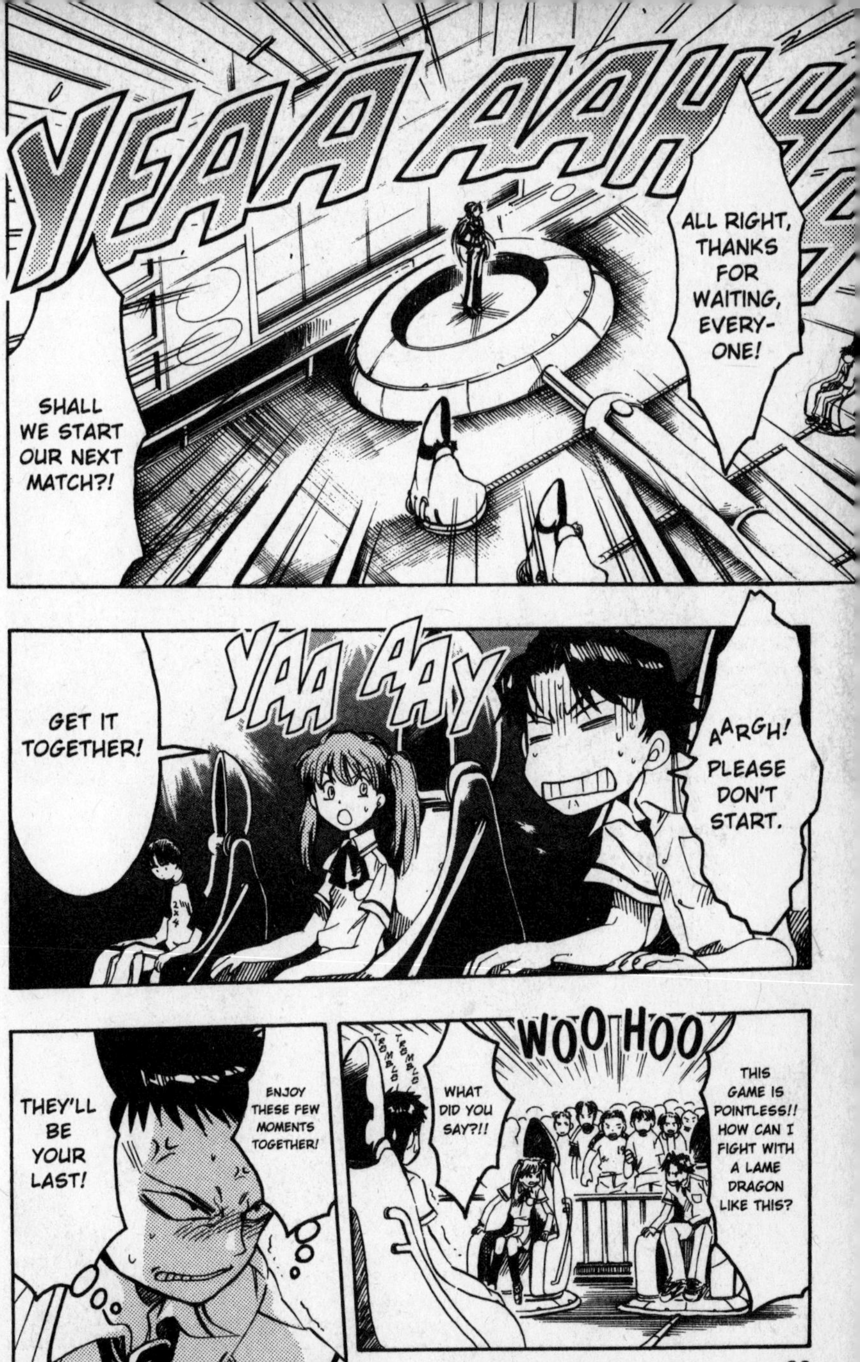
YEAAAAH
ALL RIGHT, THANKS FOR WAITING, EVERYONE!
SHALL WE START OUR NEXT MATCH?!
YAAAAY
AARGH! PLEASE DON'T START.
GET IT TOGETHER!
WOO HOO
THIS GAME IS POINTLESS!! HOW CAN I FIGHT WITH A LAME DRAGON LIKE THIS?
TREMBLE TREMBLE
WHAT DID YOU SAY?!!
ENJOY THESE FEW MOMENTS TOGETHER!
THEY'LL BE YOUR LAST!

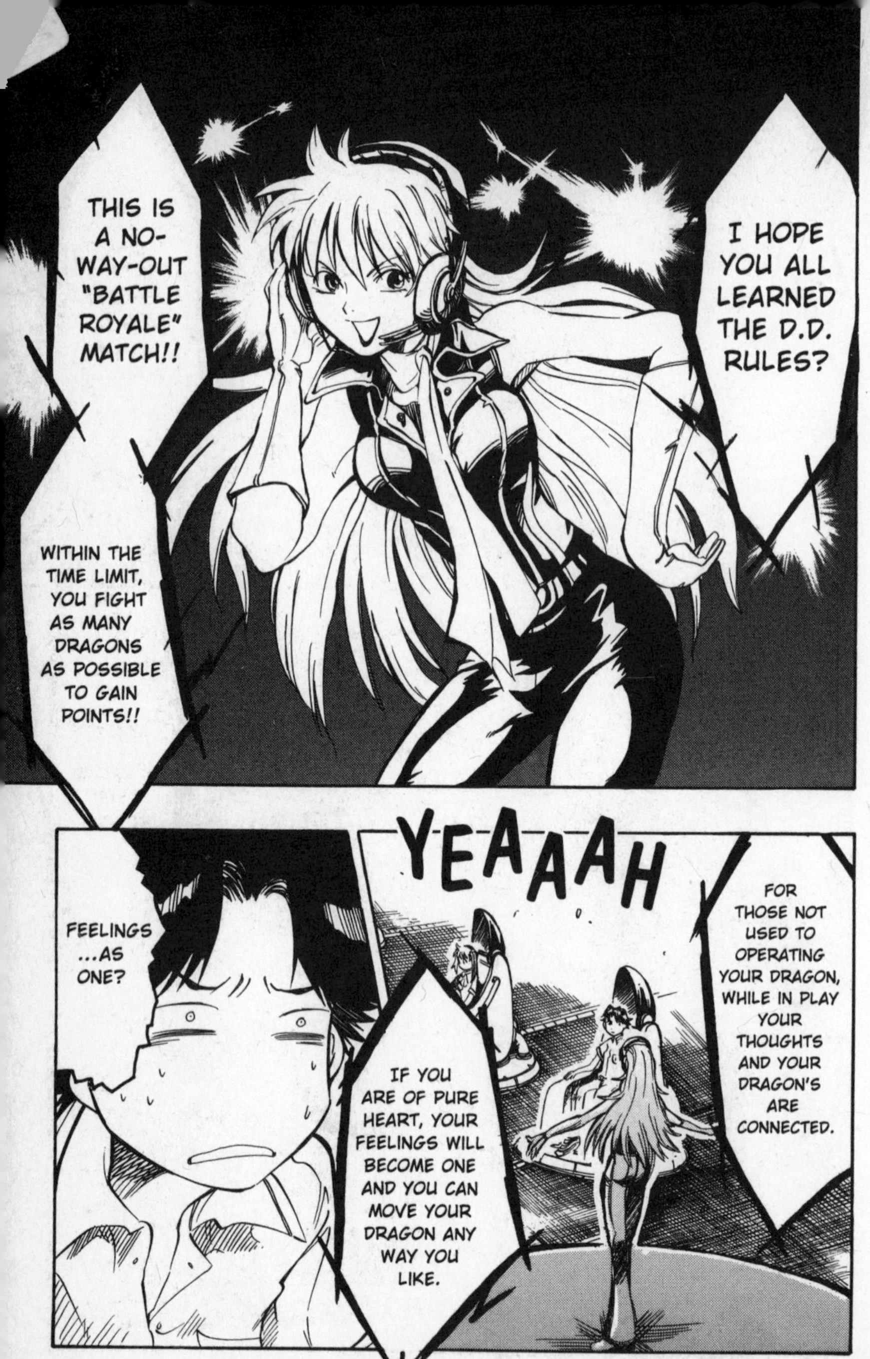
I HOPE YOU ALL LEARNED THE D.D. RULES?
THIS IS A NO-WAY-OUT "BATTLE ROYALE" MATCH!!
WITHIN THE TIME LIMIT, YOU FIGHT AS MANY DRAGONS AS POSSIBLE TO GAIN POINTS!!
YEAAAAH
FOR THOSE NOT USED TO OPERATING YOUR DRAGON, WHILE IN PLAY YOUR THOUGHTS AND YOUR DRAGON'S ARE CONNECTED.
IF YOU ARE OF PURE HEART, YOUR FEELINGS WILL BECOME ONE AND YOU CAN MOVE YOUR DRAGON ANY WAY YOU LIKE.
FEELINGS ...AS ONE?

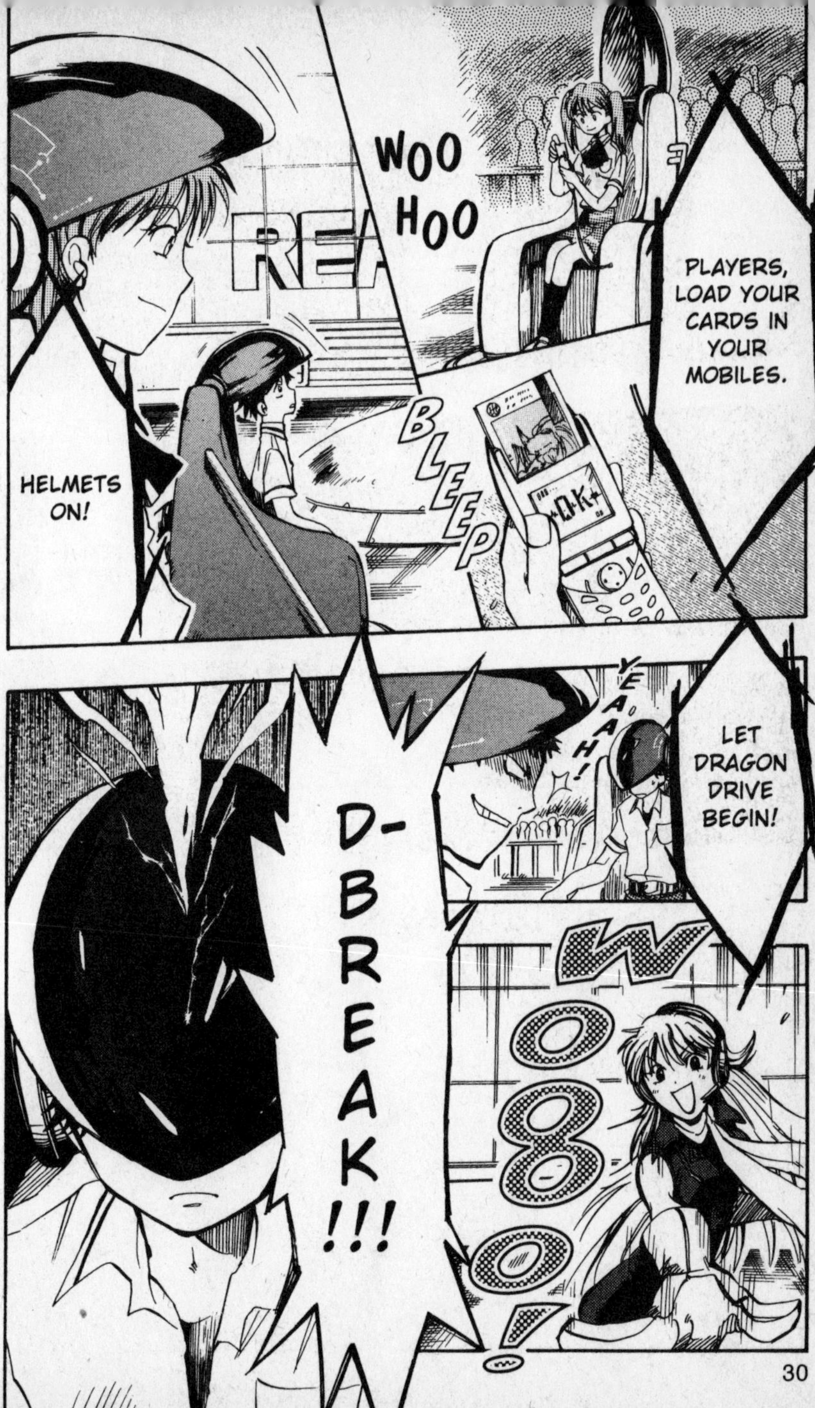

PLAYERS, LOAD YOUR CARDS IN YOUR MOBILES.
WOO HOO
BLEEP
HELMETS ON!
YEAAAH!
LET DRAGON DRIVE BEGIN!
WOOOO!
D-BREAK!!!

READ THIS WAY

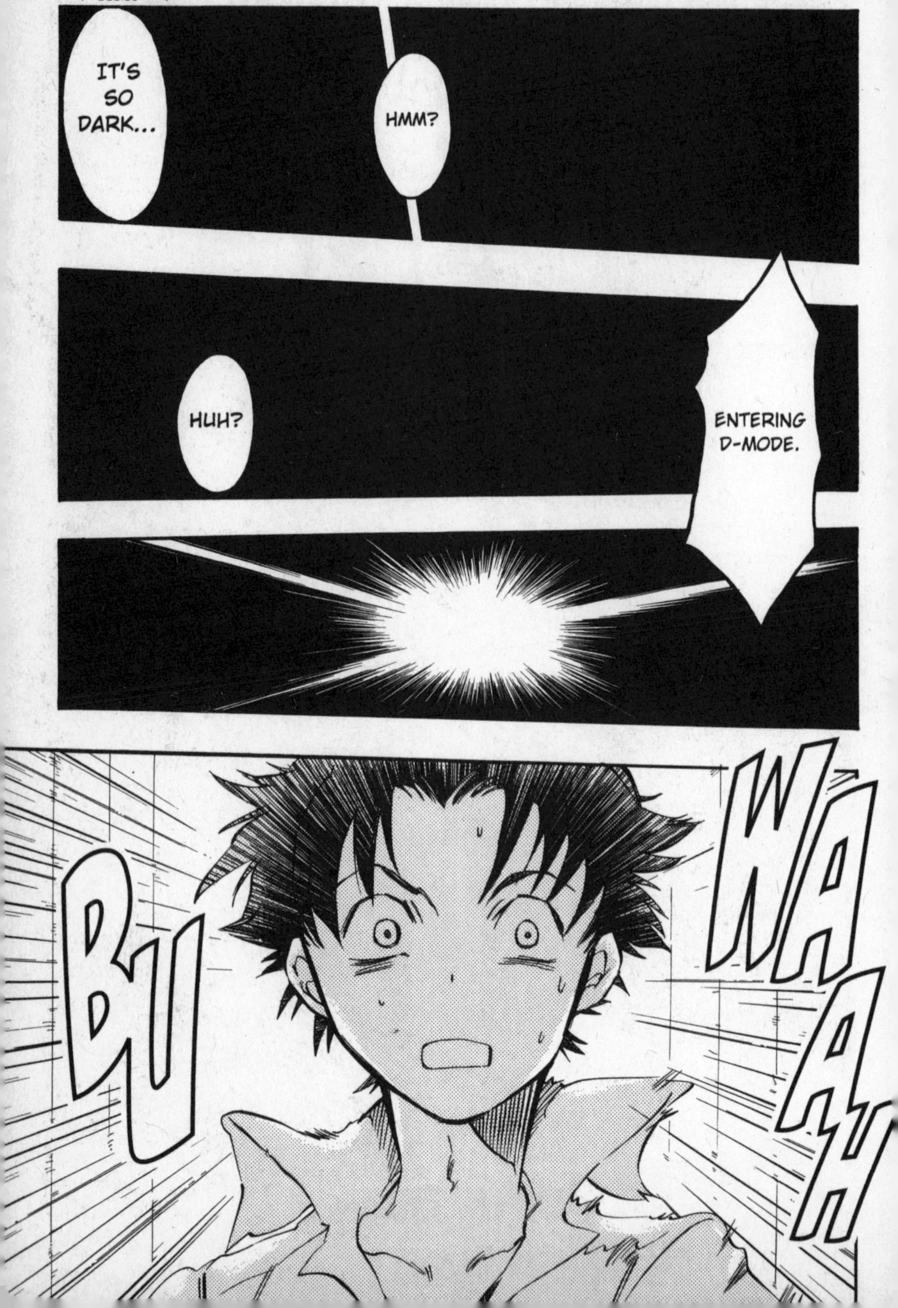
HMM?
IT'S SO DARK...
ENTERING D-MODE.
HUH?
WAAAH
BU

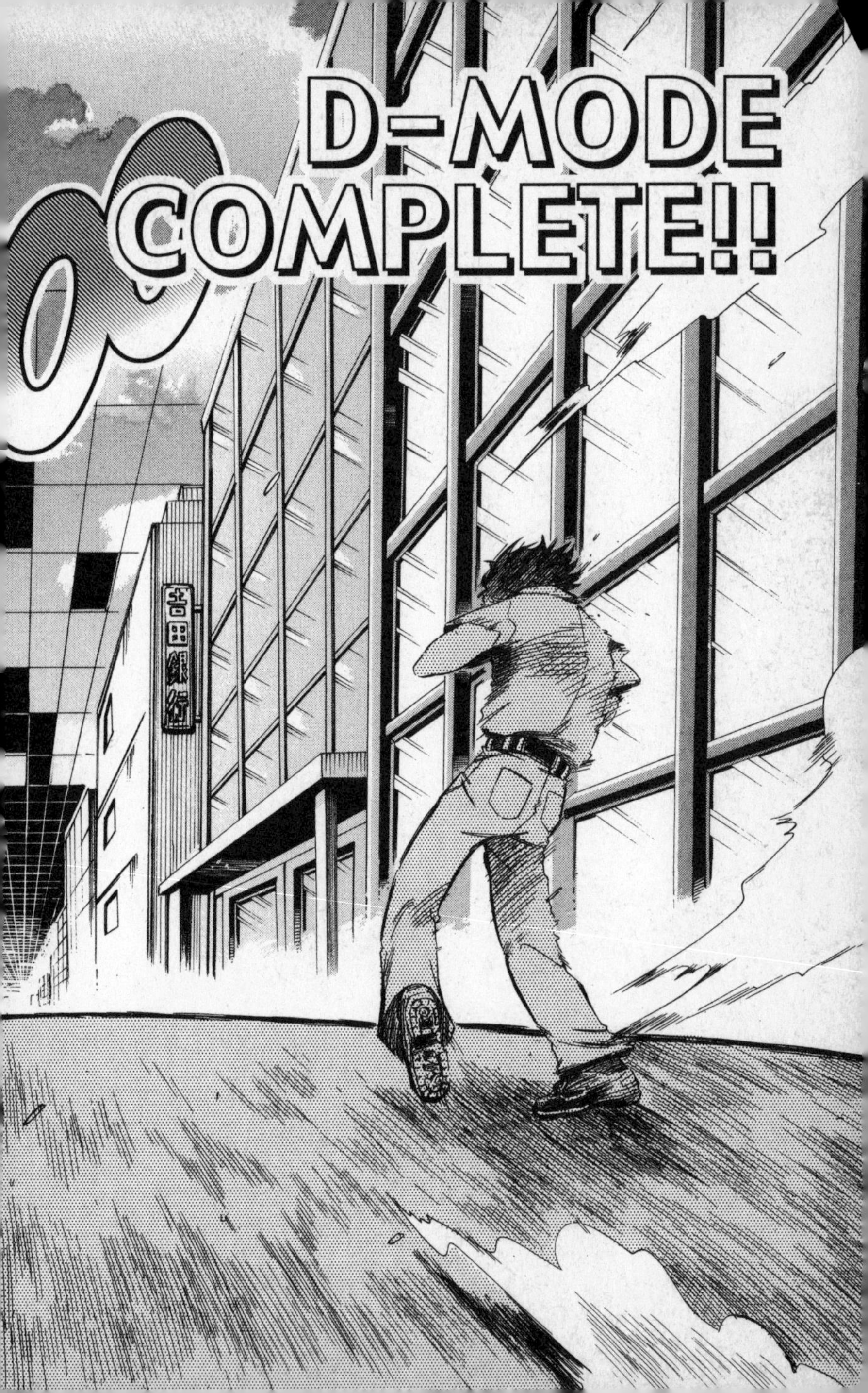
D-MODE COMPLETE!!
吉田銀行

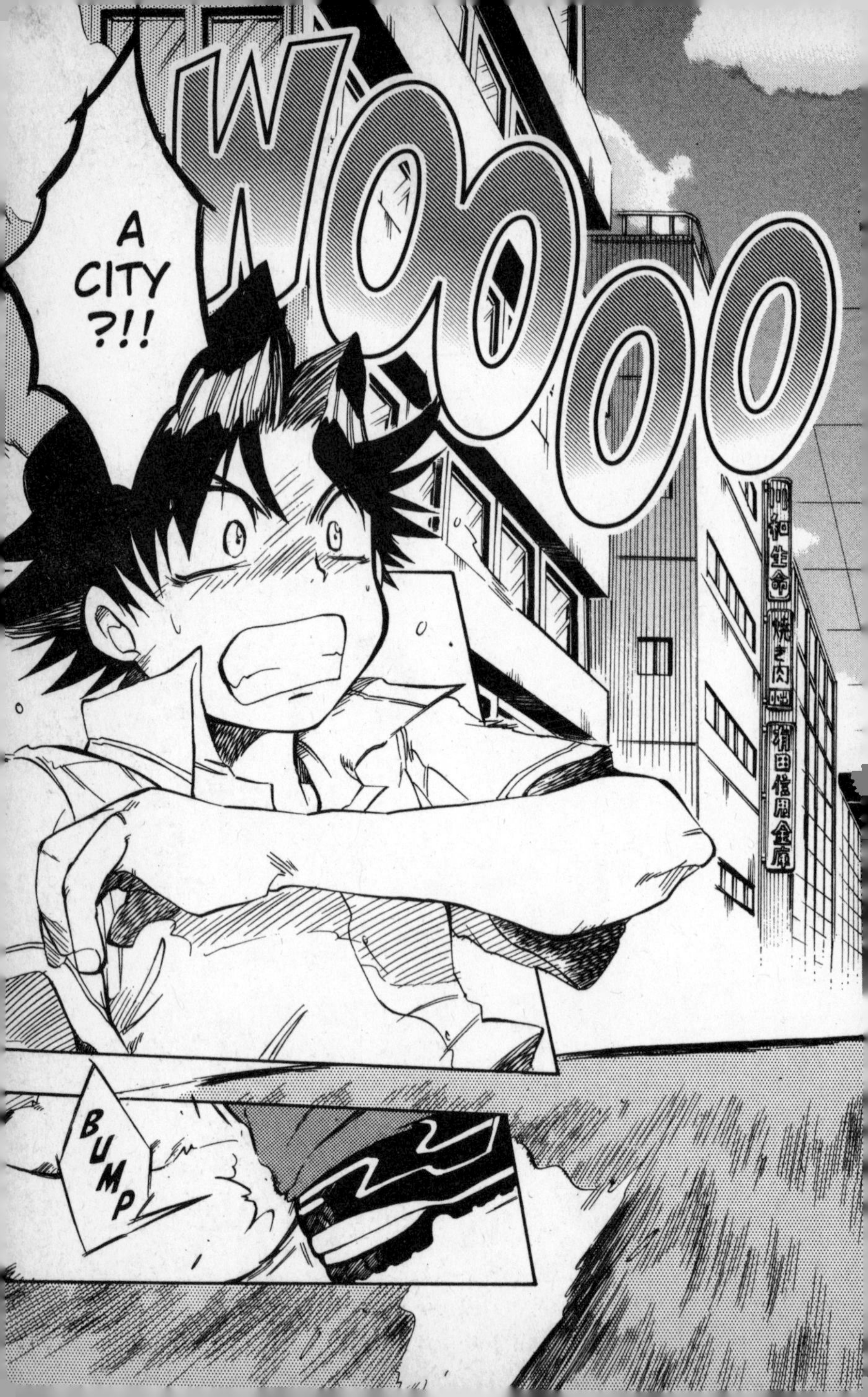
WOOOOO
A CITY ?!!
BUMP

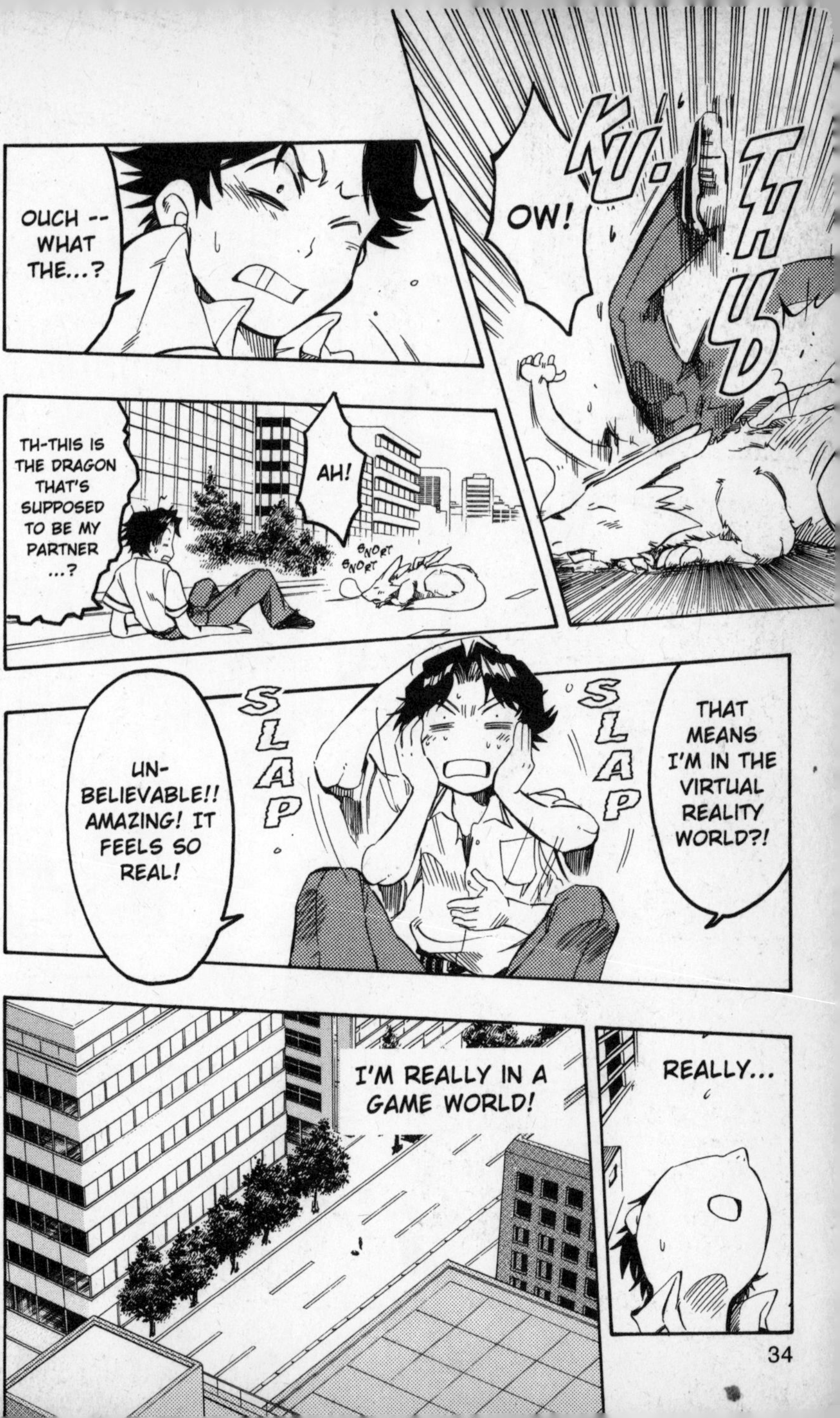
KU-THUD
OW!
OUCH -- WHAT THE...?
AH!
TH-THIS IS THE DRAGON THAT'S SUPPOSED TO BE MY PARTNER ...?
SNORT SNORT
THAT MEANS I'M IN THE VIRTUAL REALITY WORLD?!
SLAP
SLAP
UN-BELIEVABLE!! AMAZING! IT FEELS SO REAL!
REALLY...
I'M REALLY IN A GAME WORLD!

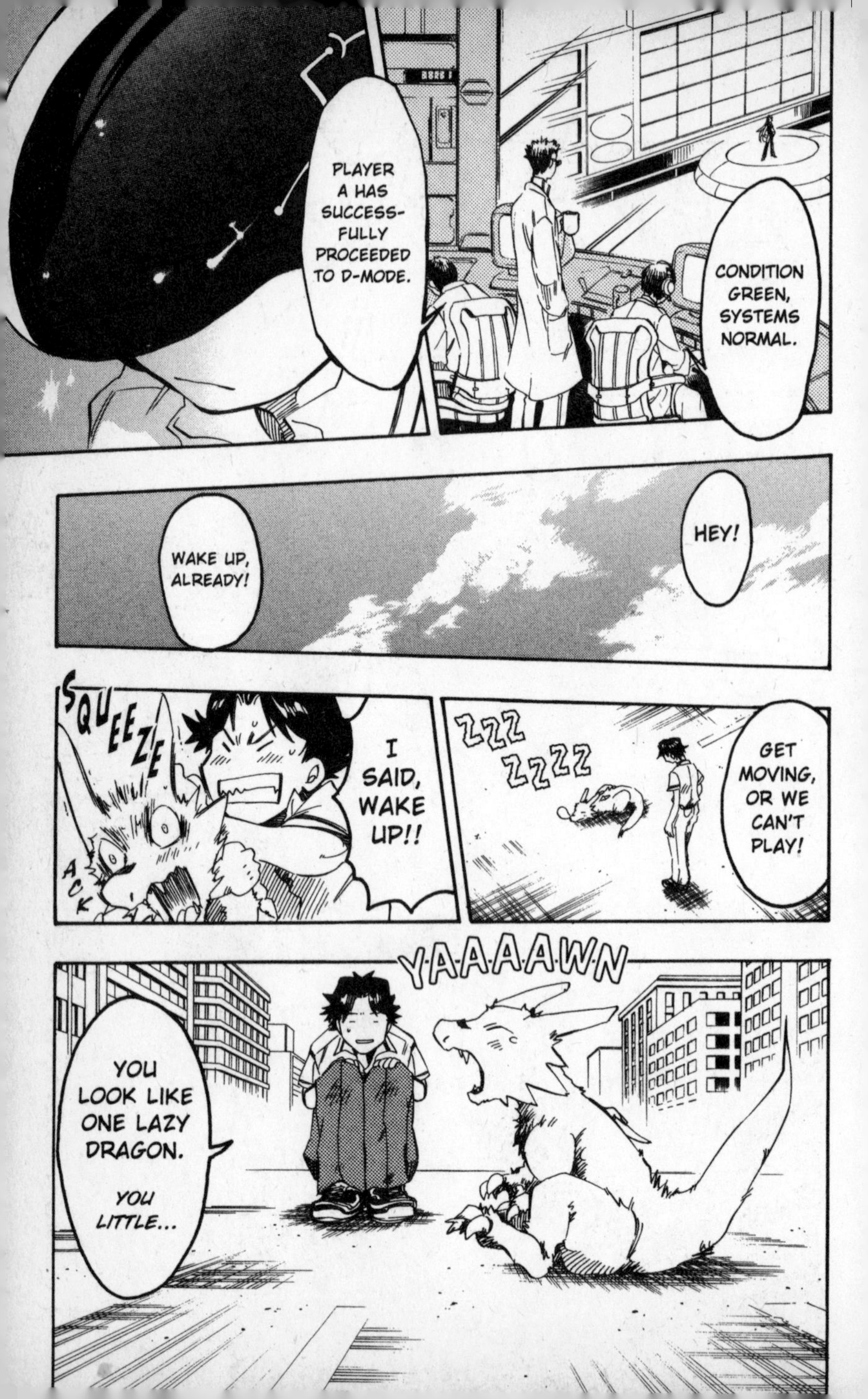
CONDITION GREEN, SYSTEMS NORMAL.
PLAYER A HAS SUCCESSFULLY PROCEEDED TO D-MODE.
HEY!
WAKE UP, ALREADY!
ZZZ ZZZZ
GET MOVING, OR WE CAN'T PLAY!
SQUEEZE
I SAID, WAKE UP!!
ACK
YAAAAWN
YOU LOOK LIKE ONE LAZY DRAGON.
YOU LITTLE...

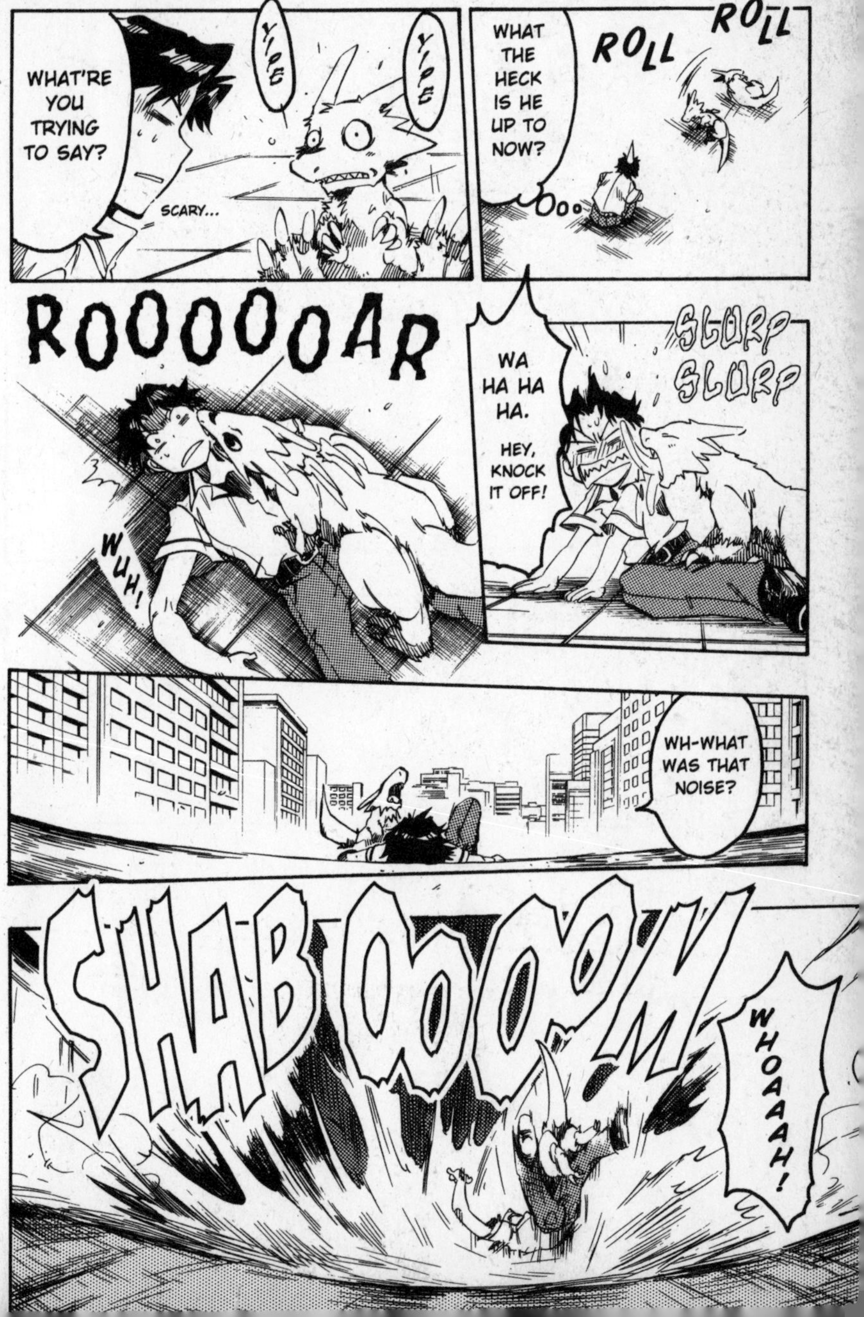
ROLL
ROLL
WHAT THE HECK IS HE UP TO NOW?
Ooo
YIPE
YIPE
WHAT'RE YOU TRYING TO SAY?
SCARY...
SLURP
SLURP
WA HA HA HA.
HEY, KNOCK IT OFF!
ROOOOOAR
WUH!
WH-WHAT WAS THAT NOISE?
WHOAAAH!
SHABOOOM

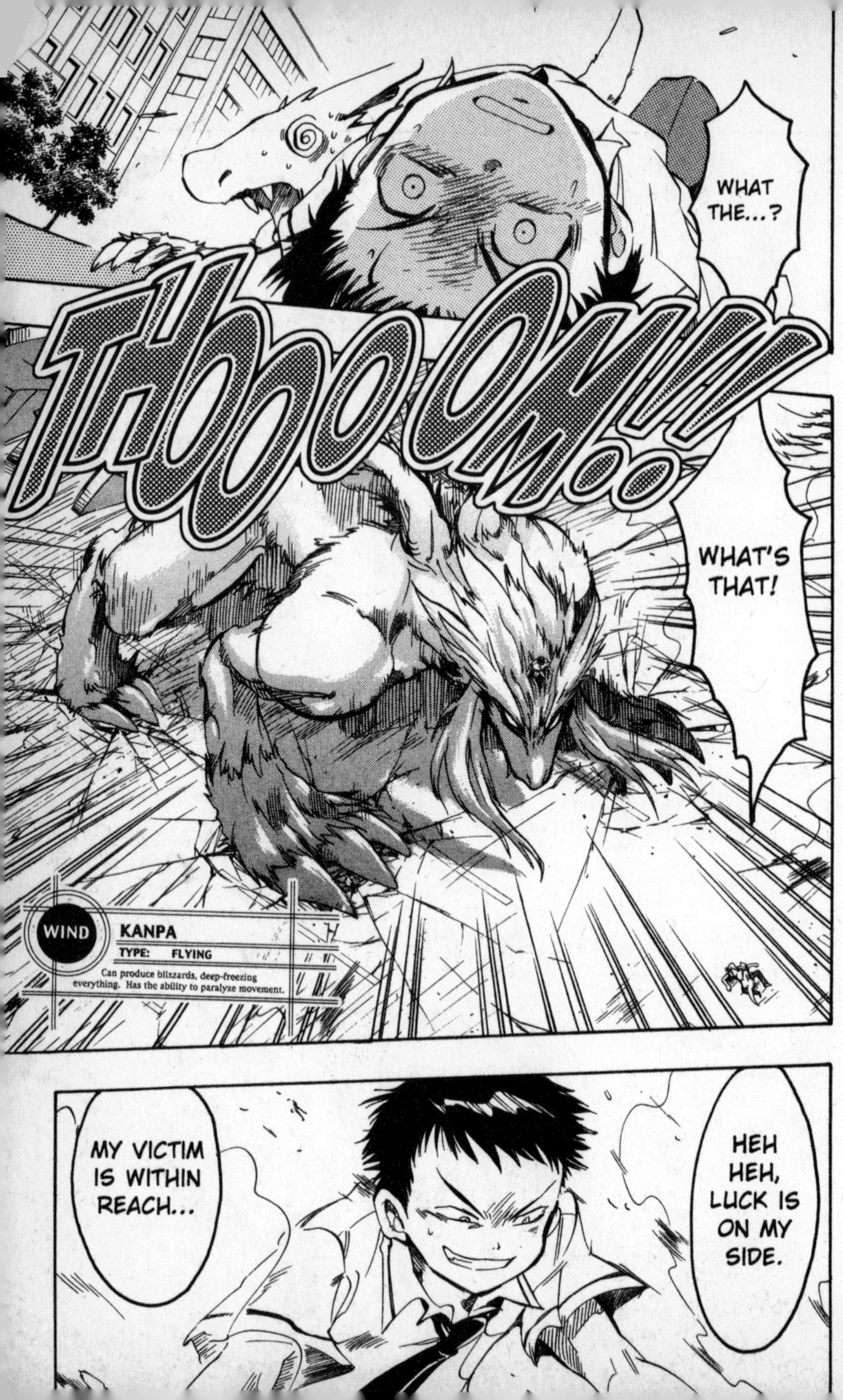
WHAT THE...?
THOOOM!!
WHAT'S THAT!
WIND
KANPA
TYPE: FLYING
Can produce blizzards, deep-freezing everything. Has the ability to paralyze movement.
HEH HEH, LUCK IS ON MY SIDE.
MY VICTIM IS WITHIN REACH...

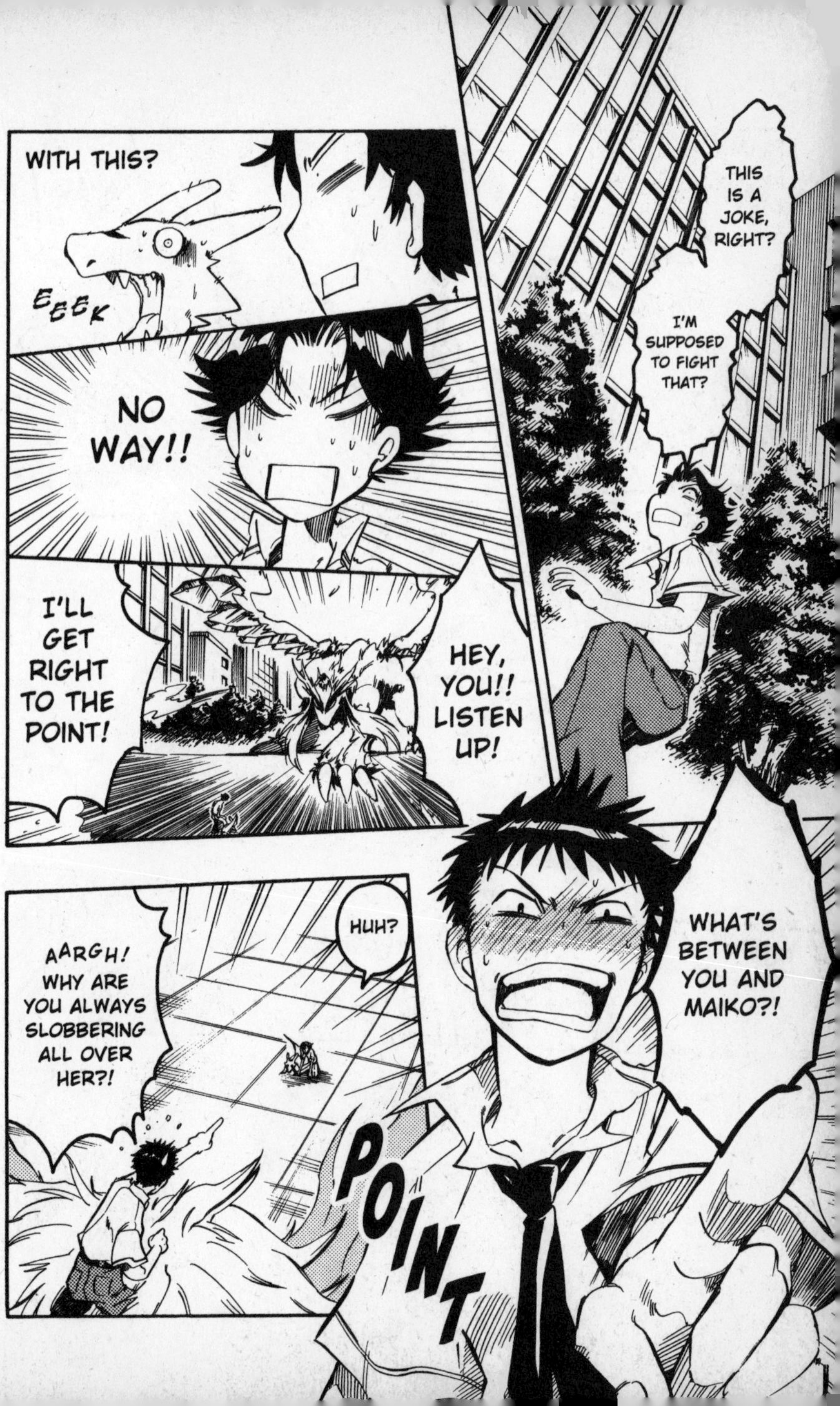
THIS IS A JOKE, RIGHT?
I'M SUPPOSED TO FIGHT THAT?
WITH THIS?
EEEK
NO WAY!!
HEY, YOU!! LISTEN UP!
I'LL GET RIGHT TO THE POINT!
WHAT'S BETWEEN YOU AND MAIKO?!
POINT
HUH?
AARGH! WHY ARE YOU ALWAYS SLOBBERING ALL OVER HER?!

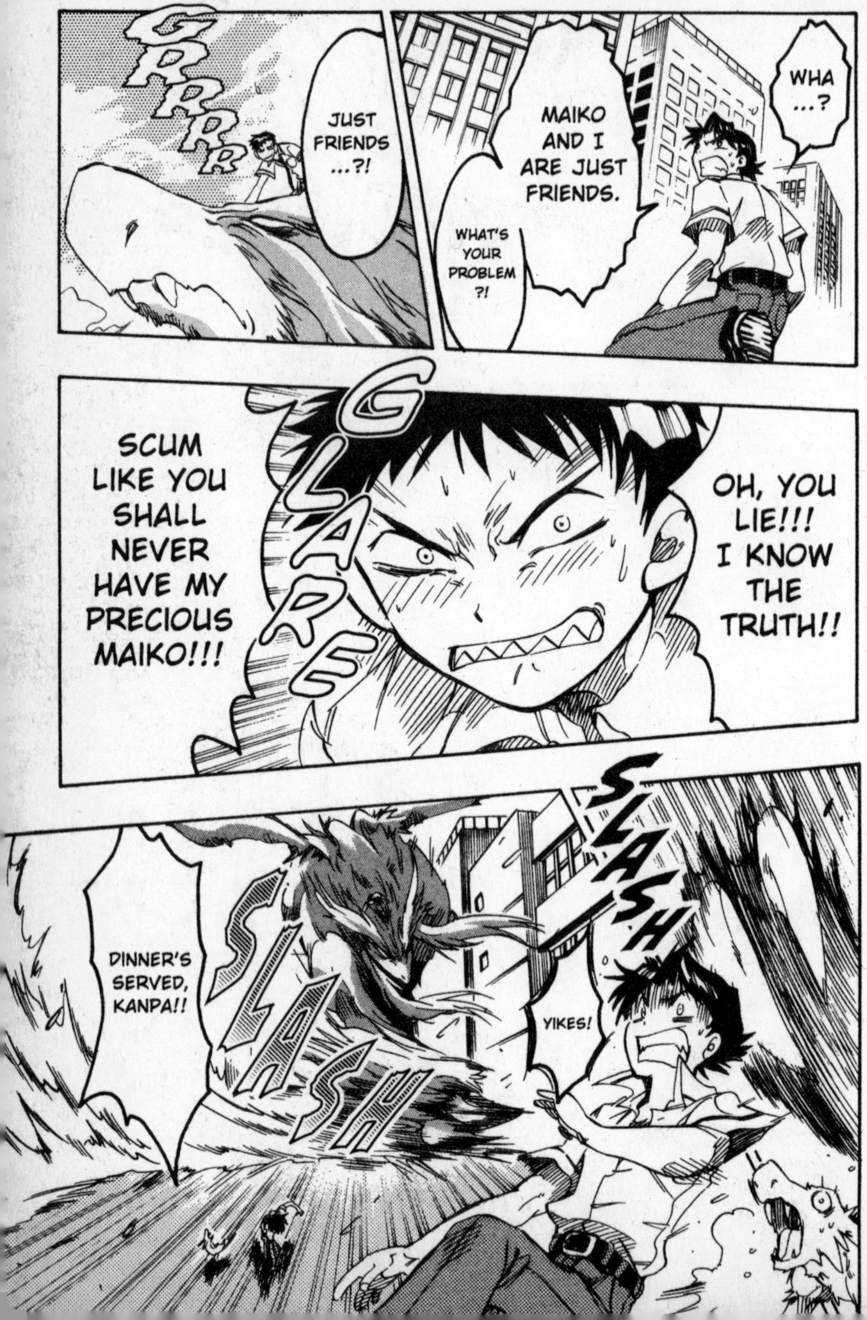
WHA ...?
MAIKO AND I ARE JUST FRIENDS.
WHAT'S YOUR PROBLEM ?!
JUST FRIENDS ...?!
GRRRR
OH, YOU LIE!!! I KNOW THE TRUTH!!
GLARE
SCUM LIKE YOU SHALL NEVER HAVE MY PRECIOUS MAIKO!!!
SLASH
YIKES!
SLASH
DINNER'S SERVED, KANPA!!

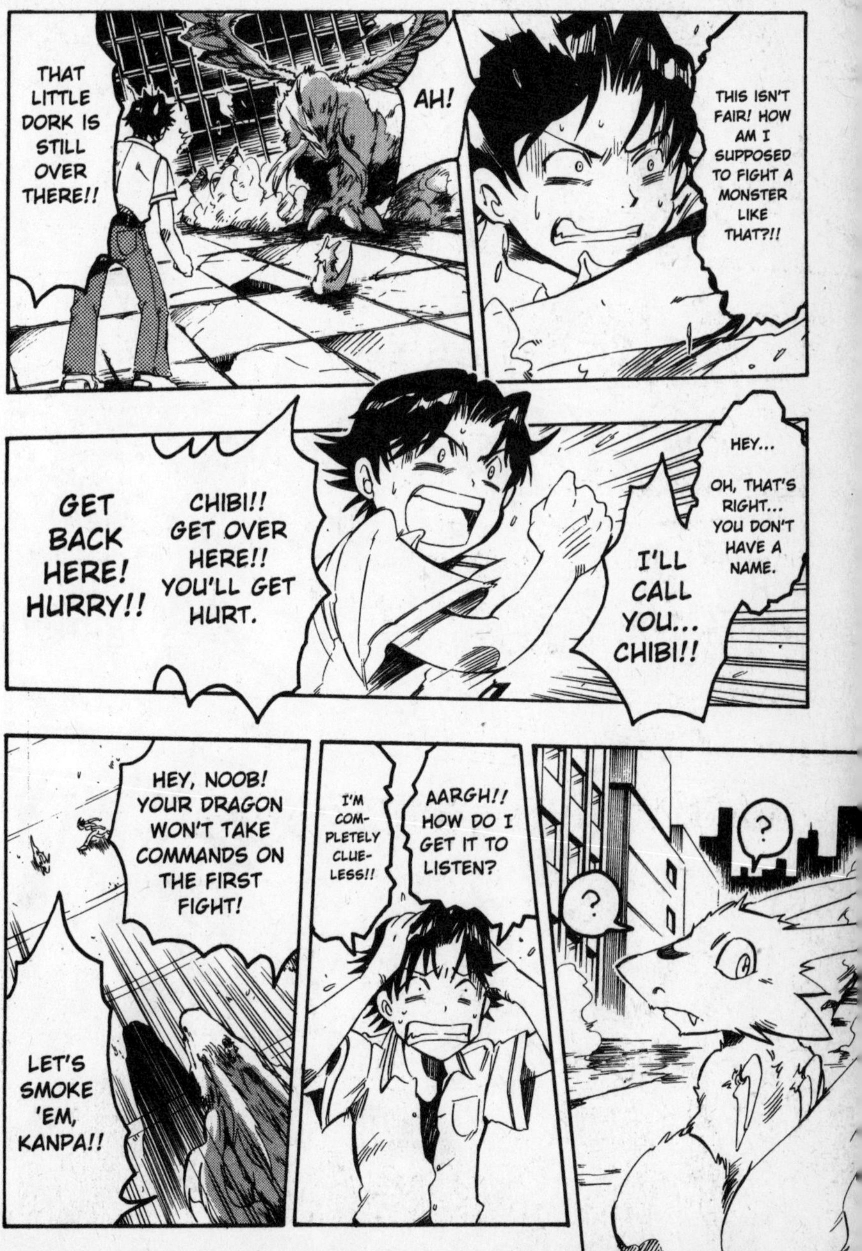
THIS ISN'T FAIR! HOW AM I SUPPOSED TO FIGHT A MONSTER LIKE THAT?!!
AH!
THAT LITTLE DORK IS STILL OVER THERE!!
HEY...
OH, THAT'S RIGHT... YOU DON'T HAVE A NAME.
I'LL CALL YOU... CHIBI!!
CHIBI!! GET OVER HERE!! YOU'LL GET HURT.
GET BACK HERE! HURRY!!
?
?
AARGH!! HOW DO I GET IT TO LISTEN?
I'M COMPLETELY CLUELESS!!
HEY, NOOB! YOUR DRAGON WON'T TAKE COMMANDS ON THE FIRST FIGHT!
LET'S SMOKE 'EM, KANPA!!

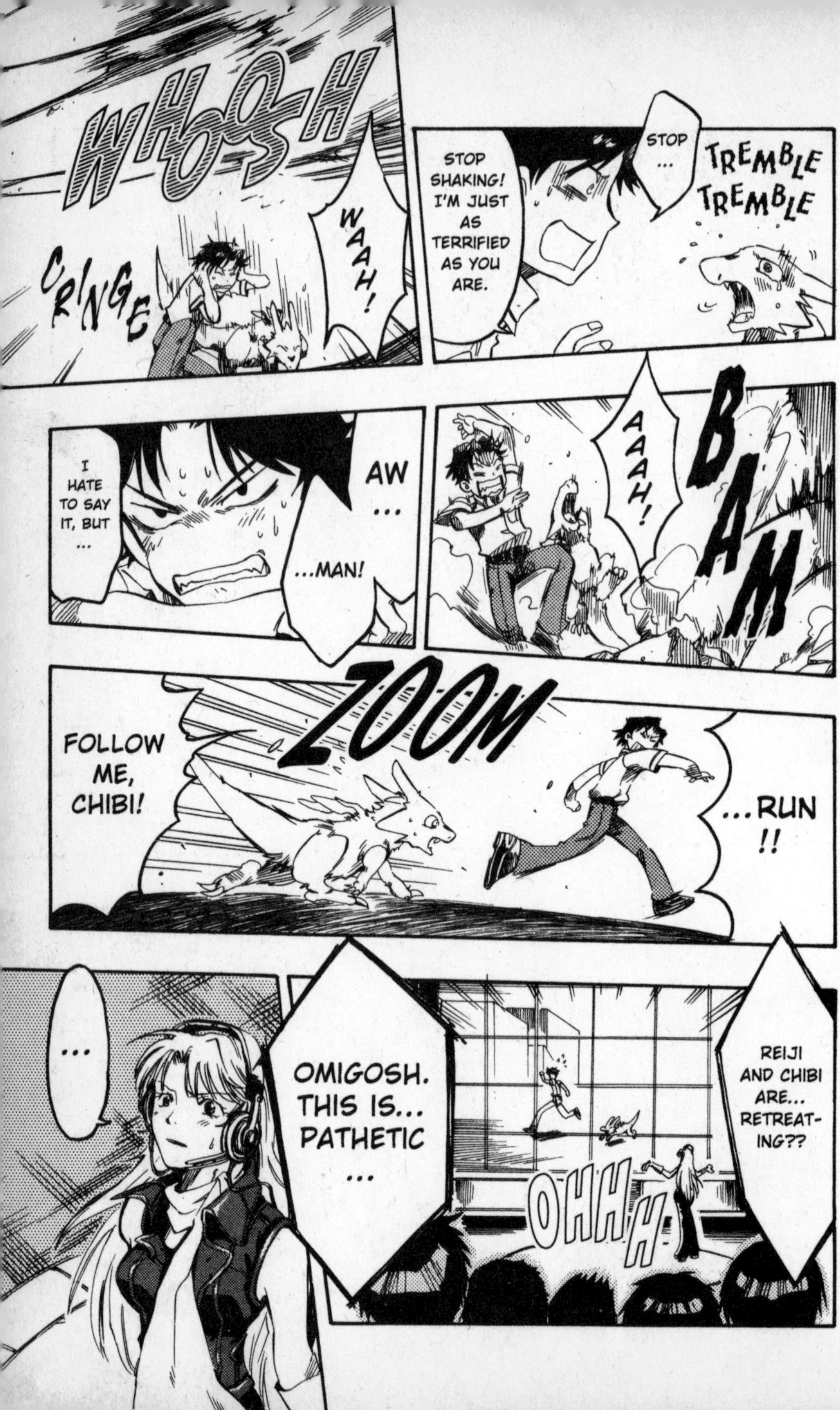
STOP ...
TREMBLE TREMBLE
STOP SHAKING! I'M JUST AS TERRIFIED AS YOU ARE.
WHOOSH
WAAAH!
CRINGE
BAM
AAAH!
AW ...
...MAN!
I HATE TO SAY IT, BUT ...
...RUN !!
ZOOM
FOLLOW ME, CHIBI!
REIJI AND CHIBI ARE... RETREATING??
OHHHH
OMIGOSH. THIS IS... PATHETIC ...
...

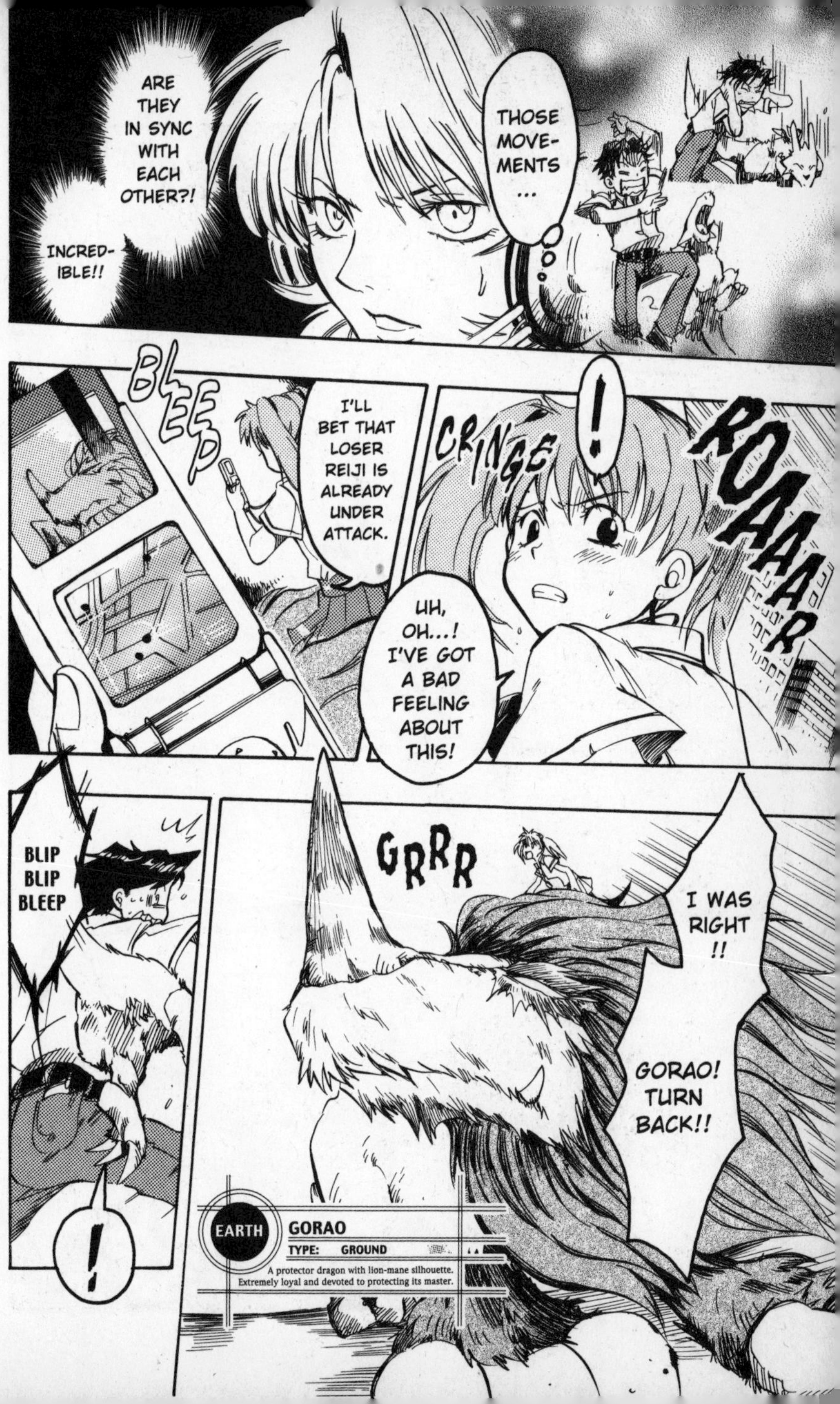
THOSE MOVEMENTS ...
ARE THEY IN SYNC WITH EACH OTHER?!
INCREDIBLE!!
ROAAAR
!
CRINGE
UH, OH...! I'VE GOT A BAD FEELING ABOUT THIS!
BLEEP
I'LL BET THAT LOSER REIJI IS ALREADY UNDER ATTACK.
GRRR
I WAS RIGHT!!
GORAO! TURN BACK!!
EARTH
GORAO
TYPE: GROUND
A protector dragon with lion-mane silhouette. Extremely loyal and devoted to protecting its master.
BLIP BLIP BLEEP
!

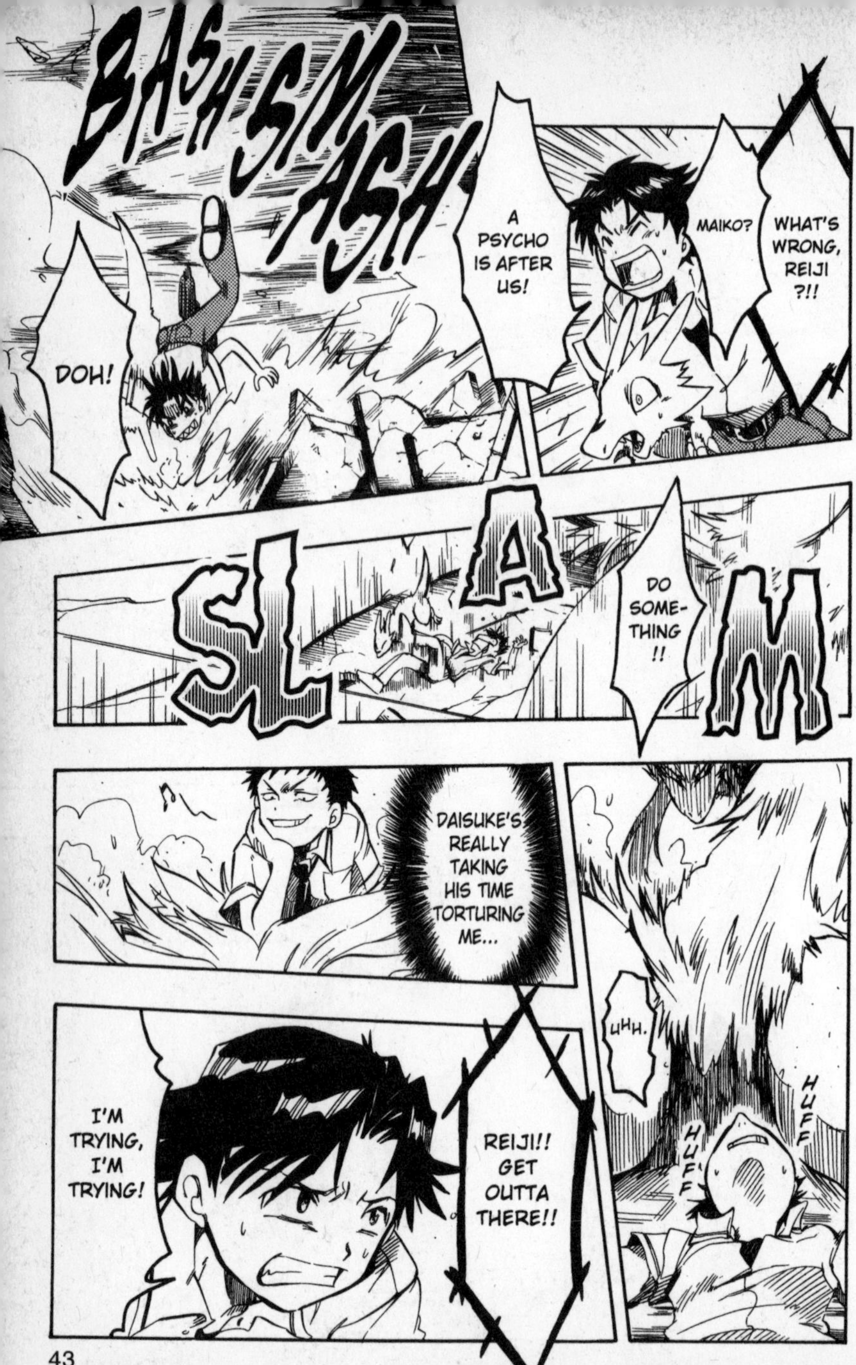
WHAT'S WRONG, REIJI ?!!
MAIKO?
A PSYCHO IS AFTER US!
BASH SMASH
DOH!
DO SOME- THING !!
SLAM
UHH.
HUFF HUFF
DAISUKE'S REALLY TAKING HIS TIME TORTURING ME...
REIJI!! GET OUTTA THERE!!
I'M TRYING, I'M TRYING!

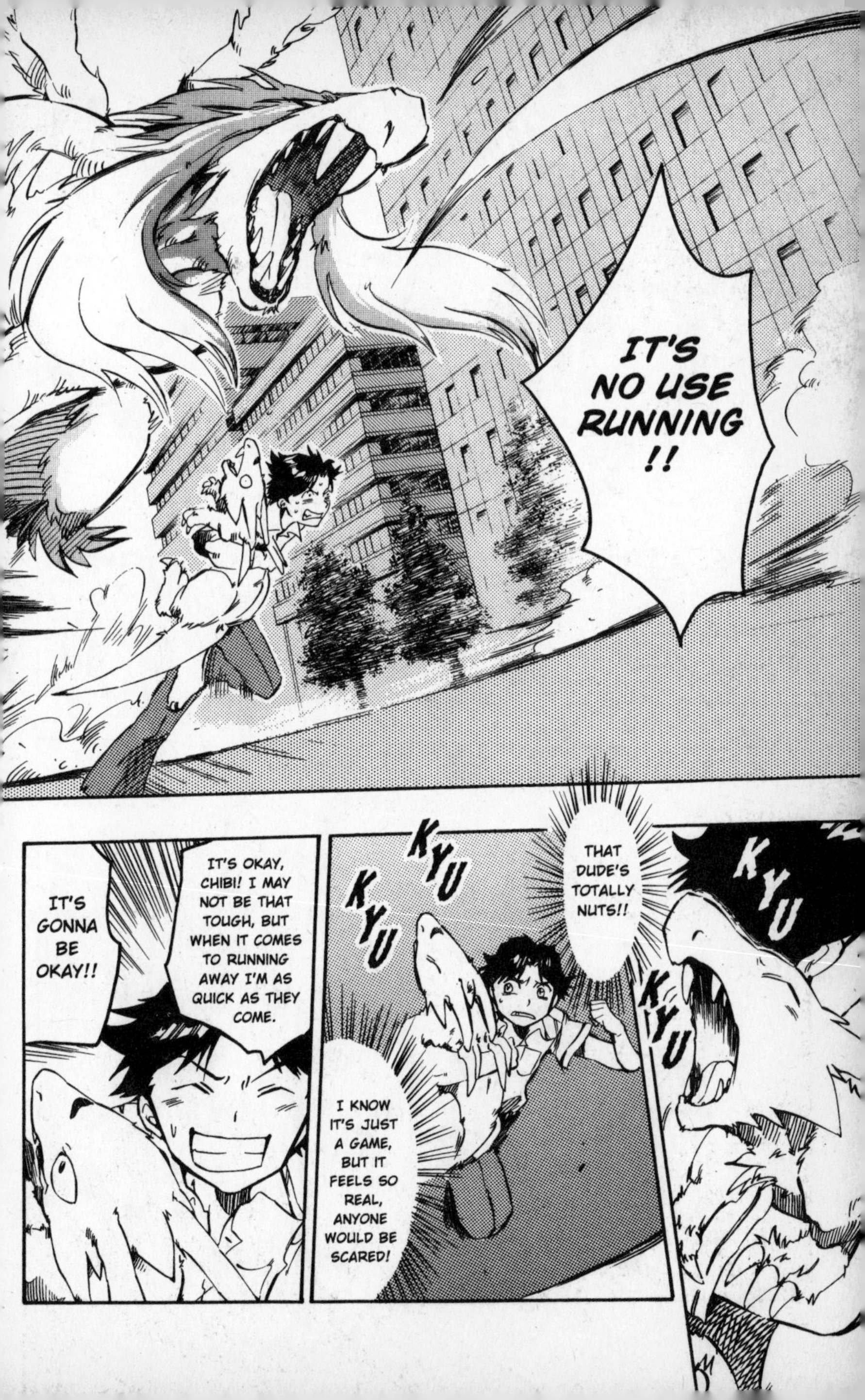
IT'S NO USE RUNNING!!
KYU KYU
KYU KYU
KYU KYU
THAT DUDE'S TOTALLY NUTS!!
I KNOW IT'S JUST A GAME, BUT IT FEELS SO REAL, ANYONE WOULD BE SCARED!
IT'S OKAY, CHIBI! I MAY NOT BE THAT TOUGH, BUT WHEN IT COMES TO RUNNING AWAY I'M AS QUICK AS THEY COME.
IT'S GONNA BE OKAY!!

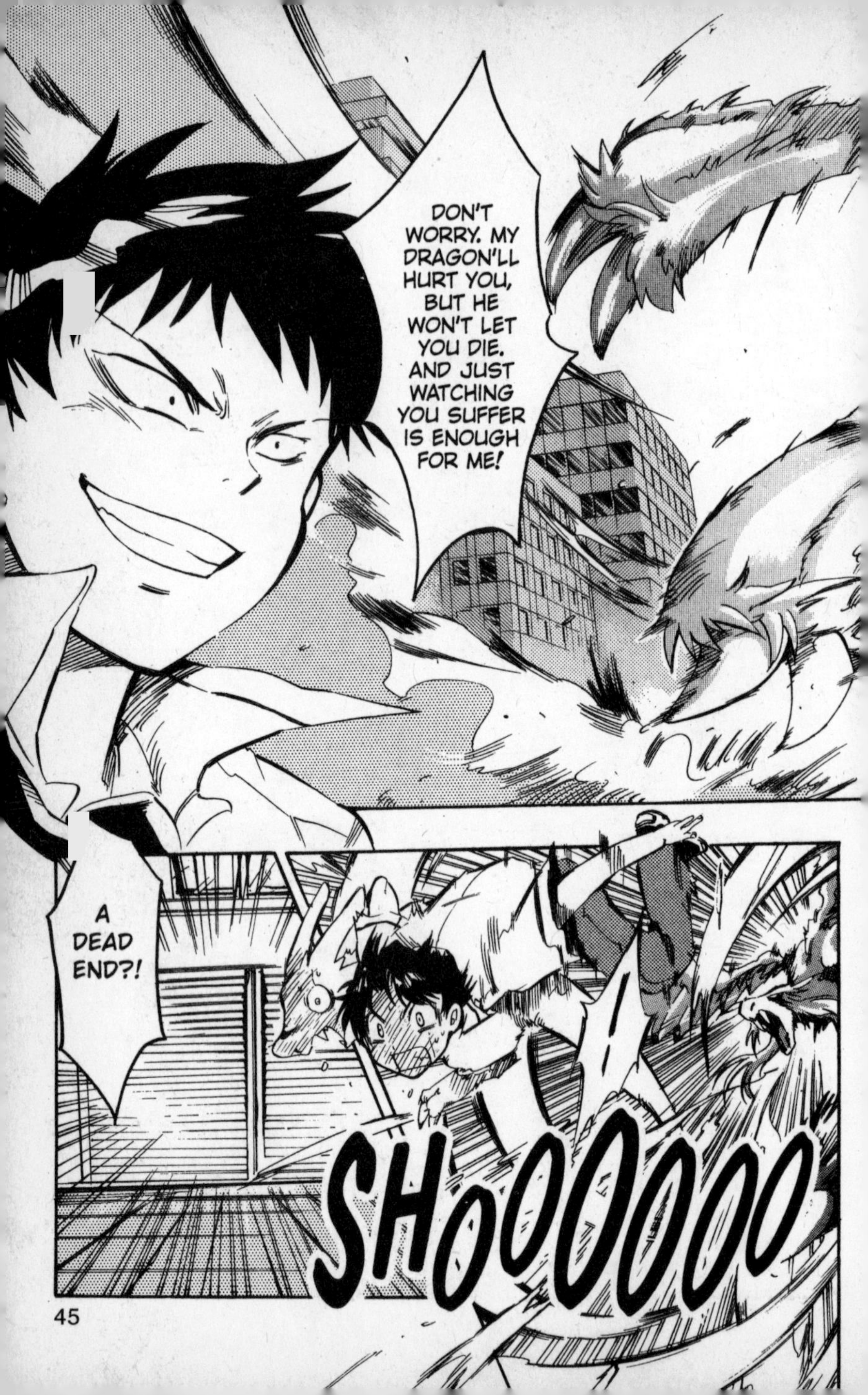
DON'T WORRY. MY DRAGON'LL HURT YOU, BUT HE WON'T LET YOU DIE. AND JUST WATCHING YOU SUFFER IS ENOUGH FOR ME!
A DEAD END?!
SHOOOOOO

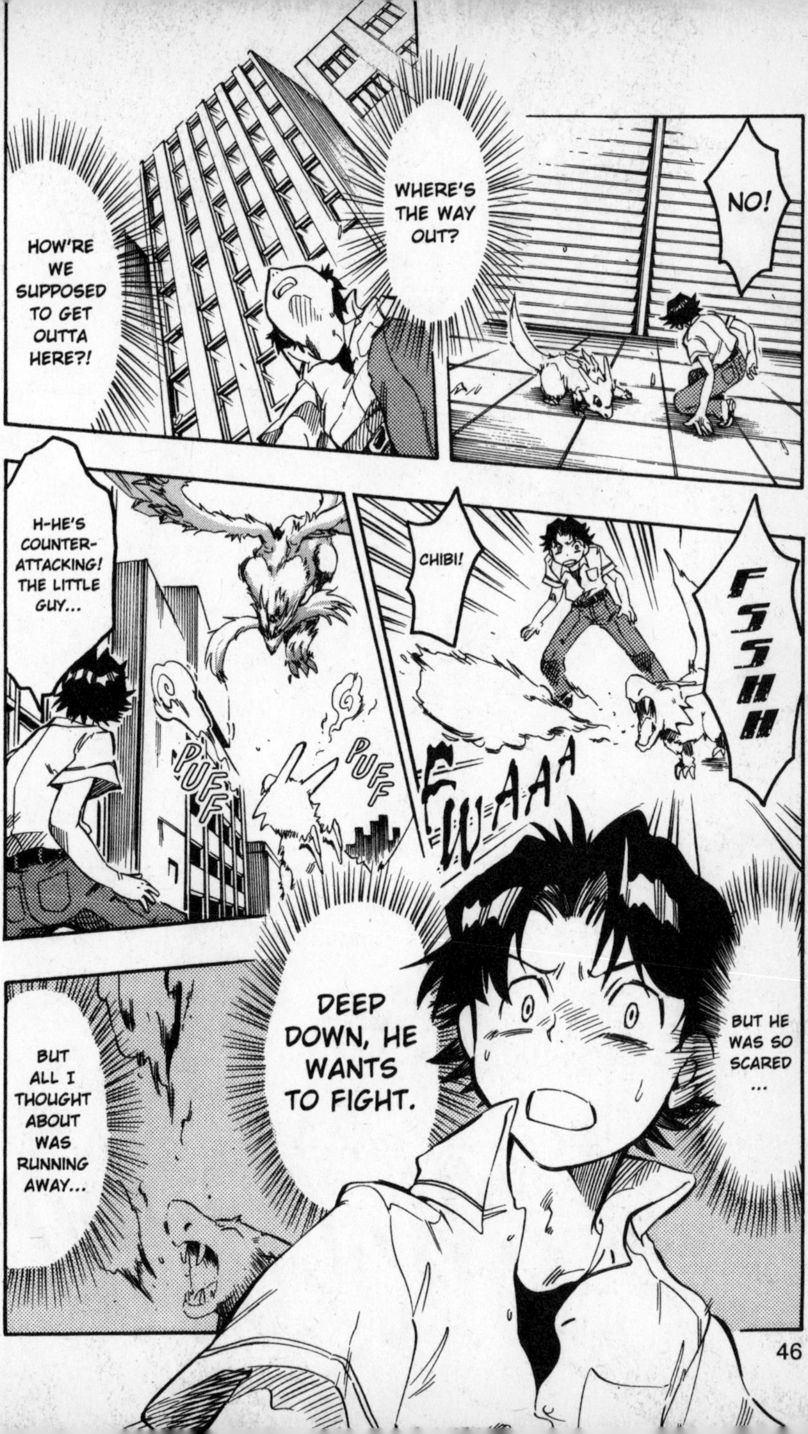
NO!
WHERE'S THE WAY OUT?
HOW'RE WE SUPPOSED TO GET OUTTA HERE?!
FSSHH
CHIBI!
FWAAA
H-HE'S COUNTER-ATTACKING! THE LITTLE GUY...
PUFF
PUFF
BUT HE WAS SO SCARED...
DEEP DOWN, HE WANTS TO FIGHT.
BUT ALL I THOUGHT ABOUT WAS RUNNING AWAY...

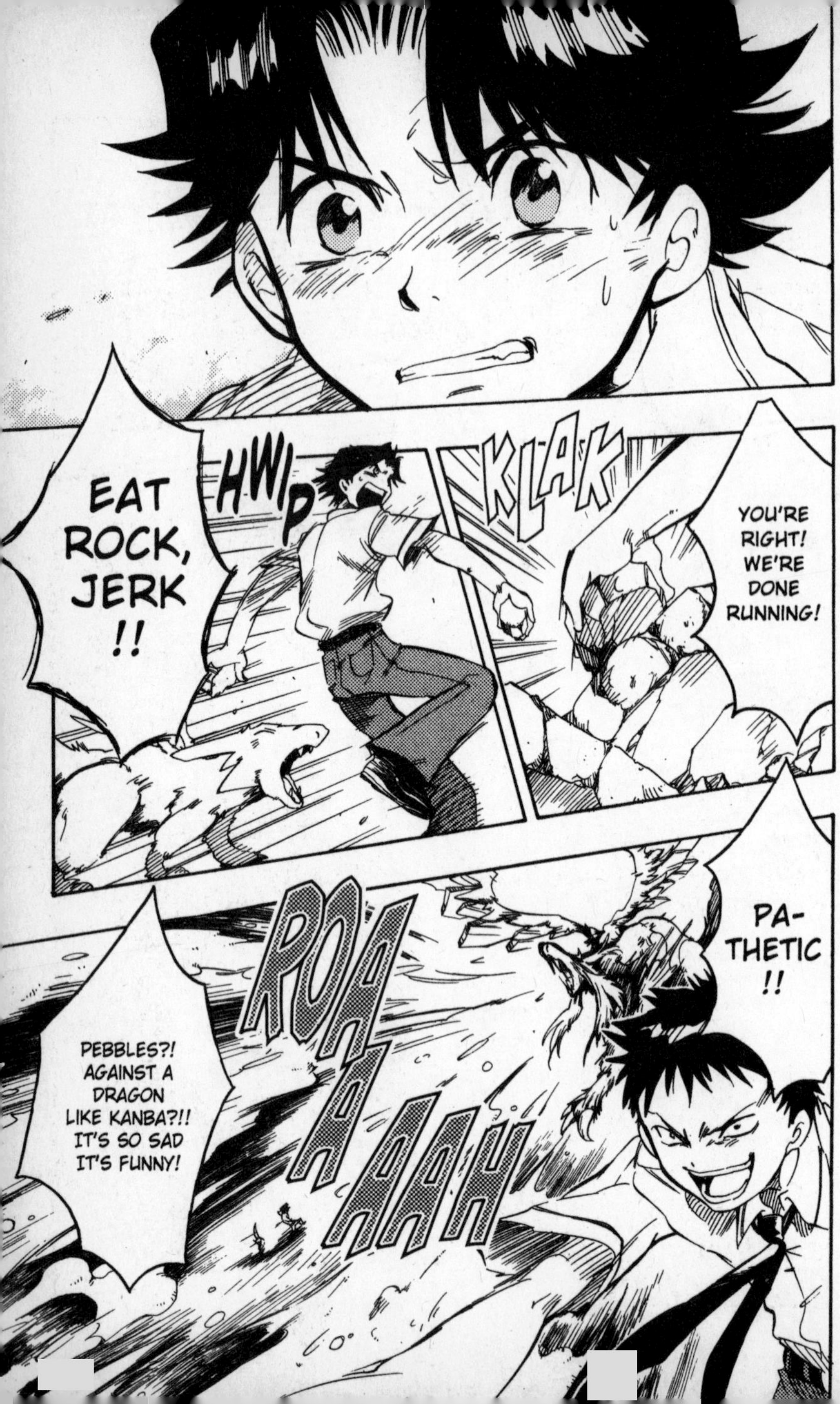
YOU'RE RIGHT! WE'RE DONE RUNNING!
KLAK
HWIP
EAT ROCK, JERK !!
PA- THETIC !!
ROAAAAH
PEBBLES?! AGAINST A DRAGON LIKE KANBA?!! IT'S SO SAD IT'S FUNNY!

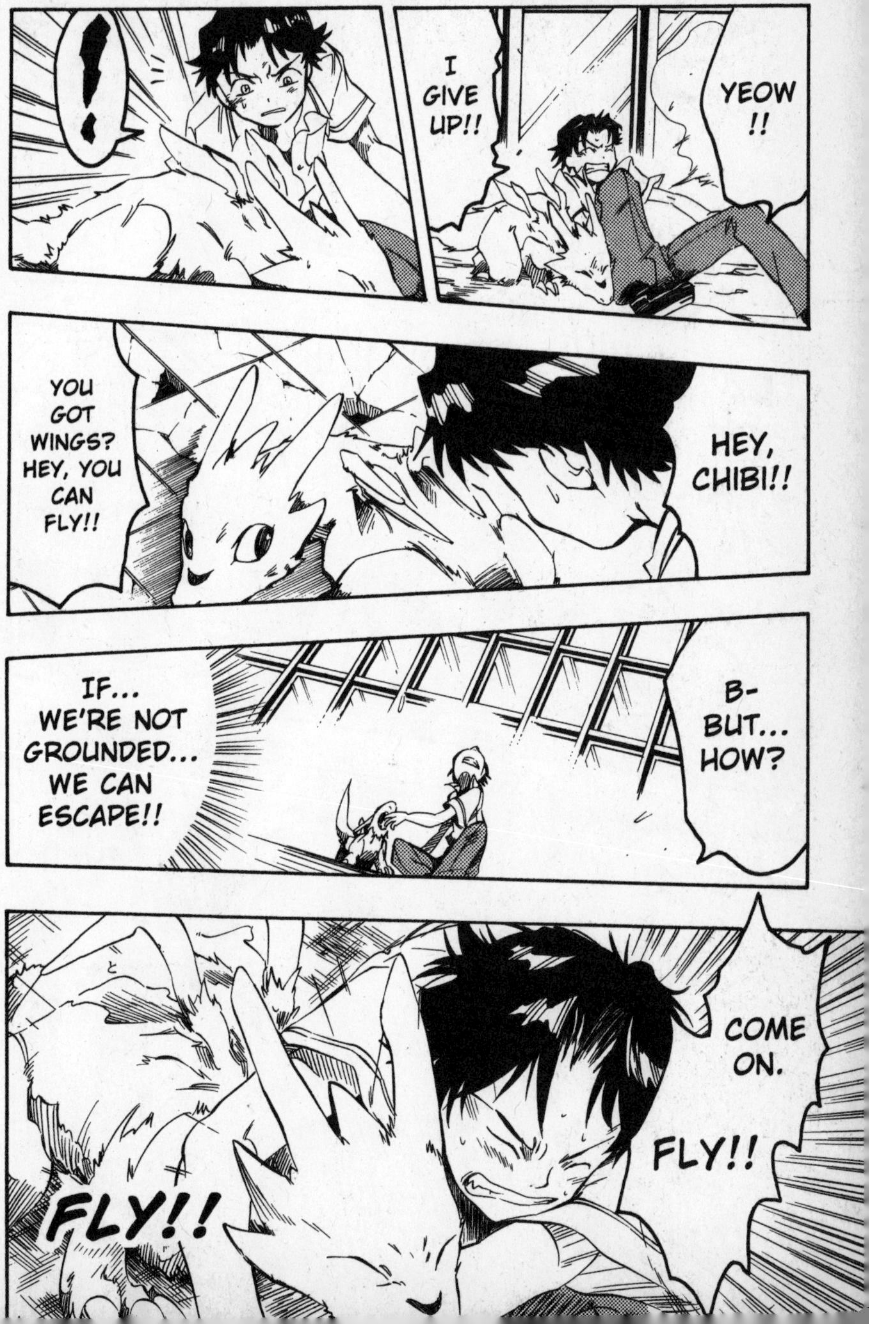
YEOW !!
I GIVE UP!!
!
HEY, CHIBI!!
YOU GOT WINGS? HEY, YOU CAN FLY!!
B-BUT... HOW?
IF... WE'RE NOT GROUNDED... WE CAN ESCAPE!!
COME ON.
FLY!!
FLY!!

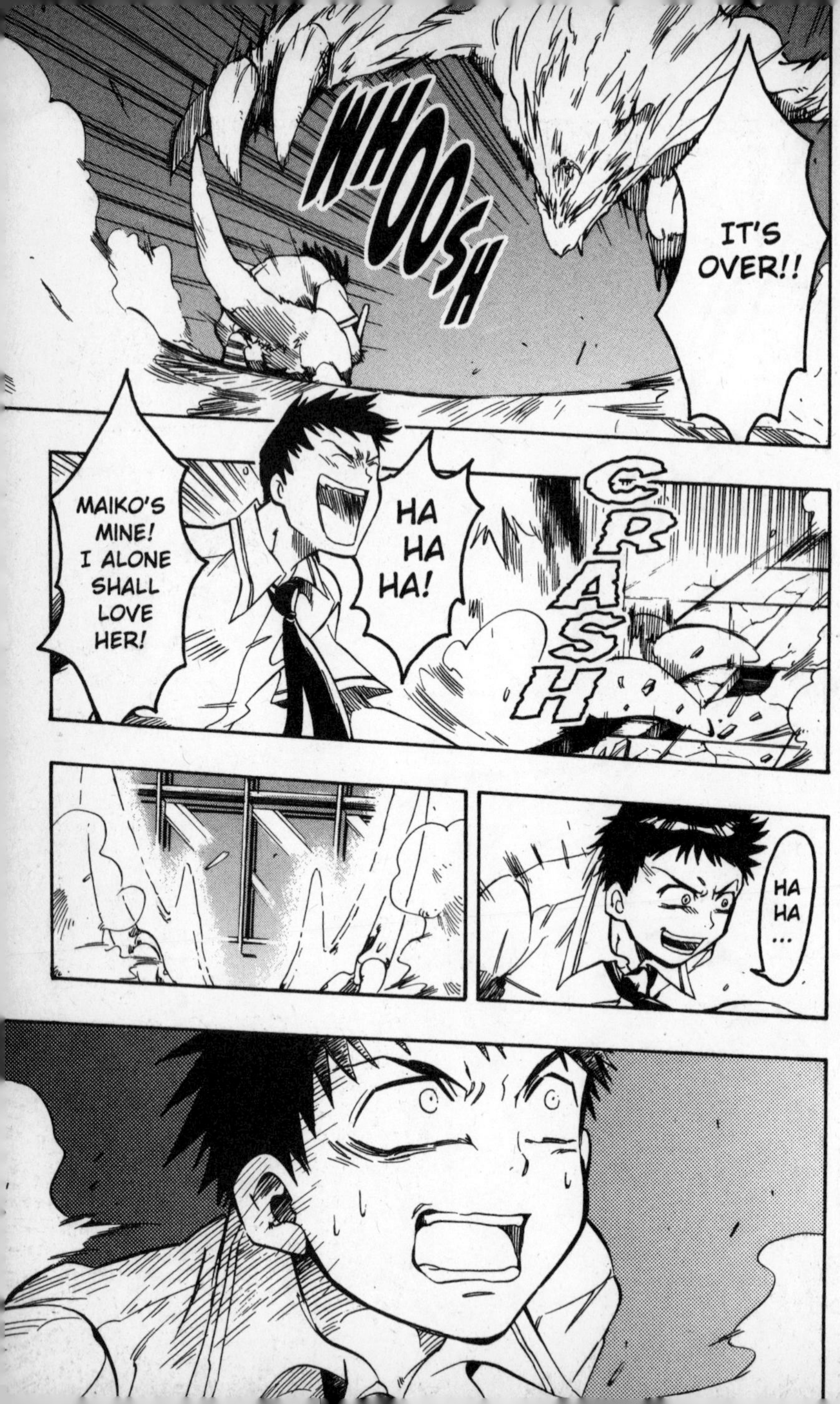
IT'S OVER!!
WHOOSH
CRASH
HA HA HA!
MAIKO'S MINE! I ALONE SHALL LOVE HER!
HA HA ...

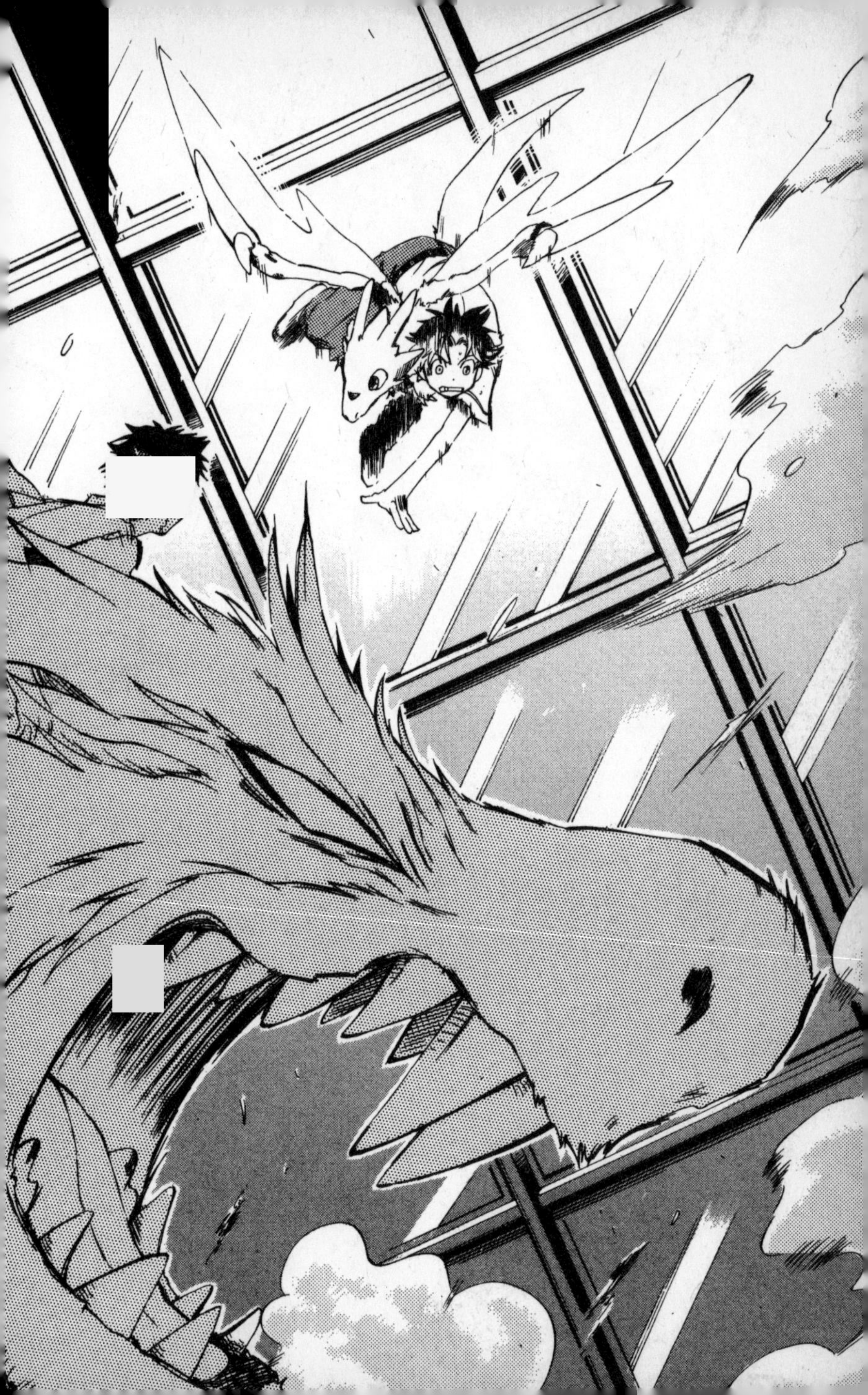

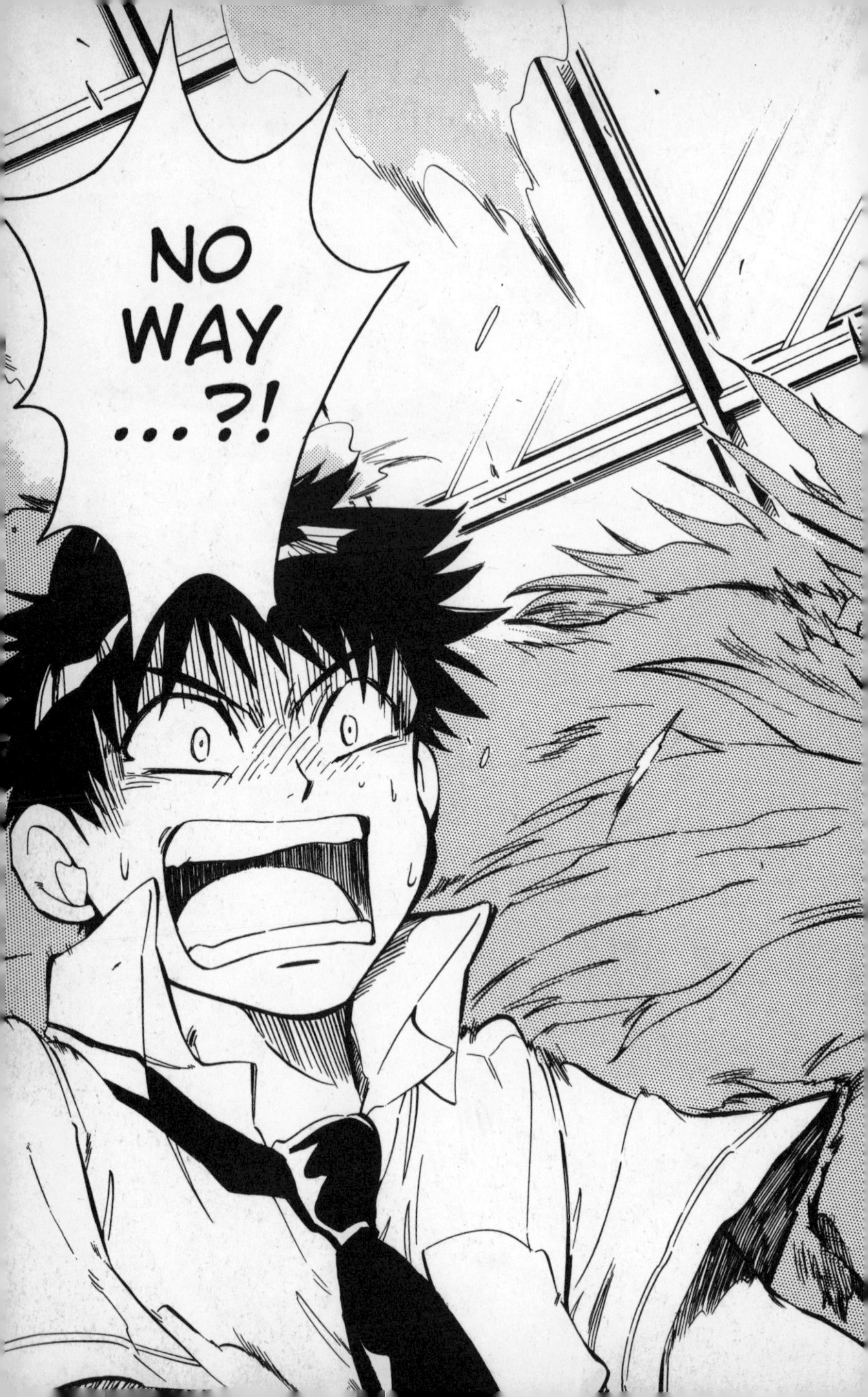
NO WAY ...?!

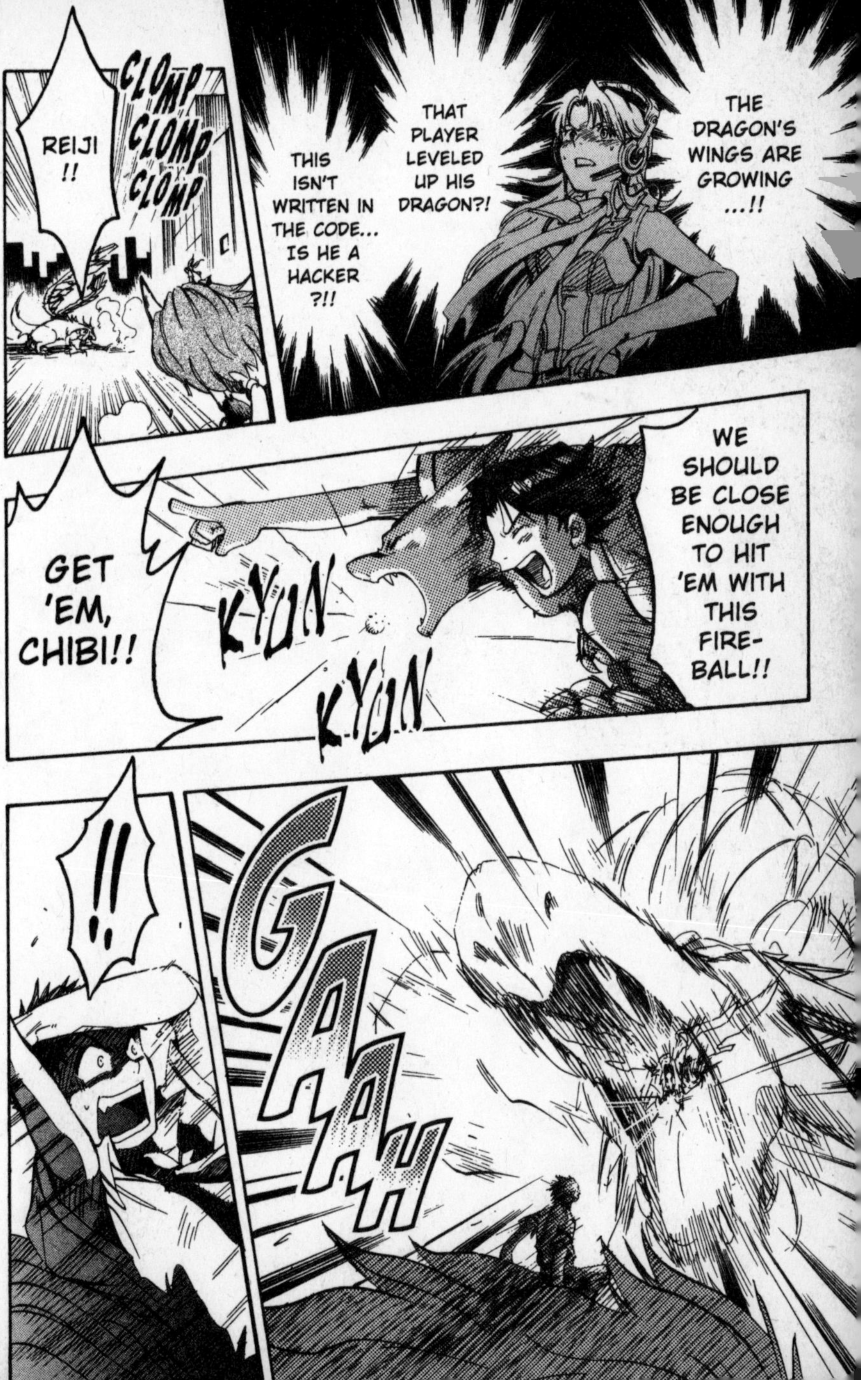
THE DRAGON'S WINGS ARE GROWING ...!!
THAT PLAYER LEVELED UP HIS DRAGON?!
THIS ISN'T WRITTEN IN THE CODE... IS HE A HACKER ?!!
REIJI !!
CLOMP CLOMP CLOMP
WE SHOULD BE CLOSE ENOUGH TO HIT 'EM WITH THIS FIRE-BALL!!
GET 'EM, CHIBI!!
KYUN
KYUN
GAAH
!!

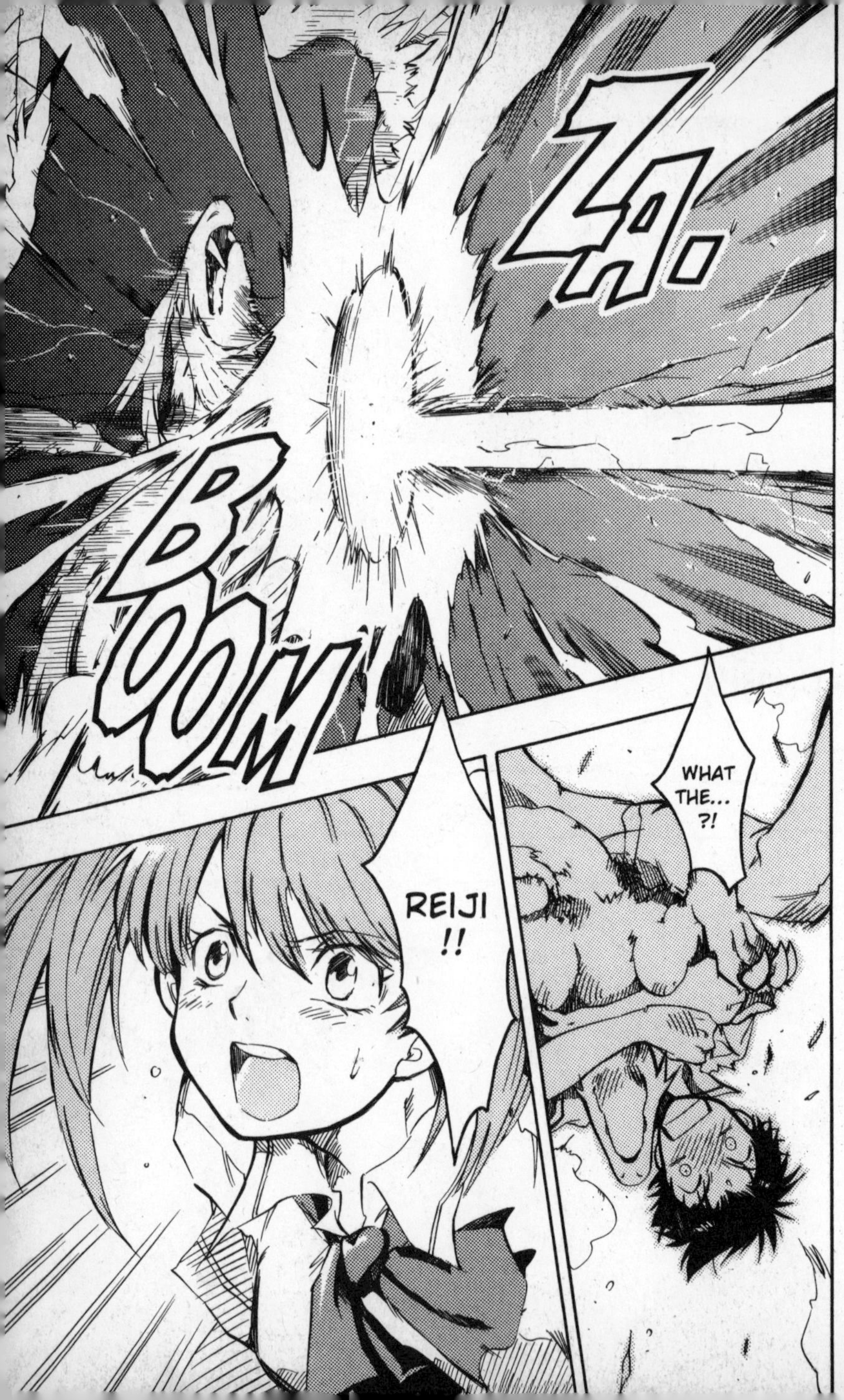
ZA.
BOOM
WHAT THE... ?!
REIJI !!

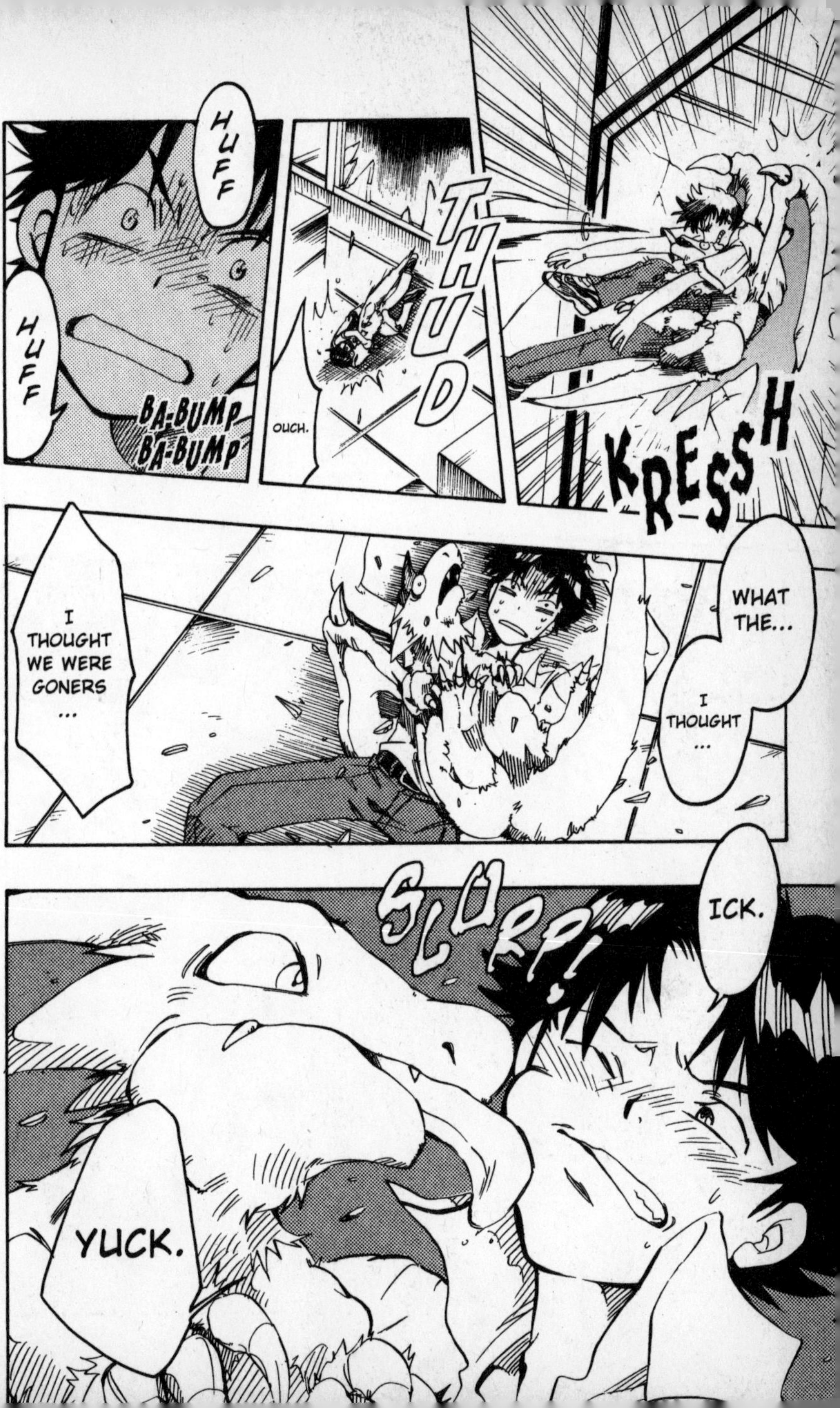
KRESSH
THUD
OUCH.
HUFF
HUFF
BA-BUMP BA-BUMP
WHAT THE...
I THOUGHT ...
I THOUGHT WE WERE GONERS ...
ICK.
SLURP!
YUCK.

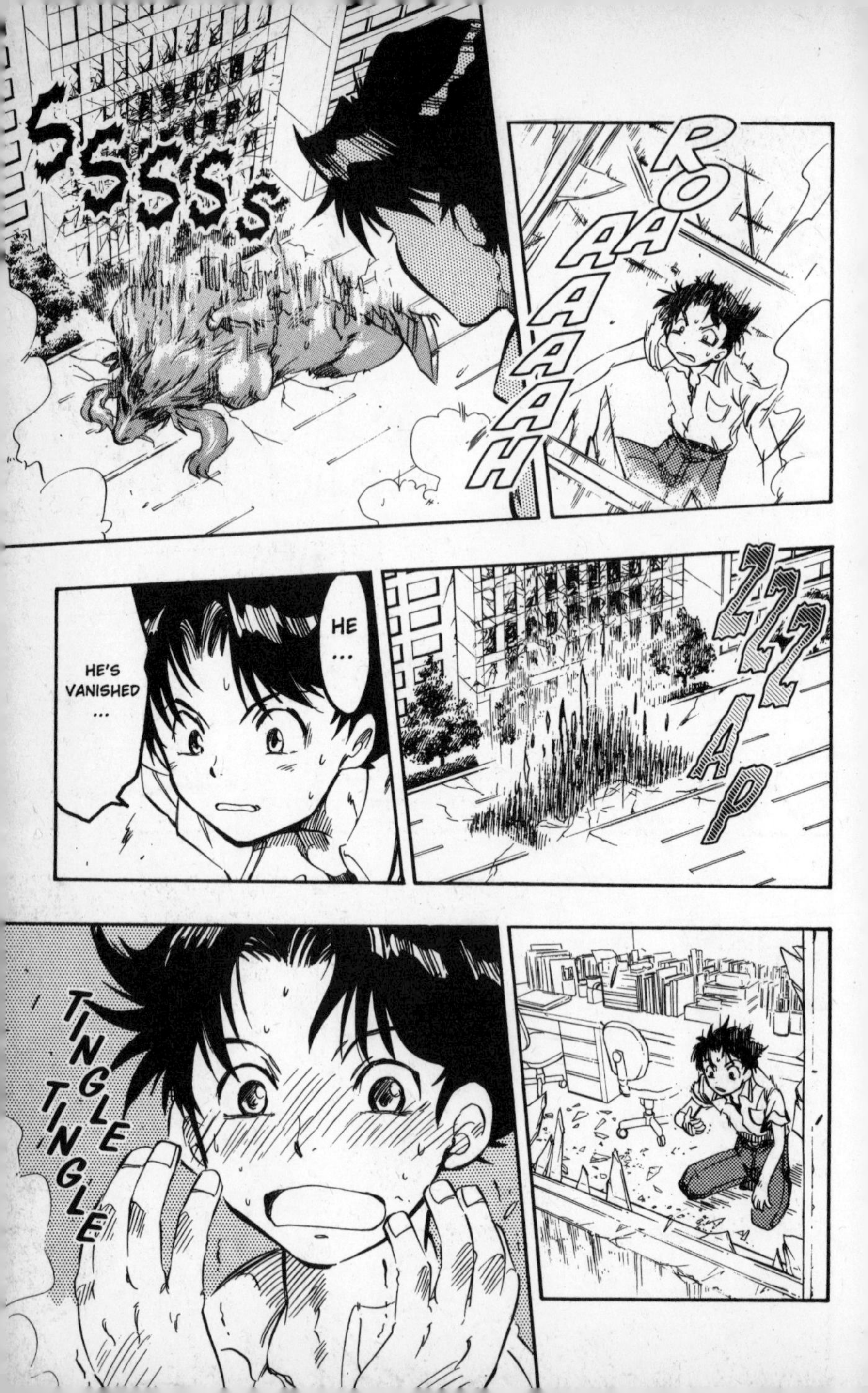
ROAAAAAAAH
SSSSSS
ZZZAP
HE ...
HE'S VANISHED ...
TINGLE TINGLE

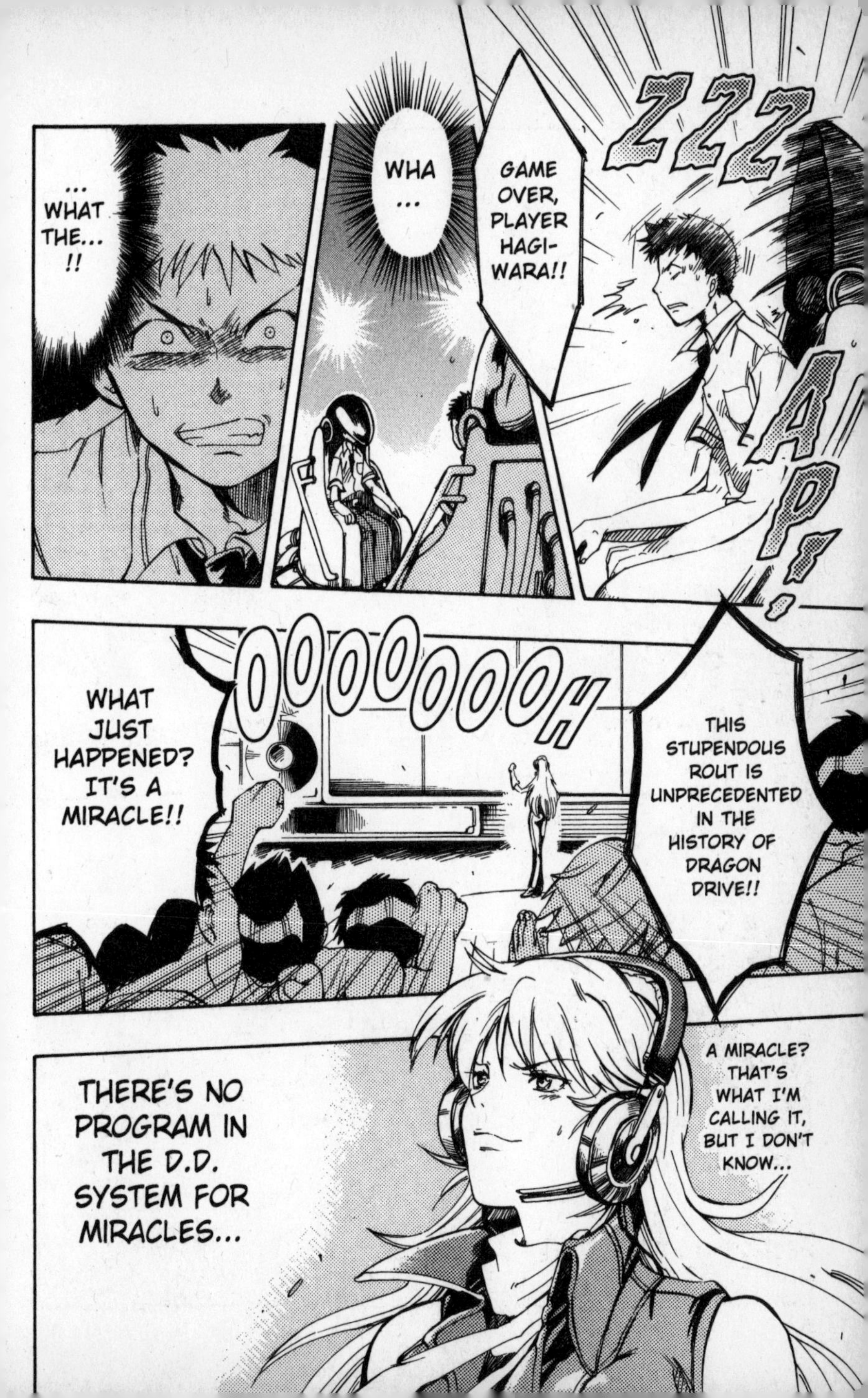
ZZZAP!!
GAME OVER, PLAYER HAGI-WARA!!
WHA ...
... WHAT THE... !!
THIS STUPENDOUS ROUT IS UNPRECEDENTED IN THE HISTORY OF DRAGON DRIVE!!
OOOOOOOOH
WHAT JUST HAPPENED? IT'S A MIRACLE!!
A MIRACLE? THAT'S WHAT I'M CALLING IT, BUT I DON'T KNOW...
THERE'S NO PROGRAM IN THE D.D. SYSTEM FOR MIRACLES...

READ THIS WAY

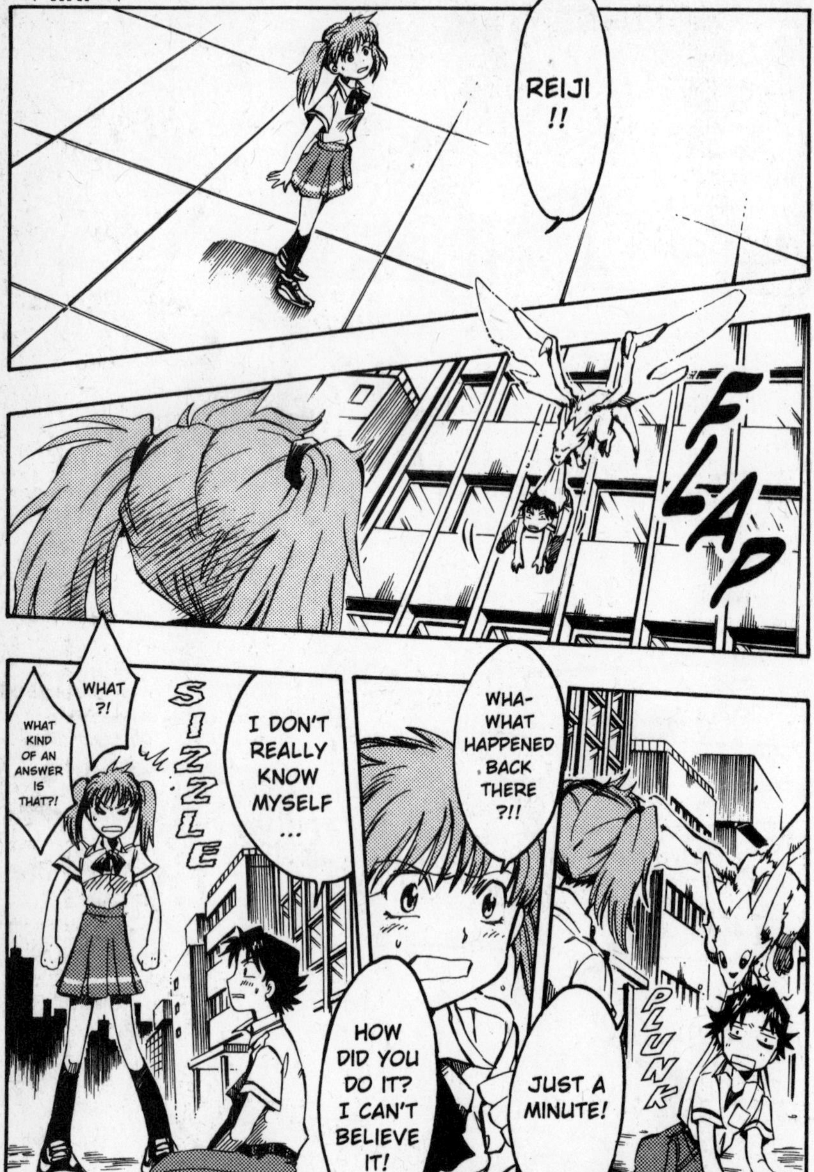

REIJI !!
FLAP
WHA- WHAT HAPPENED BACK THERE ?!!
PLUNK
JUST A MINUTE!
HOW DID YOU DO IT? I CAN'T BELIEVE IT!
I DON'T REALLY KNOW MYSELF ...
SIZZLE
WHAT ?!
WHAT KIND OF AN ANSWER IS THAT?!

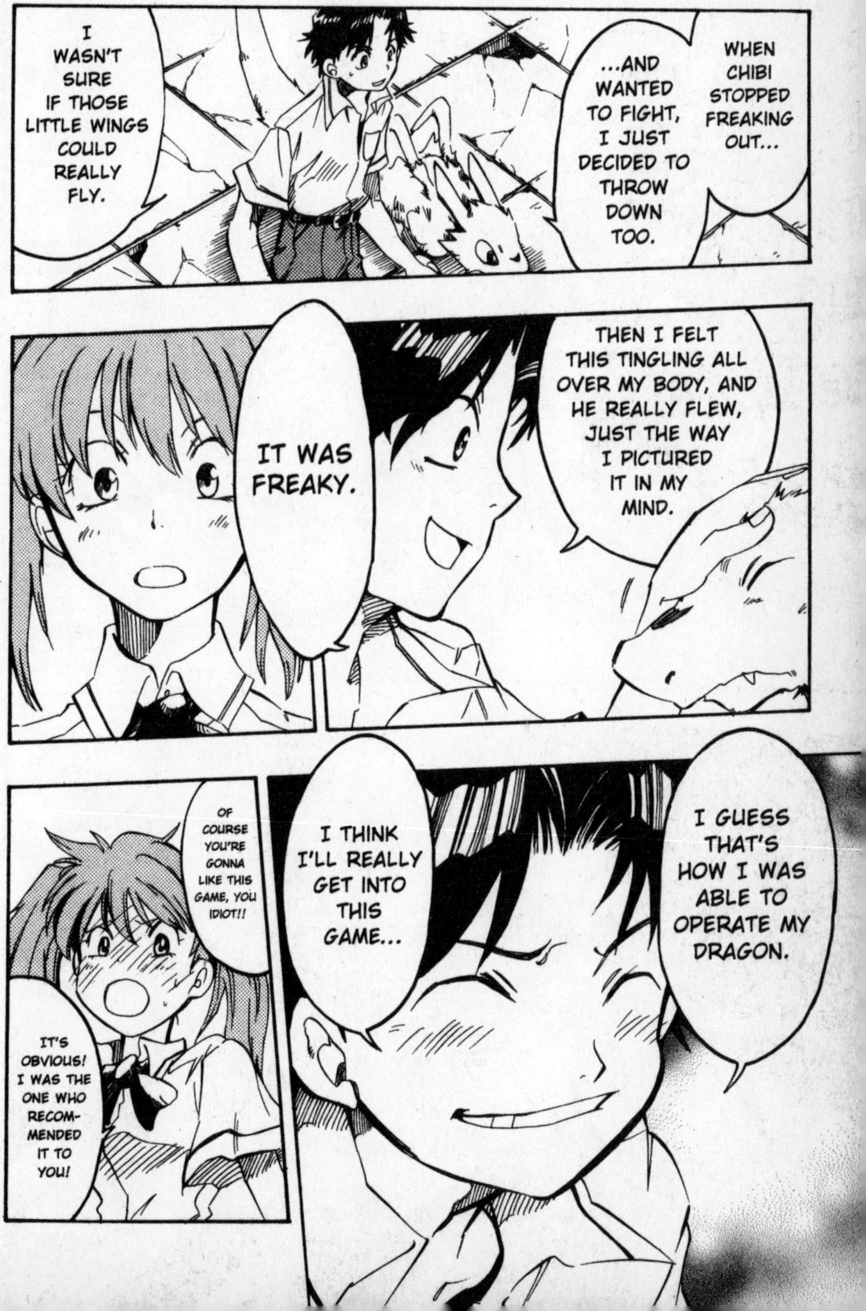
WHEN CHIBI STOPPED FREAKING OUT...
...AND WANTED TO FIGHT, I JUST DECIDED TO THROW DOWN TOO.
I WASN'T SURE IF THOSE LITTLE WINGS COULD REALLY FLY.
THEN I FELT THIS TINGLING ALL OVER MY BODY, AND HE REALLY FLEW, JUST THE WAY I PICTURED IT IN MY MIND.
IT WAS FREAKY.
I GUESS THAT'S HOW I WAS ABLE TO OPERATE MY DRAGON.
I THINK I'LL REALLY GET INTO THIS GAME...
OF COURSE YOU'RE GONNA LIKE THIS GAME, YOU IDIOT!!
IT'S OBVIOUS! I WAS THE ONE WHO RECOMMENDED IT TO YOU!

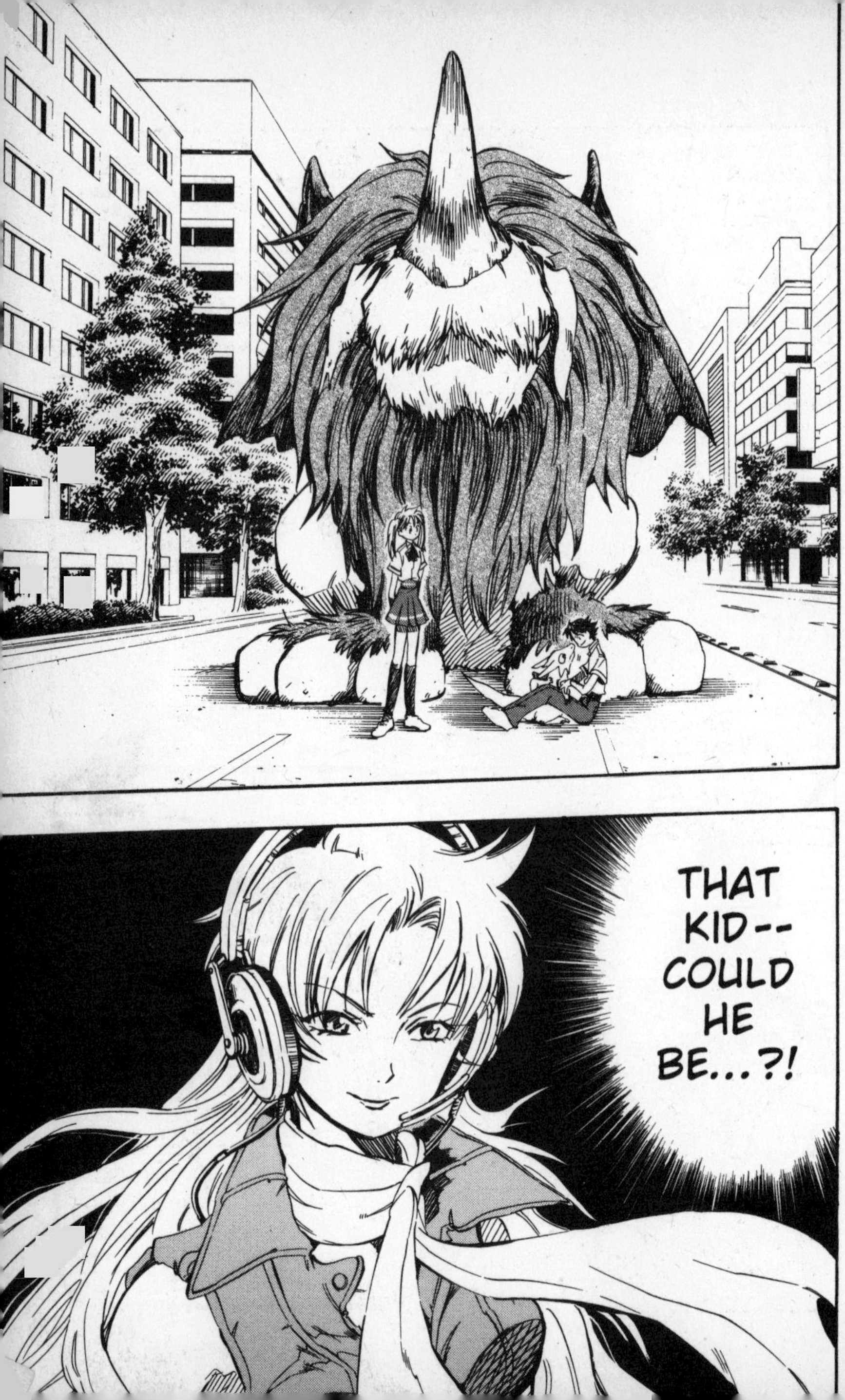
THAT KID-- COULD HE BE...?!

GORAO

EARTH

PLAYER: MAIKO YUKINO
TYPE: GROUND

A protector dragon with lion-mane
silhouette. Extremely loyal and devoted
to protecting its master.

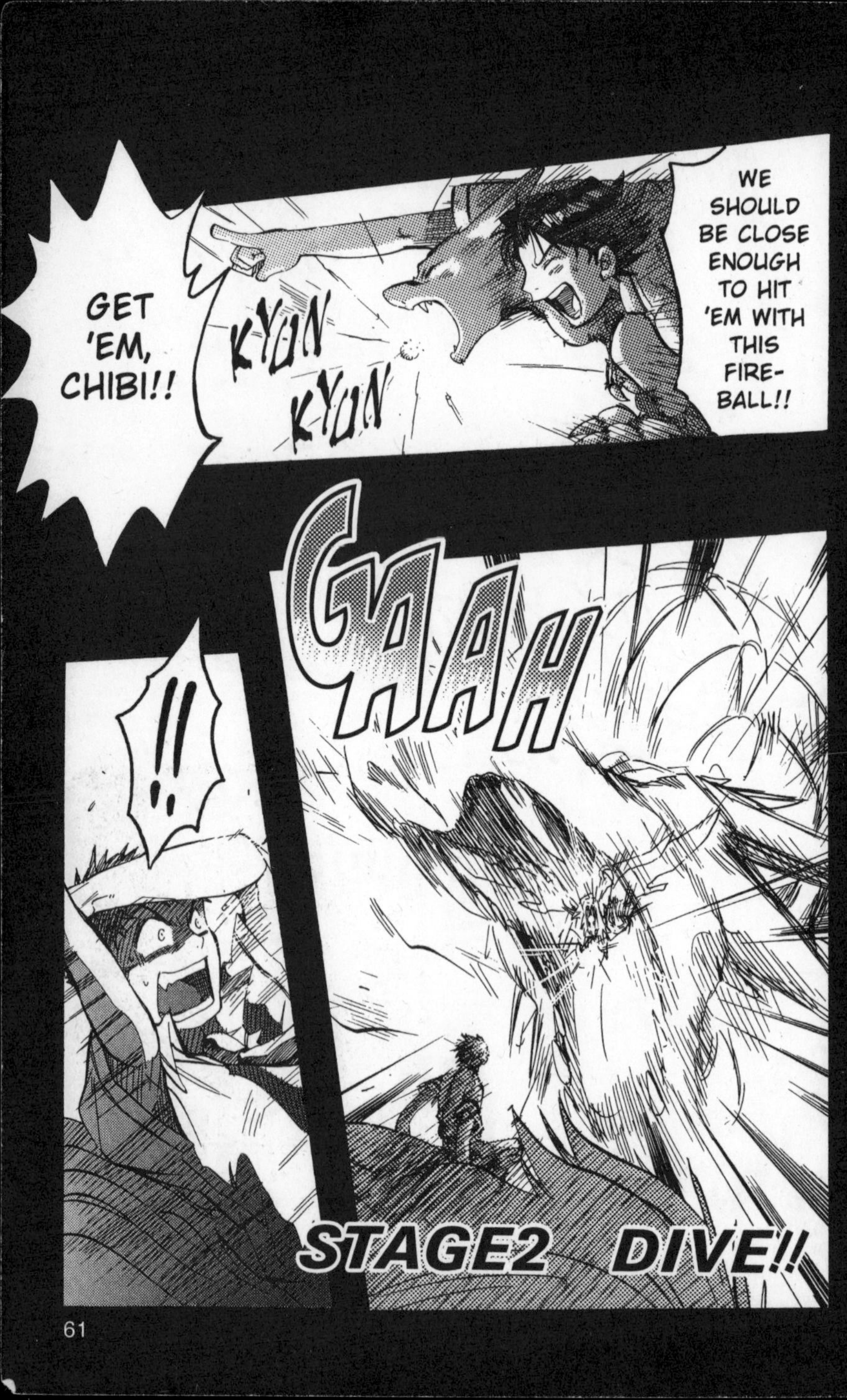
WE SHOULD BE CLOSE ENOUGH TO HIT 'EM WITH THIS FIRE-BALL!!
KYUN KYUN
GET 'EM, CHIBI!!
GWAAH
STAGE2 DIVE!!
!!

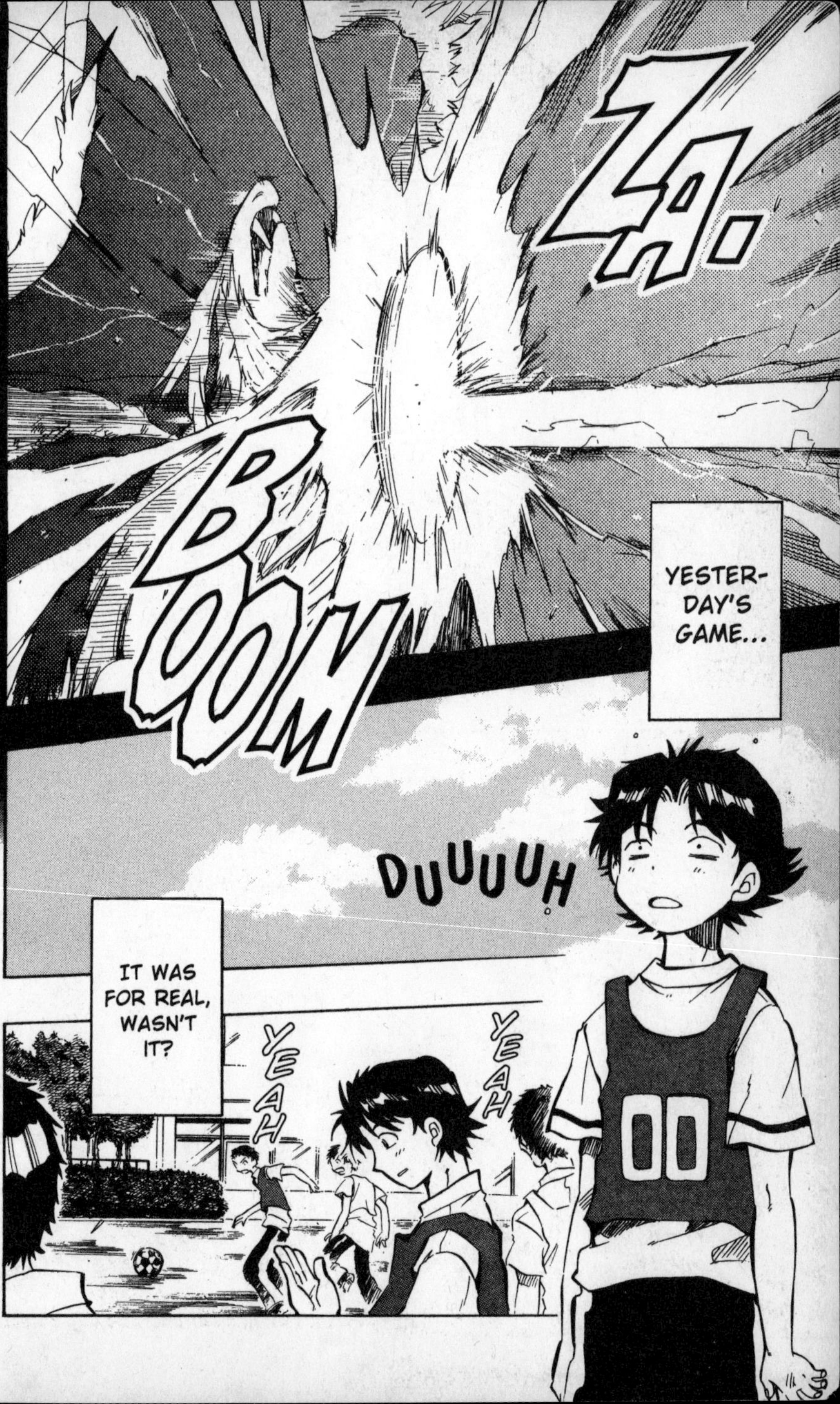
ZA.
BOOOM
YESTER-DAY'S GAME...
DUUUUH
IT WAS FOR REAL, WASN'T IT?
YEAH
YEAH

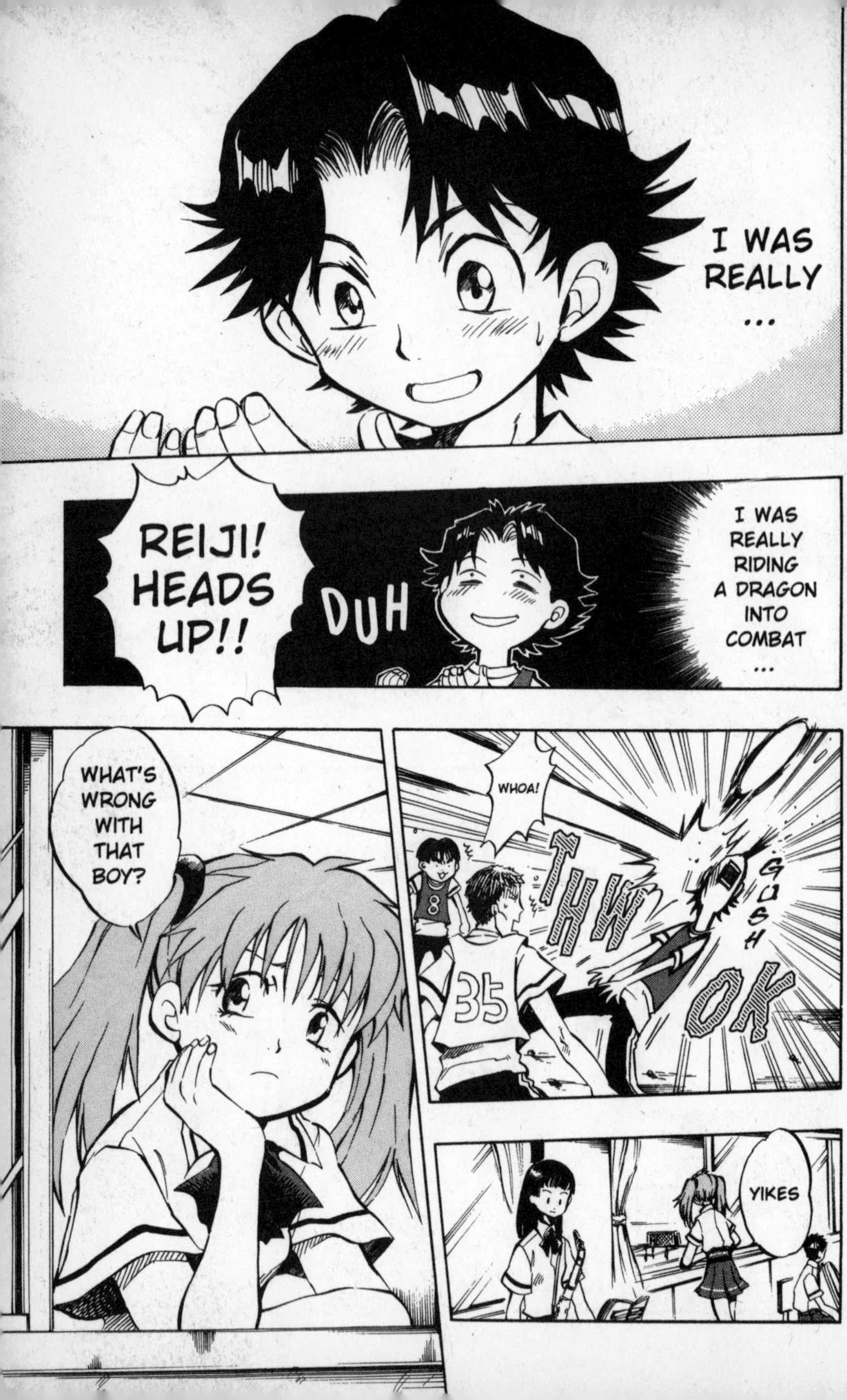

I WAS REALLY ...
I WAS REALLY RIDING A DRAGON INTO COMBAT ...
DUH
REIJI! HEADS UP!!
WHOA!
THWOK
GUSH
YIKES
WHAT'S WRONG WITH THAT BOY?

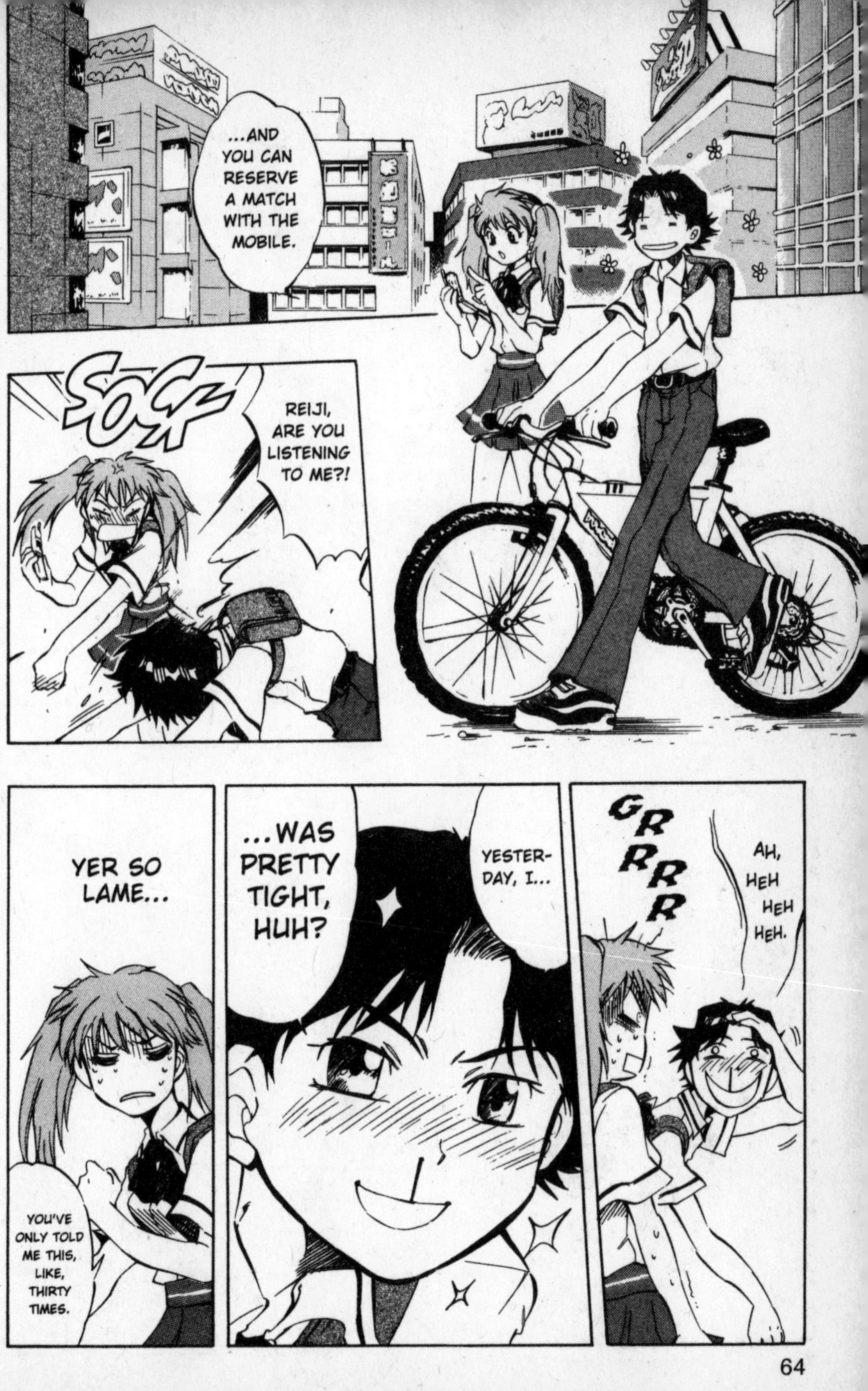
...AND YOU CAN RESERVE A MATCH WITH THE MOBILE.
SOCK
REIJI, ARE YOU LISTENING TO ME?!
GRRRR
AH, HEH HEH HEH.
YESTER-DAY, I...
...WAS PRETTY TIGHT, HUH?
YER SO LAME...
YOU'VE ONLY TOLD ME THIS, LIKE, THIRTY TIMES.

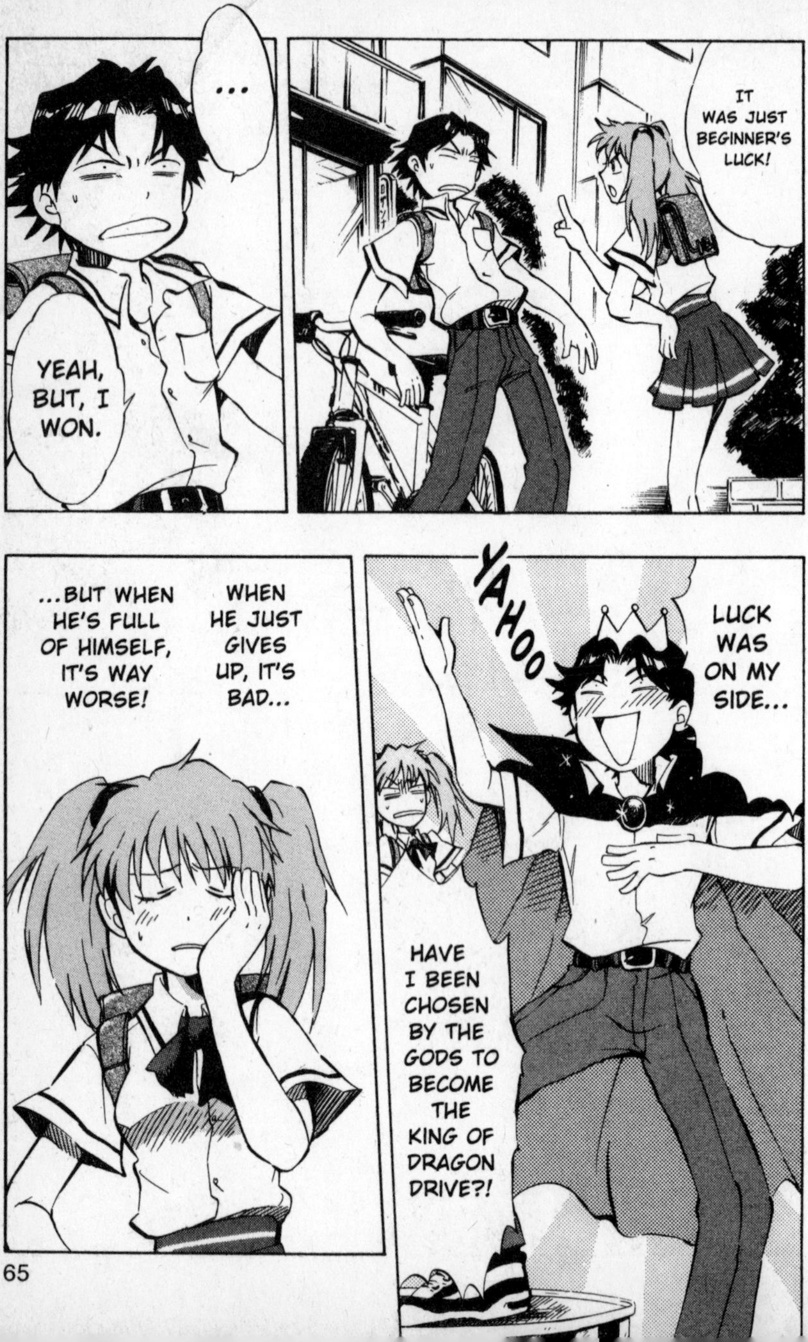
IT WAS JUST BEGINNER'S LUCK!
...
YEAH, BUT, I WON.
YAHOO
LUCK WAS ON MY SIDE...
HAVE I BEEN CHOSEN BY THE GODS TO BECOME THE KING OF DRAGON DRIVE?!
WHEN HE JUST GIVES UP, IT'S BAD...
...BUT WHEN HE'S FULL OF HIMSELF, IT'S WAY WORSE!

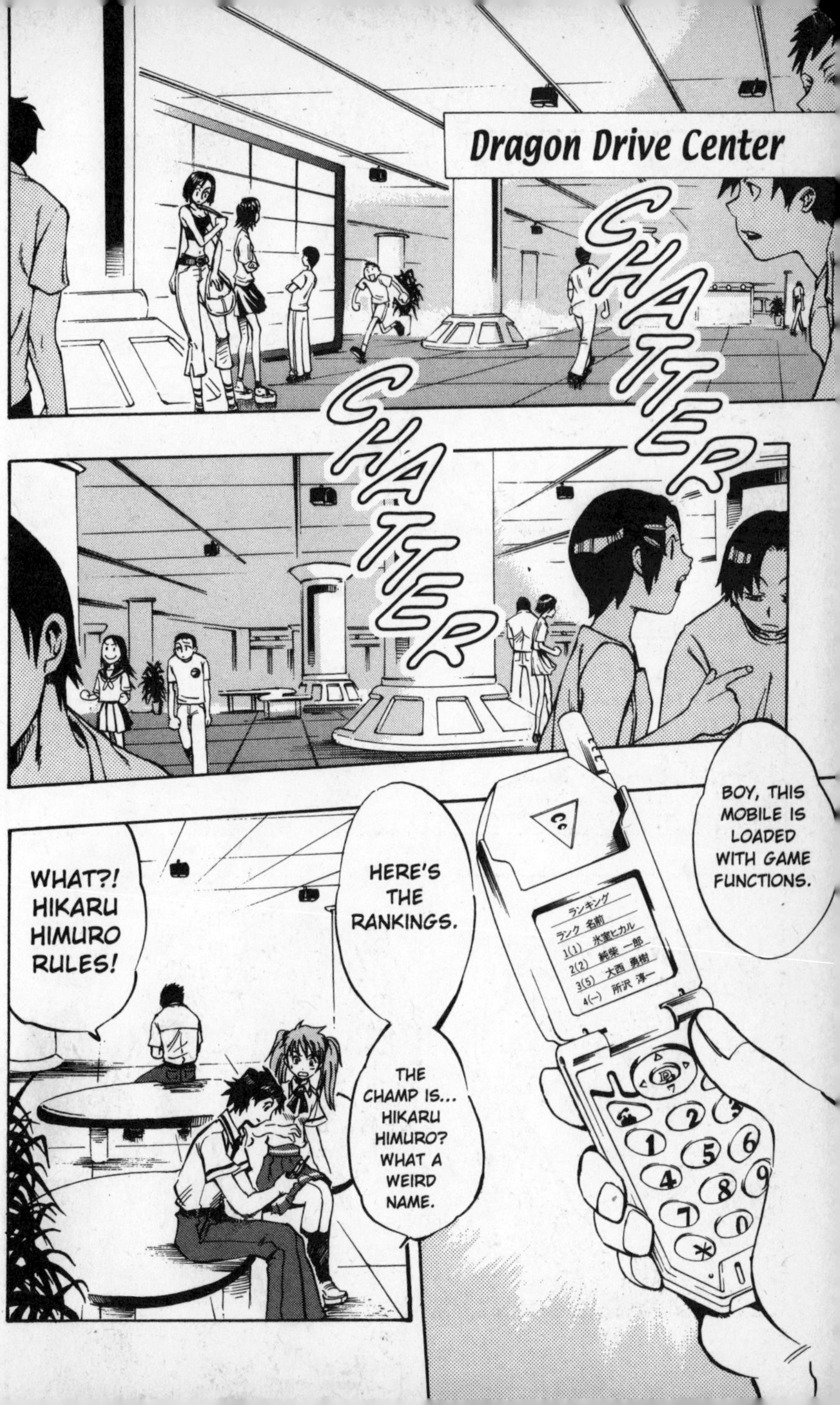
Dragon Drive Center
CHATTER
CHATTER
BOY, THIS MOBILE IS LOADED WITH GAME FUNCTIONS.
ランキング
ランク 名前
1(1) 氷室ヒカル
2(2) 純柴 一郎
3(5) 大西 勇樹
4(ー) 所沢 淳一
HERE'S THE RANKINGS.
THE CHAMP IS... HIKARU HIMURO? WHAT A WEIRD NAME.
WHAT?! HIKARU HIMURO RULES!

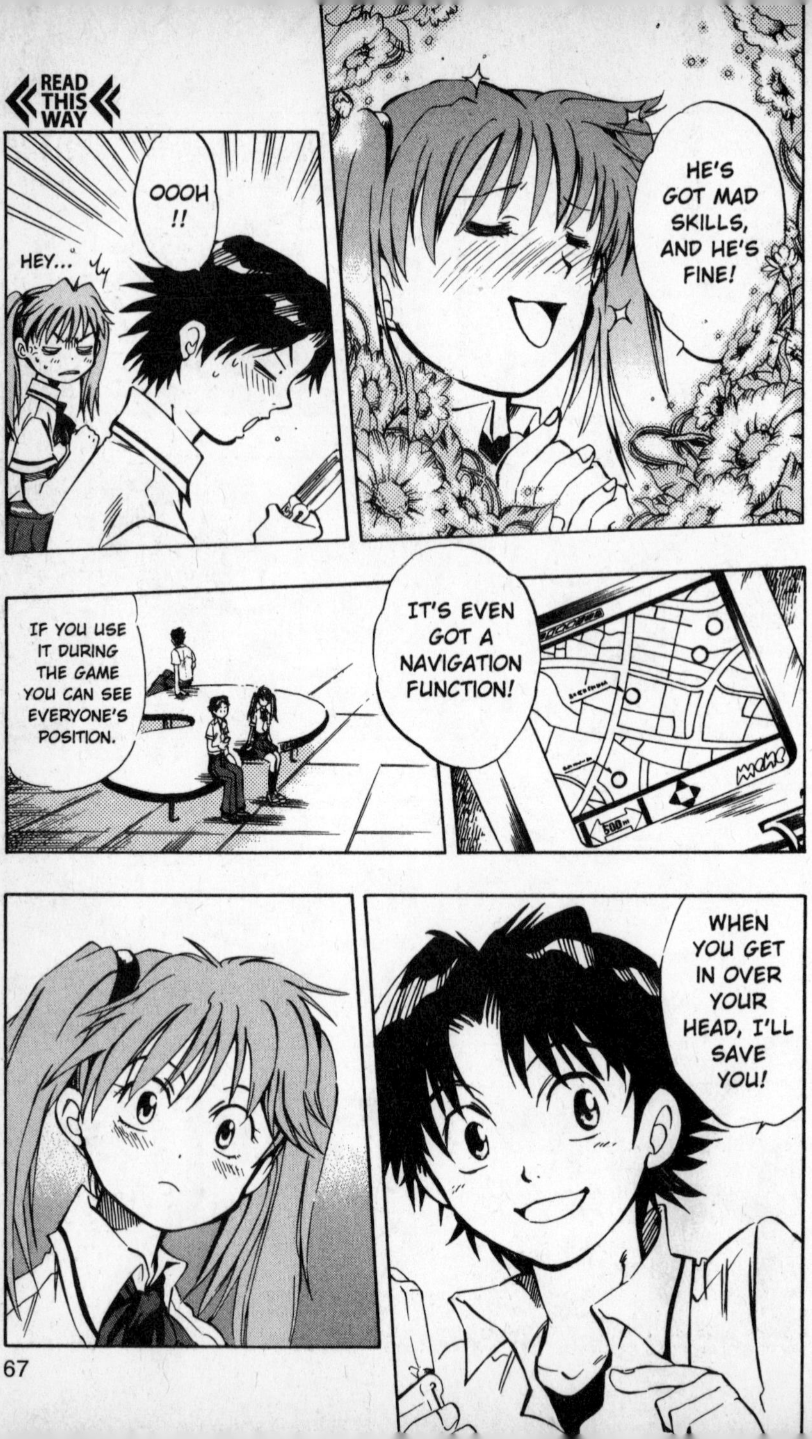
READ THIS WAY
HE'S GOT MAD SKILLS, AND HE'S FINE!
OOOH !!
HEY...
IT'S EVEN GOT A NAVIGATION FUNCTION!
IF YOU USE IT DURING THE GAME YOU CAN SEE EVERYONE'S POSITION.
WHEN YOU GET IN OVER YOUR HEAD, I'LL SAVE YOU!

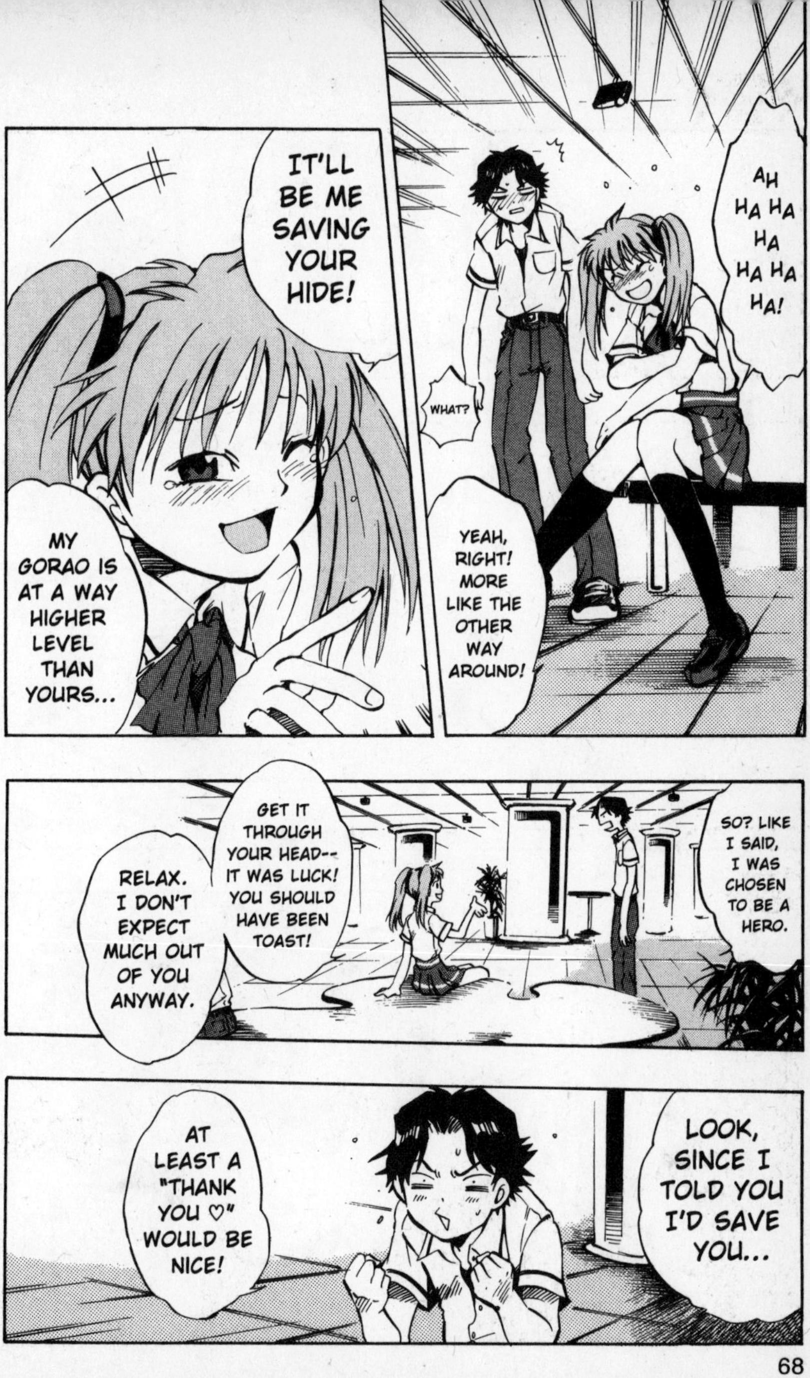
AH HA HA HA HA HA HA!
WHAT?
YEAH, RIGHT! MORE LIKE THE OTHER WAY AROUND!
IT'LL BE ME SAVING YOUR HIDE!
MY GORAO IS AT A WAY HIGHER LEVEL THAN YOURS...
SO? LIKE I SAID, I WAS CHOSEN TO BE A HERO.
GET IT THROUGH YOUR HEAD-- IT WAS LUCK! YOU SHOULD HAVE BEEN TOAST!
RELAX. I DON'T EXPECT MUCH OUT OF YOU ANYWAY.
LOOK, SINCE I TOLD YOU I'D SAVE YOU...
AT LEAST A "THANK YOU ♡" WOULD BE NICE!

READ THIS WAY

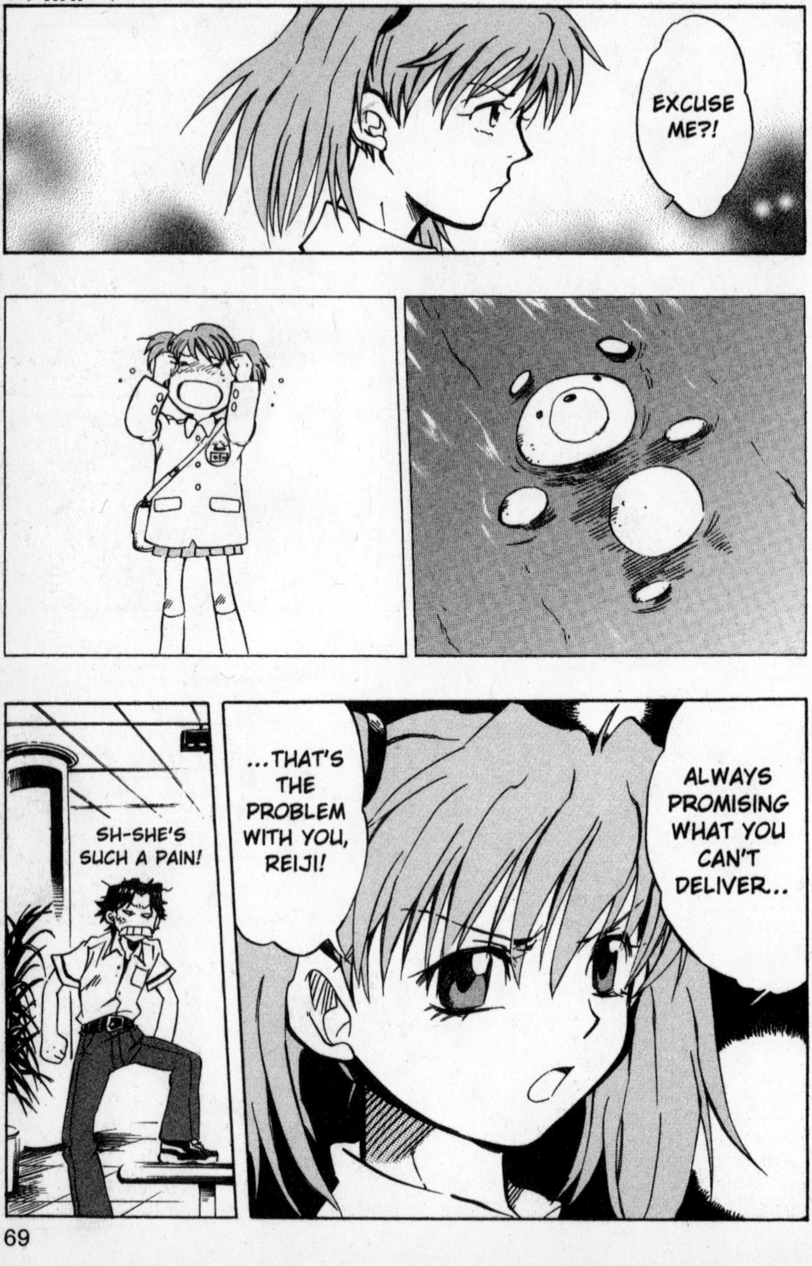
EXCUSE ME?!
ALWAYS PROMISING WHAT YOU CAN'T DELIVER...
...THAT'S THE PROBLEM WITH YOU, REIJI!
SH-SHE'S SUCH A PAIN!

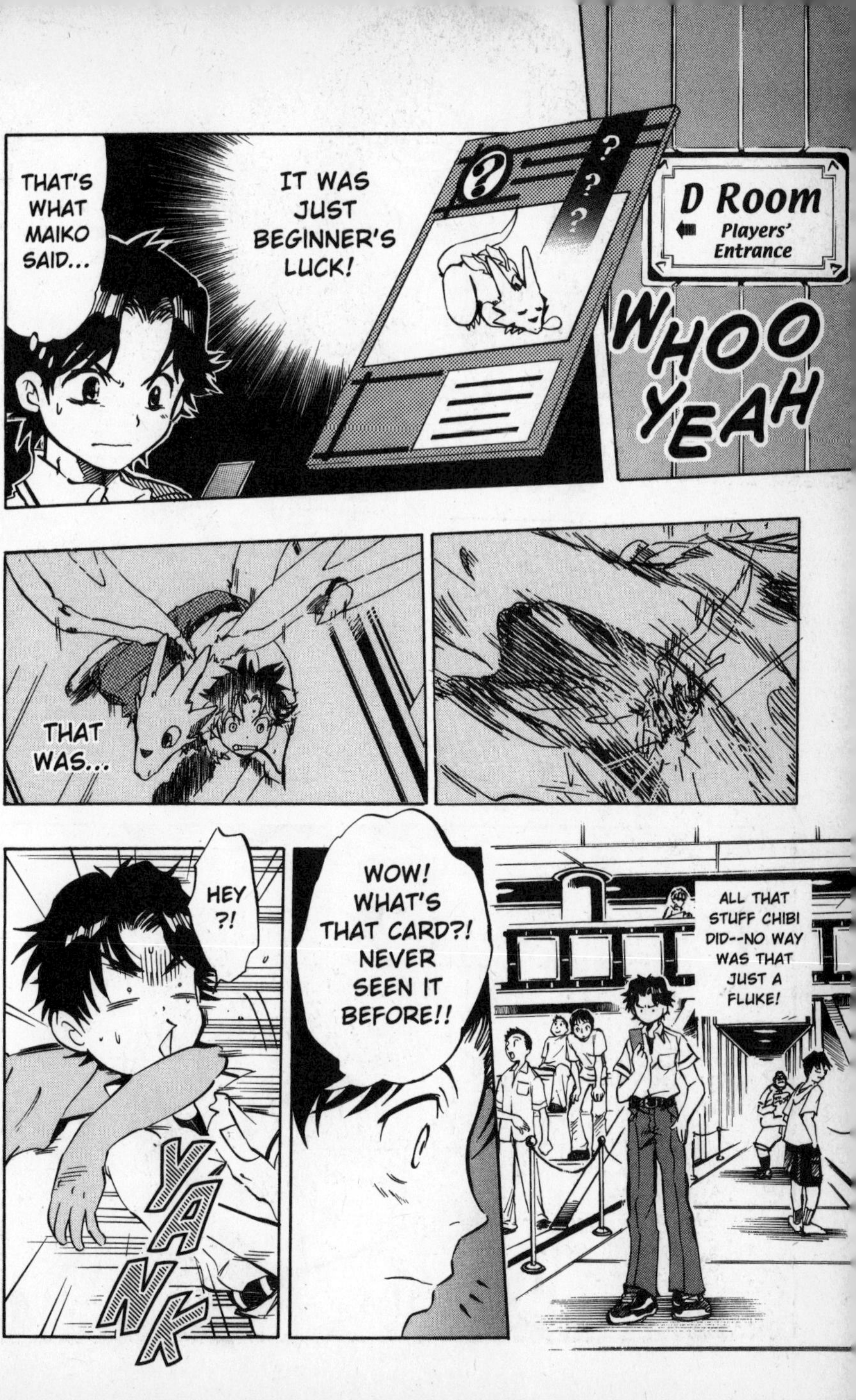
D Room
Players' Entrance
WHOO YEAH
IT WAS JUST BEGINNER'S LUCK!
THAT'S WHAT MAIKO SAID...
THAT WAS...
ALL THAT STUFF CHIBI DID--NO WAY WAS THAT JUST A FLUKE!
WOW! WHAT'S THAT CARD?! NEVER SEEN IT BEFORE!!
HEY ?!
YANK

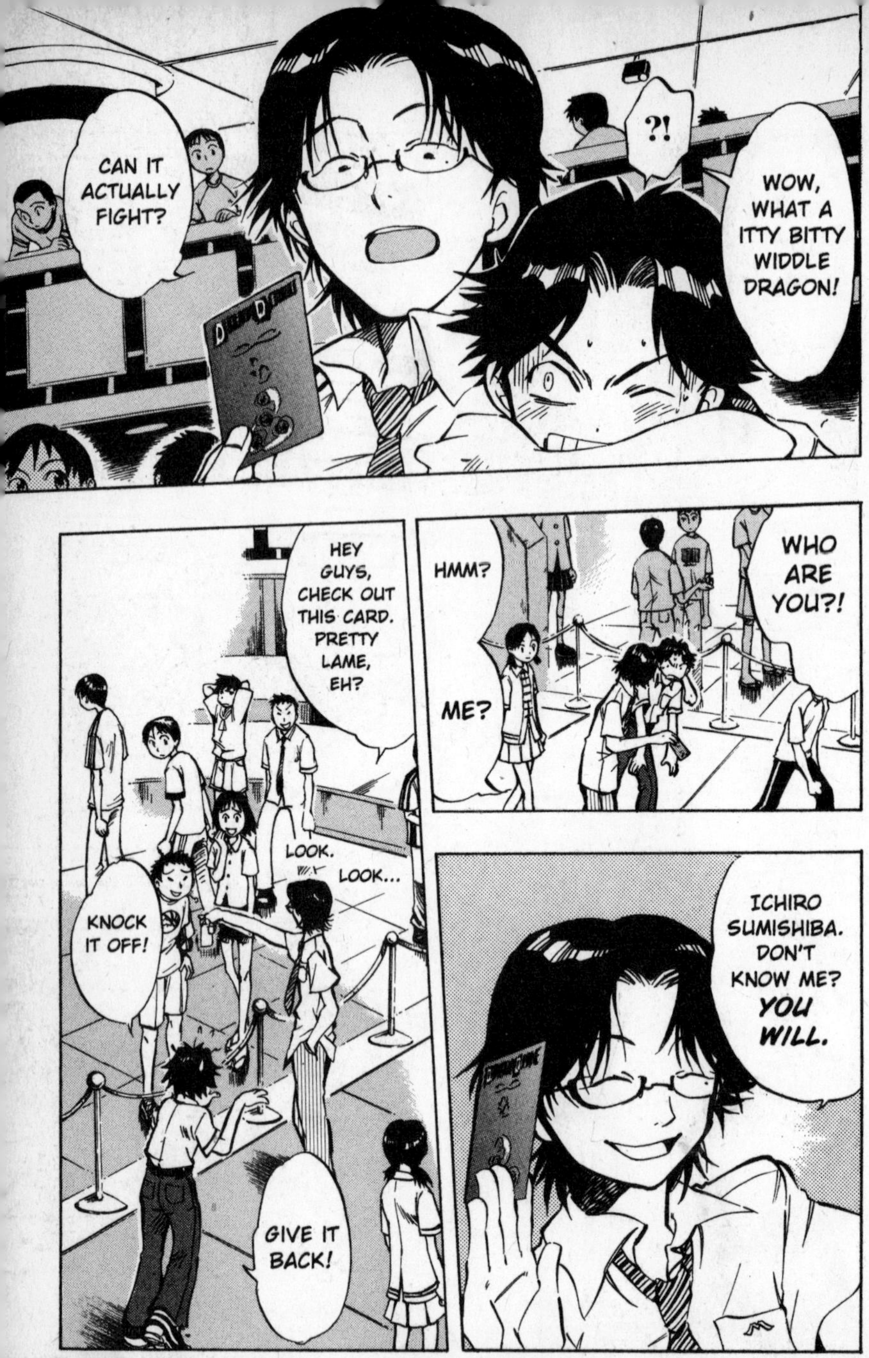
?!
WOW, WHAT A ITTY BITTY WIDDLE DRAGON!
CAN IT ACTUALLY FIGHT?
WHO ARE YOU?!
HMM?
ME?
ICHIRO SUMISHIBA. DON'T KNOW ME? YOU WILL.
HEY GUYS, CHECK OUT THIS CARD. PRETTY LAME, EH?
LOOK.
LOOK...
KNOCK IT OFF!
GIVE IT BACK!

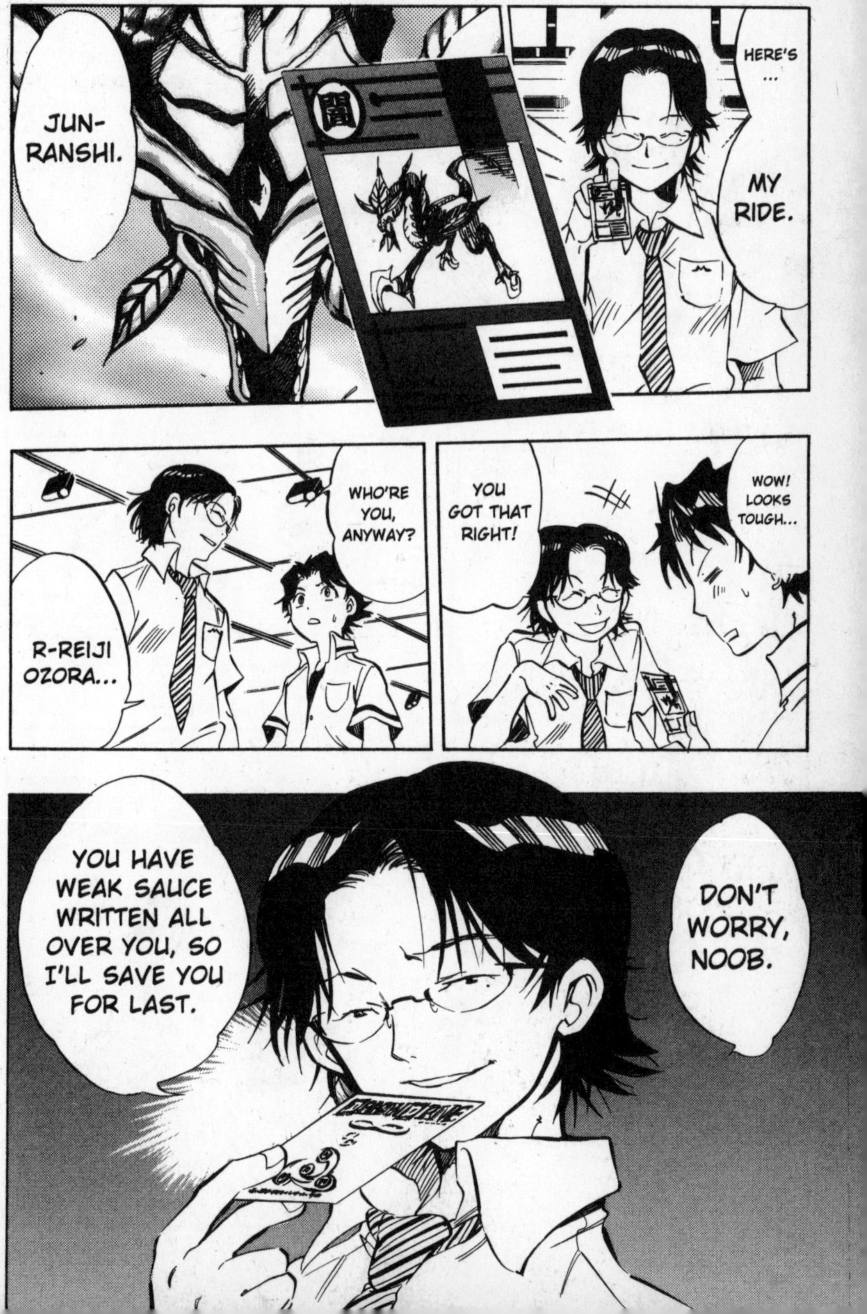
HERE'S...
MY RIDE.
JUN-RANSHI.
WOW! LOOKS TOUGH...
YOU GOT THAT RIGHT!
WHO'RE YOU, ANYWAY?
R-REIJI OZORA...
DON'T WORRY, NOOB.
YOU HAVE WEAK SAUCE WRITTEN ALL OVER YOU, SO I'LL SAVE YOU FOR LAST.

READ THIS WAY

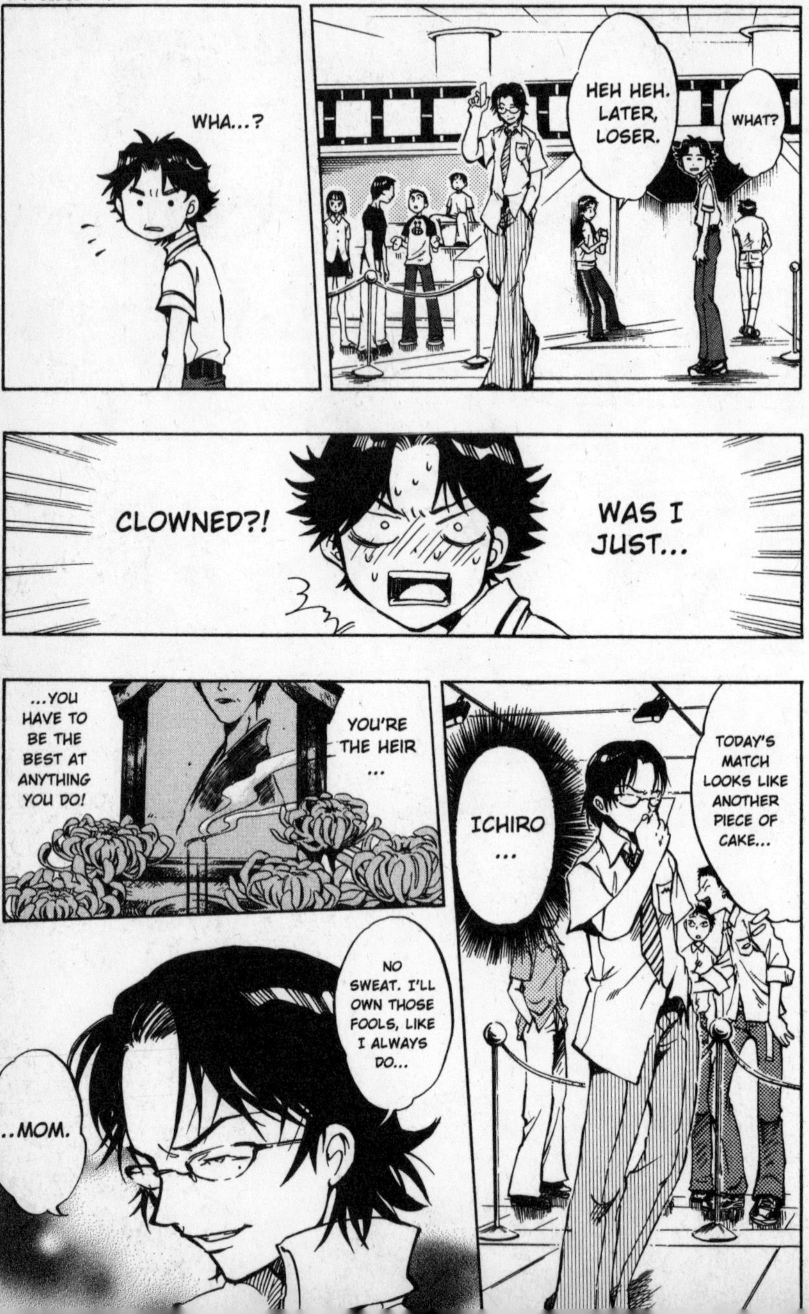
HEH HEH. LATER, LOSER.
WHAT?
WHA...?
WAS I JUST...
CLOWNED?!
TODAY'S MATCH LOOKS LIKE ANOTHER PIECE OF CAKE...
ICHIRO...
YOU'RE THE HEIR...
...YOU HAVE TO BE THE BEST AT ANYTHING YOU DO!
NO SWEAT. I'LL OWN THOSE FOOLS, LIKE I ALWAYS DO...
...MOM.

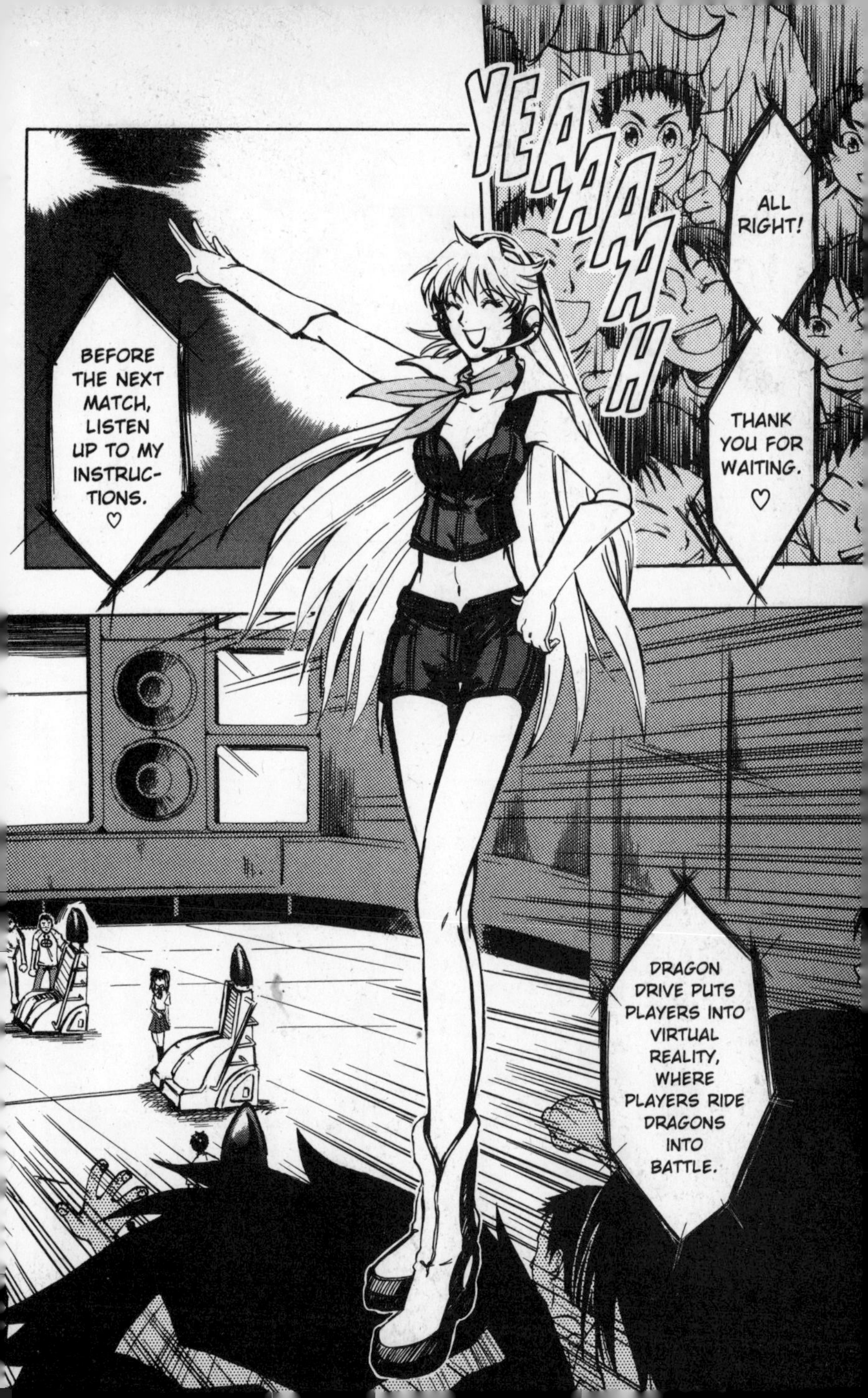
YEAAAAH
ALL RIGHT!
THANK YOU FOR WAITING. ♡
BEFORE THE NEXT MATCH, LISTEN UP TO MY INSTRUC- TIONS. ♡
DRAGON DRIVE PUTS PLAYERS INTO VIRTUAL REALITY, WHERE PLAYERS RIDE DRAGONS INTO BATTLE.

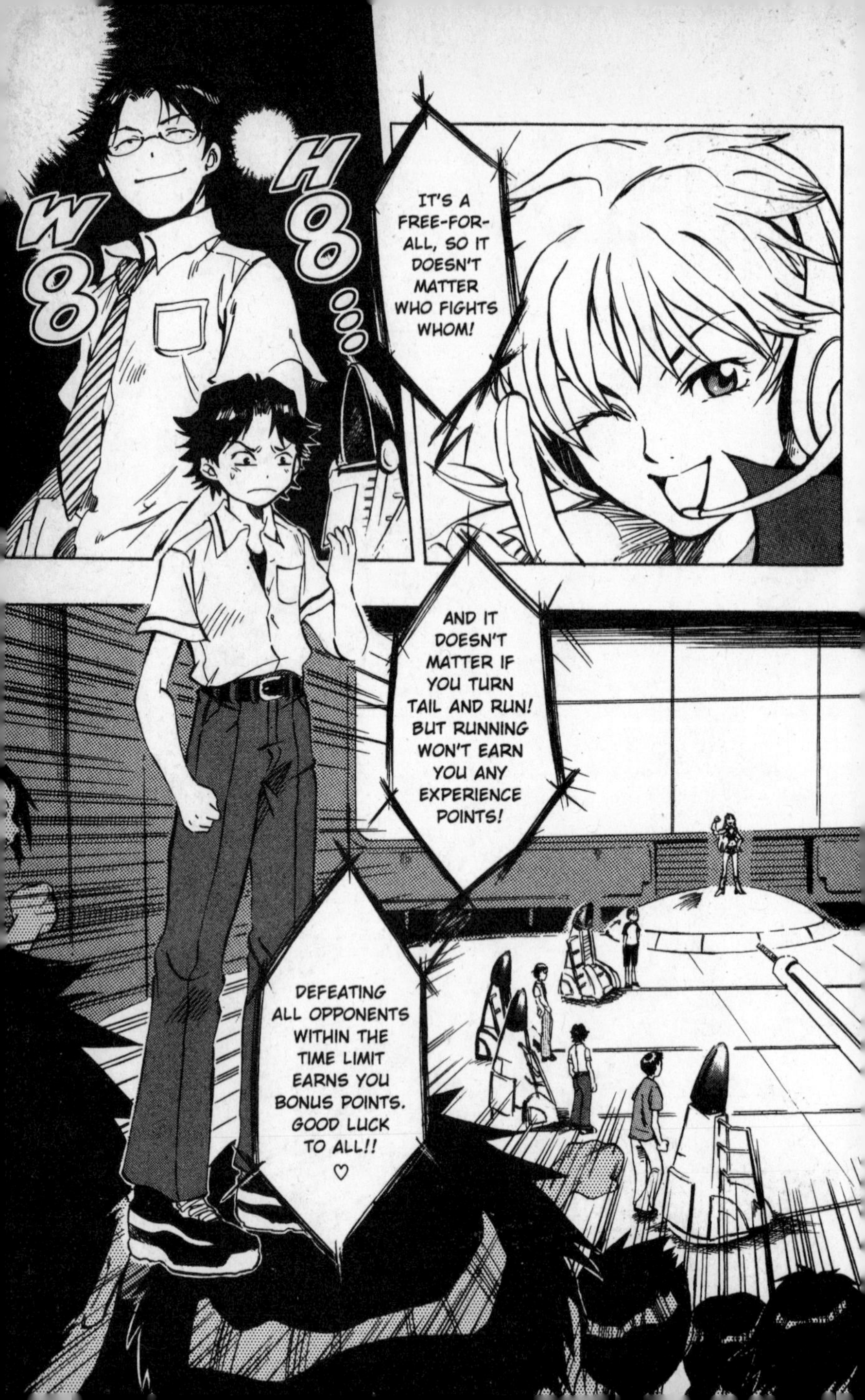
IT'S A FREE-FOR-ALL, SO IT DOESN'T MATTER WHO FIGHTS WHOM!
H88...
W88
AND IT DOESN'T MATTER IF YOU TURN TAIL AND RUN! BUT RUNNING WON'T EARN YOU ANY EXPERIENCE POINTS!
DEFEATING ALL OPPONENTS WITHIN THE TIME LIMIT EARNS YOU BONUS POINTS. GOOD LUCK TO ALL!! ♡

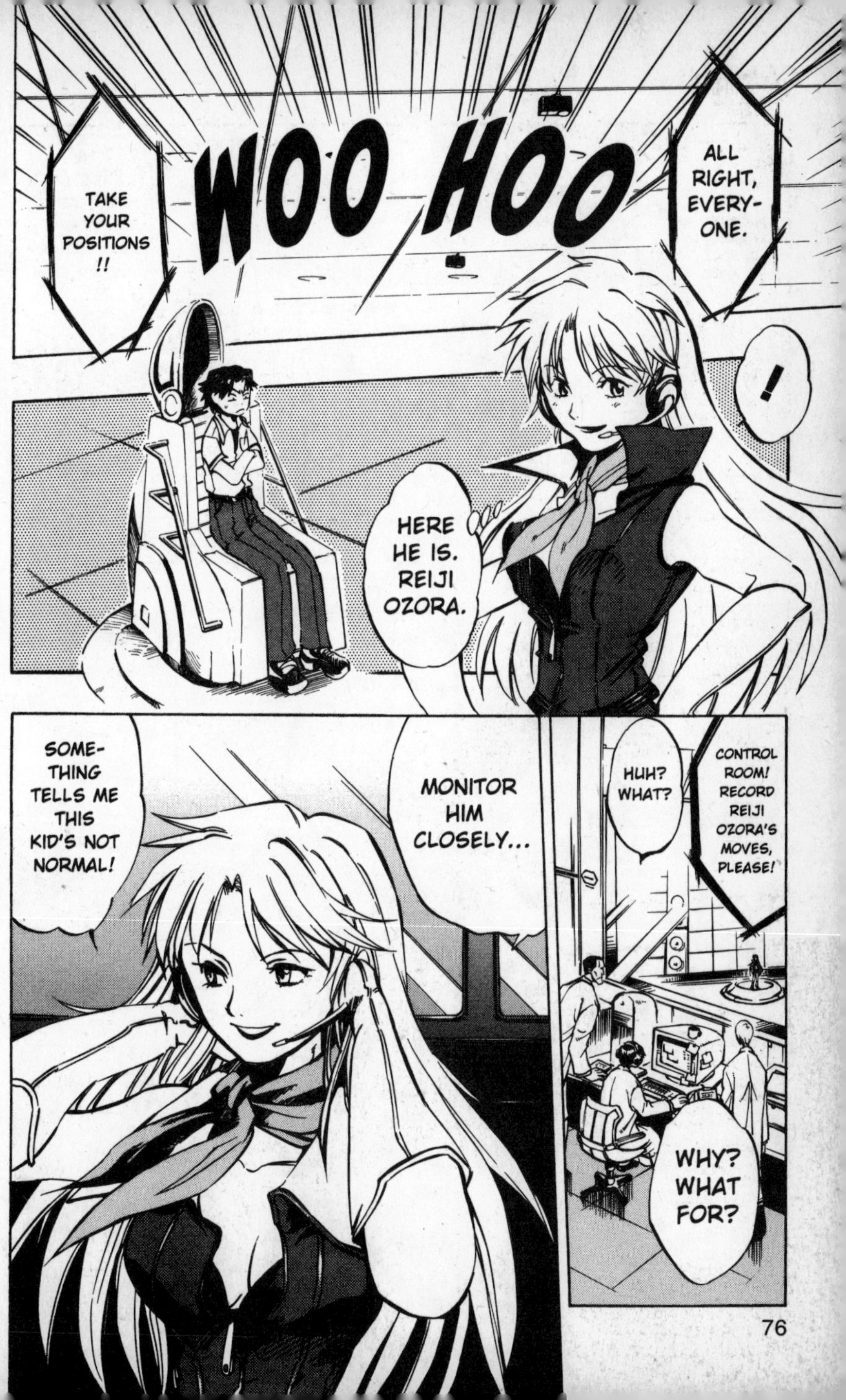
ALL RIGHT, EVERYONE.
WOO HOO
TAKE YOUR POSITIONS !!
!
HERE HE IS. REIJI OZORA.
CONTROL ROOM! RECORD REIJI OZORA'S MOVES, PLEASE!
HUH? WHAT?
WHY? WHAT FOR?
MONITOR HIM CLOSELY...
SOMETHING TELLS ME THIS KID'S NOT NORMAL!

READ THIS WAY

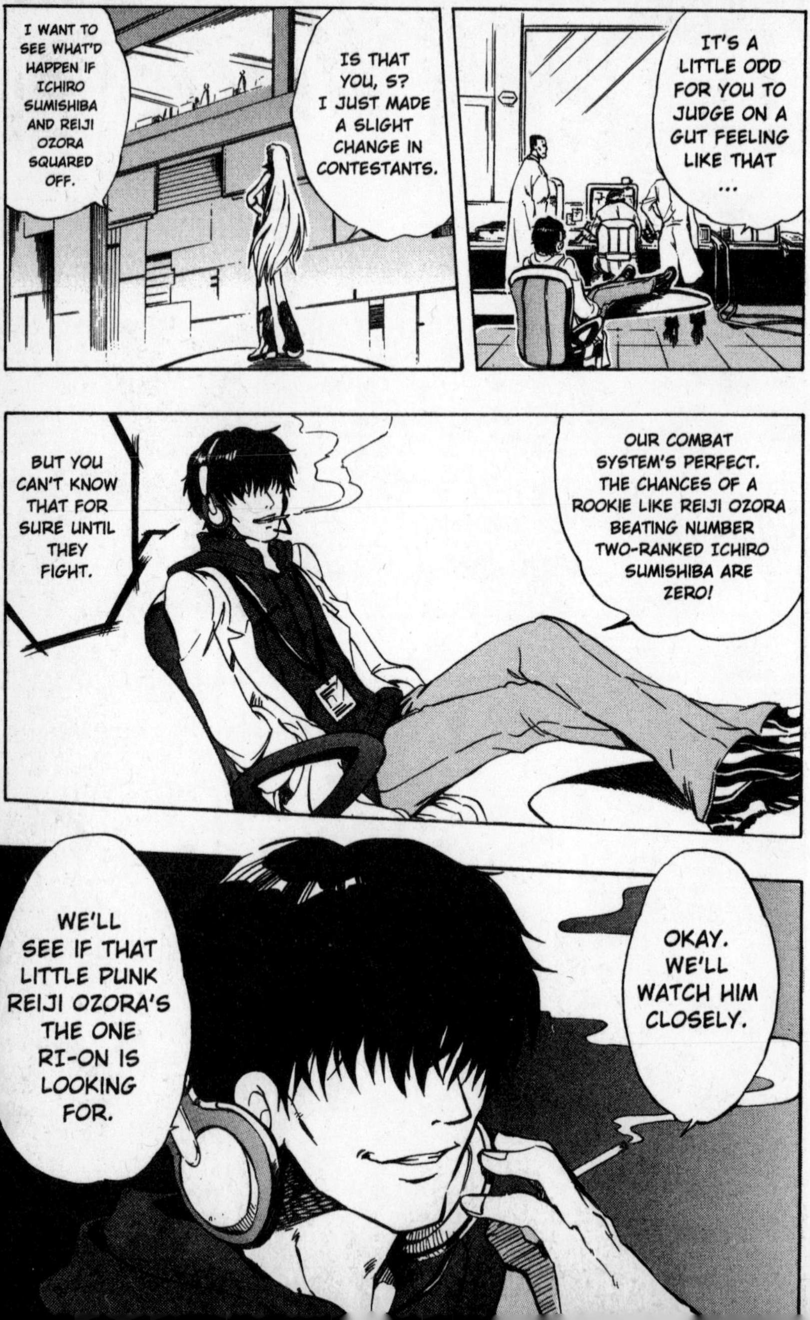
IT'S A LITTLE ODD FOR YOU TO JUDGE ON A GUT FEELING LIKE THAT ...
IS THAT YOU, S? I JUST MADE A SLIGHT CHANGE IN CONTESTANTS.
I WANT TO SEE WHAT'D HAPPEN IF ICHIRO SUMISHIBA AND REIJI OZORA SQUARED OFF.
OUR COMBAT SYSTEM'S PERFECT. THE CHANCES OF A ROOKIE LIKE REIJI OZORA BEATING NUMBER TWO-RANKED ICHIRO SUMISHIBA ARE ZERO!
BUT YOU CAN'T KNOW THAT FOR SURE UNTIL THEY FIGHT.
OKAY. WE'LL WATCH HIM CLOSELY.
WE'LL SEE IF THAT LITTLE PUNK REIJI OZORA'S THE ONE RI-ON IS LOOKING FOR.

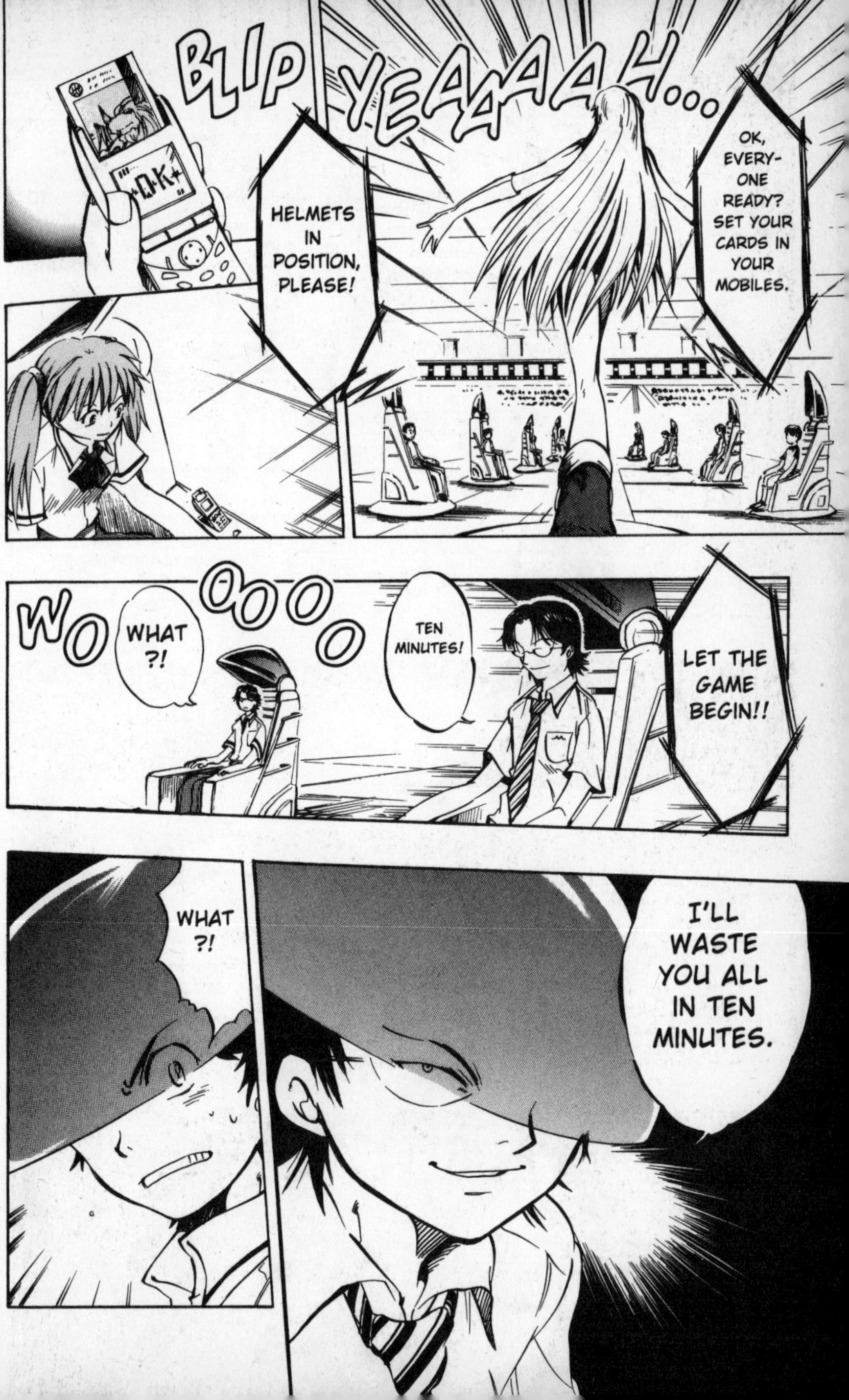
YEAAAAH...
OK, EVERYONE READY? SET YOUR CARDS IN YOUR MOBILES.
HELMETS IN POSITION, PLEASE!
BLIP
OK
LET THE GAME BEGIN!!
TEN MINUTES!
WOOOOO
WHAT?!
I'LL WASTE YOU ALL IN TEN MINUTES.
WHAT?!

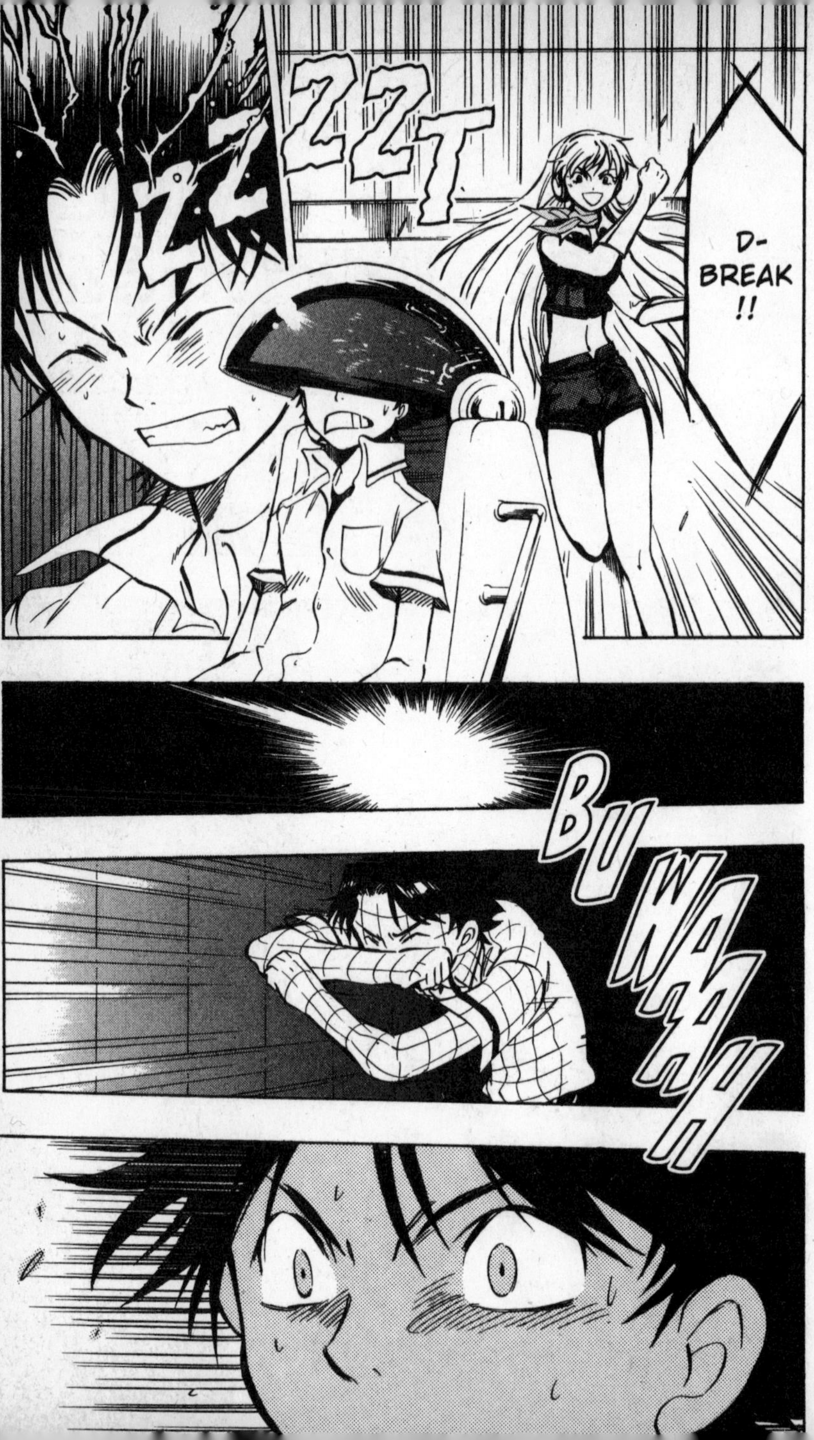
D-BREAK!!
ZZZZT
BUWAAAH

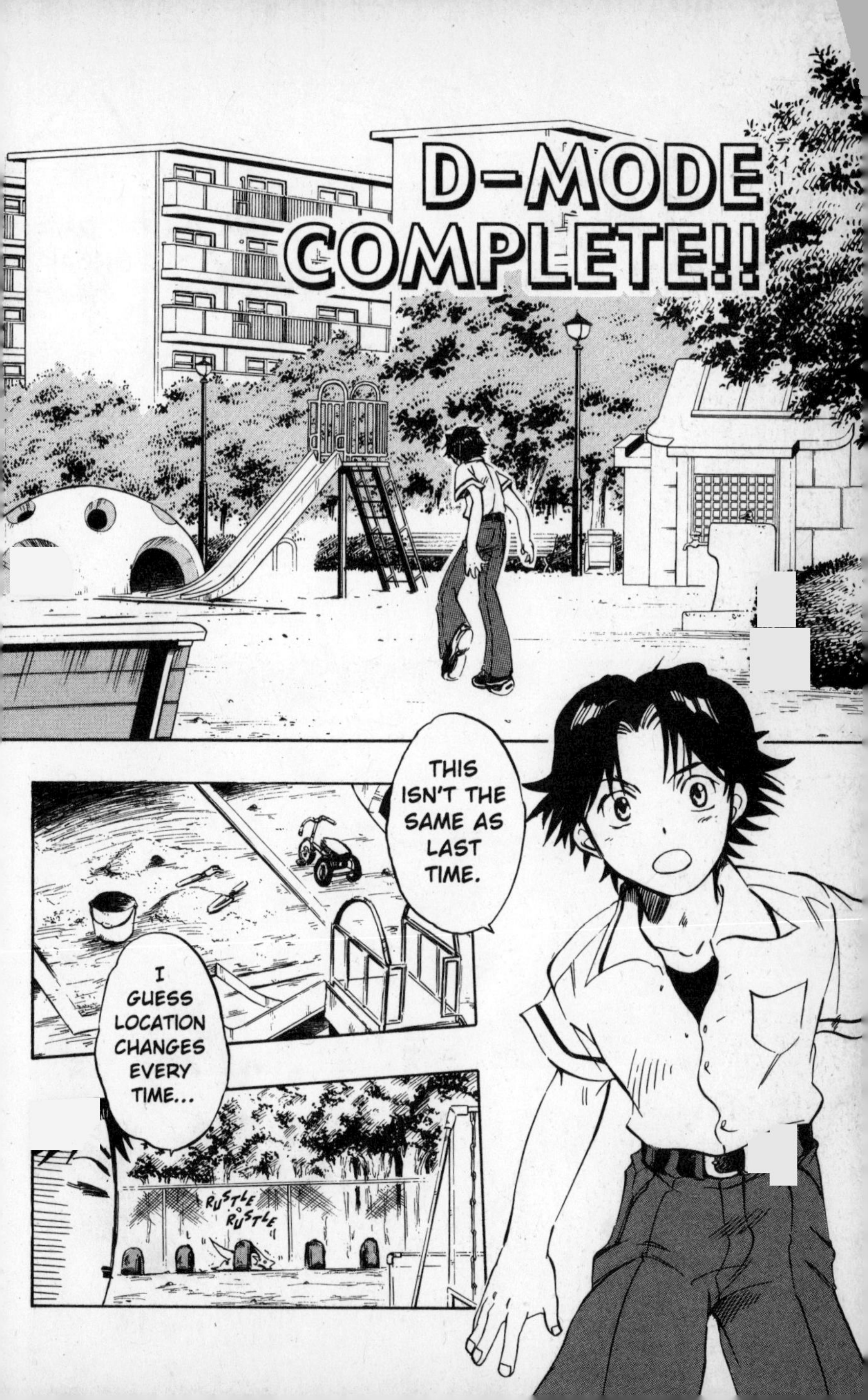
D-MODE COMPLETE!!
THIS ISN'T THE SAME AS LAST TIME.
I GUESS LOCATION CHANGES EVERY TIME...
RUSTLE RUSTLE

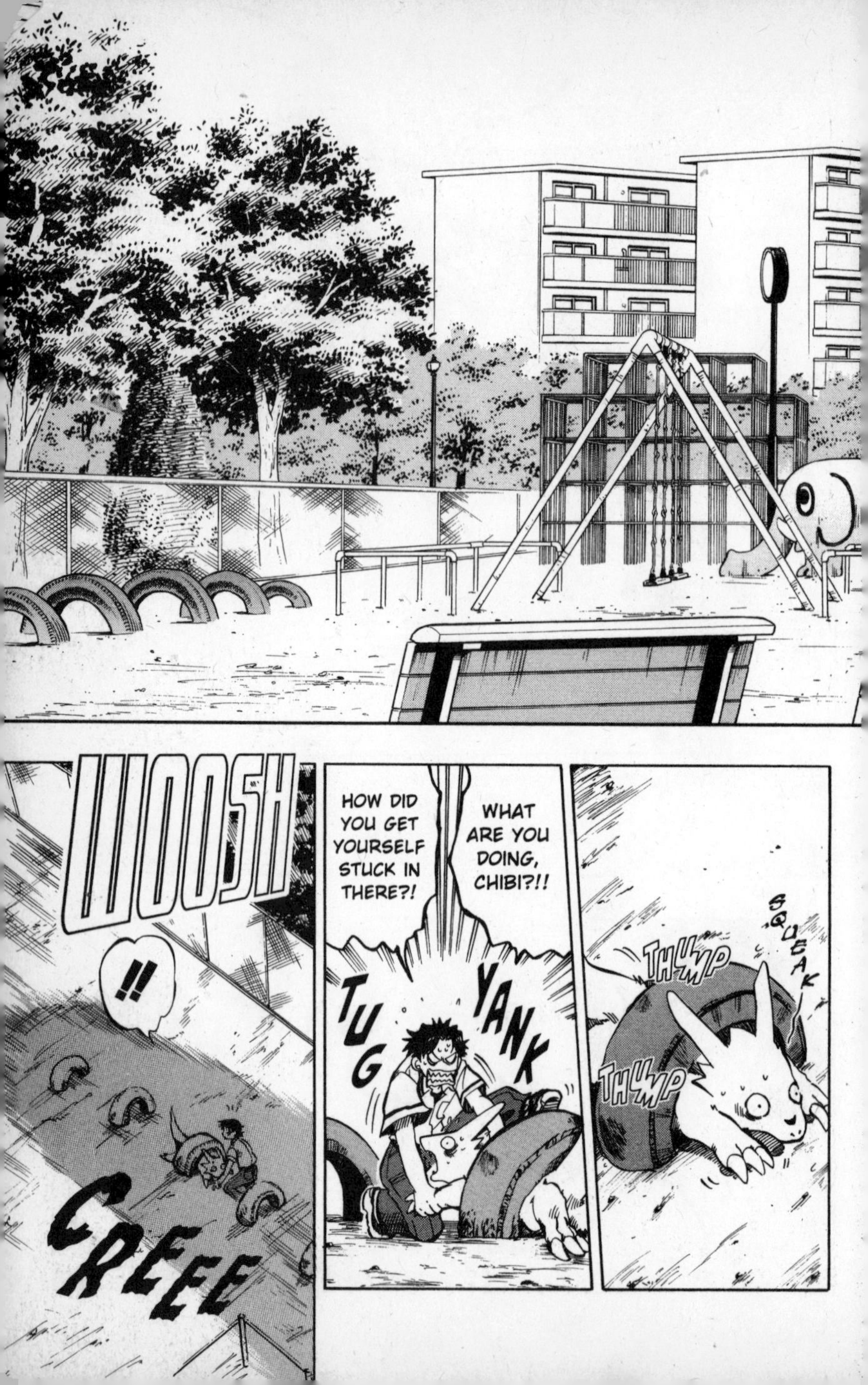
SQUEAK
THUMP
THUMP
WHAT ARE YOU DOING, CHIBI?!!
HOW DID YOU GET YOURSELF STUCK IN THERE?!
YANK
TUG
WOOSH
!!
CREEE

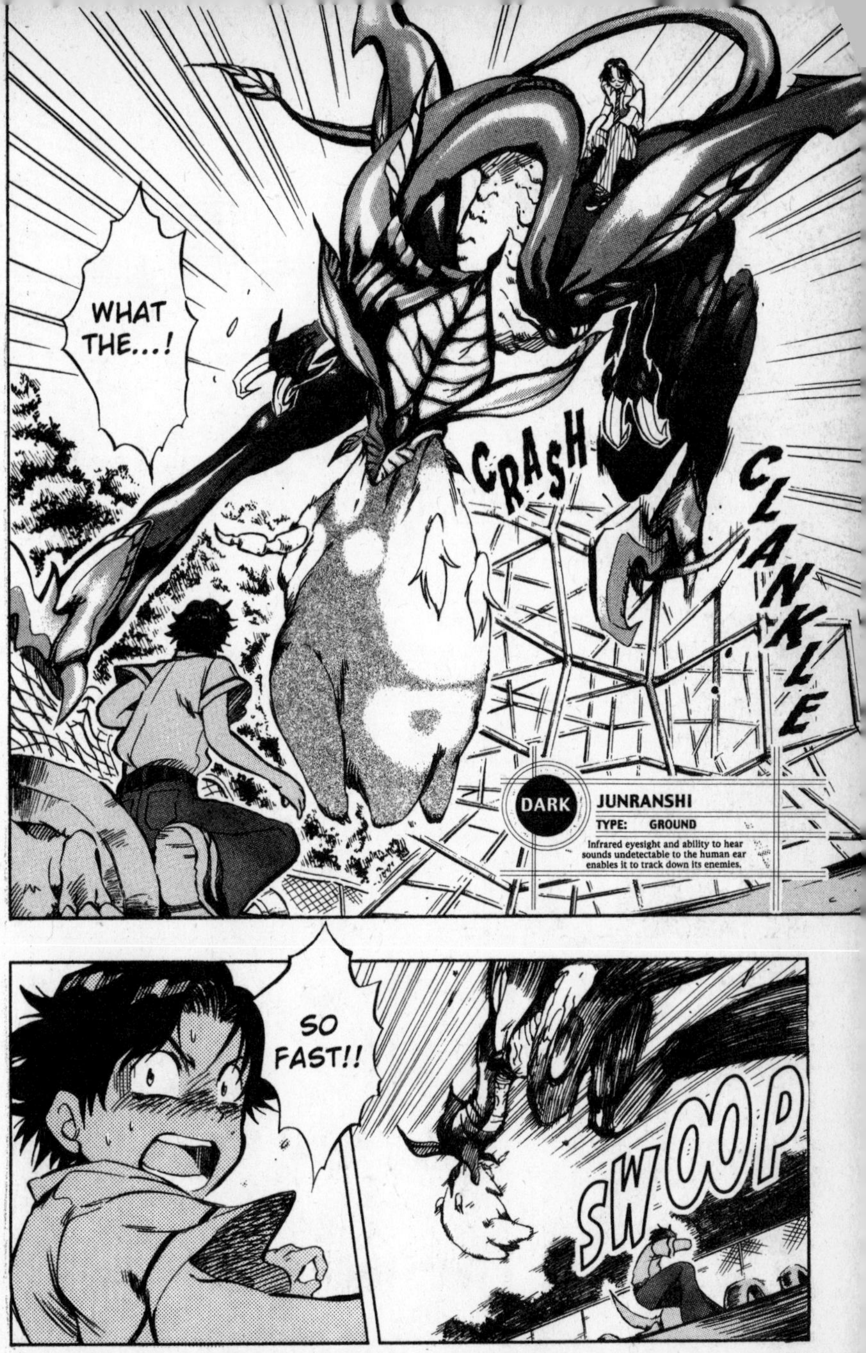
WHAT THE...!
CRASH
CLANKLE
DARK
JUNRANSHI
TYPE: GROUND
Infrared eyesight and ability to hear sounds undetectable to the human ear enables it to track down its enemies.
SWOOP
SO FAST!!

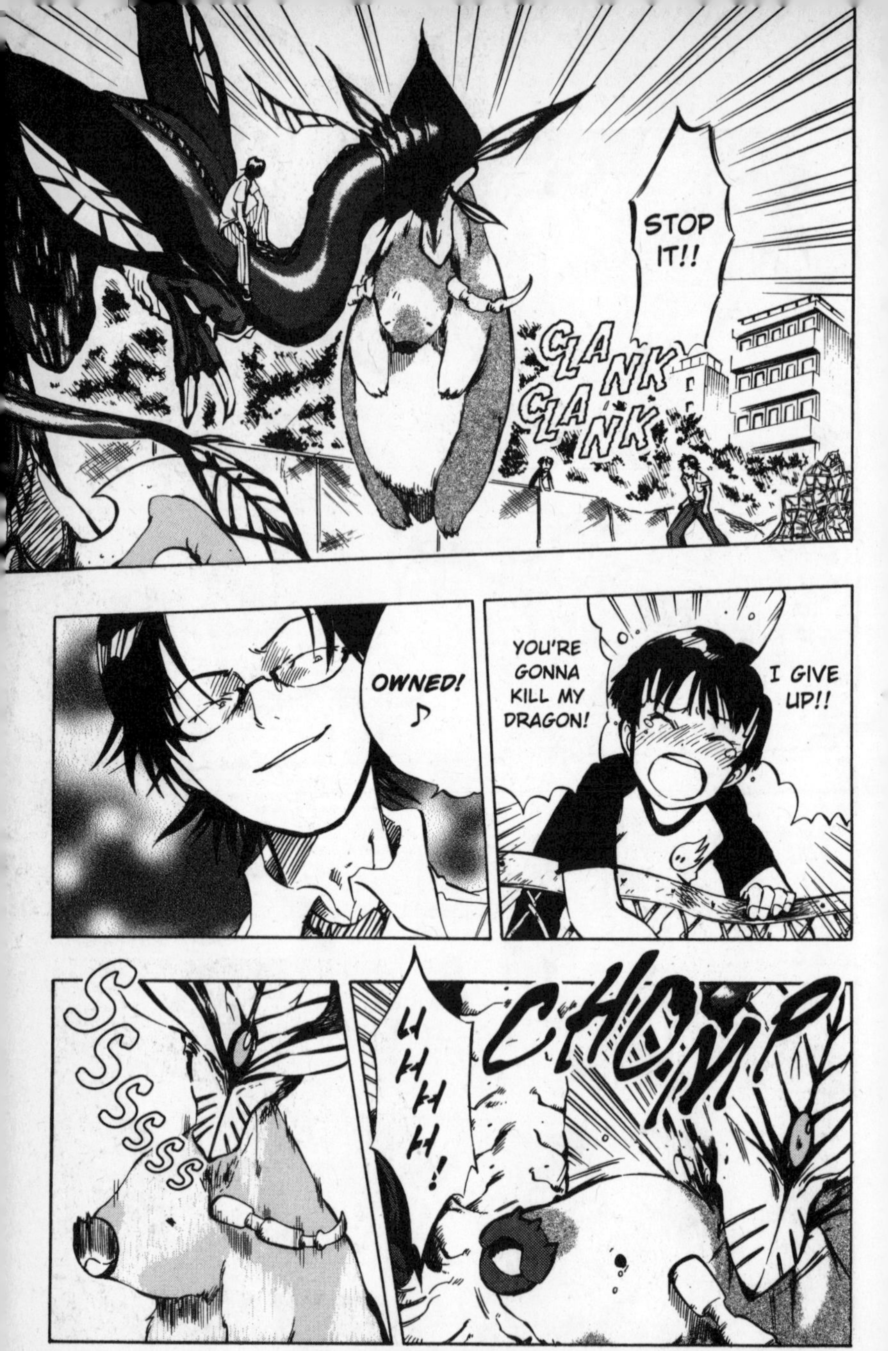
STOP IT!!
CLANK CLANK
I GIVE UP!!
YOU'RE GONNA KILL MY DRAGON!
OWNED! ♪
CHOMP
UHHHH!
SSSSSS

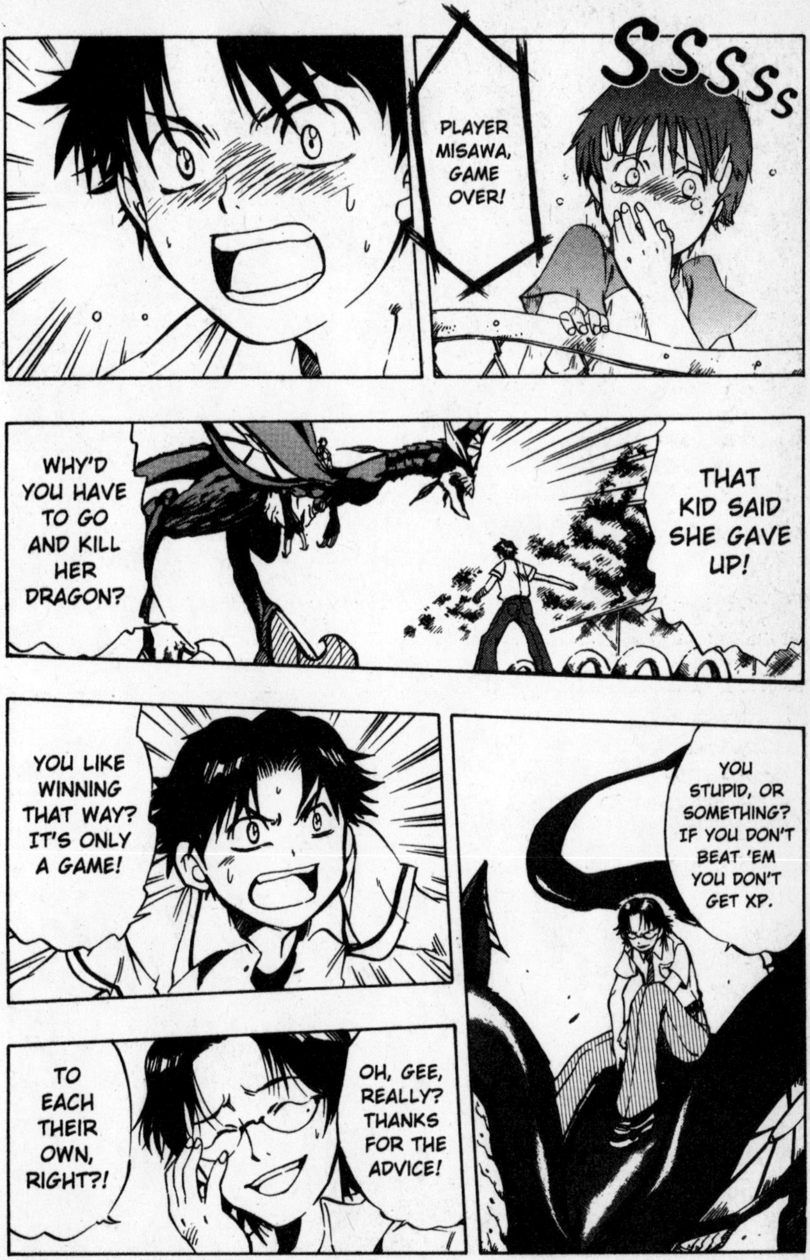
SSSSS
PLAYER MISAWA, GAME OVER!
THAT KID SAID SHE GAVE UP!
WHY'D YOU HAVE TO GO AND KILL HER DRAGON?
YOU STUPID, OR SOMETHING? IF YOU DON'T BEAT 'EM YOU DON'T GET XP.
YOU LIKE WINNING THAT WAY? IT'S ONLY A GAME!
OH, GEE, REALLY? THANKS FOR THE ADVICE!
TO EACH THEIR OWN, RIGHT?!

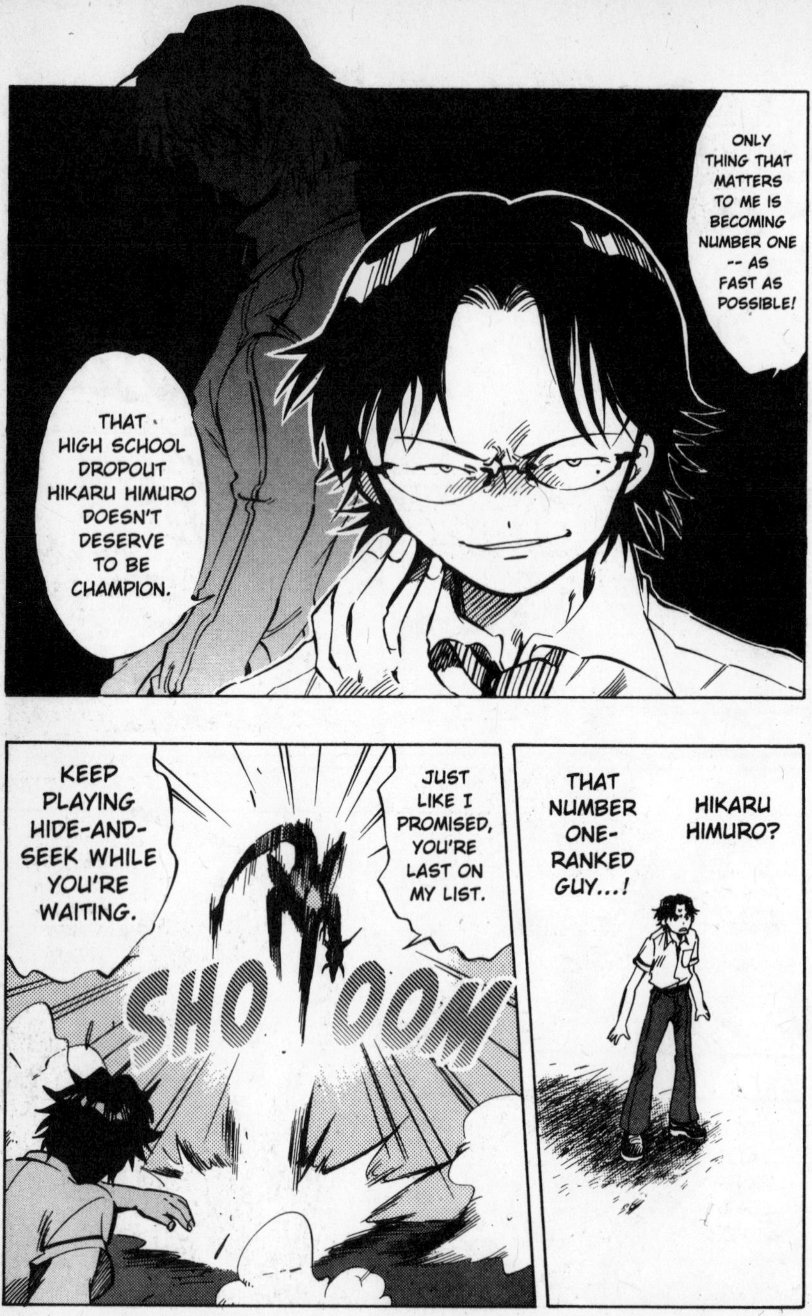
ONLY THING THAT MATTERS TO ME IS BECOMING NUMBER ONE -- AS FAST AS POSSIBLE!
THAT HIGH SCHOOL DROPOUT HIKARU HIMURO DOESN'T DESERVE TO BE CHAMPION.
HIKARU HIMURO?
THAT NUMBER ONE-RANKED GUY...!
JUST LIKE I PROMISED, YOU'RE LAST ON MY LIST.
KEEP PLAYING HIDE-AND-SEEK WHILE YOU'RE WAITING.
SHOOOM

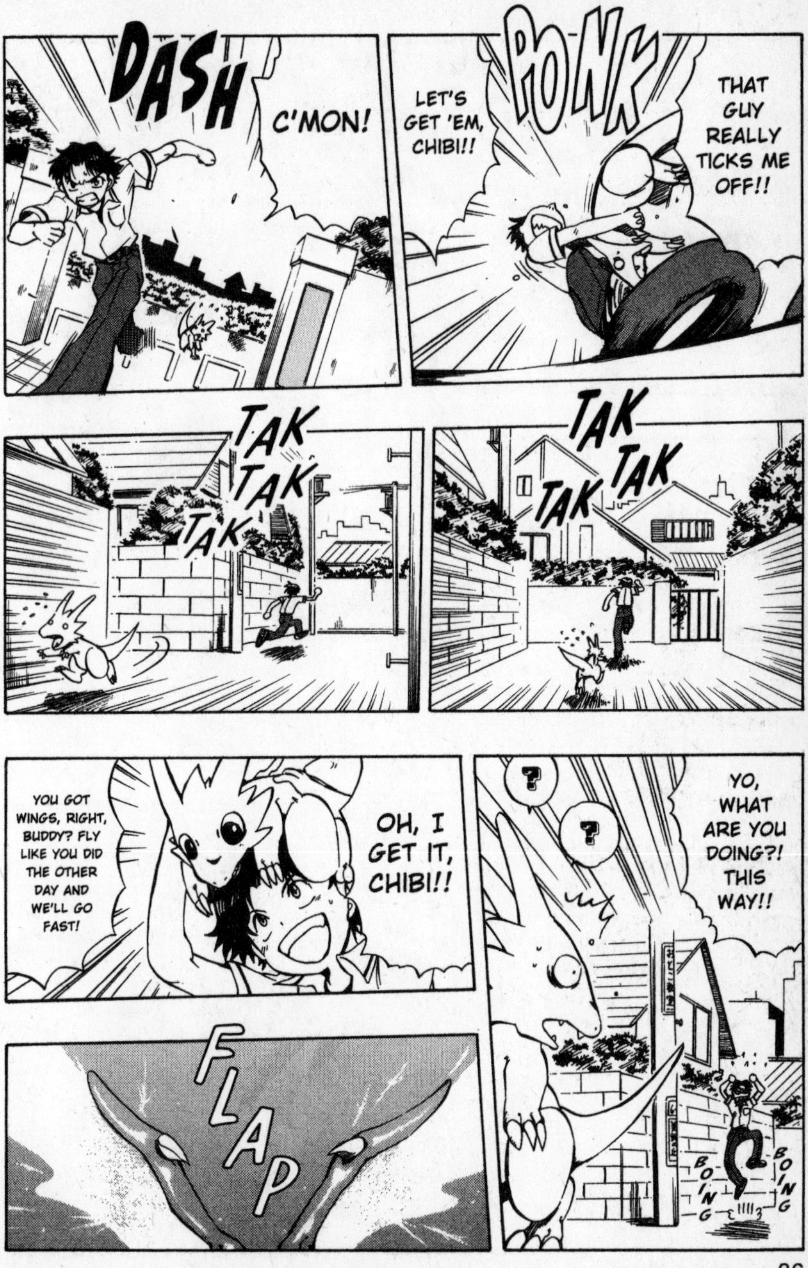
PONK
THAT GUY REALLY TICKS ME OFF!!
LET'S GET 'EM, CHIBI!!
DASH
C'MON!
TAK TAK TAK
TAK TAK TAK
YO, WHAT ARE YOU DOING?! THIS WAY!!
?
?
BOING
BOING
OH, I GET IT, CHIBI!!
YOU GOT WINGS, RIGHT, BUDDY? FLY LIKE YOU DID THE OTHER DAY AND WE'LL GO FAST!
FLAP

READ THIS WAY

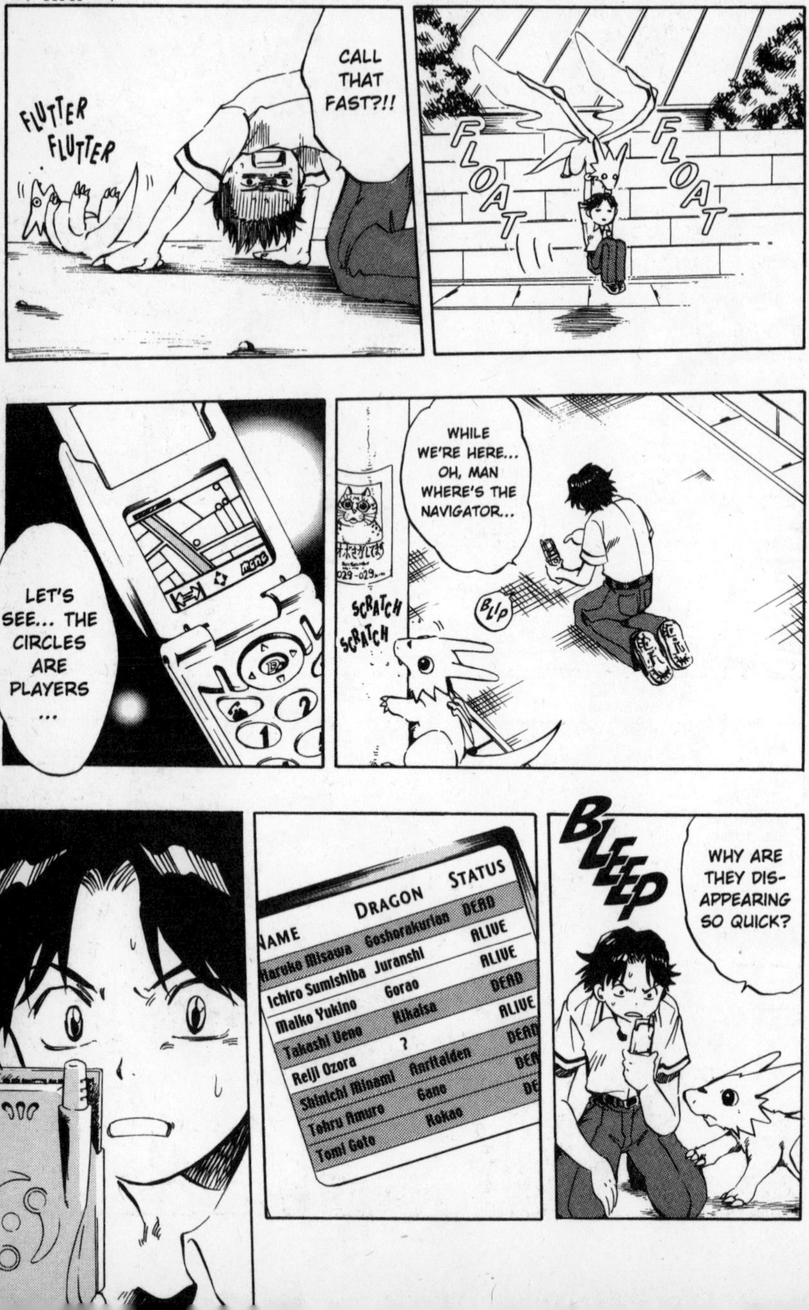
FLOAT
FLOAT
CALL THAT FAST?!!
FLUTTER FLUTTER
WHILE WE'RE HERE... OH, MAN WHERE'S THE NAVIGATOR...
BLIP
SCRATCH SCRATCH
LET'S SEE... THE CIRCLES ARE PLAYERS ...
BLEEP
WHY ARE THEY DIS-APPEARING SO QUICK?
NAME DRAGON STATUS
Haruko Misawa Goshorakurian DEAD
Ichiro Sumishiba Juranshi ALIVE
Maiko Yukino Gorao ALIVE
Takashi Ueno Rikaisa DEAD
Reiji Ozora ? ALIVE
Shinichi Minami Aarftalden DEAD
Tohru Amuro Gano DEA
Tomi Goto Kokao DE

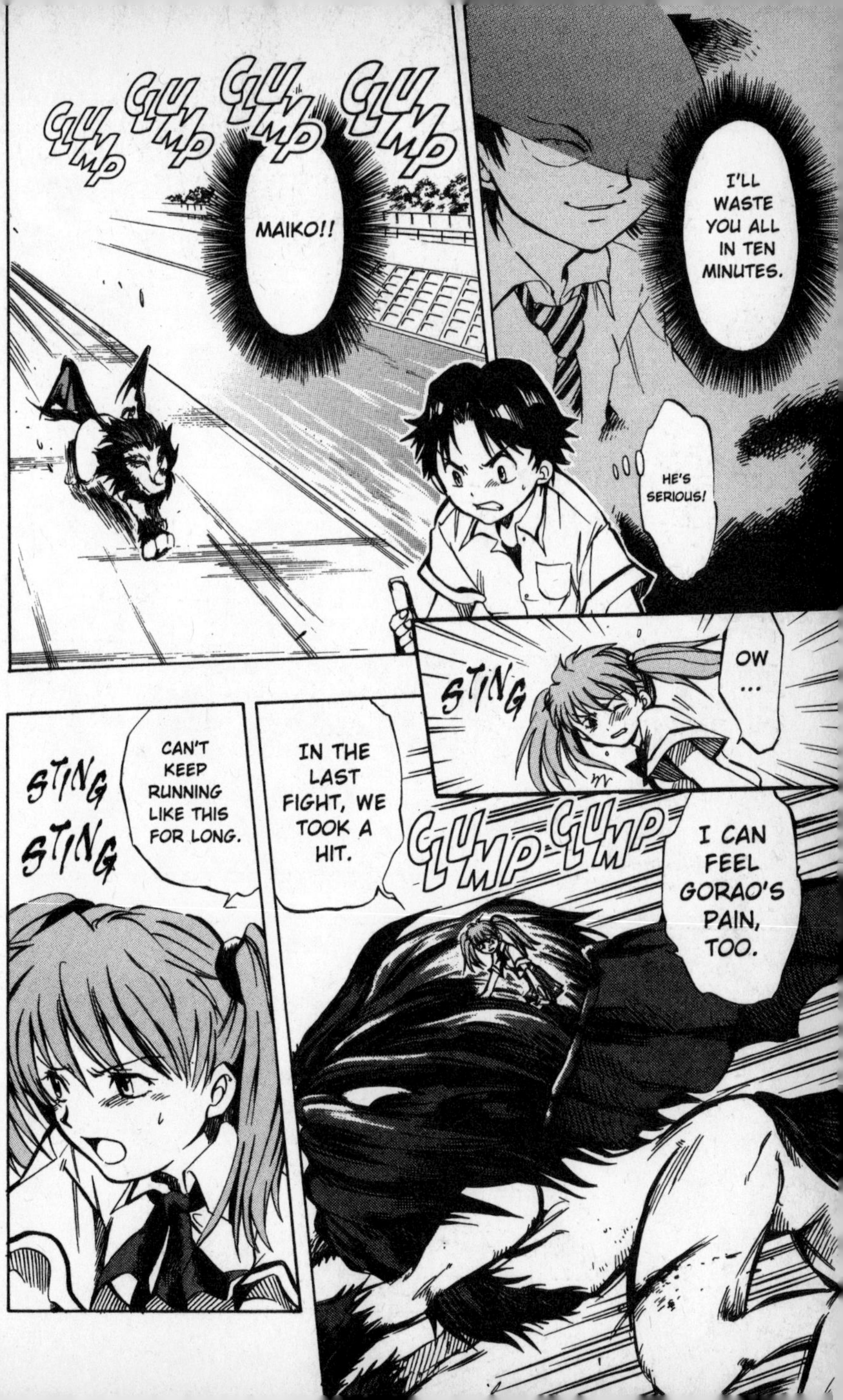
I'LL WASTE YOU ALL IN TEN MINUTES.
HE'S SERIOUS!
CLUMP CLUMP CLUMP CLUMP
MAIKO!!
STING
OW...
I CAN FEEL GORAO'S PAIN, TOO.
CLUMP CLUMP
IN THE LAST FIGHT, WE TOOK A HIT.
CAN'T KEEP RUNNING LIKE THIS FOR LONG.
STING STING

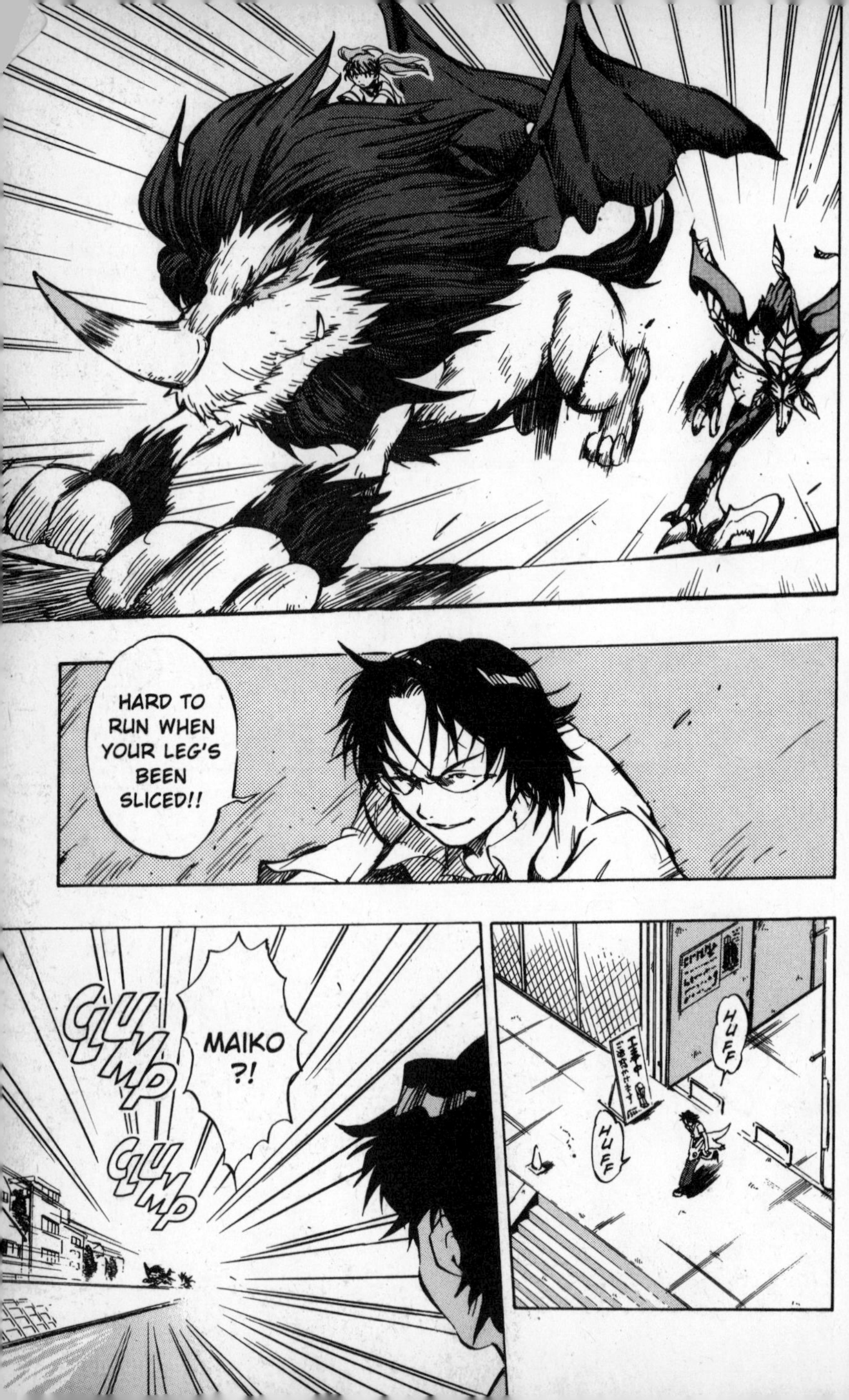
HARD TO RUN WHEN YOUR LEG'S BEEN SLICED!!
HUFF
HUFF
MAIKO ?!
CLUMP
CLUMP

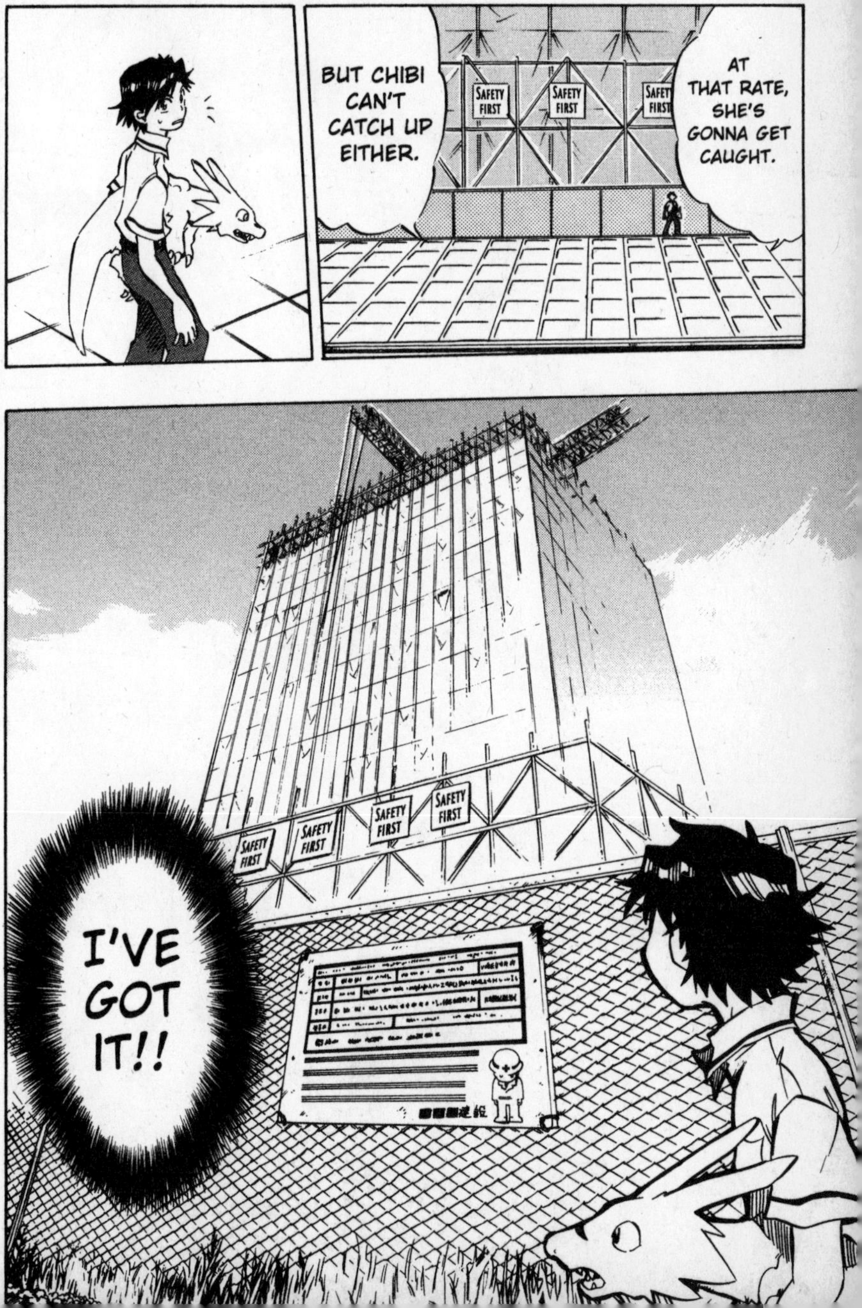
AT THAT RATE, SHE'S GONNA GET CAUGHT.
BUT CHIBI CAN'T CATCH UP EITHER.
I'VE GOT IT!!

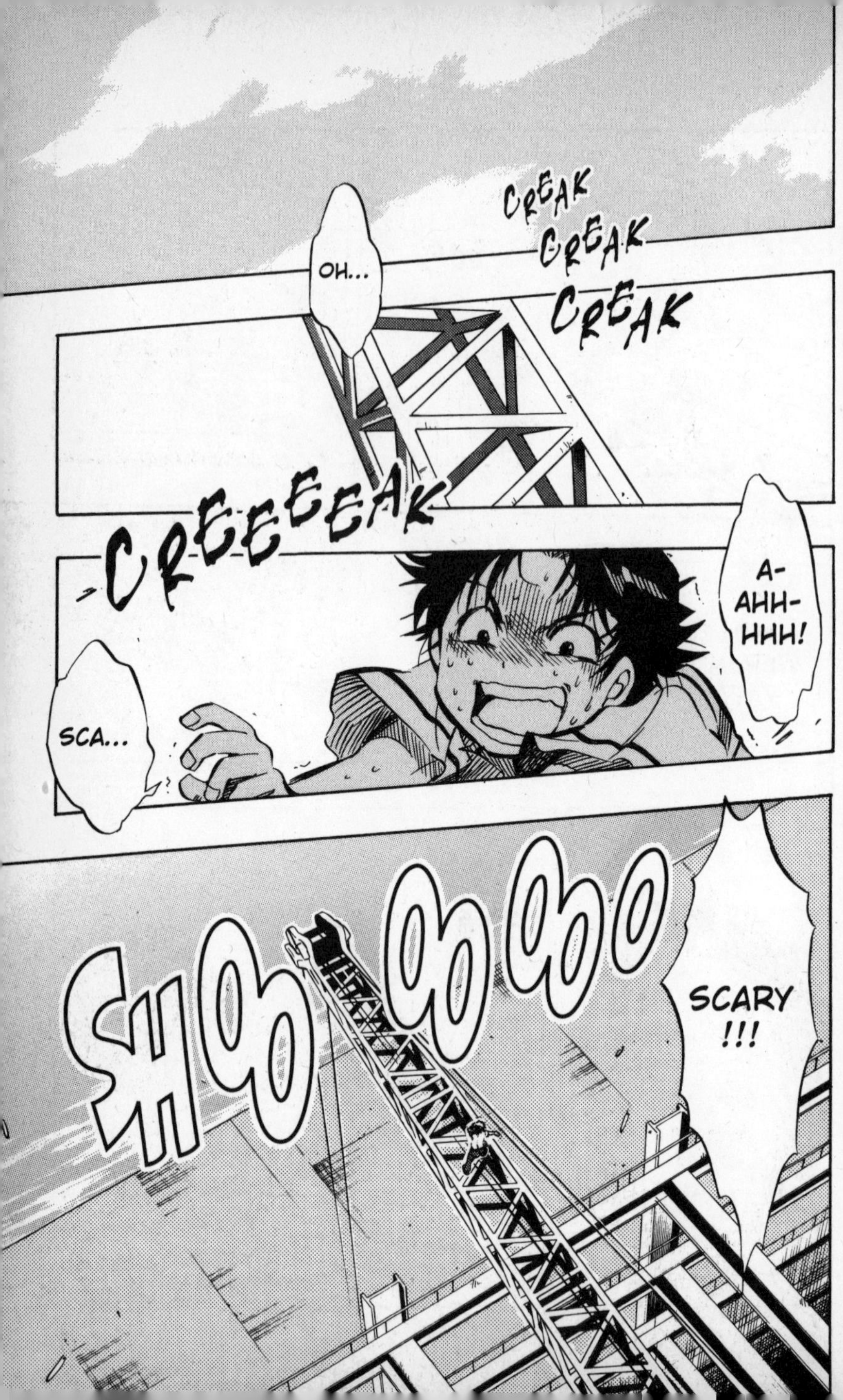
CREAK
CREAK
CREAK
OH...
CREEEEAK
A-AHH-HHH!
SCA...
SCARY!!!
SHOOOOOO

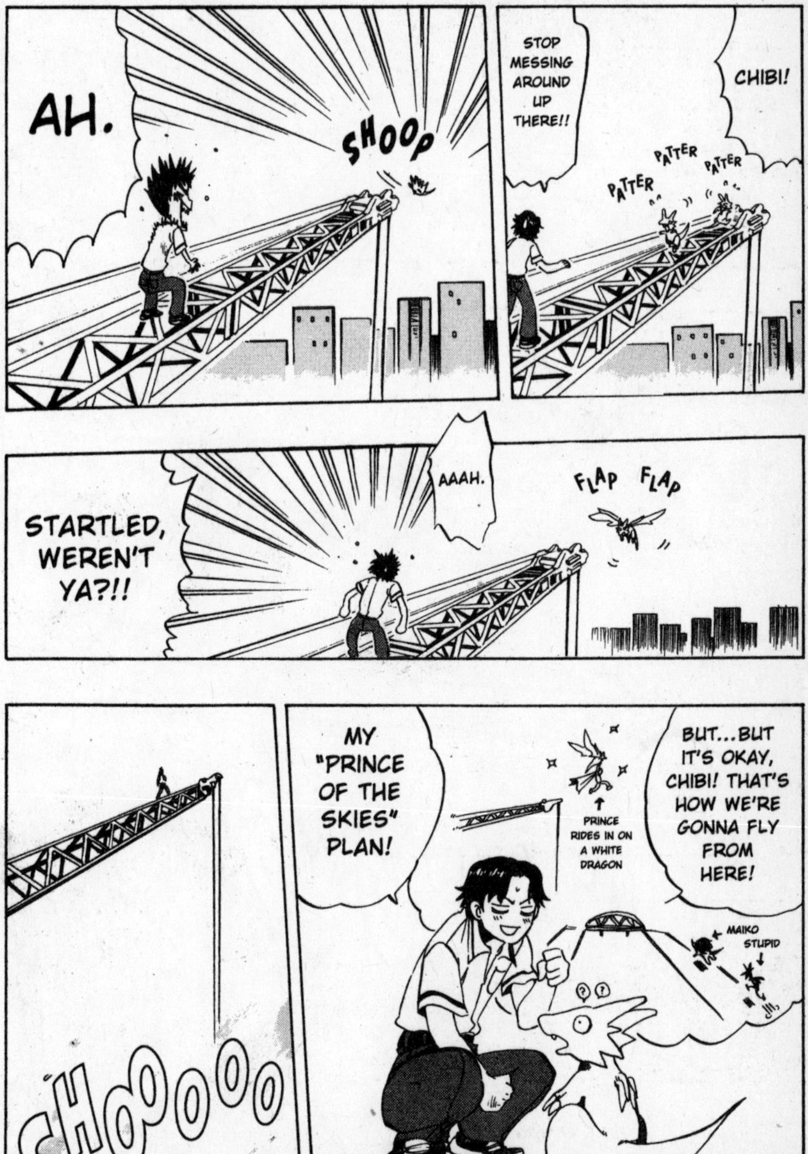
CHIBI!
STOP MESSING AROUND UP THERE!!
PATTER
PATTER
PATTER
SHOOP
AH.
FLAP FLAP
AAAH.
STARTLED, WEREN'T YA?!!
BUT...BUT IT'S OKAY, CHIBI! THAT'S HOW WE'RE GONNA FLY FROM HERE!
PRINCE RIDES IN ON A WHITE DRAGON
MY "PRINCE OF THE SKIES" PLAN!
MAIKO
STUPID
SHOOOOO

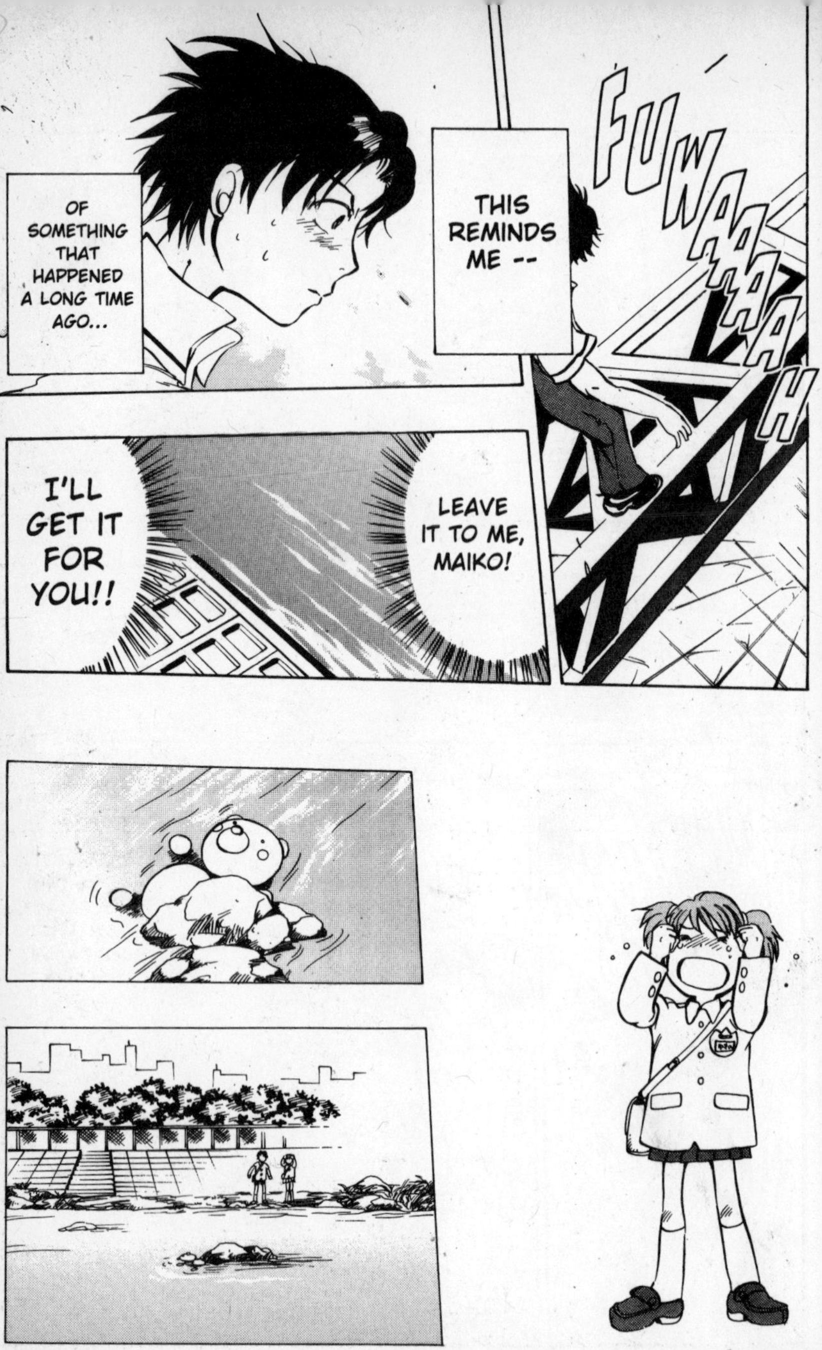
FUWAAAAAH
THIS REMINDS ME --
OF SOMETHING THAT HAPPENED A LONG TIME AGO...
LEAVE IT TO ME, MAIKO!
I'LL GET IT FOR YOU!!

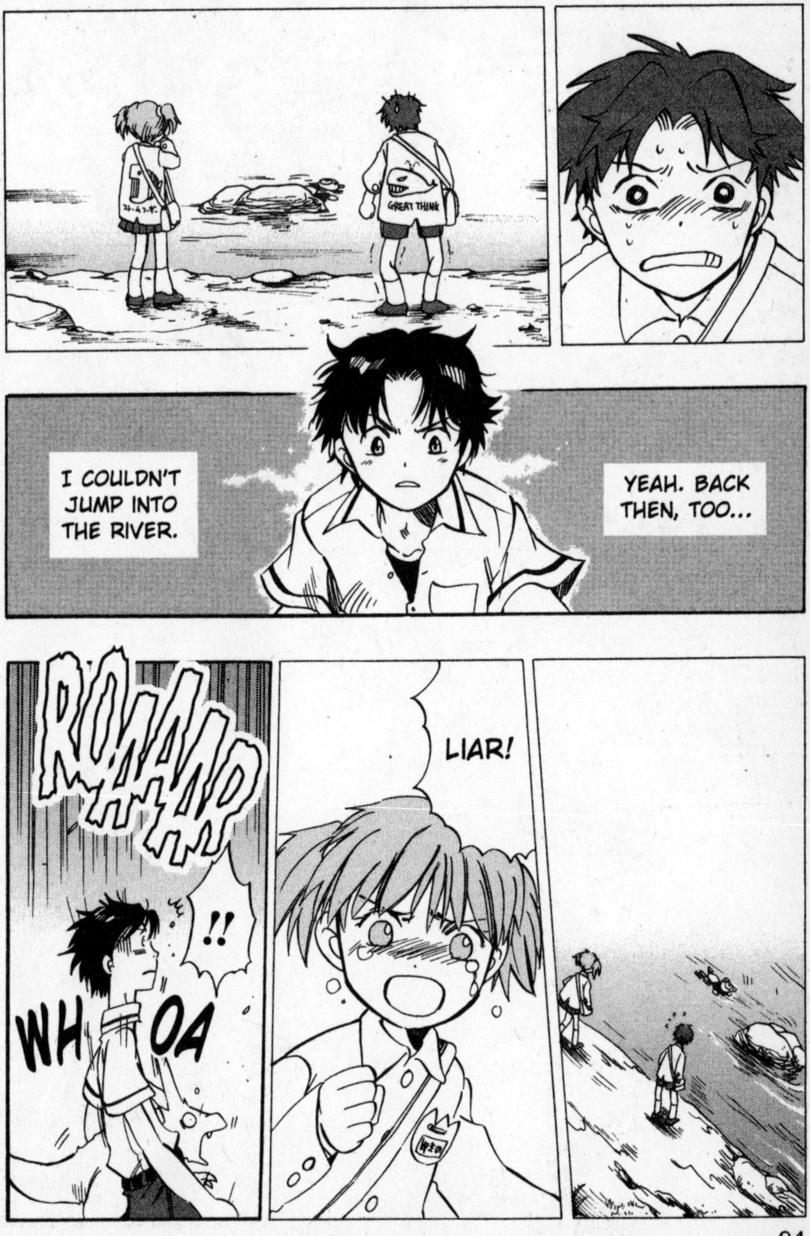
GREAT THING
YEAH. BACK THEN, TOO...
I COULDN'T JUMP INTO THE RIVER.
LIAR!
ROAAAR
!!
WHOA

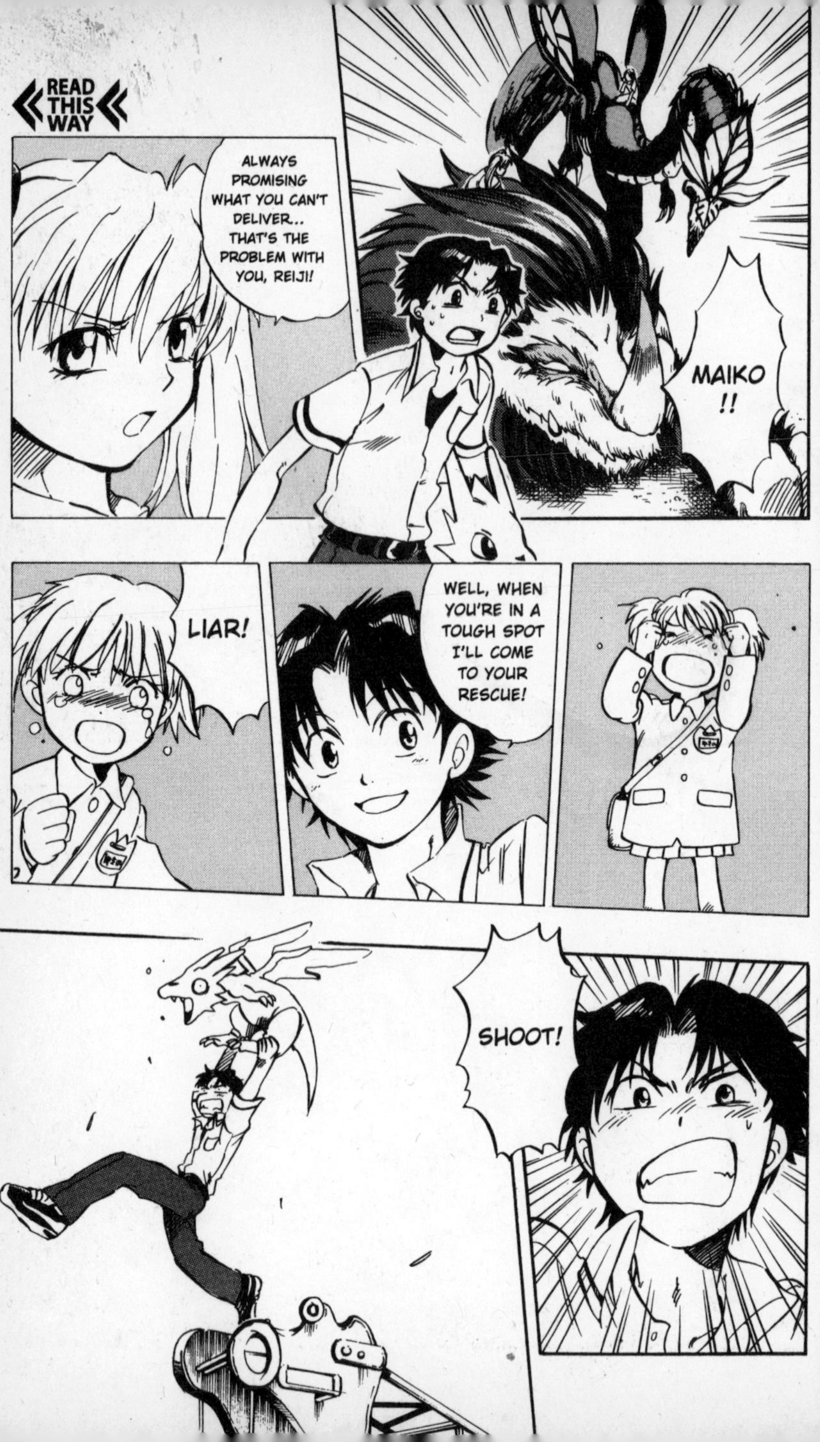
READ THIS WAY
MAIKO !!
ALWAYS PROMISING WHAT YOU CAN'T DELIVER... THAT'S THE PROBLEM WITH YOU, REIJI!
WELL, WHEN YOU'RE IN A TOUGH SPOT I'LL COME TO YOUR RESCUE!
LIAR!
SHOOT!

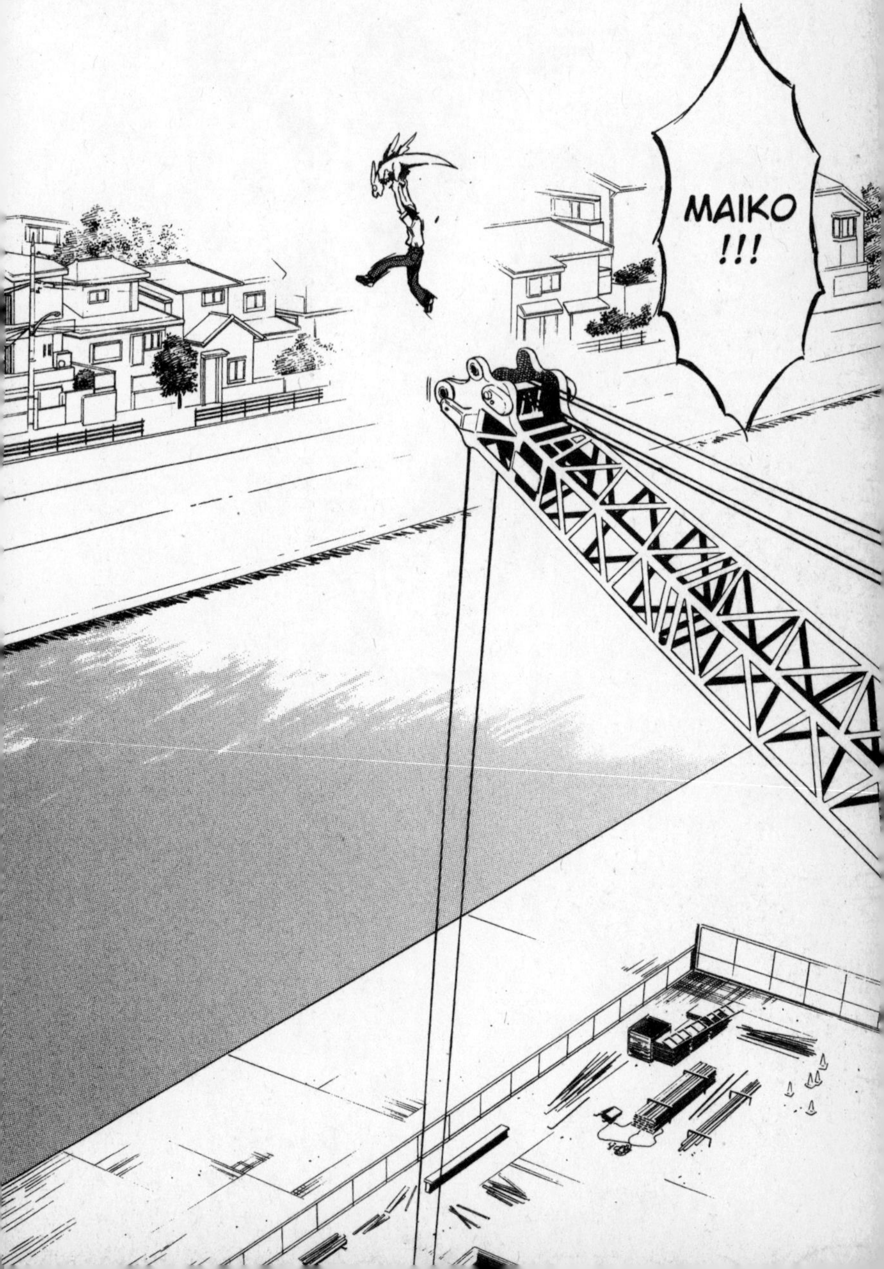
MAIKO
!!!

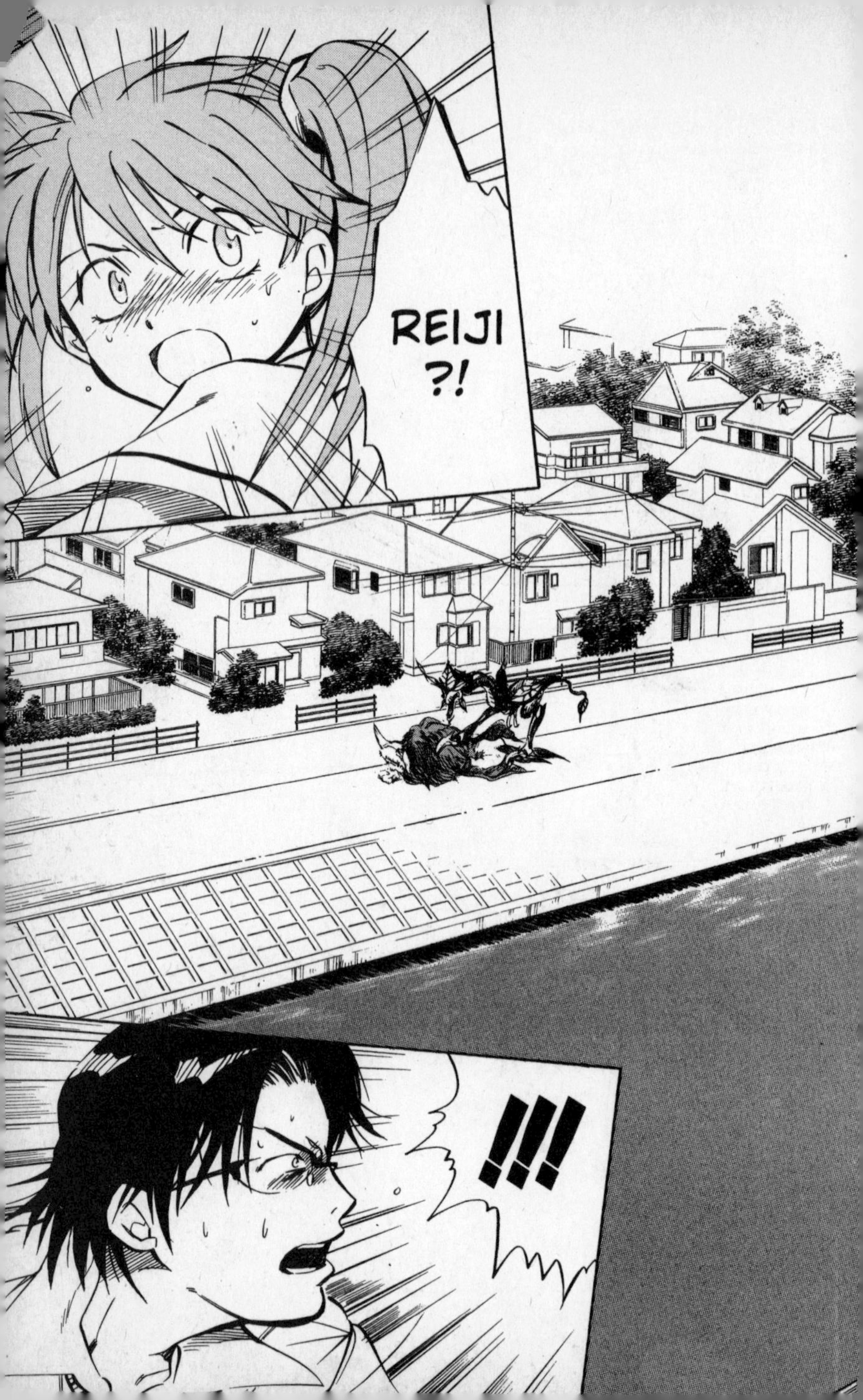
REIJI ?!
!!!

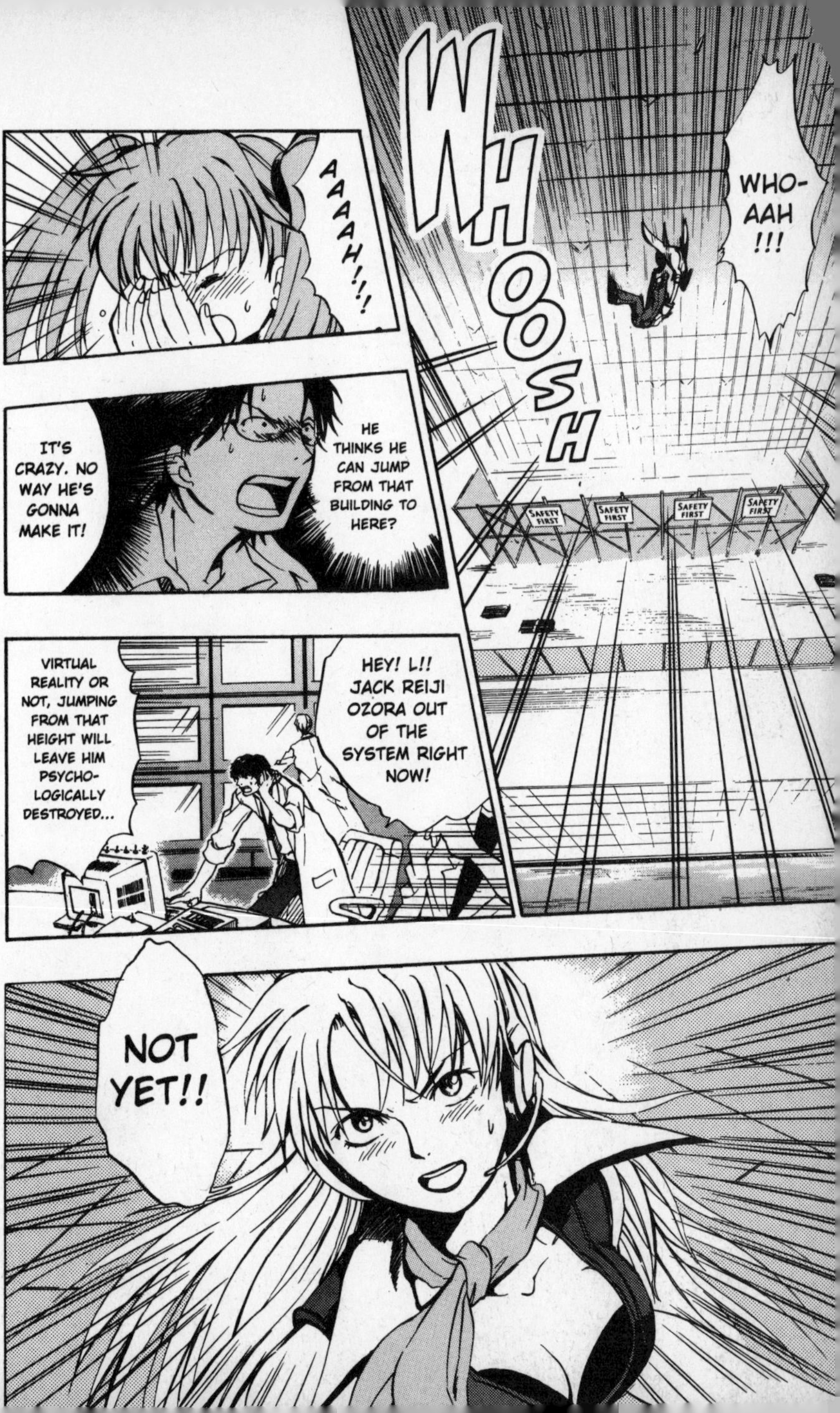

WHO-AAH!!!
WHOOSH
SAFETY FIRST
SAFETY FIRST
SAFETY FIRST
SAFETY FIRST
AAAAH!!!
HE THINKS HE CAN JUMP FROM THAT BUILDING TO HERE?
IT'S CRAZY. NO WAY HE'S GONNA MAKE IT!
HEY! L!! JACK REIJI OZORA OUT OF THE SYSTEM RIGHT NOW!
VIRTUAL REALITY OR NOT, JUMPING FROM THAT HEIGHT WILL LEAVE HIM PSYCHO-LOGICALLY DESTROYED...
NOT YET!!

READ THIS WAY

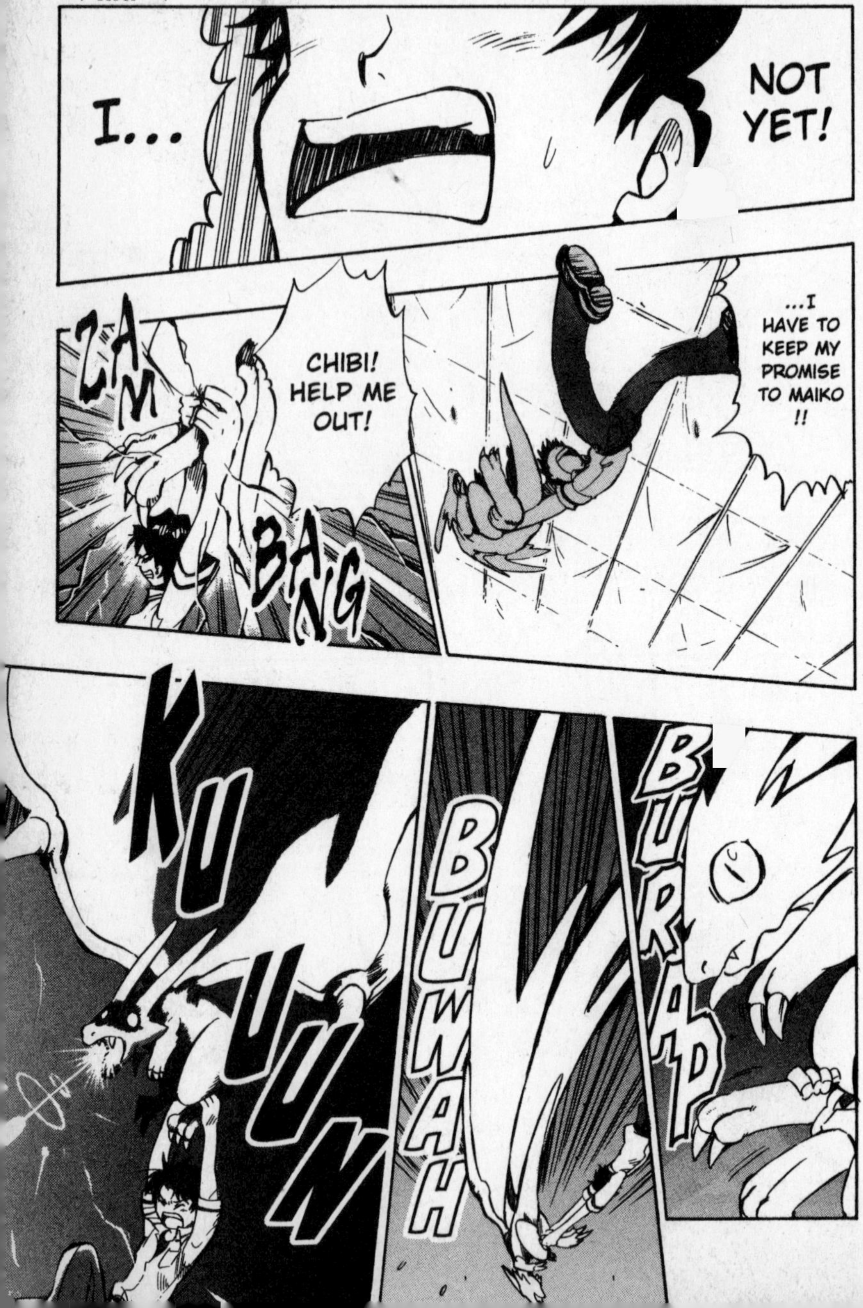
NOT YET!
I...
...I HAVE TO KEEP MY PROMISE TO MAIKO !!
CHIBI! HELP ME OUT!
ZAM
BANG
BURAP
BUWAH
KUUUN

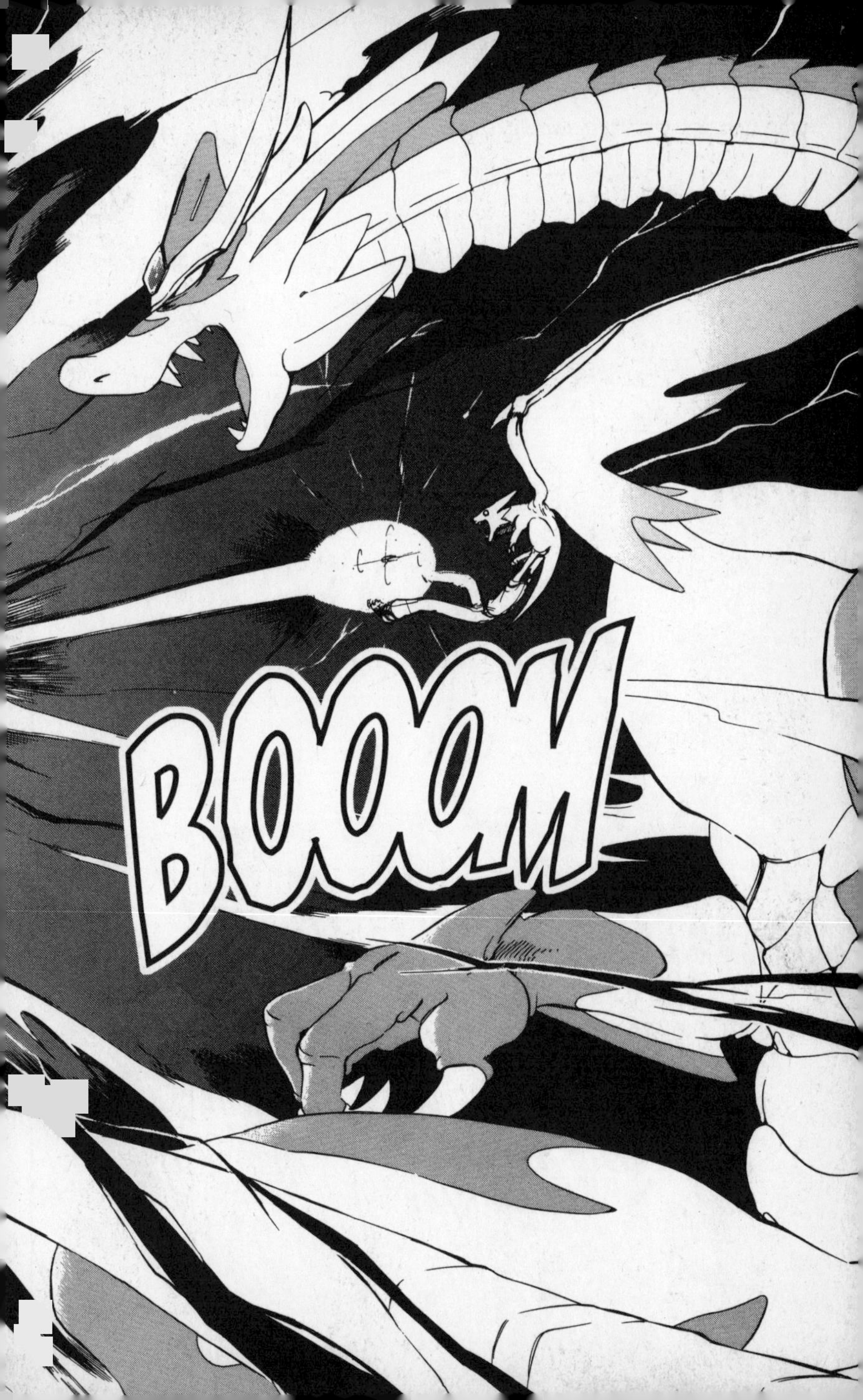
BOOOM

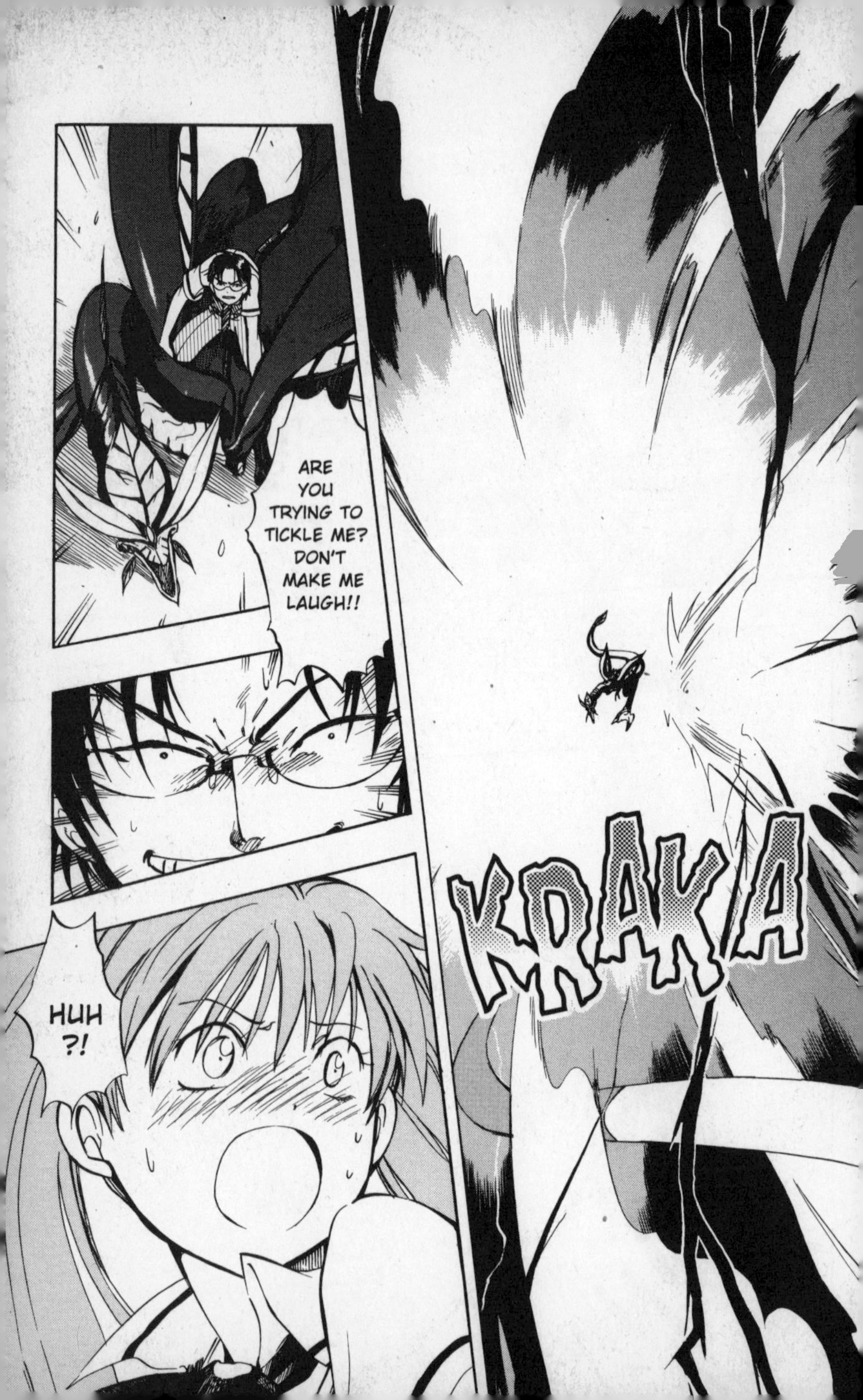
KRAKA
ARE YOU TRYING TO TICKLE ME? DON'T MAKE ME LAUGH!!
HUH ?!

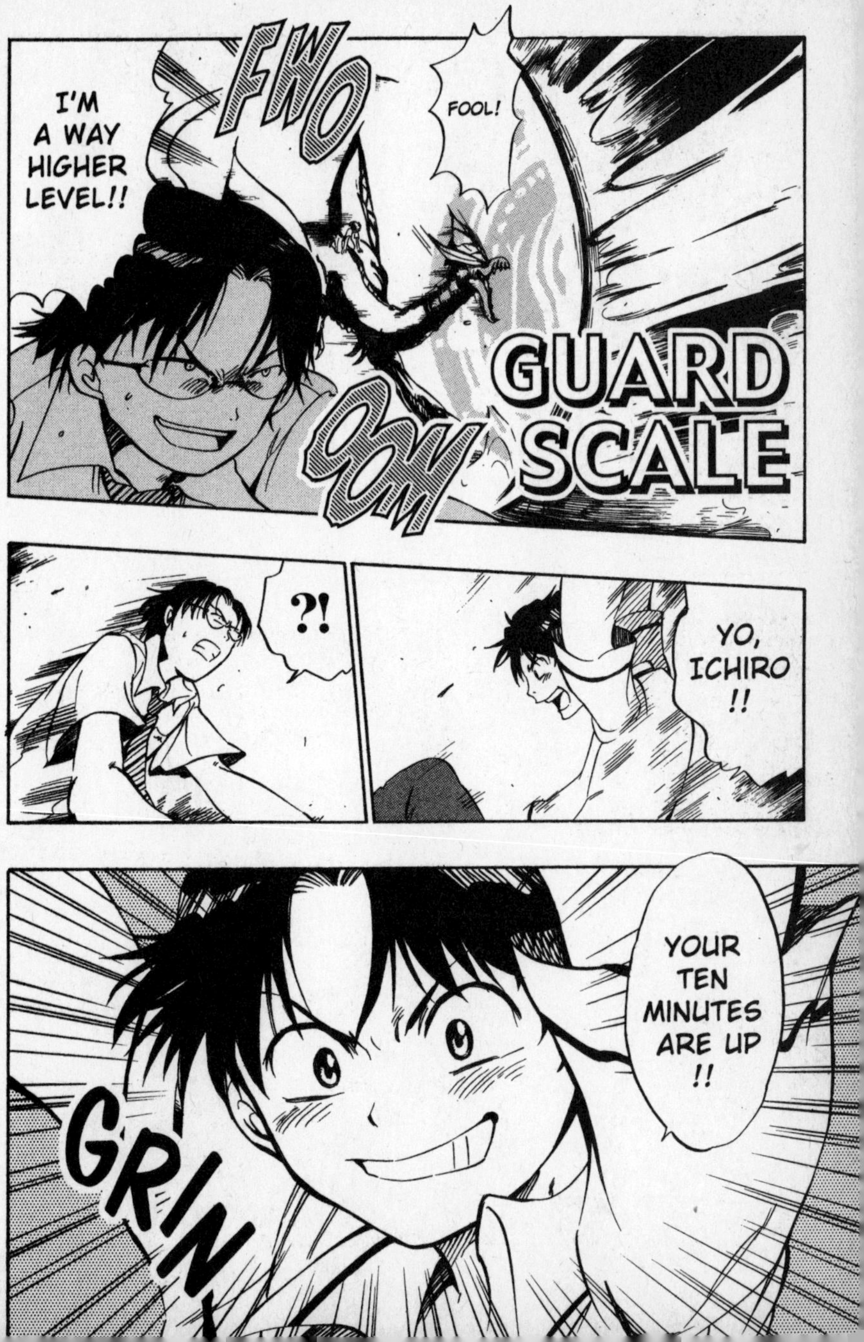
FOOL!
FWO
I'M A WAY HIGHER LEVEL!!
GUARD SCALE
OOM
YO, ICHIRO!!
?!
YOUR TEN MINUTES ARE UP!!
GRIN

READ THIS WAY

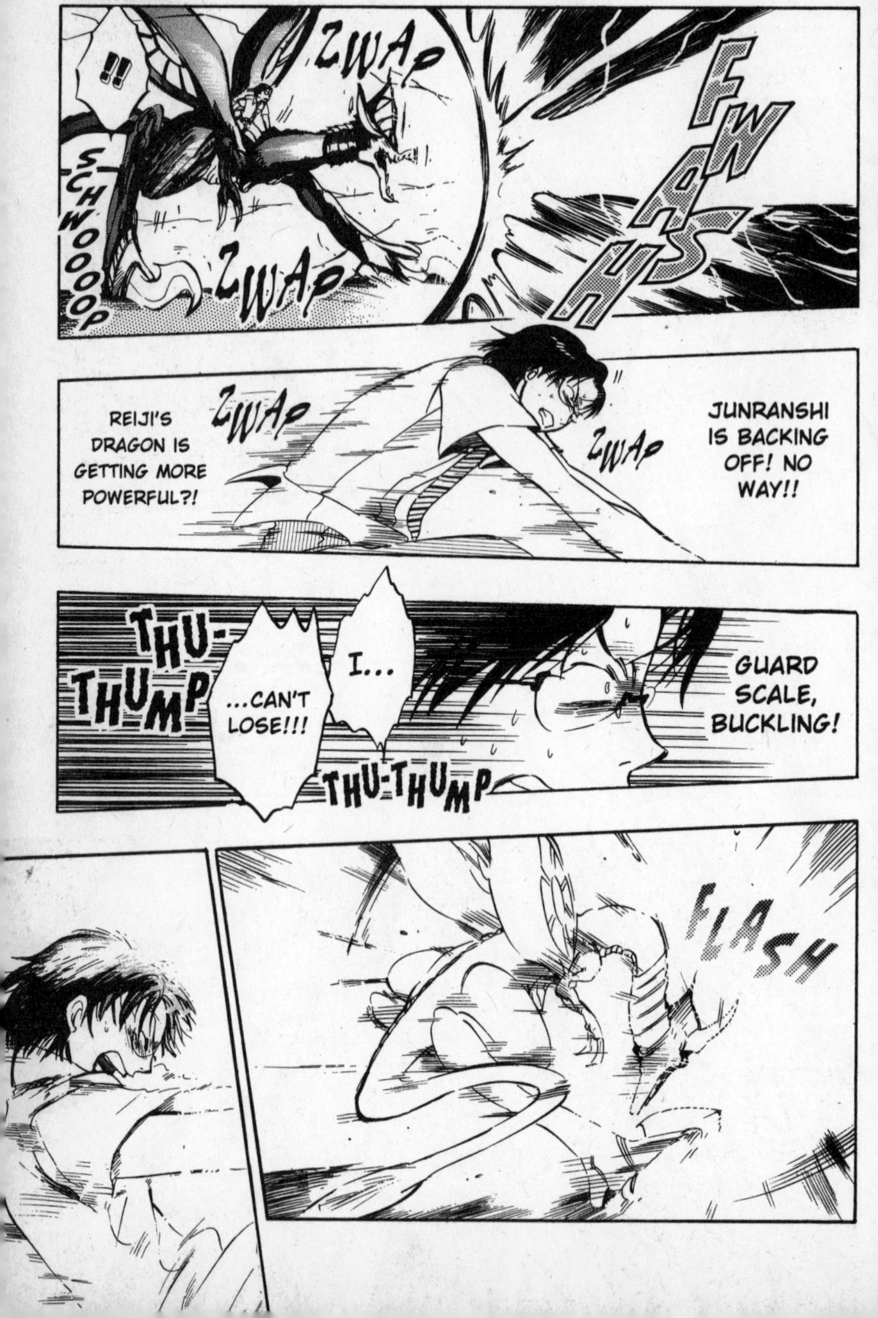
FWASH
ZWAP
!!
ZWAP
SCHWOOOOOP
JUNRANSHI IS BACKING OFF! NO WAY!!
ZWAP
ZWAP
REIJI'S DRAGON IS GETTING MORE POWERFUL?!
GUARD SCALE, BUCKLING!
I...
...CAN'T LOSE!!!
THU-THUMP
THU-THUMP
FLASH

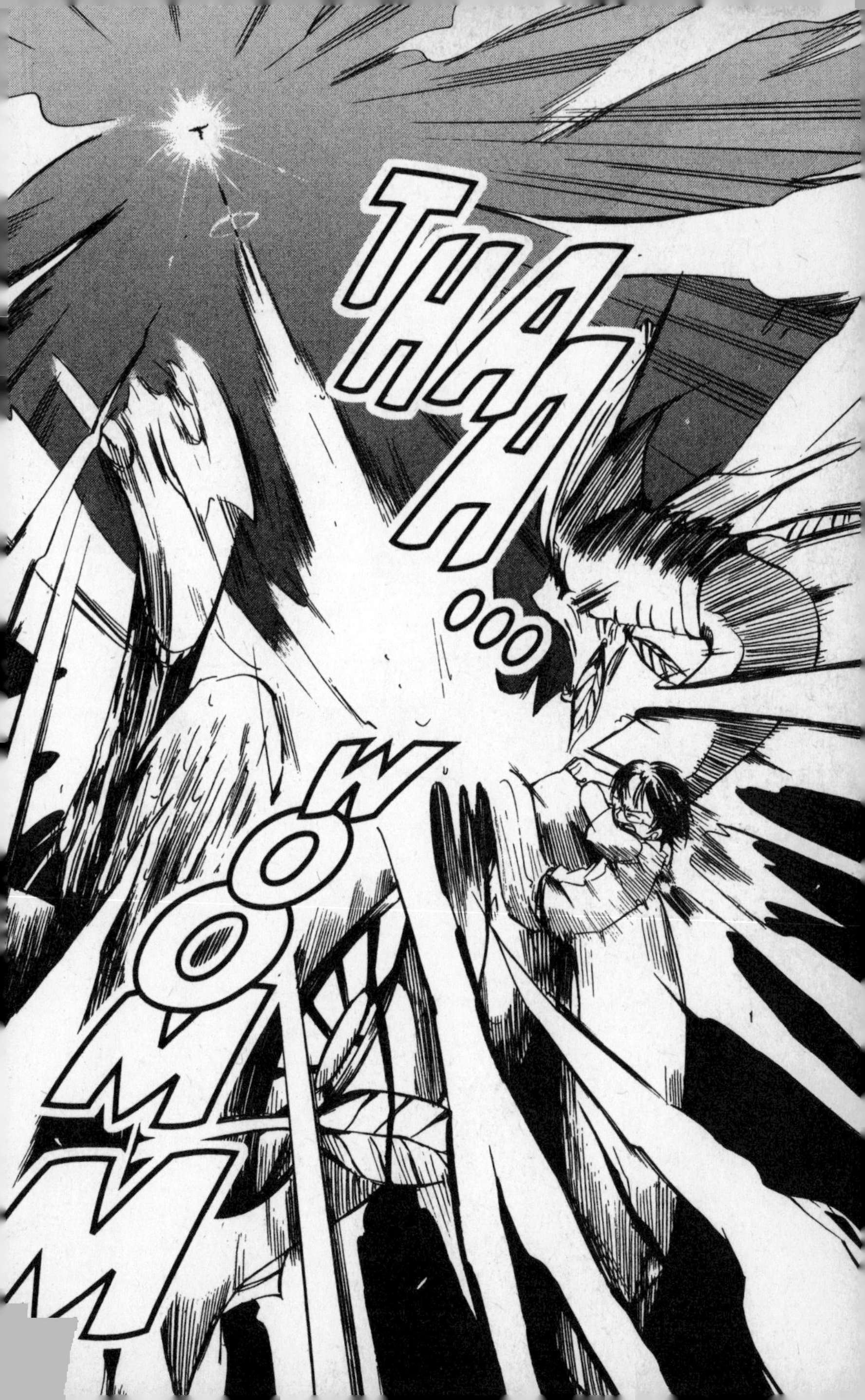
THAAOOO
WOOMM

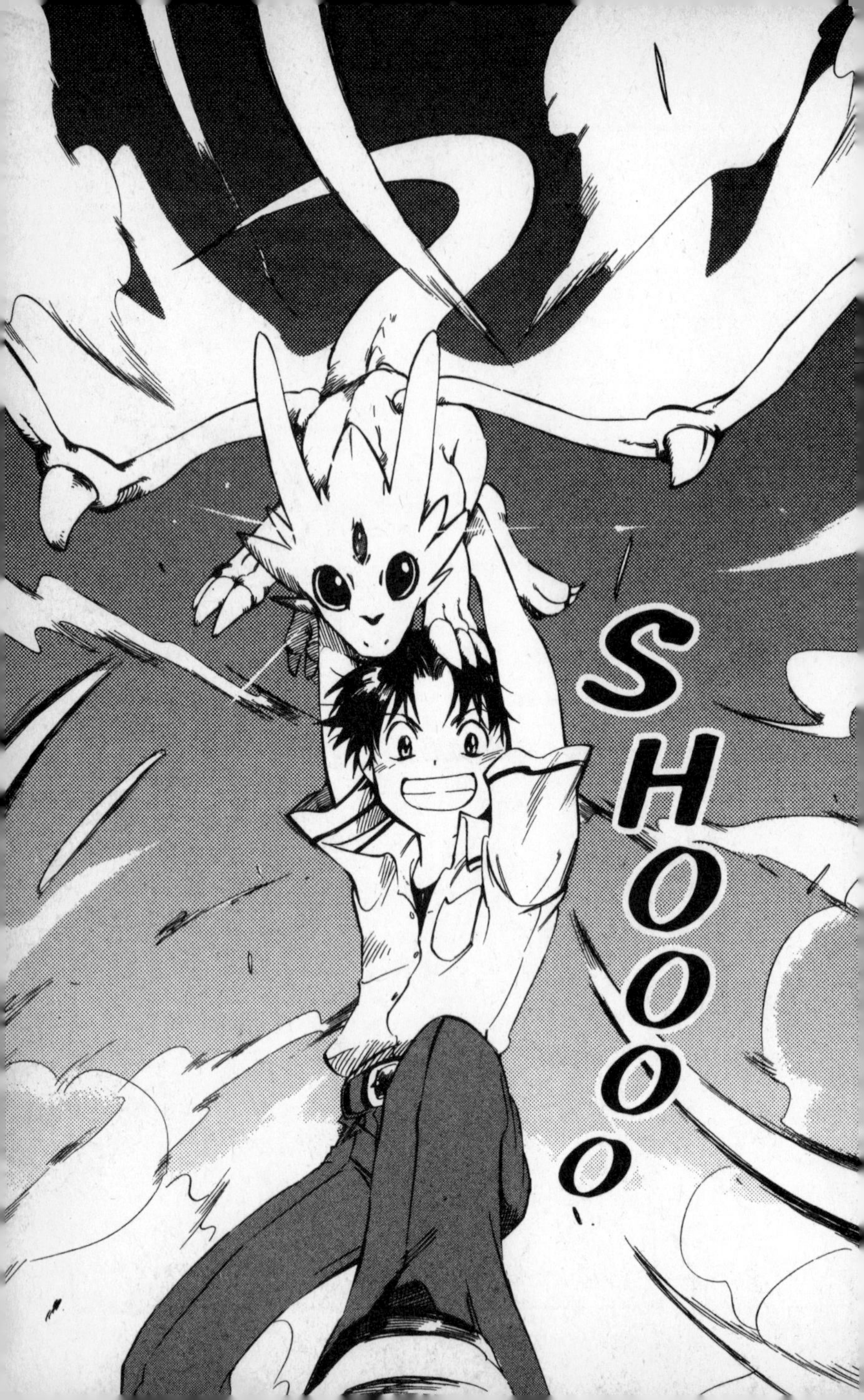
SHOOOO.

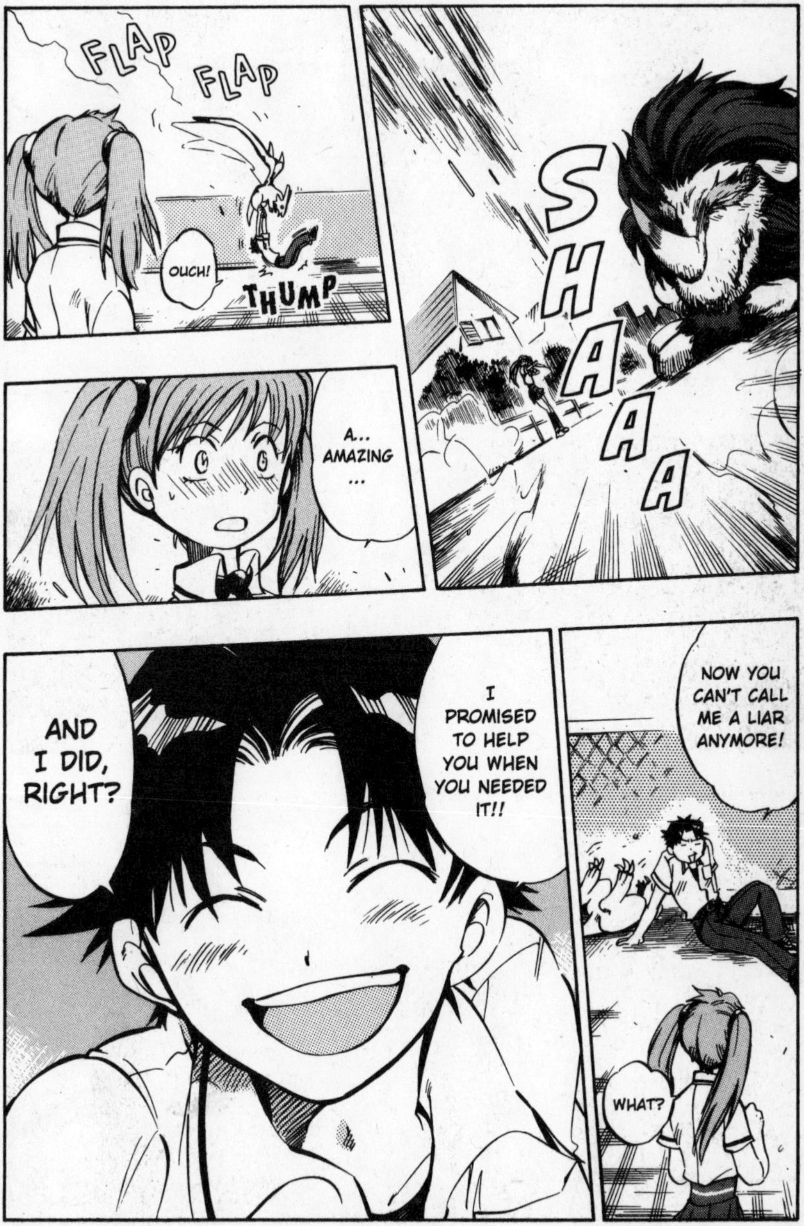
SHAAAA
FLAP FLAP
OUCH!
THUMP
A... AMAZING ...
NOW YOU CAN'T CALL ME A LIAR ANYMORE!
WHAT?
I PROMISED TO HELP YOU WHEN YOU NEEDED IT!!
AND I DID, RIGHT?

READ THIS WAY

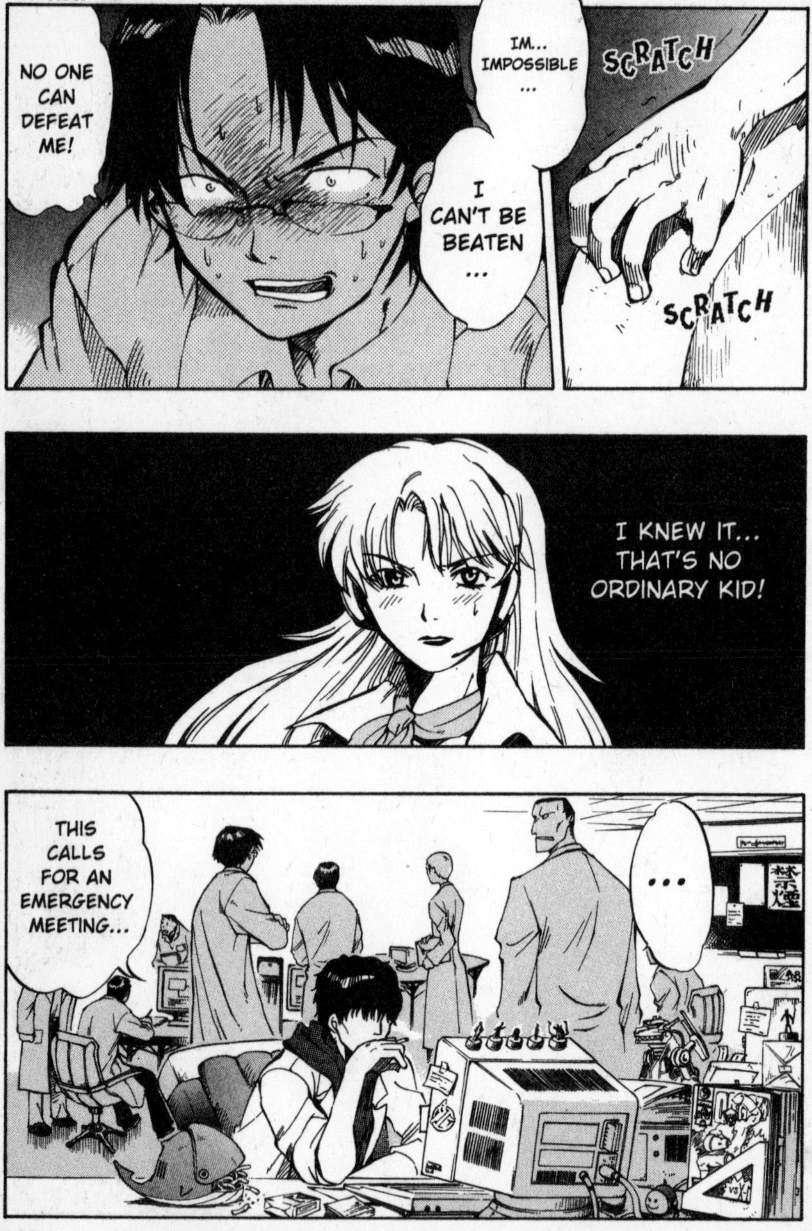
SCRATCH
SCRATCH
IM... IMPOSSIBLE...
I CAN'T BE BEATEN...
NO ONE CAN DEFEAT ME!
I KNEW IT... THAT'S NO ORDINARY KID!
...
THIS CALLS FOR AN EMERGENCY MEETING...

KANPA

WIND

PLAYER: DAISUKE
HAGIWARA
TYPE: FLYING
Can produce blizzards, deep-freezing
everything. Has the ability to paralyze
movement on a molecular level.

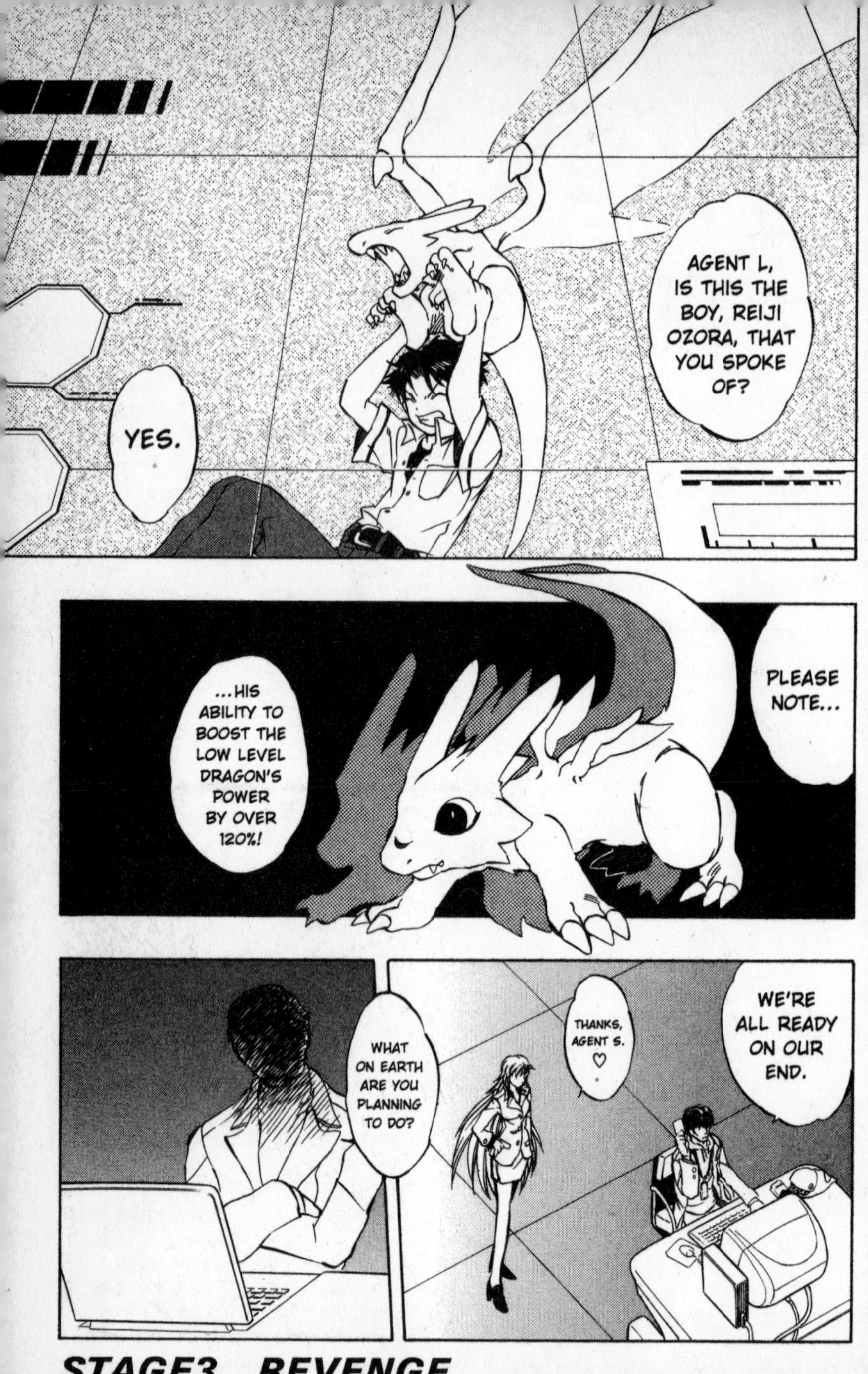
AGENT L, IS THIS THE BOY, REIJI OZORA, THAT YOU SPOKE OF?
YES.
PLEASE NOTE...
...HIS ABILITY TO BOOST THE LOW LEVEL DRAGON'S POWER BY OVER 120%!
WE'RE ALL READY ON OUR END.
THANKS, AGENT S. ♡
WHAT ON EARTH ARE YOU PLANNING TO DO?

STAGE3 REVENGE

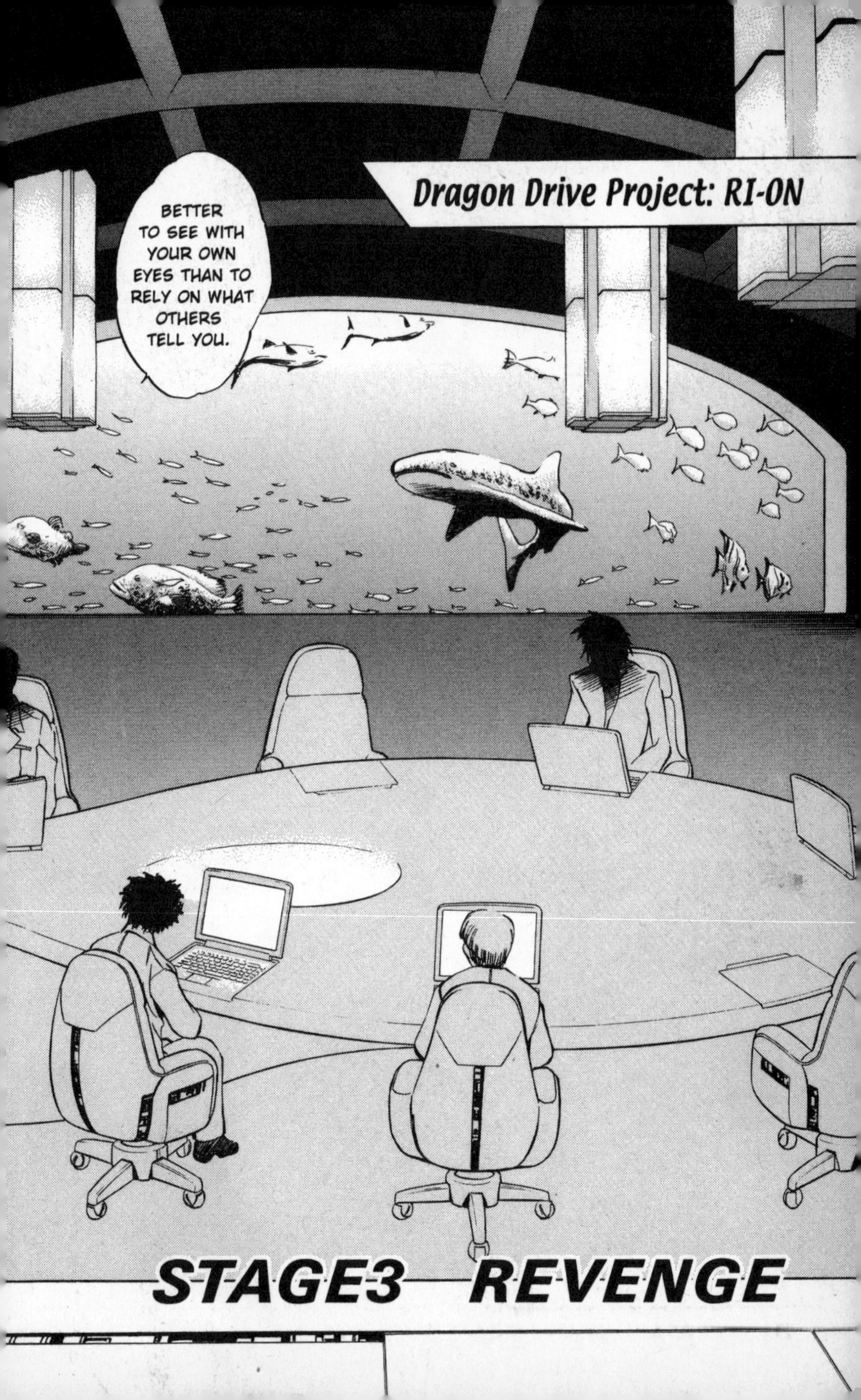
Dragon Drive Project: RI-ON
BETTER TO SEE WITH YOUR OWN EYES THAN TO RELY ON WHAT OTHERS TELL YOU.
STAGE3 REVENGE

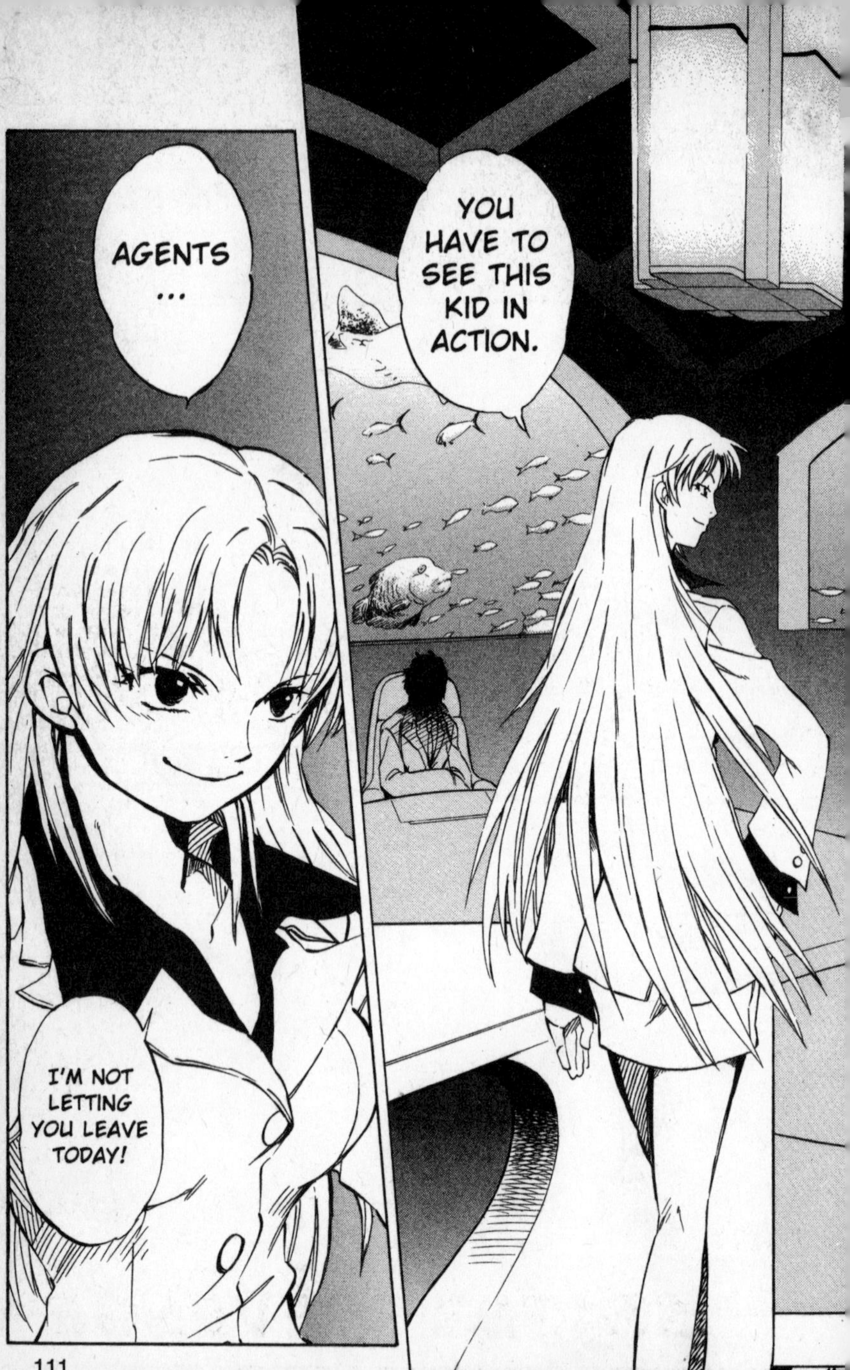
YOU HAVE TO SEE THIS KID IN ACTION.
AGENTS ...
I'M NOT LETTING YOU LEAVE TODAY!

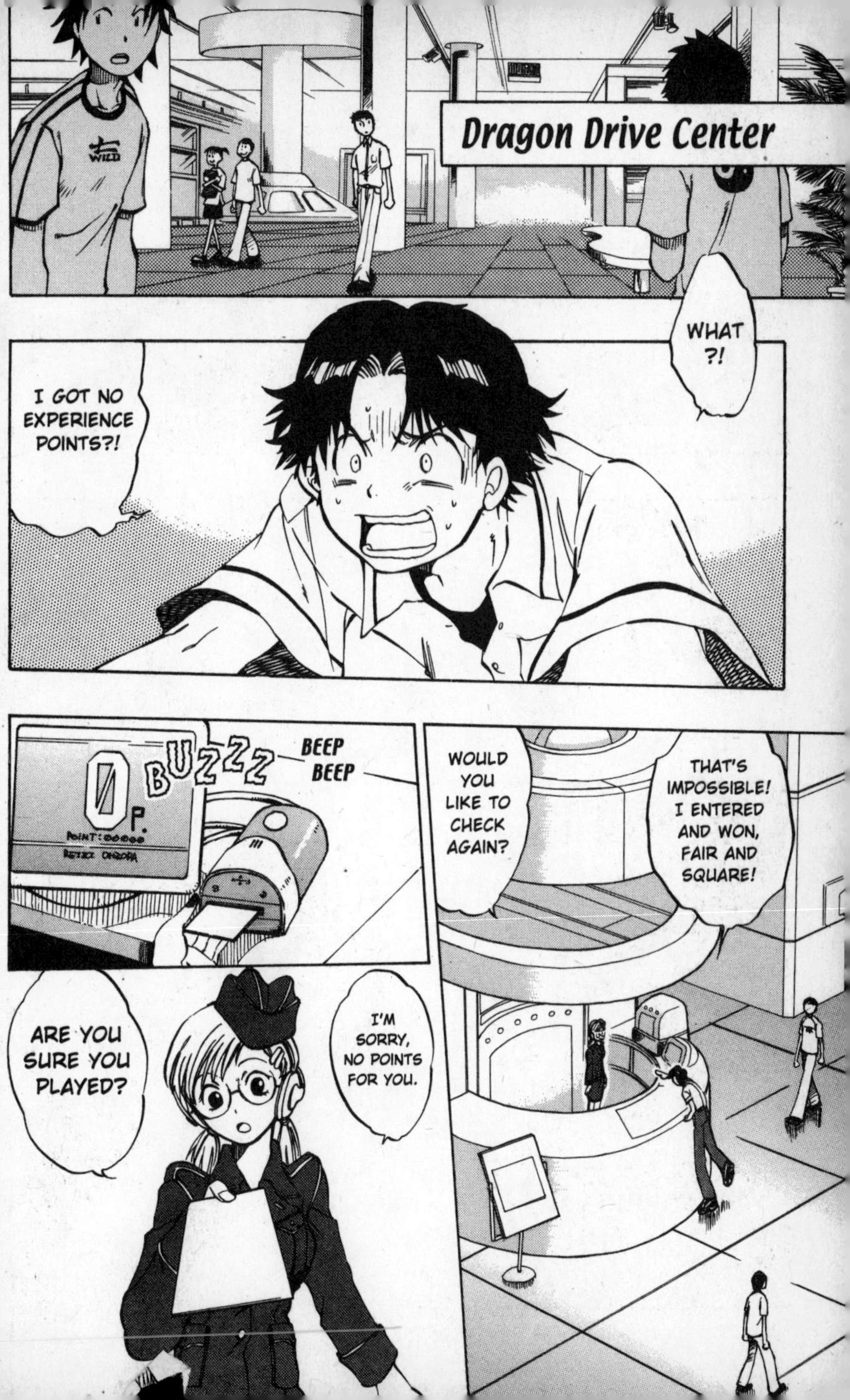
Dragon Drive Center
WHAT?!
I GOT NO EXPERIENCE POINTS?!
THAT'S IMPOSSIBLE! I ENTERED AND WON, FAIR AND SQUARE!
WOULD YOU LIKE TO CHECK AGAIN?
0 P.
BEEP BEEP
BUZZZ
I'M SORRY, NO POINTS FOR YOU.
ARE YOU SURE YOU PLAYED?

READ THIS WAY

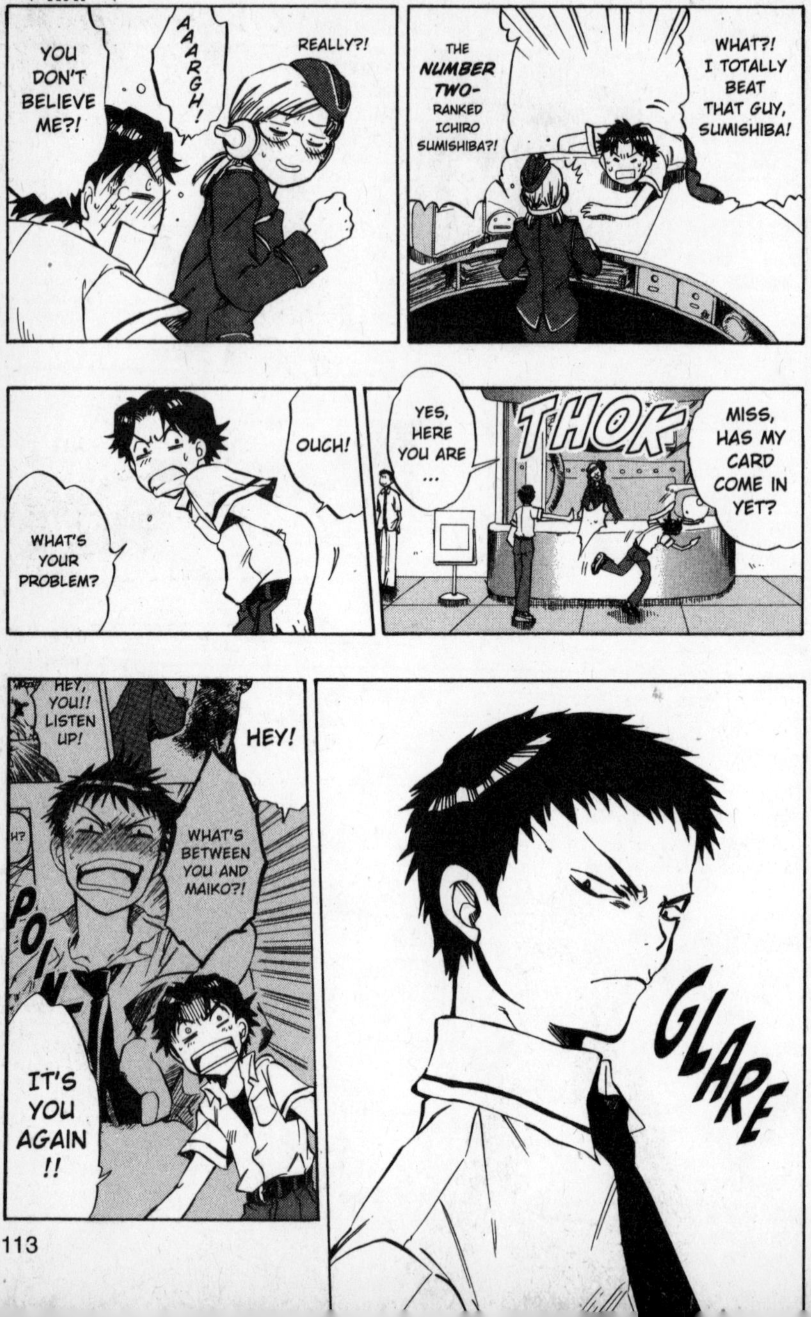

WHAT?! I TOTALLY BEAT THAT GUY, SUMISHIBA!
THE NUMBER TWO-RANKED ICHIRO SUMISHIBA?!
REALLY?!
AAAARGH!
YOU DON'T BELIEVE ME?!
MISS, HAS MY CARD COME IN YET?
THOK
YES, HERE YOU ARE ...
OUCH!
WHAT'S YOUR PROBLEM?
GLARE
HEY!
HEY, YOU!! LISTEN UP!
WHAT'S BETWEEN YOU AND MAIKO?!
POIN
IT'S YOU AGAIN !!

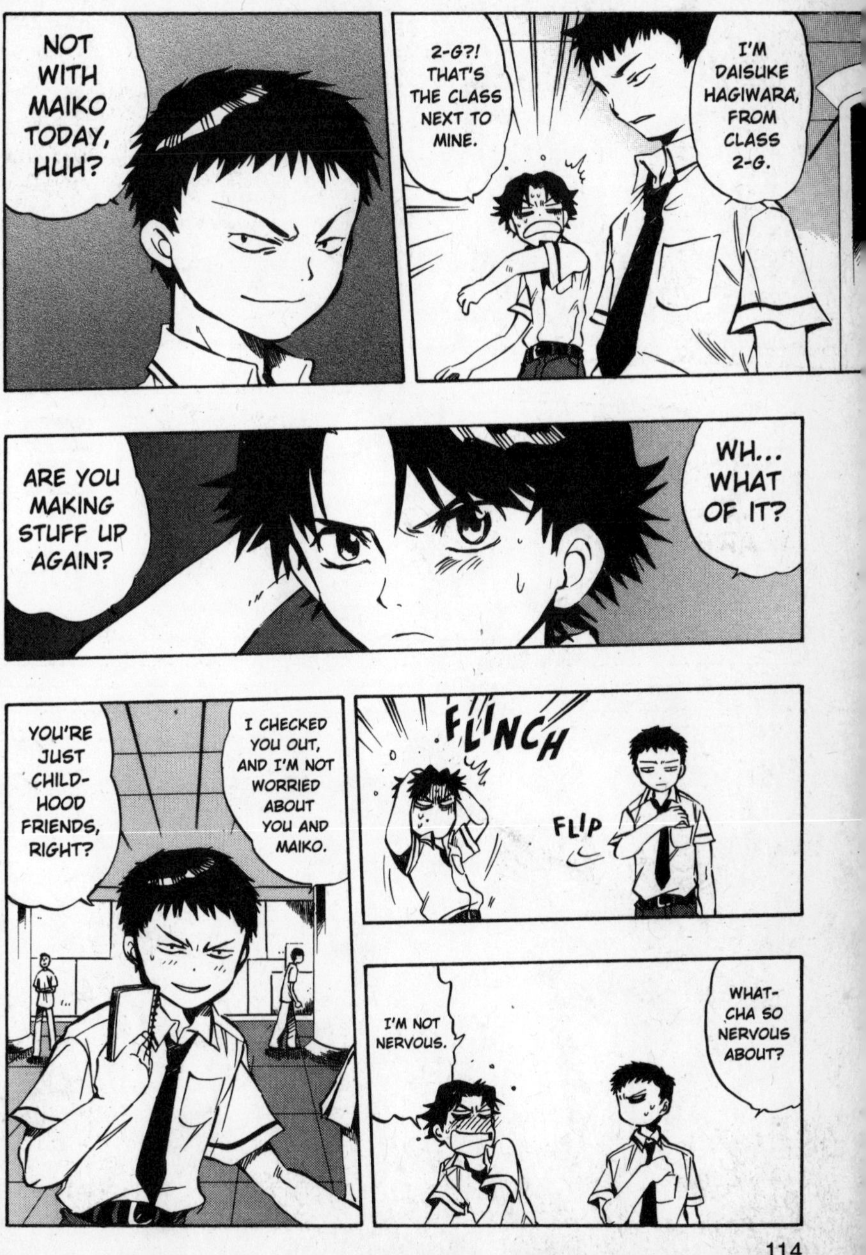
I'M DAISUKE HAGIWARA, FROM CLASS 2-G.
2-G?! THAT'S THE CLASS NEXT TO MINE.
NOT WITH MAIKO TODAY, HUH?
WH... WHAT OF IT?
ARE YOU MAKING STUFF UP AGAIN?
FLINCH
FLIP
WHAT-CHA SO NERVOUS ABOUT?
I'M NOT NERVOUS.
I CHECKED YOU OUT, AND I'M NOT WORRIED ABOUT YOU AND MAIKO.
YOU'RE JUST CHILD-HOOD FRIENDS, RIGHT?

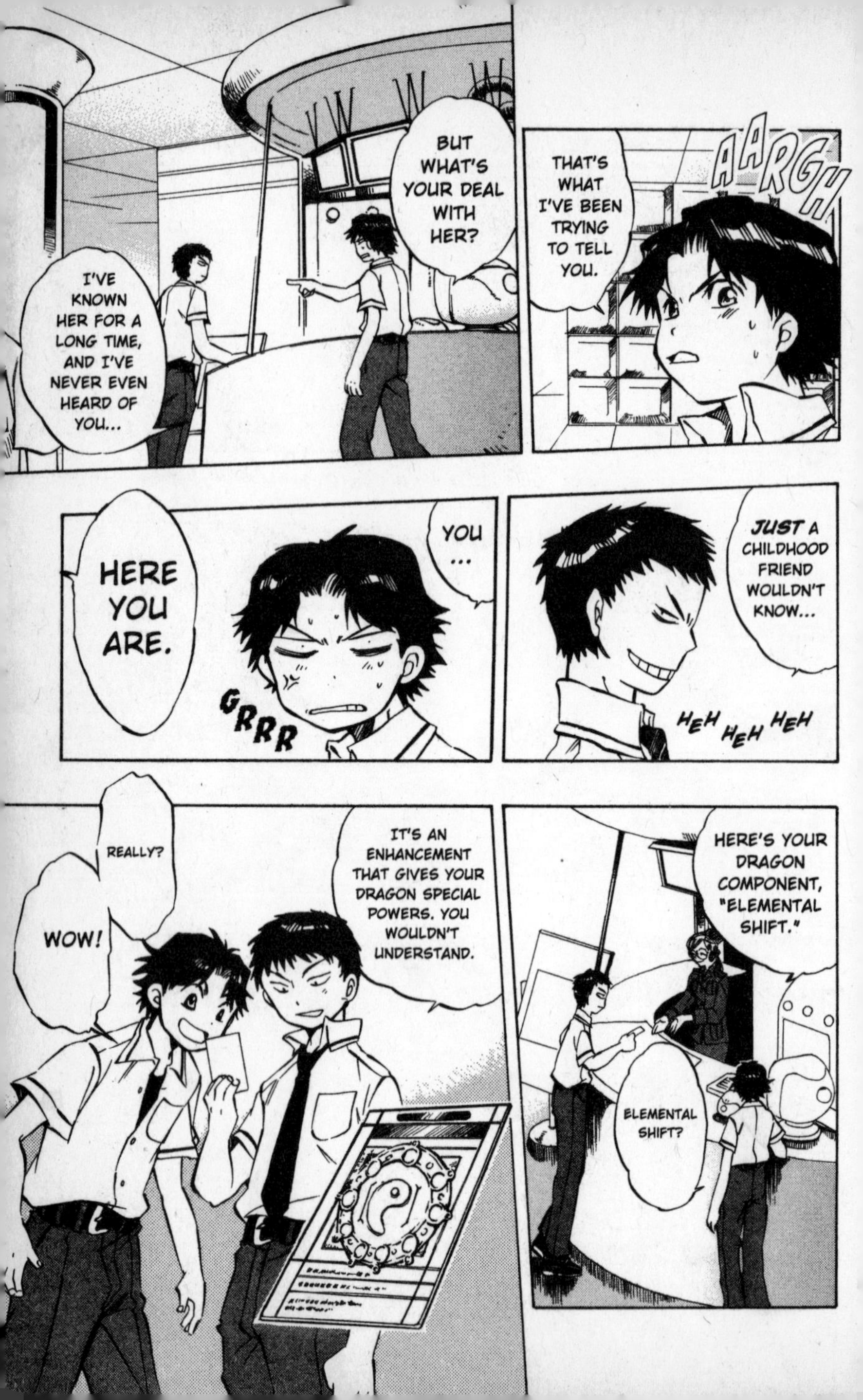
AARGH
THAT'S WHAT I'VE BEEN TRYING TO TELL YOU.
BUT WHAT'S YOUR DEAL WITH HER?
I'VE KNOWN HER FOR A LONG TIME, AND I'VE NEVER EVEN HEARD OF YOU...
JUST A CHILDHOOD FRIEND WOULDN'T KNOW...
HEH HEH HEH
YOU...
GRRR
HERE YOU ARE.
HERE'S YOUR DRAGON COMPONENT, "ELEMENTAL SHIFT."
ELEMENTAL SHIFT?
IT'S AN ENHANCEMENT THAT GIVES YOUR DRAGON SPECIAL POWERS. YOU WOULDN'T UNDERSTAND.
REALLY?
WOW!

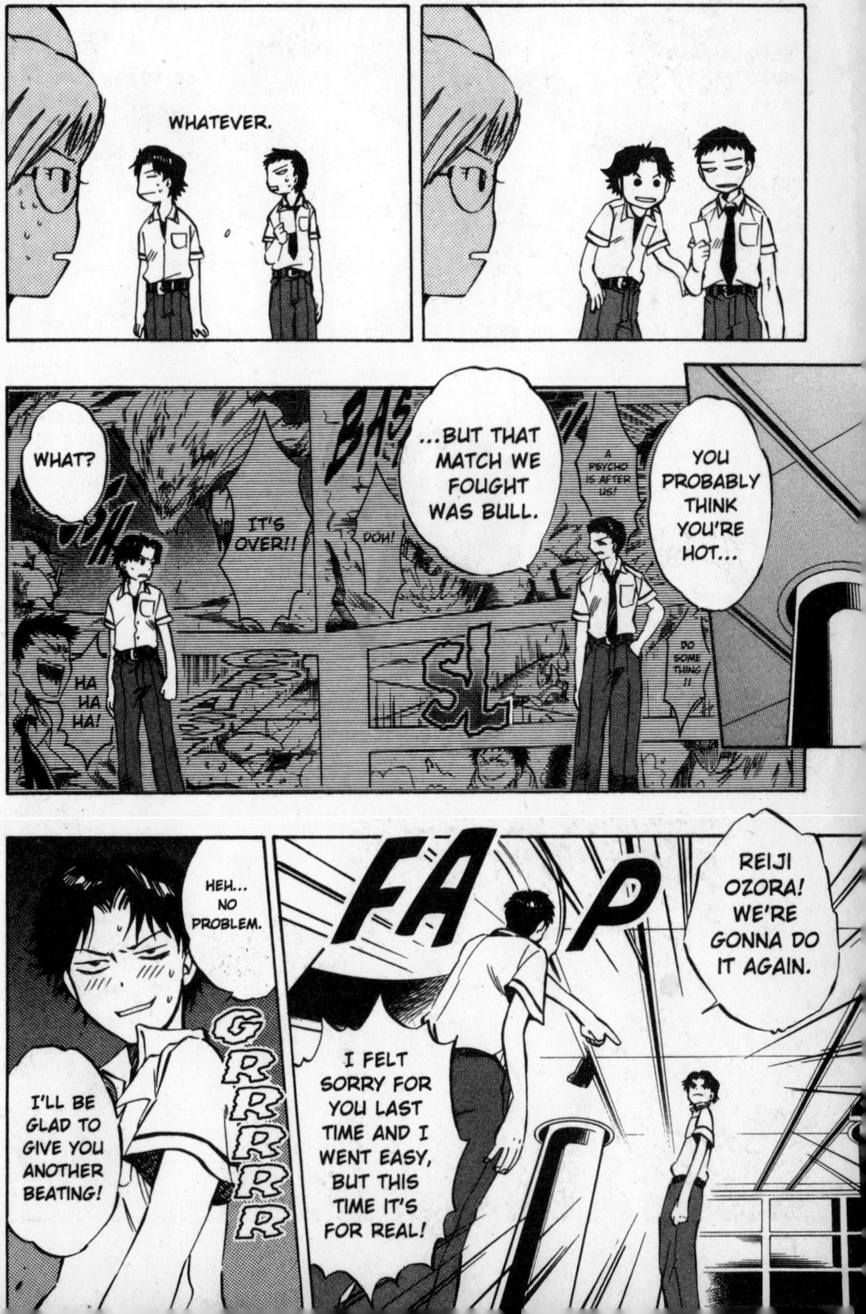
WHATEVER.
YOU PROBABLY THINK YOU'RE HOT...
A PSYCHO IS AFTER US!
DO SOME THING!!
...BUT THAT MATCH WE FOUGHT WAS BULL.
BAS
DOH!
SL
IT'S OVER!!
WHAT?
HA HA HA!
REIJI OZORA! WE'RE GONNA DO IT AGAIN.
FA P
I FELT SORRY FOR YOU LAST TIME AND I WENT EASY, BUT THIS TIME IT'S FOR REAL!
HEH... NO PROBLEM.
GRRRRR
I'LL BE GLAD TO GIVE YOU ANOTHER BEATING!

READ THIS WAY

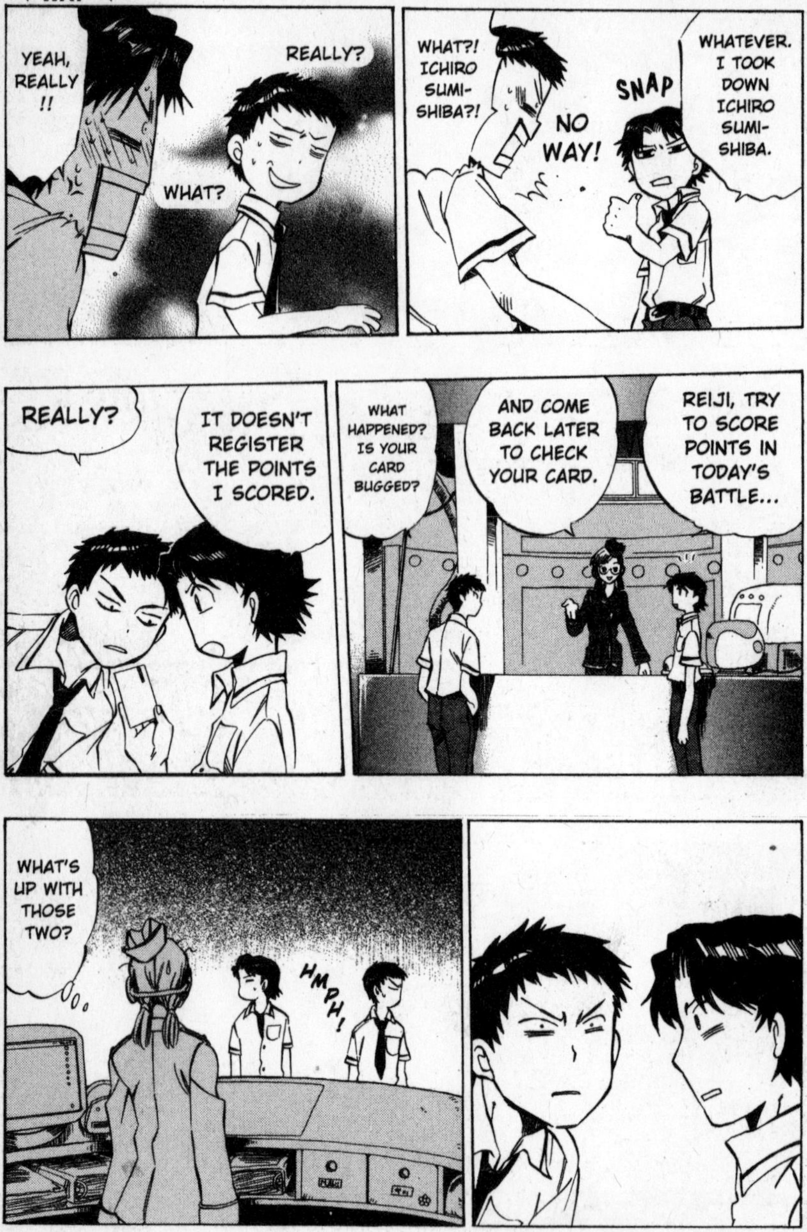
WHATEVER. I TOOK DOWN ICHIRO SUMI-SHIBA.
SNAP
WHAT?! ICHIRO SUMI-SHIBA?!
NO WAY!
REALLY?
YEAH, REALLY !!
WHAT?
REIJI, TRY TO SCORE POINTS IN TODAY'S BATTLE...
AND COME BACK LATER TO CHECK YOUR CARD.
WHAT HAPPENED? IS YOUR CARD BUGGED?
IT DOESN'T REGISTER THE POINTS I SCORED.
REALLY?
WHAT'S UP WITH THOSE TWO?
HMPH!

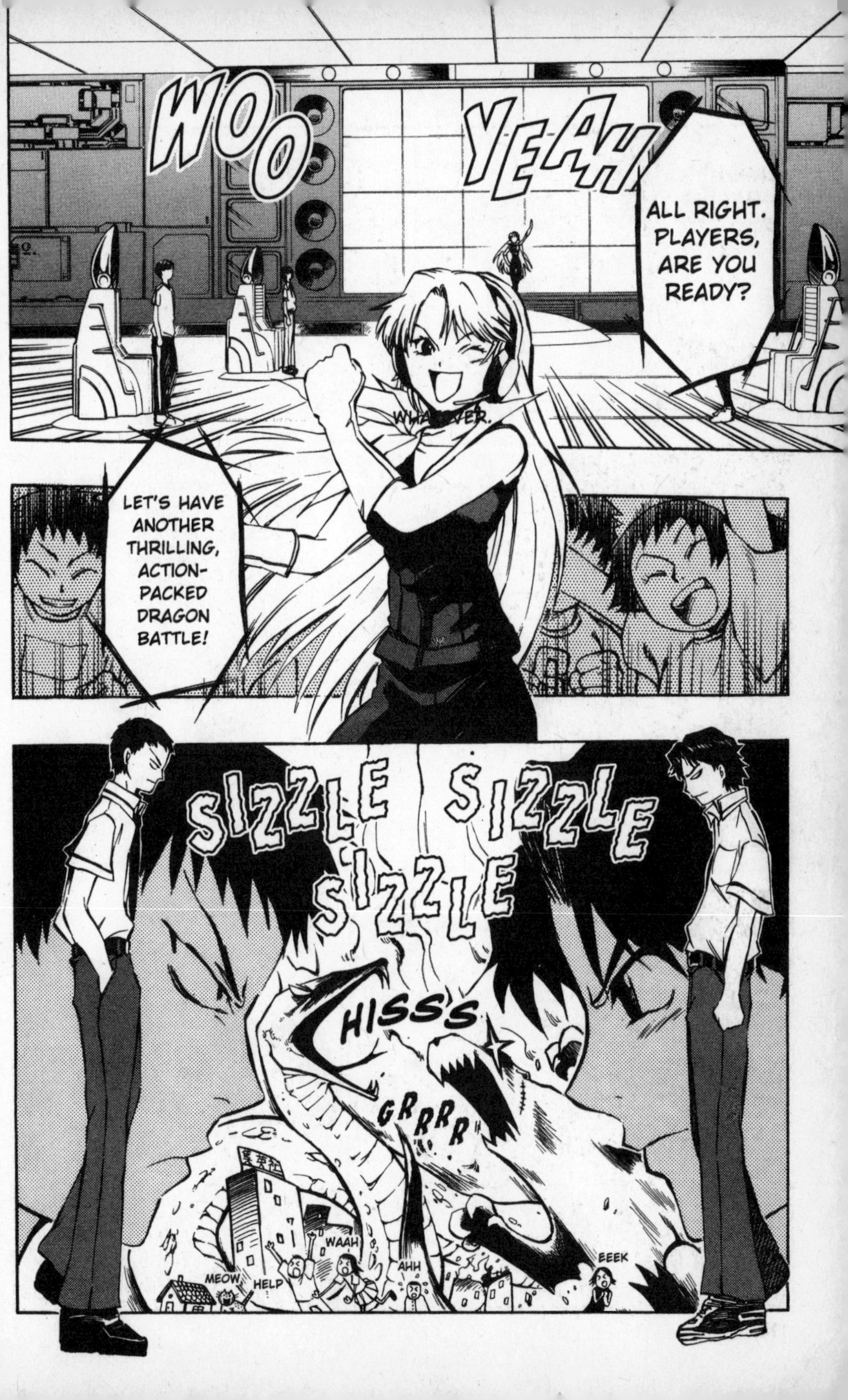
ALL RIGHT. PLAYERS, ARE YOU READY?
YEAH
WOO
LET'S HAVE ANOTHER THRILLING, ACTION-PACKED DRAGON BATTLE!
SIZZLE
SIZZLE
SIZZLE
HISS'S
GRRRR
EEEK
AHH
WAAH
HELP
MEOW

READ THIS WAY

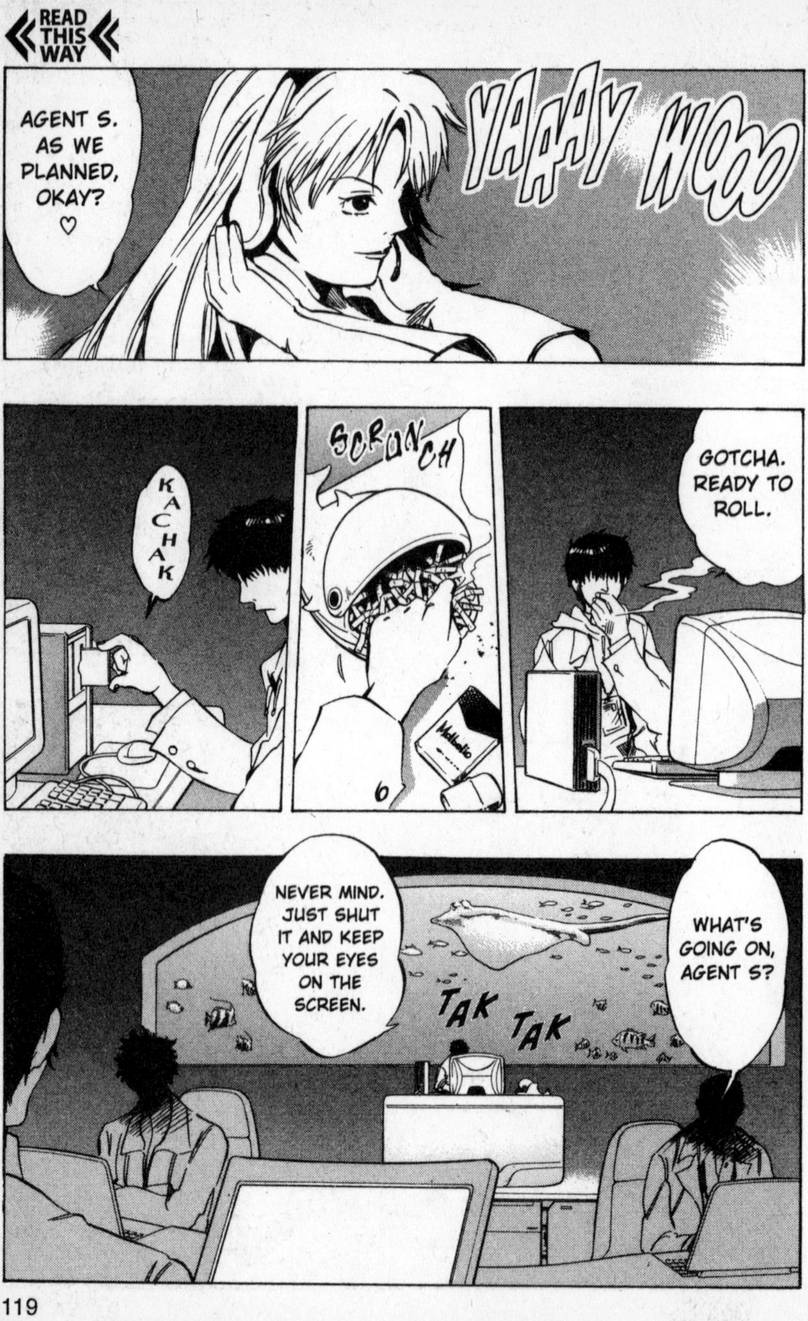

YAAAY WOOO
AGENT S. AS WE PLANNED, OKAY? ♡
GOTCHA. READY TO ROLL.
SCRUNCH
KACHAK
WHAT'S GOING ON, AGENT S?
NEVER MIND. JUST SHUT IT AND KEEP YOUR EYES ON THE SCREEN.
TAK TAK

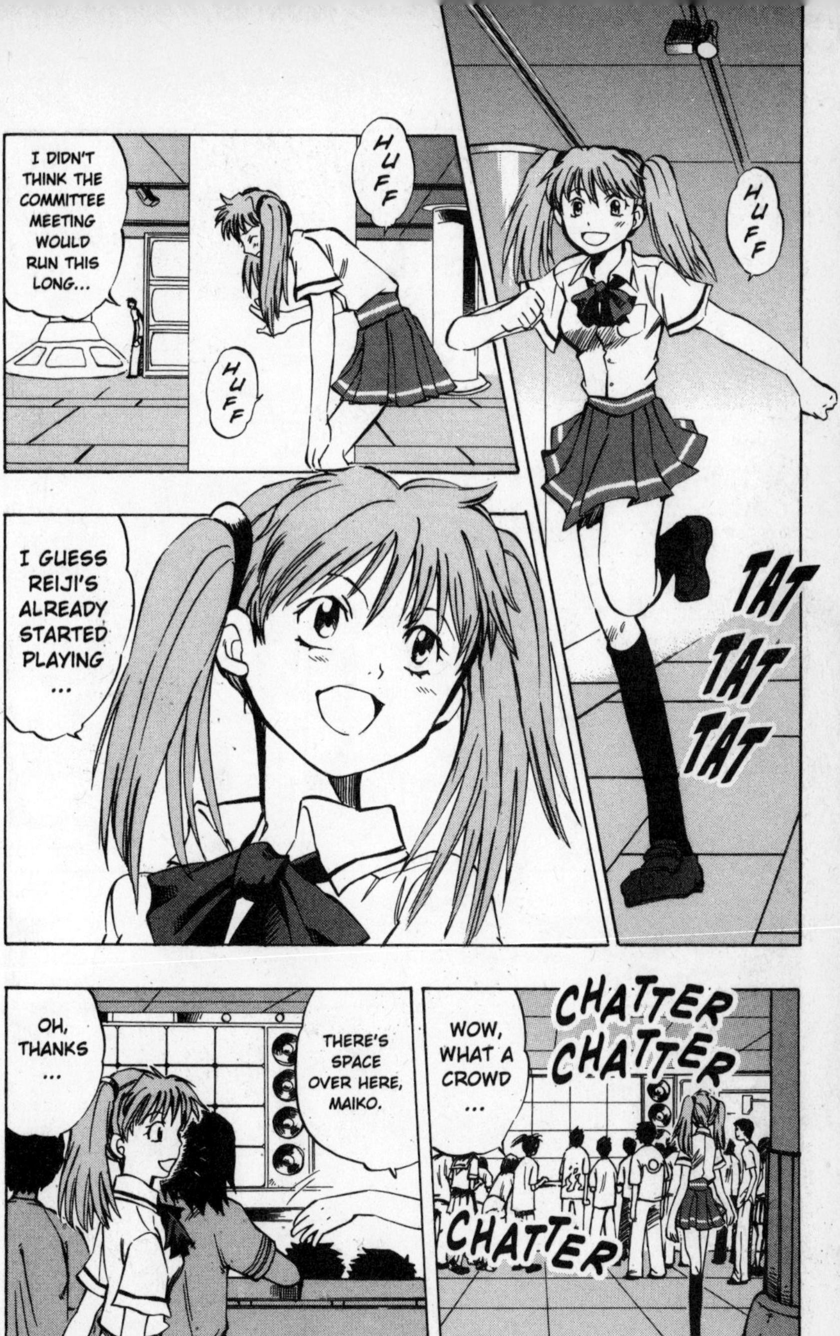
HUFF
TAT TAT TAT
HUFF
HUFF
I DIDN'T THINK THE COMMITTEE MEETING WOULD RUN THIS LONG...
I GUESS REIJI'S ALREADY STARTED PLAYING...
CHATTER CHATTER
WOW, WHAT A CROWD...
CHATTER
THERE'S SPACE OVER HERE, MAIKO.
OH, THANKS...

READ THIS WAY

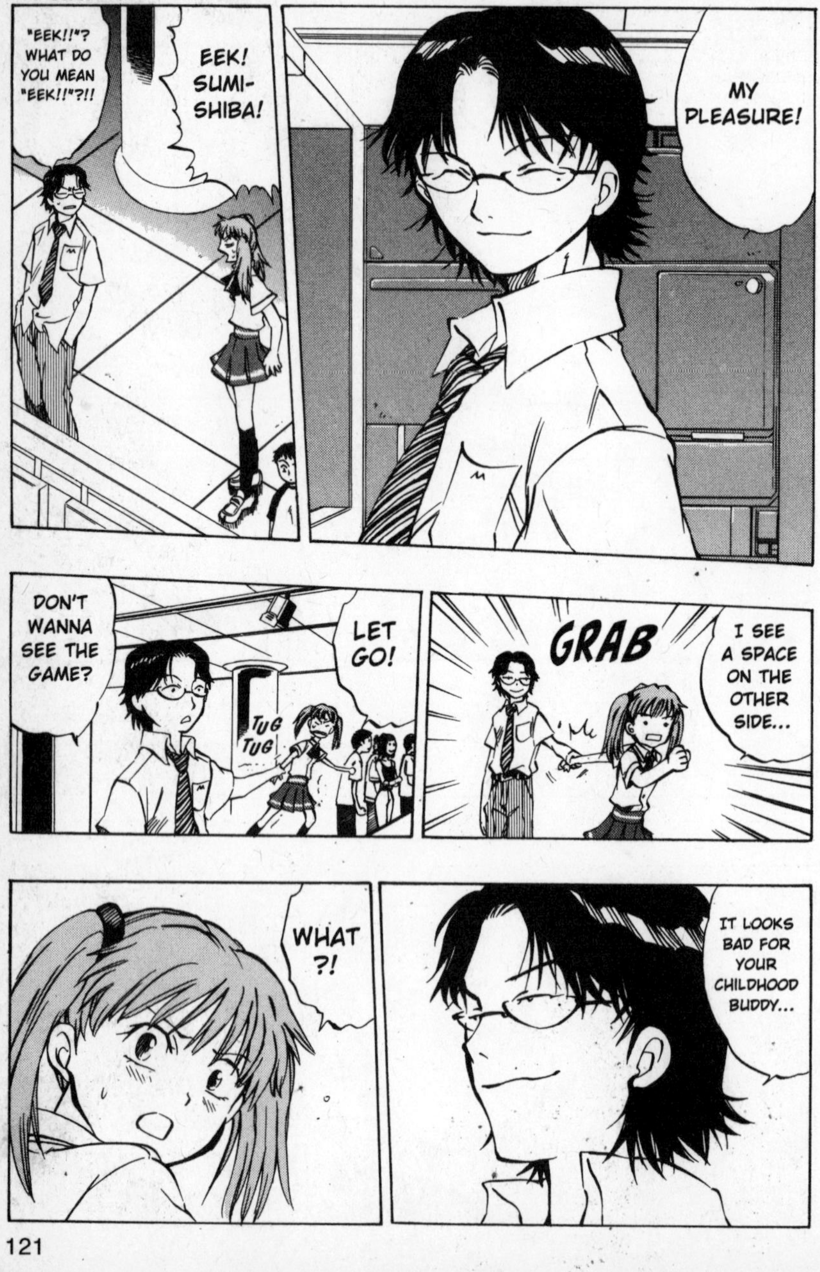
MY PLEASURE!
EEK! SUMI-SHIBA!
"EEK!!"? WHAT DO YOU MEAN "EEK!!"?!!
I SEE A SPACE ON THE OTHER SIDE...
GRAB
LET GO!
DON'T WANNA SEE THE GAME?
TUG TUG
IT LOOKS BAD FOR YOUR CHILDHOOD BUDDY...
WHAT ?!

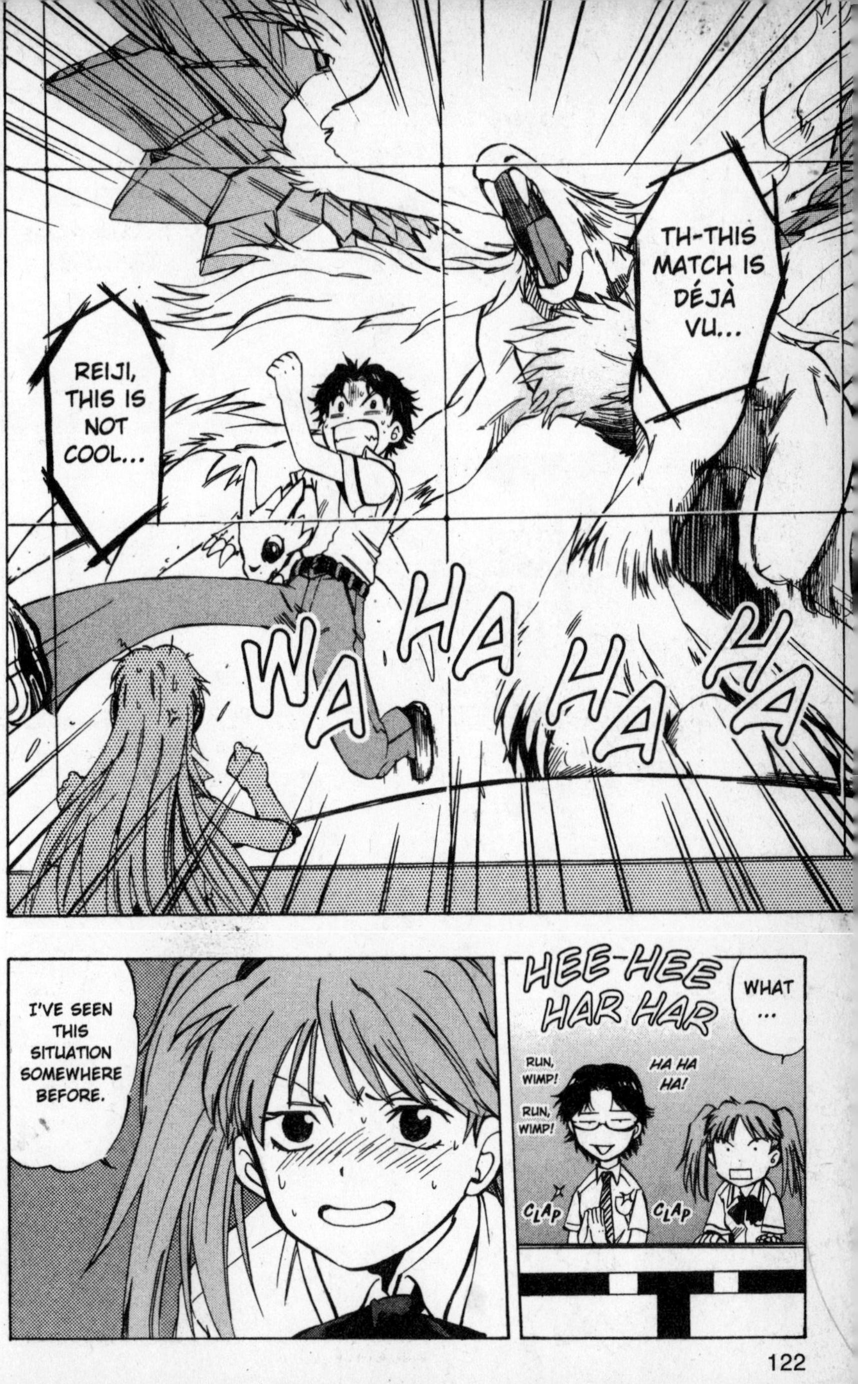
TH-THIS MATCH IS DÉJÀ VU...
REIJI, THIS IS NOT COOL...
WA HA HA HA HA
HEE-HEE HAR HAR
WHAT ...
HA HA HA!
RUN, WIMP!
RUN, WIMP!
CLAP
CLAP
I'VE SEEN THIS SITUATION SOMEWHERE BEFORE.

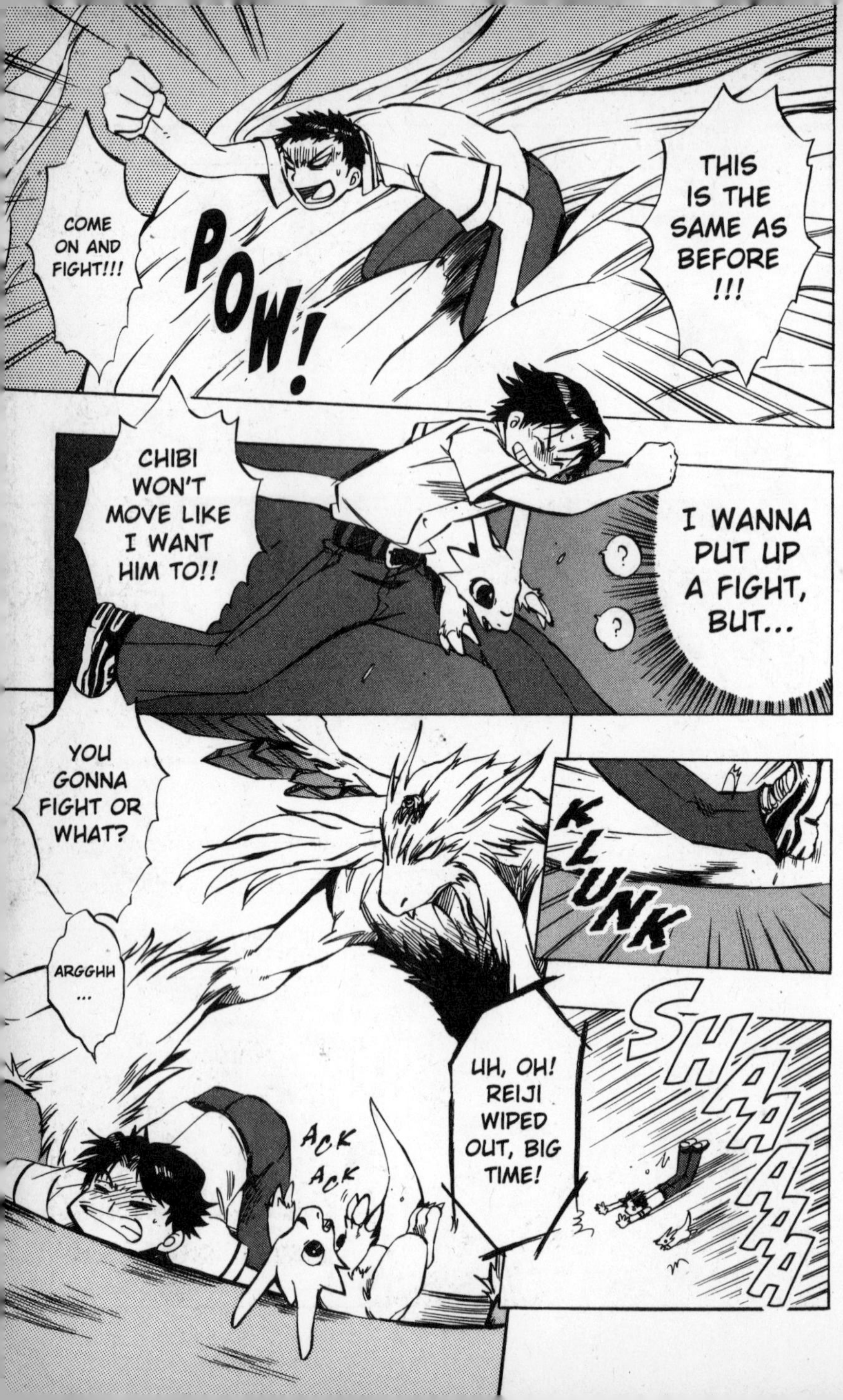
THIS IS THE SAME AS BEFORE!!!
POW!
COME ON AND FIGHT!!!
I WANNA PUT UP A FIGHT, BUT...
?
?
CHIBI WON'T MOVE LIKE I WANT HIM TO!!
KLUNK
SHAAAA
UH, OH! REIJI WIPED OUT, BIG TIME!
YOU GONNA FIGHT OR WHAT?
ARGGHH...
ACK
ACK

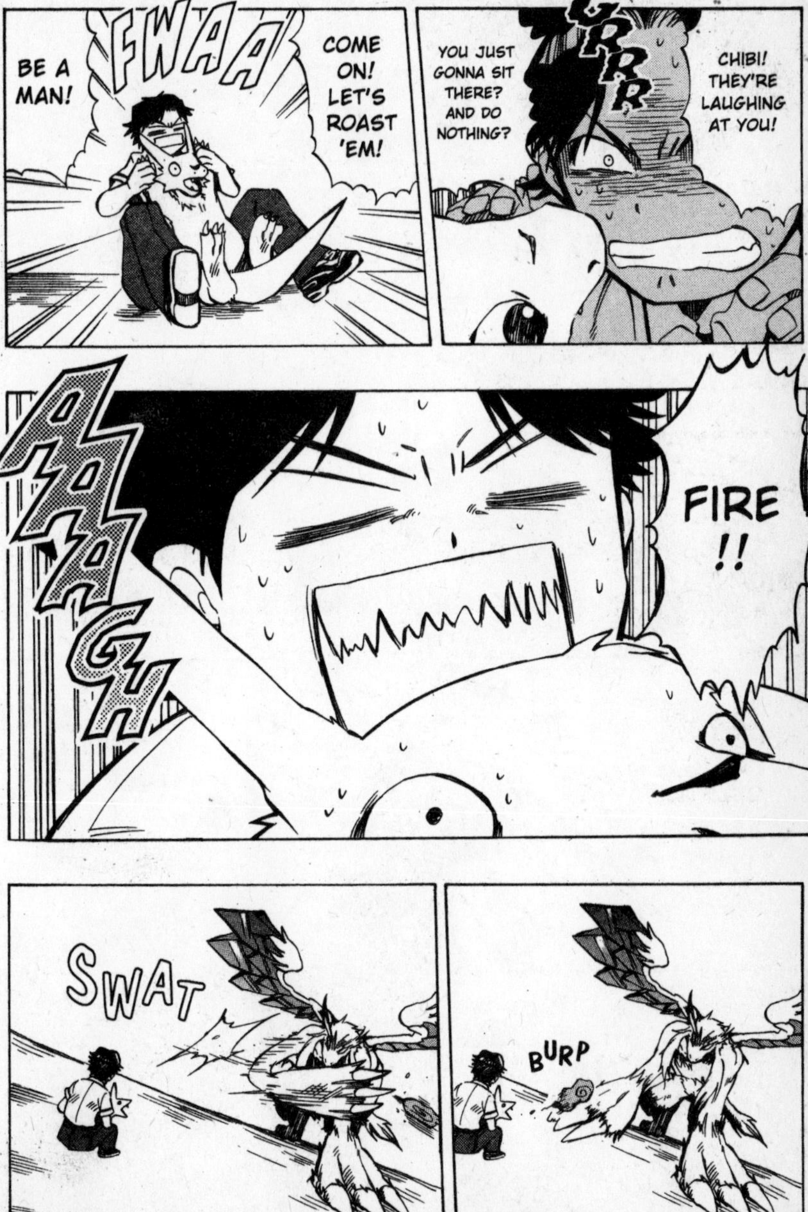
CHIBI! THEY'RE LAUGHING AT YOU!
GRRR
YOU JUST GONNA SIT THERE? AND DO NOTHING?
COME ON! LET'S ROAST 'EM!
FWAA
BE A MAN!
FIRE!!
AAAAGH
BURP
SWAT

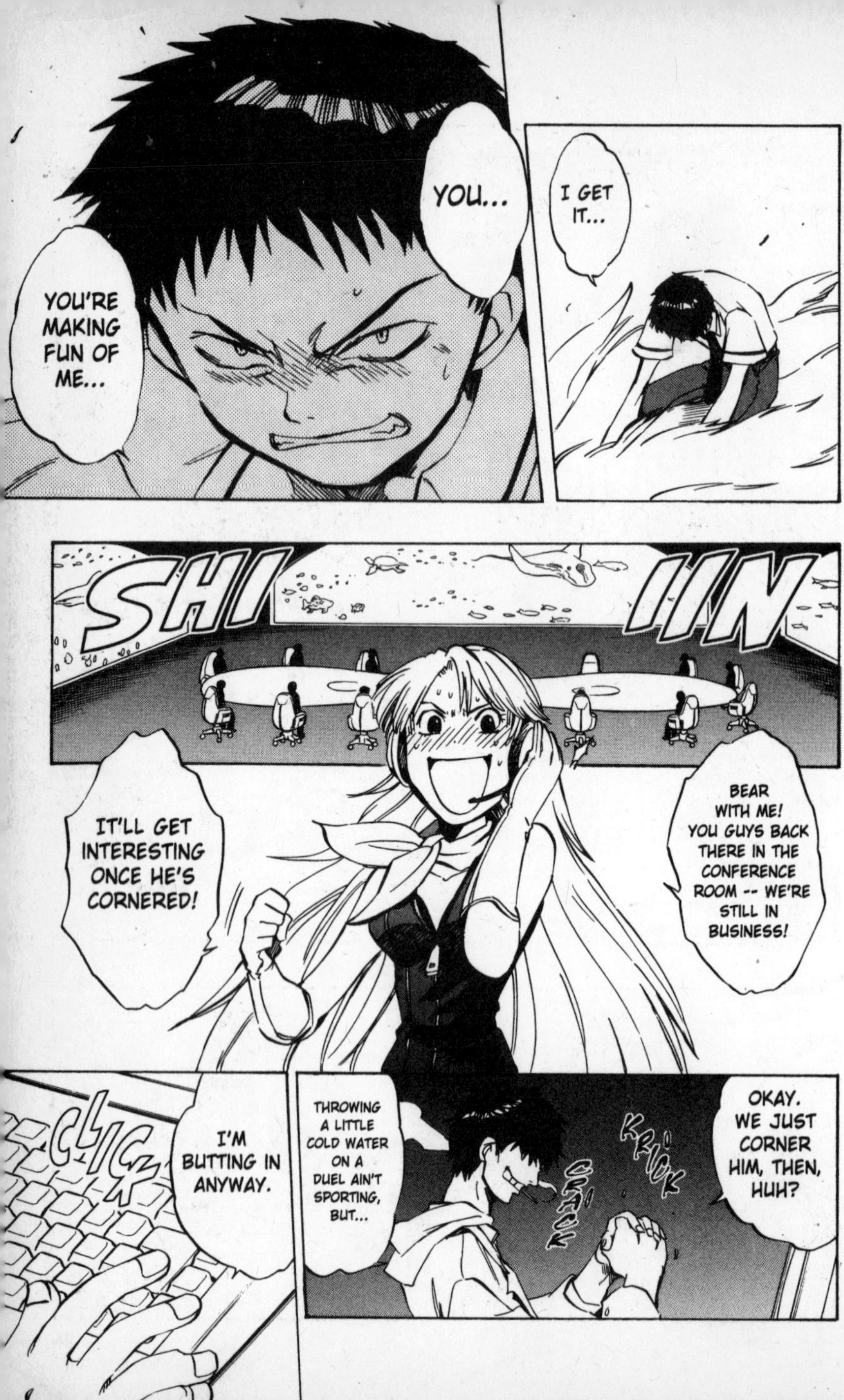
I GET IT...
YOU...
YOU'RE MAKING FUN OF ME...
SHI IIN
BEAR WITH ME! YOU GUYS BACK THERE IN THE CONFERENCE ROOM -- WE'RE STILL IN BUSINESS!
IT'LL GET INTERESTING ONCE HE'S CORNERED!
OKAY. WE JUST CORNER HIM, THEN, HUH?
KRICK
CRACK
THROWING A LITTLE COLD WATER ON A DUEL AIN'T SPORTING, BUT...
CLICK
I'M BUTTING IN ANYWAY.

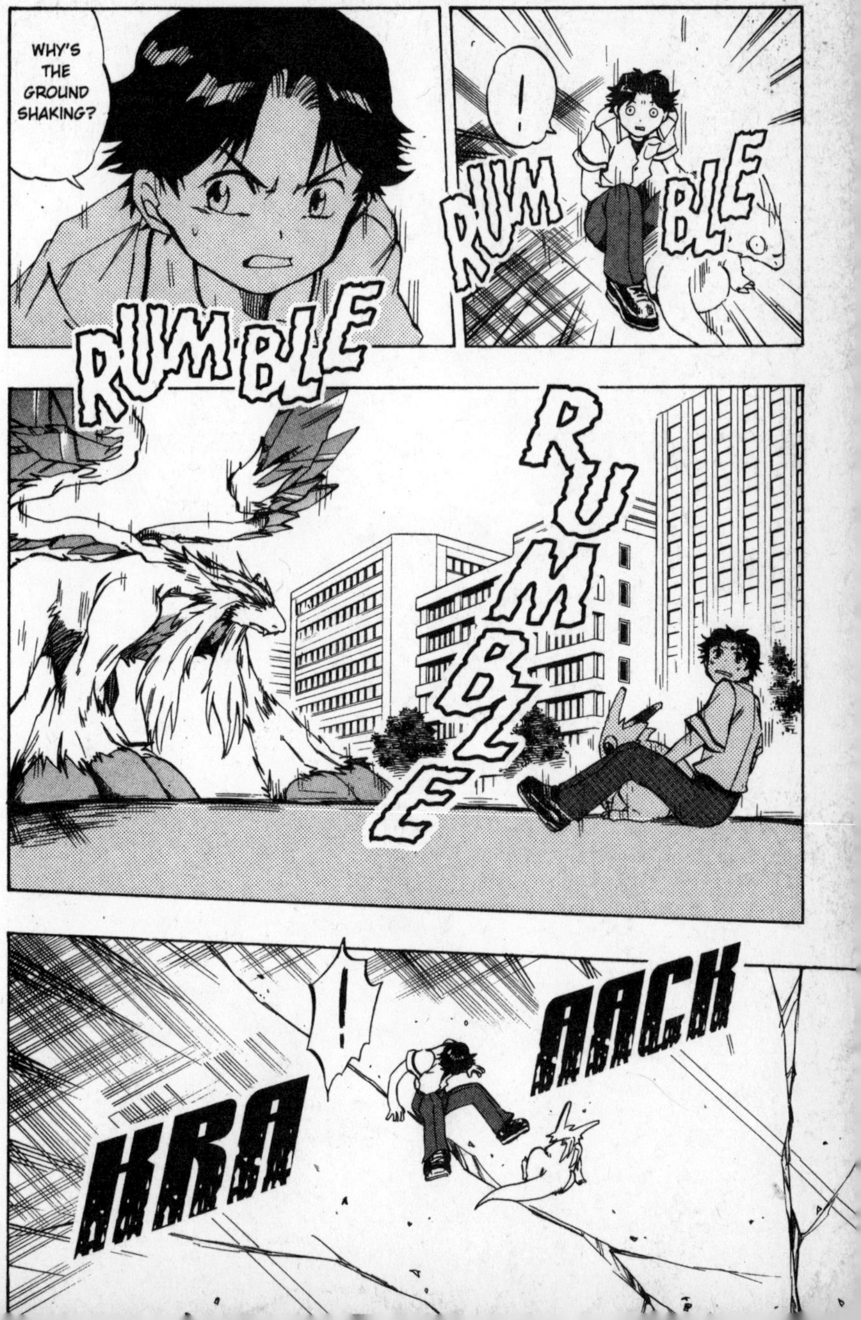
!
RUMBLE
WHY'S THE GROUND SHAKING?
RUMBLE
RUMBLE
!
KRAAACK

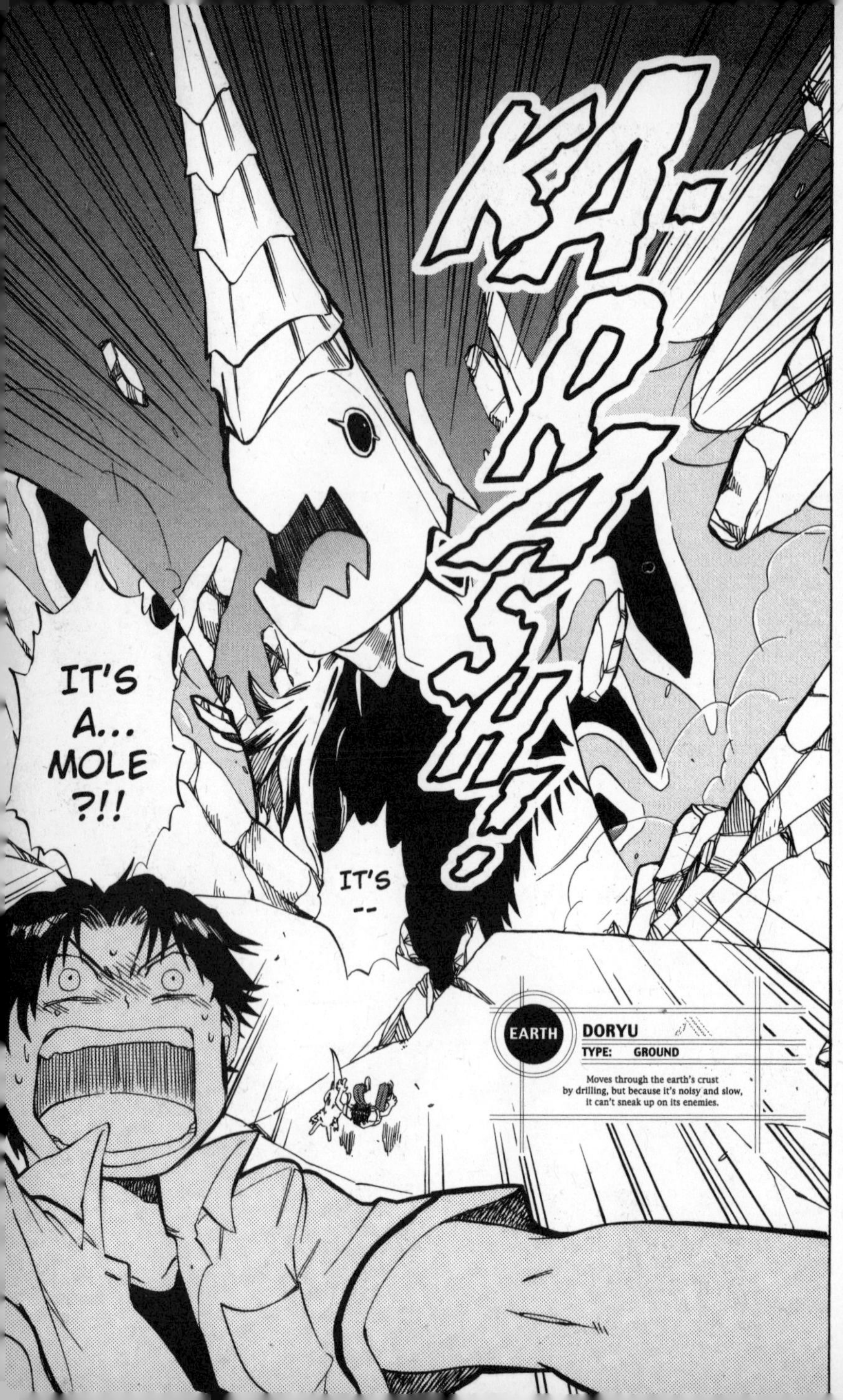
KA-KRASH!!
IT'S A... MOLE?!!
IT'S --
EARTH
DORYU
TYPE: GROUND
Moves through the earth's crust by drilling, but because it's noisy and slow, it can't sneak up on its enemies.

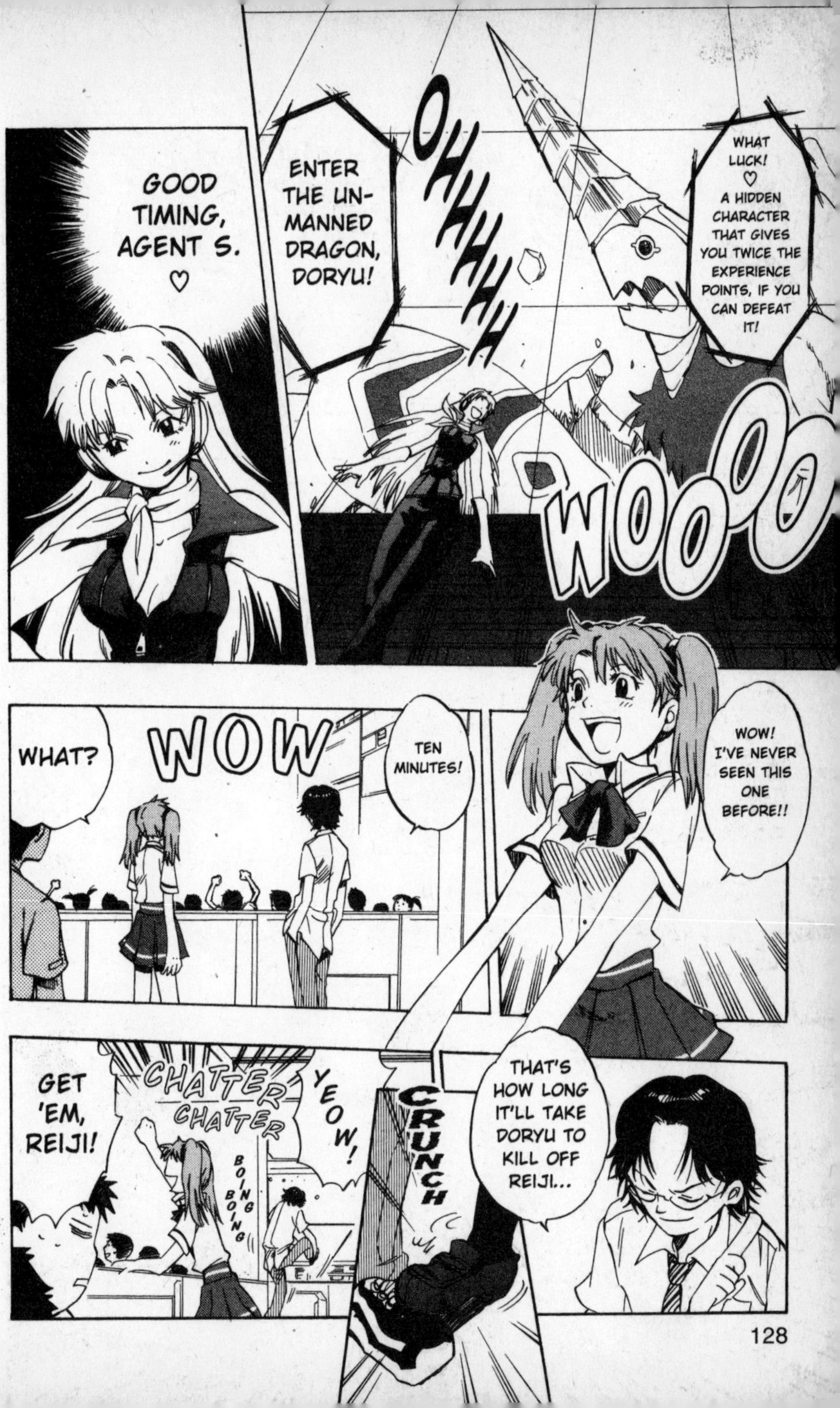
WHAT LUCK! ♡ A HIDDEN CHARACTER THAT GIVES YOU TWICE THE EXPERIENCE POINTS, IF YOU CAN DEFEAT IT!
OHHHHHH
ENTER THE UN-MANNED DRAGON, DORYU!
WOOOOOO
GOOD TIMING, AGENT S. ♡
WOW! I'VE NEVER SEEN THIS ONE BEFORE!!
TEN MINUTES!
WOW
WHAT?
THAT'S HOW LONG IT'LL TAKE DORYU TO KILL OFF REIJI...
CRUNCH
YEOW!
CHATTER CHATTER
BOING BOING
GET 'EM, REIJI!

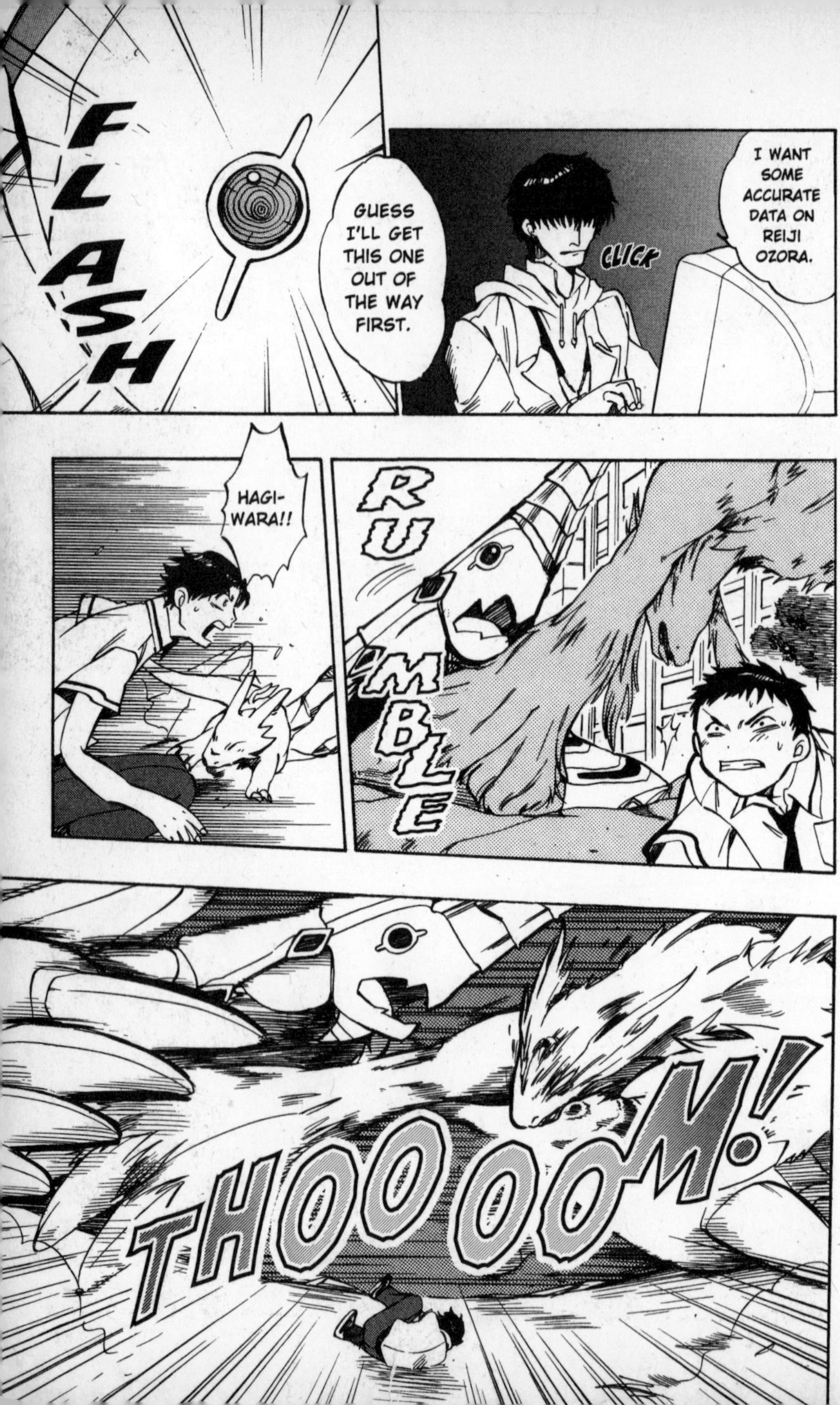
I WANT SOME ACCURATE DATA ON REIJI OZORA.
CLICK
GUESS I'LL GET THIS ONE OUT OF THE WAY FIRST.
FLASH
RUMBLE
HAGI-WARA!!
THOOOOM!

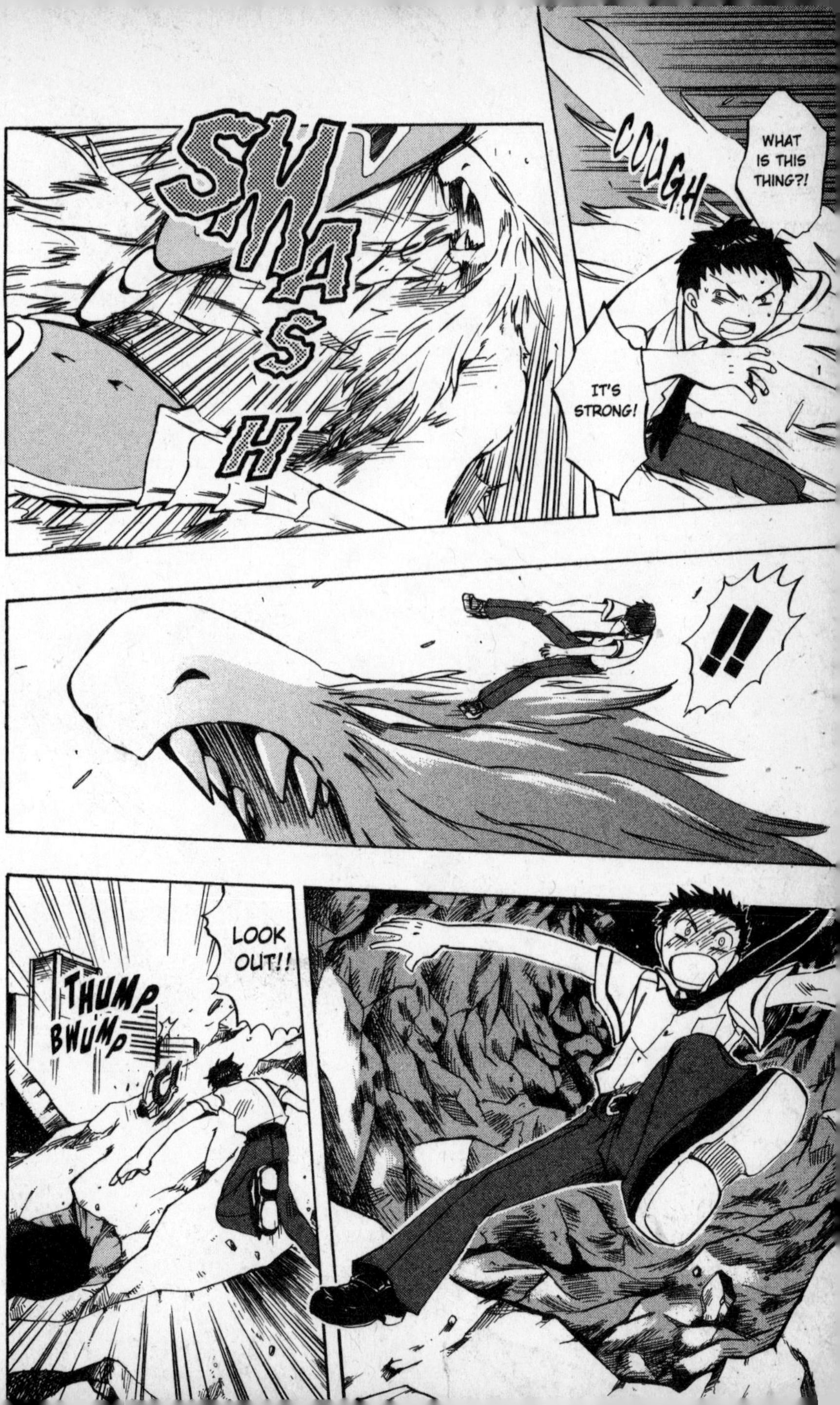
COUGH
WHAT IS THIS THING?!
IT'S STRONG!
SWASH
!!
LOOK OUT!!
THUMP
BWUMP

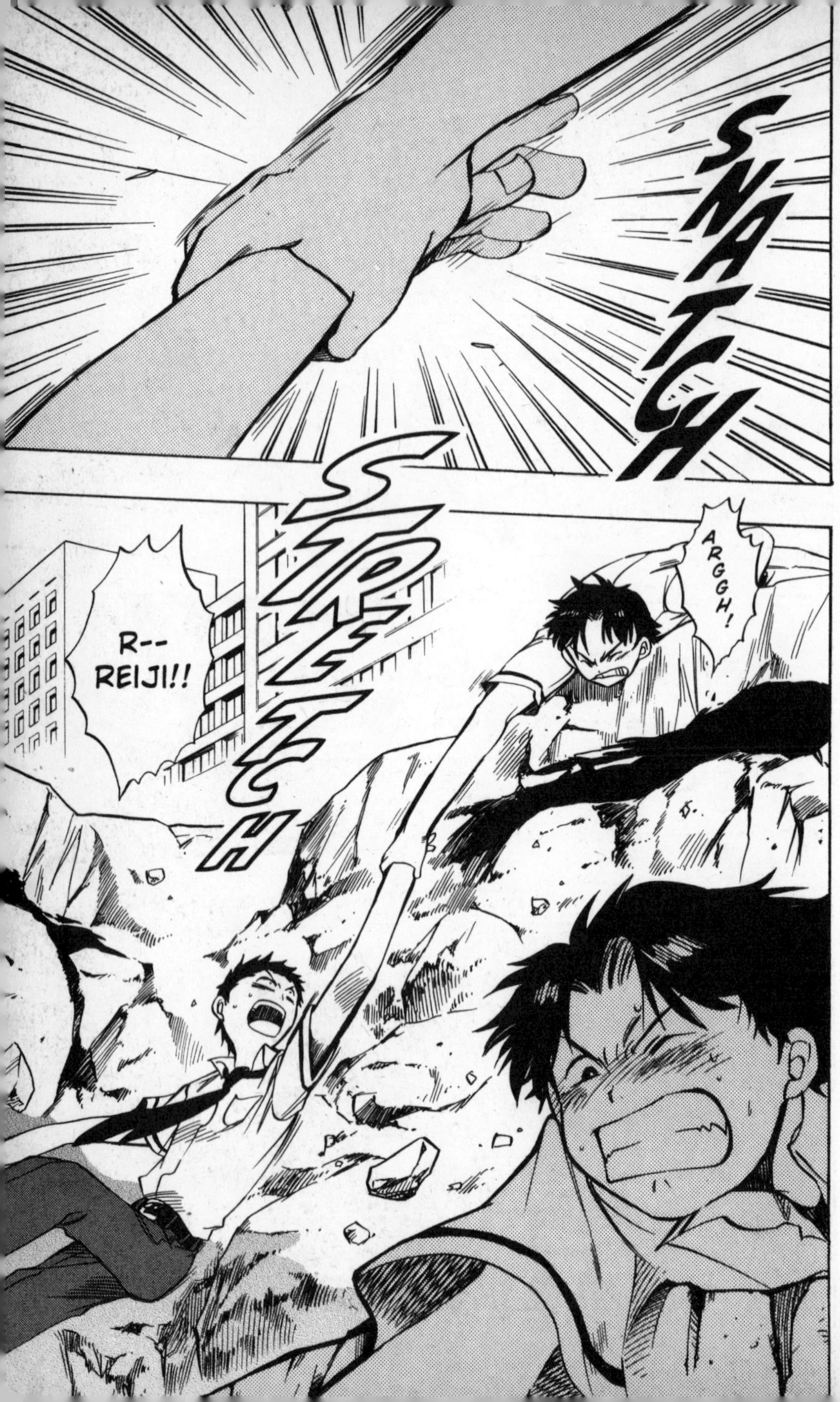
SNATCH
STRETCH
ARGGH!
R--
REIJI!!

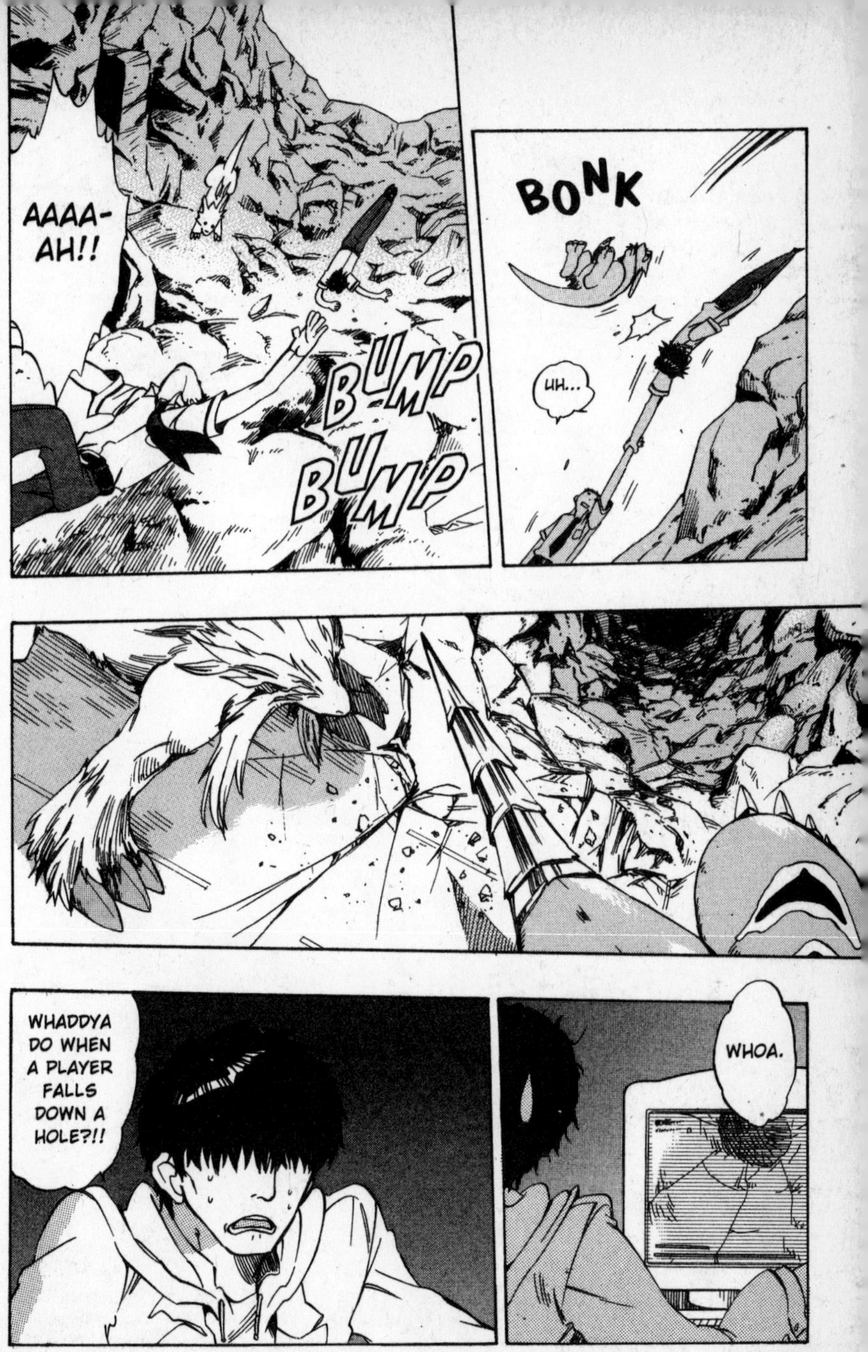
BONK
UH...
AAAA-AH!!
BUMP
BUMP
WHOA.
WHADDYA DO WHEN A PLAYER FALLS DOWN A HOLE?!!

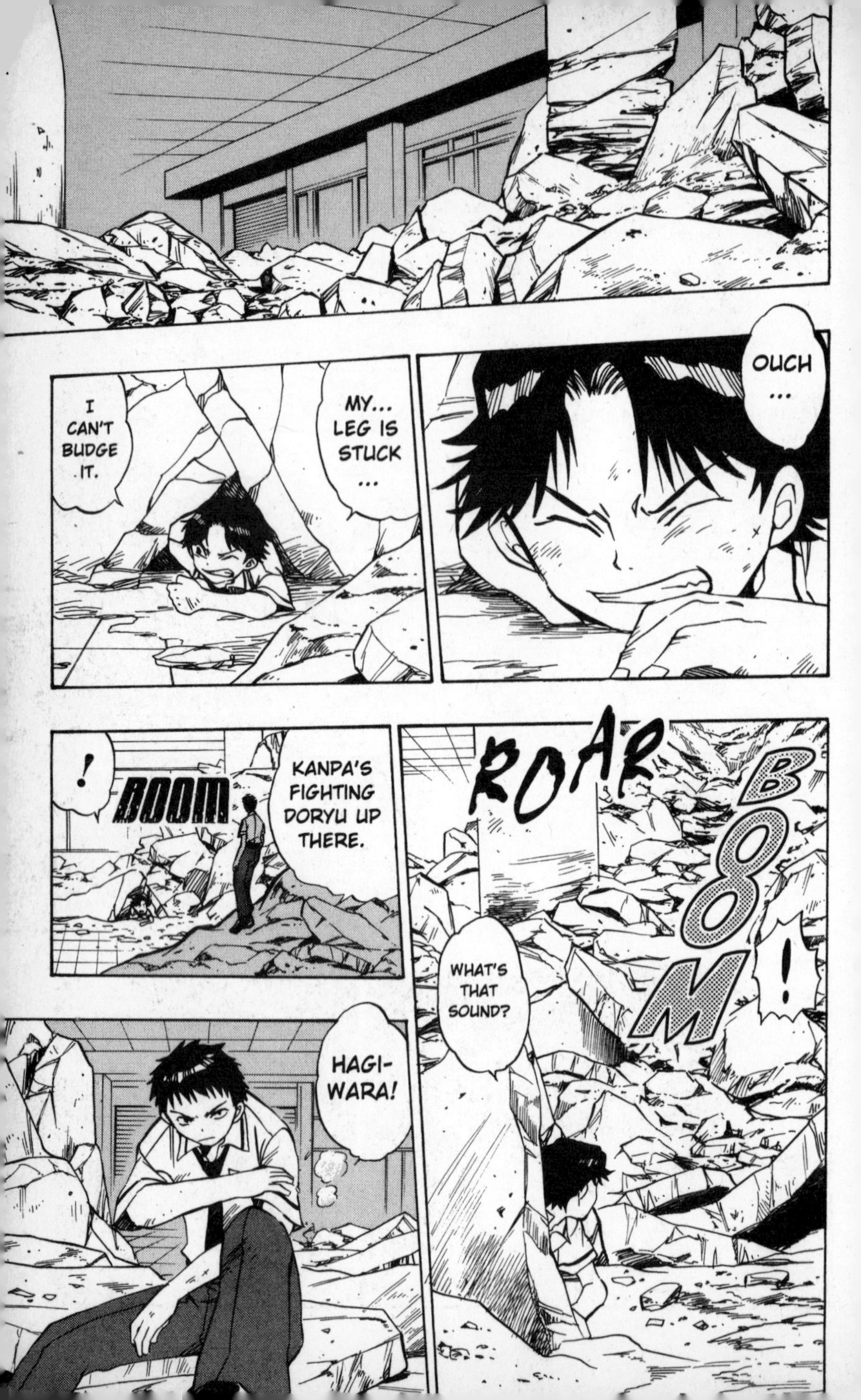
OUCH...
MY... LEG IS STUCK...
I CAN'T BUDGE IT.
BOOM
ROAR
!
WHAT'S THAT SOUND?
KANPA'S FIGHTING DORYU UP THERE.
!
BOOM
HAGI-WARA!

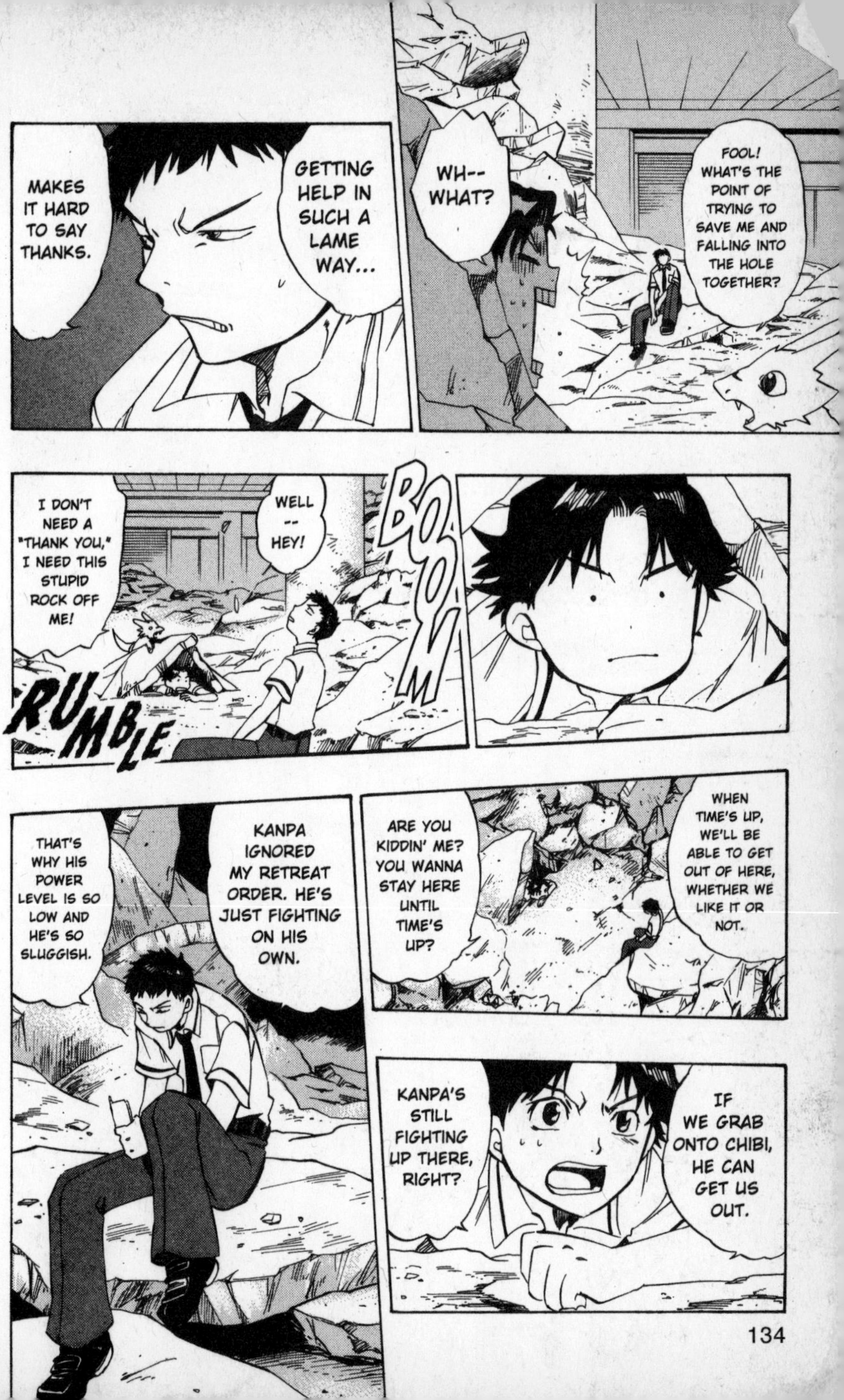
FOOL! WHAT'S THE POINT OF TRYING TO SAVE ME AND FALLING INTO THE HOLE TOGETHER?
WH-- WHAT?
GETTING HELP IN SUCH A LAME WAY...
MAKES IT HARD TO SAY THANKS.
BOOM
WELL -- HEY!
I DON'T NEED A "THANK YOU," I NEED THIS STUPID ROCK OFF ME!
RUMBLE
WHEN TIME'S UP, WE'LL BE ABLE TO GET OUT OF HERE, WHETHER WE LIKE IT OR NOT.
ARE YOU KIDDIN' ME? YOU WANNA STAY HERE UNTIL TIME'S UP?
IF WE GRAB ONTO CHIBI, HE CAN GET US OUT.
KANPA'S STILL FIGHTING UP THERE, RIGHT?
KANPA IGNORED MY RETREAT ORDER. HE'S JUST FIGHTING ON HIS OWN.
THAT'S WHY HIS POWER LEVEL IS SO LOW AND HE'S SO SLUGGISH.

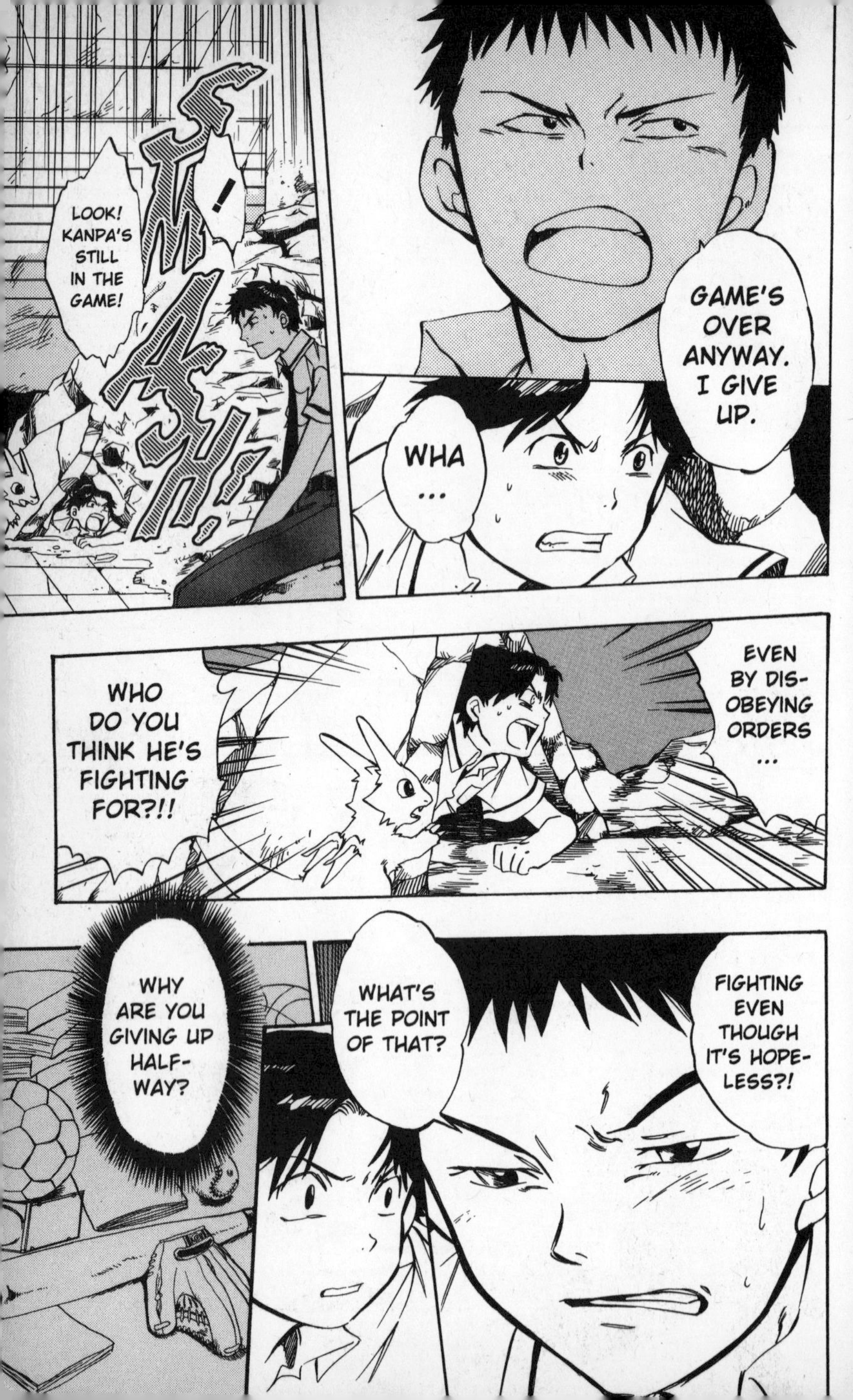
GAME'S OVER ANYWAY. I GIVE UP.
WHA ...
!
LOOK! KANPA'S STILL IN THE GAME!
EVEN BY DIS-OBEYING ORDERS ...
WHO DO YOU THINK HE'S FIGHTING FOR?!!
FIGHTING EVEN THOUGH IT'S HOPE-LESS?!
WHAT'S THE POINT OF THAT?
WHY ARE YOU GIVING UP HALF-WAY?

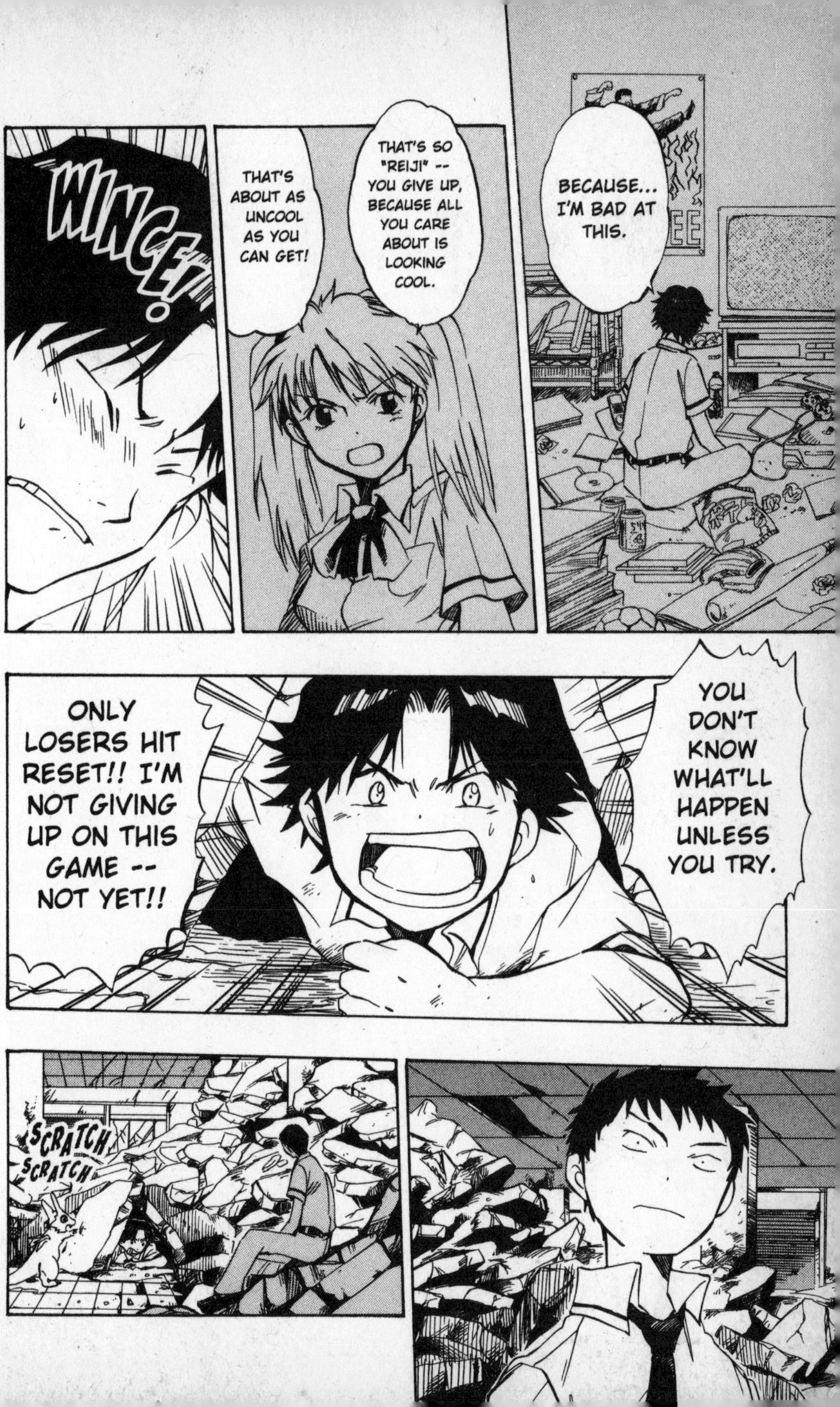
BECAUSE... I'M BAD AT THIS.
THAT'S SO "REIJI" -- YOU GIVE UP, BECAUSE ALL YOU CARE ABOUT IS LOOKING COOL.
THAT'S ABOUT AS UNCOOL AS YOU CAN GET!
WINCE!
YOU DON'T KNOW WHAT'LL HAPPEN UNLESS YOU TRY.
ONLY LOSERS HIT RESET!! I'M NOT GIVING UP ON THIS GAME -- NOT YET!!
SCRATCH
SCRATCH

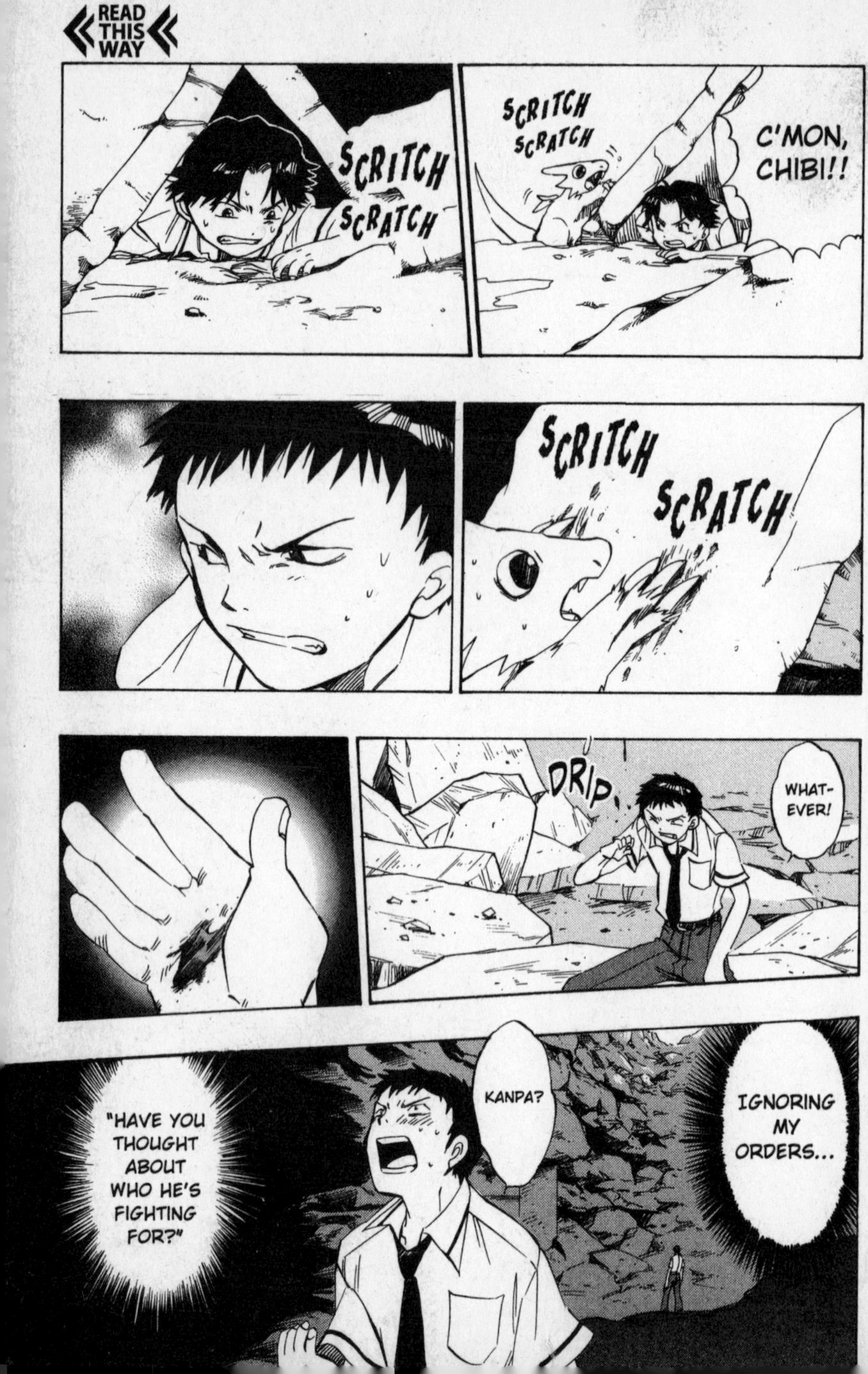
READ THIS WAY
SCRITCH SCRATCH
C'MON, CHIBI!!
SCRITCH SCRATCH
SCRITCH SCRATCH
DRIP
WHAT-EVER!
IGNORING MY ORDERS...
KANPA?
"HAVE YOU THOUGHT ABOUT WHO HE'S FIGHTING FOR?"

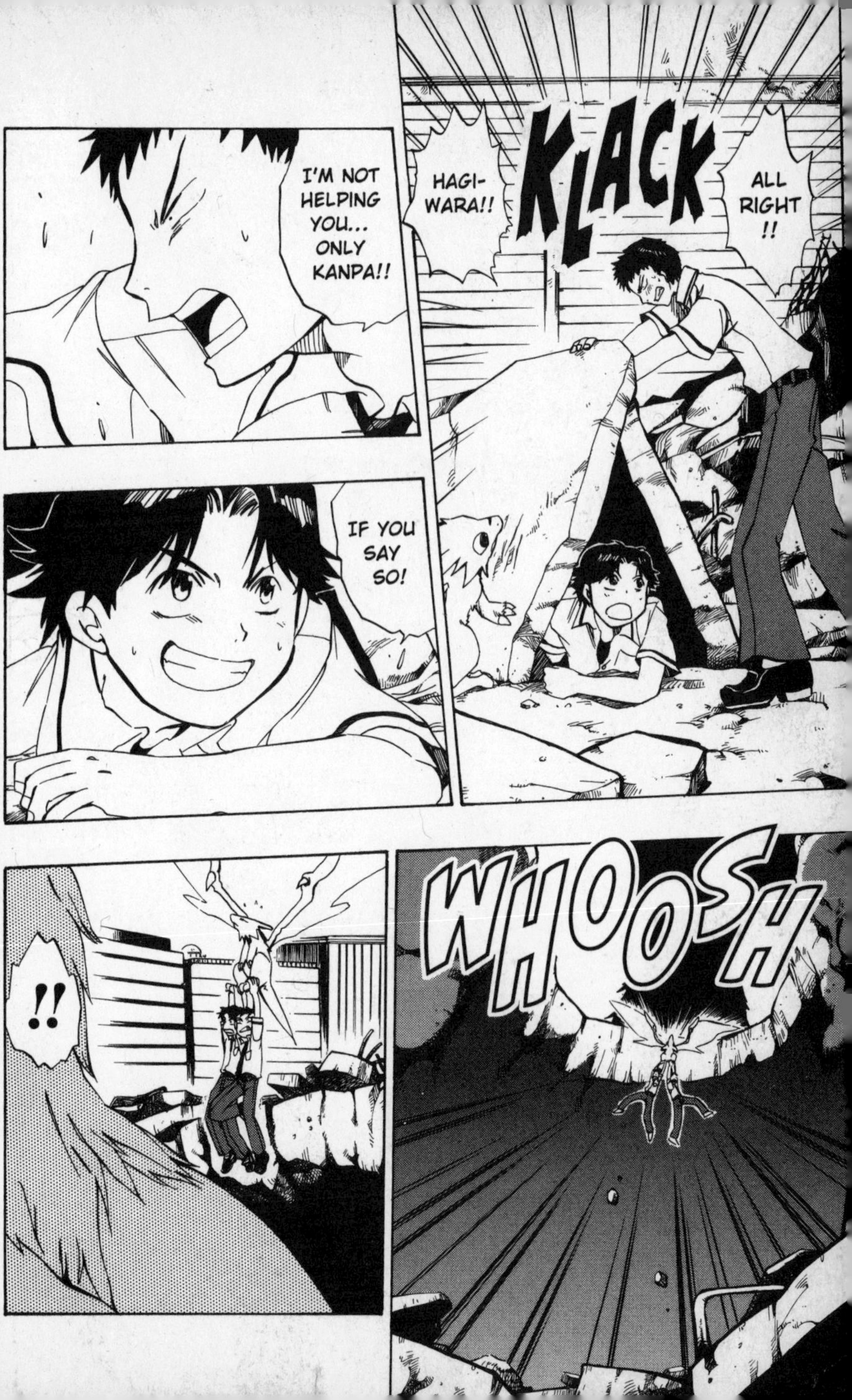
ALL RIGHT!!
KLACK
HAGIWARA!!
I'M NOT HELPING YOU... ONLY KANPA!!
IF YOU SAY SO!
WHOOSH
!!

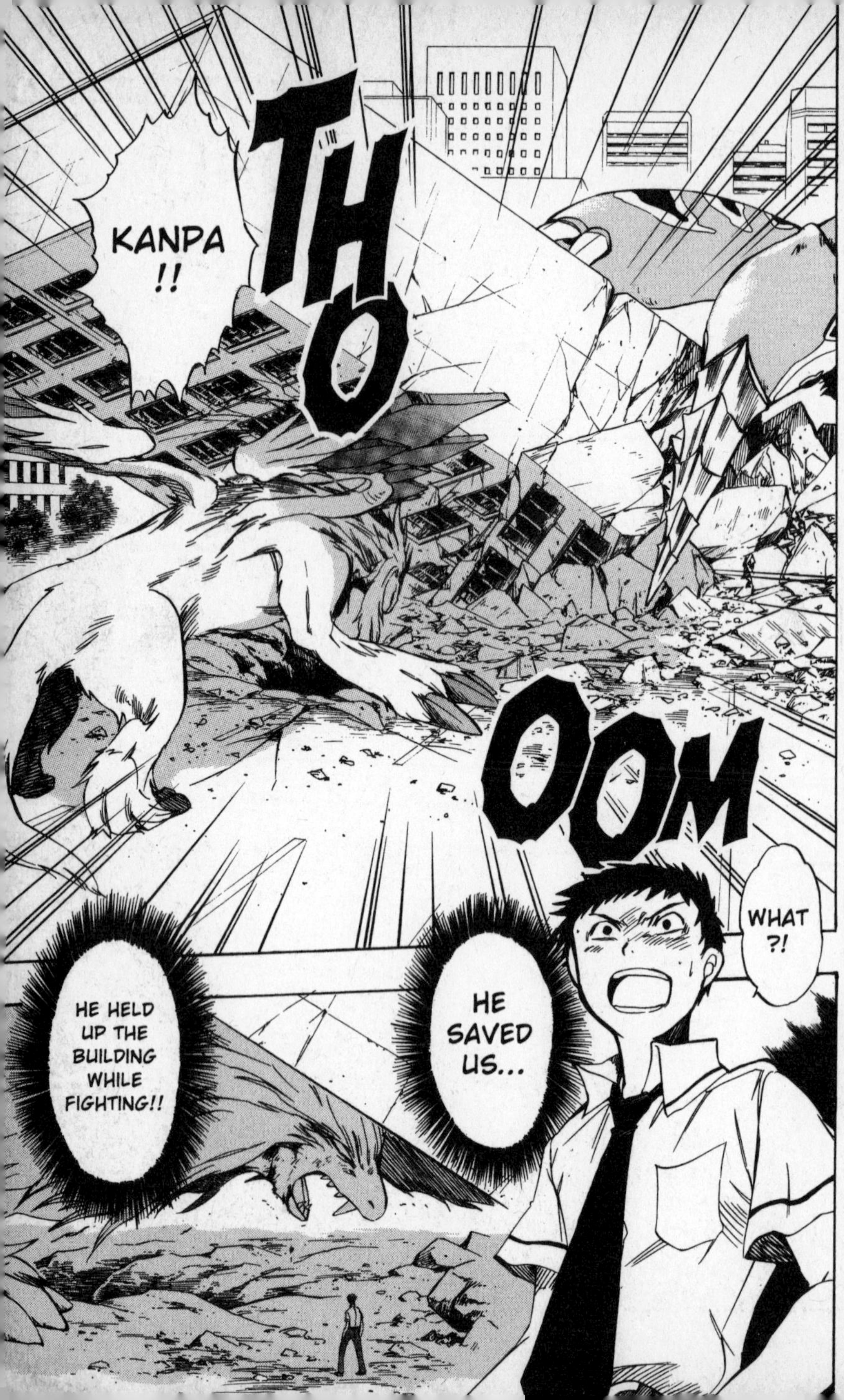
THOOOM
KANPA !!
WHAT ?!
HE SAVED US...
HE HELD UP THE BUILDING WHILE FIGHTING!!

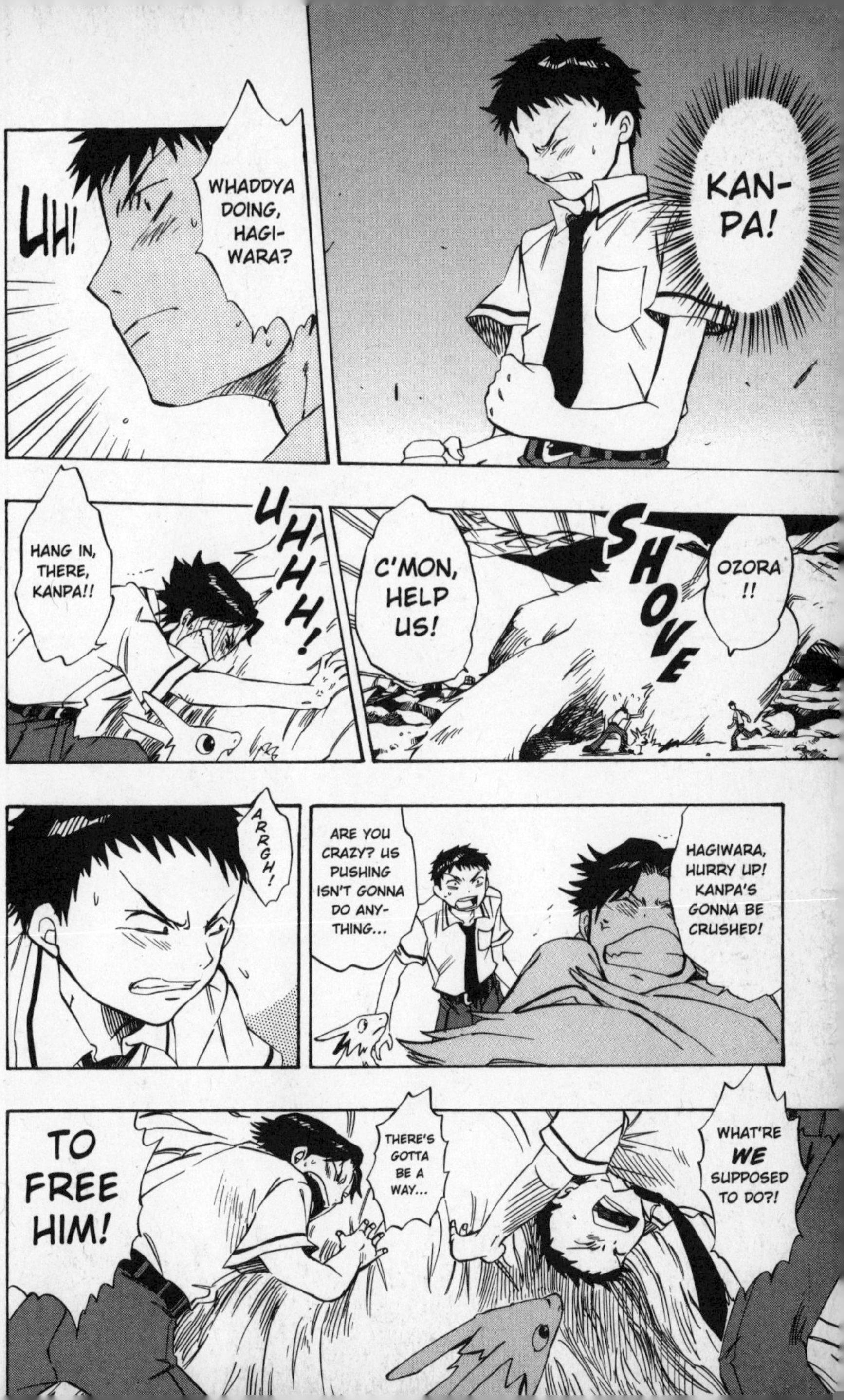
KAN-PA!
WHADDYA DOING, HAGI-WARA?
UH!
OZORA !!
SHOVE
C'MON, HELP US!
UHHHH!
HANG IN, THERE, KANPA!!
HAGIWARA, HURRY UP! KANPA'S GONNA BE CRUSHED!
ARE YOU CRAZY? US PUSHING ISN'T GONNA DO ANY-THING...
ARRGH!
WHAT'RE *WE* SUPPOSED TO DO?!
THERE'S GOTTA BE A WAY...
TO FREE HIM!

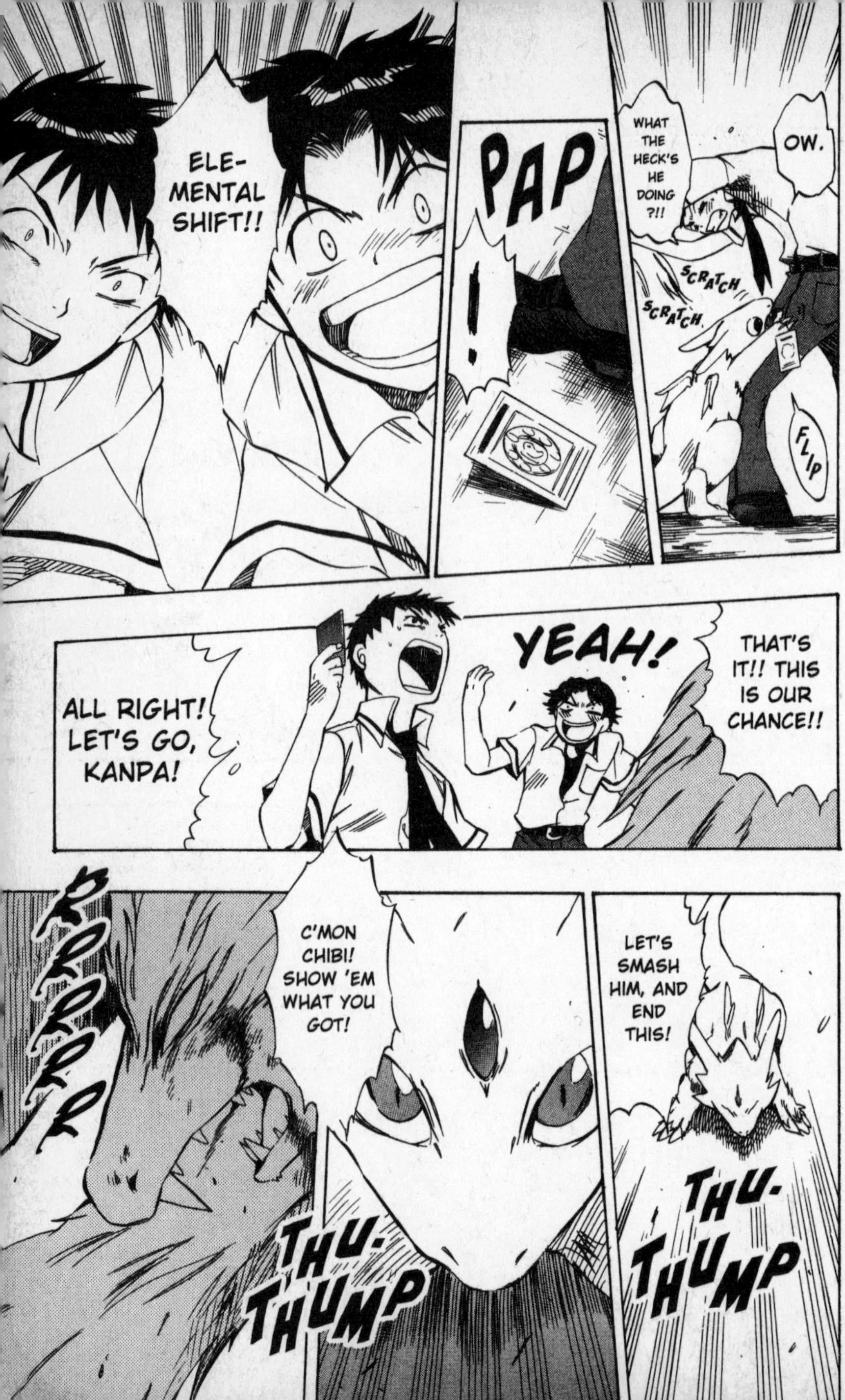
OW.
WHAT THE HECK'S HE DOING ?!!
SCRATCH
SCRATCH
FLIP
PAP
!
ELE-MENTAL SHIFT!!
THAT'S IT!! THIS IS OUR CHANCE!!
YEAH!
ALL RIGHT! LET'S GO, KANPA!
LET'S SMASH HIM, AND END THIS!
THU-THUMP
C'MON CHIBI! SHOW 'EM WHAT YOU GOT!
THU-THUMP
RRRRRRR

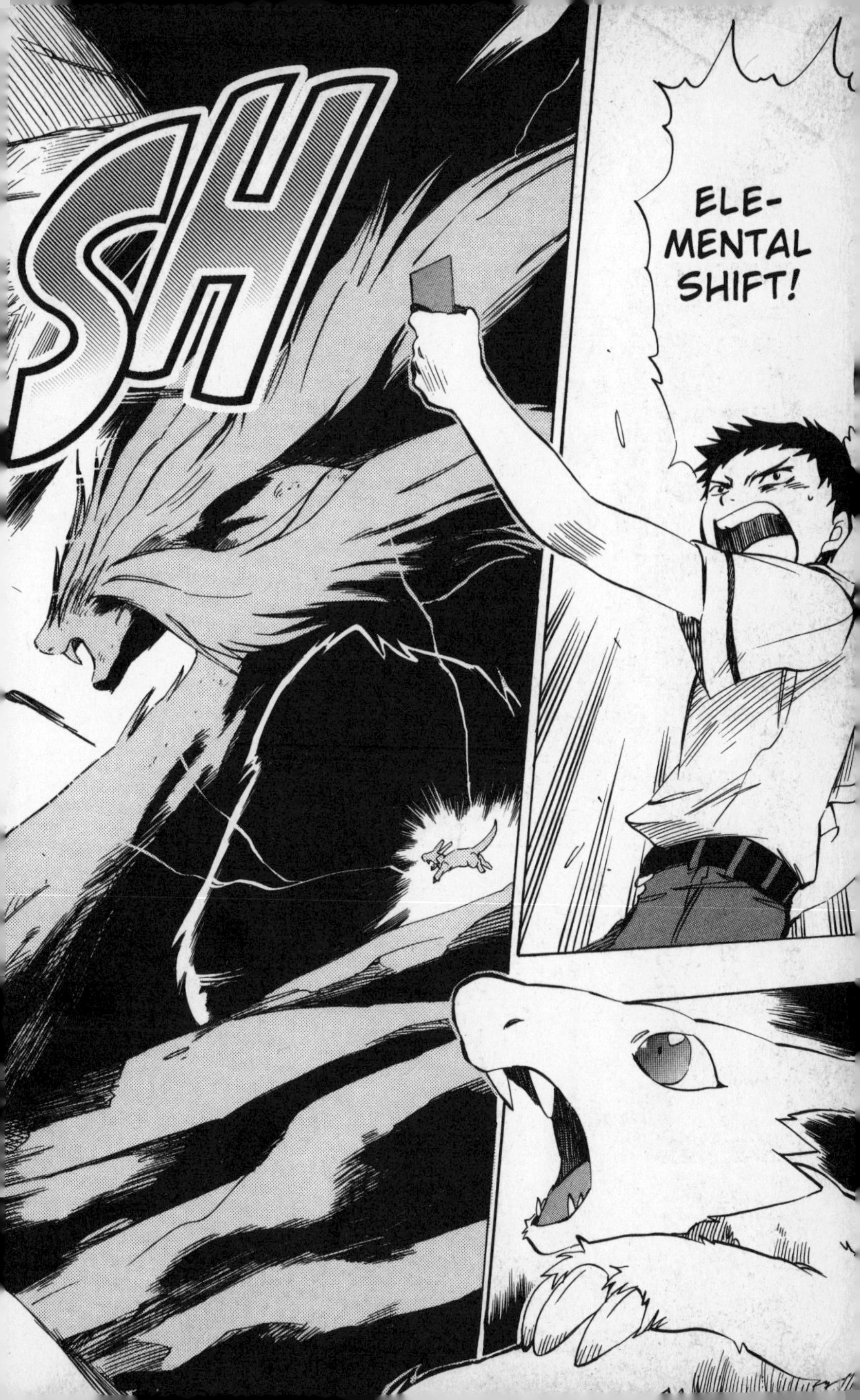
ELE-
MENTAL
SHIFT!
SH

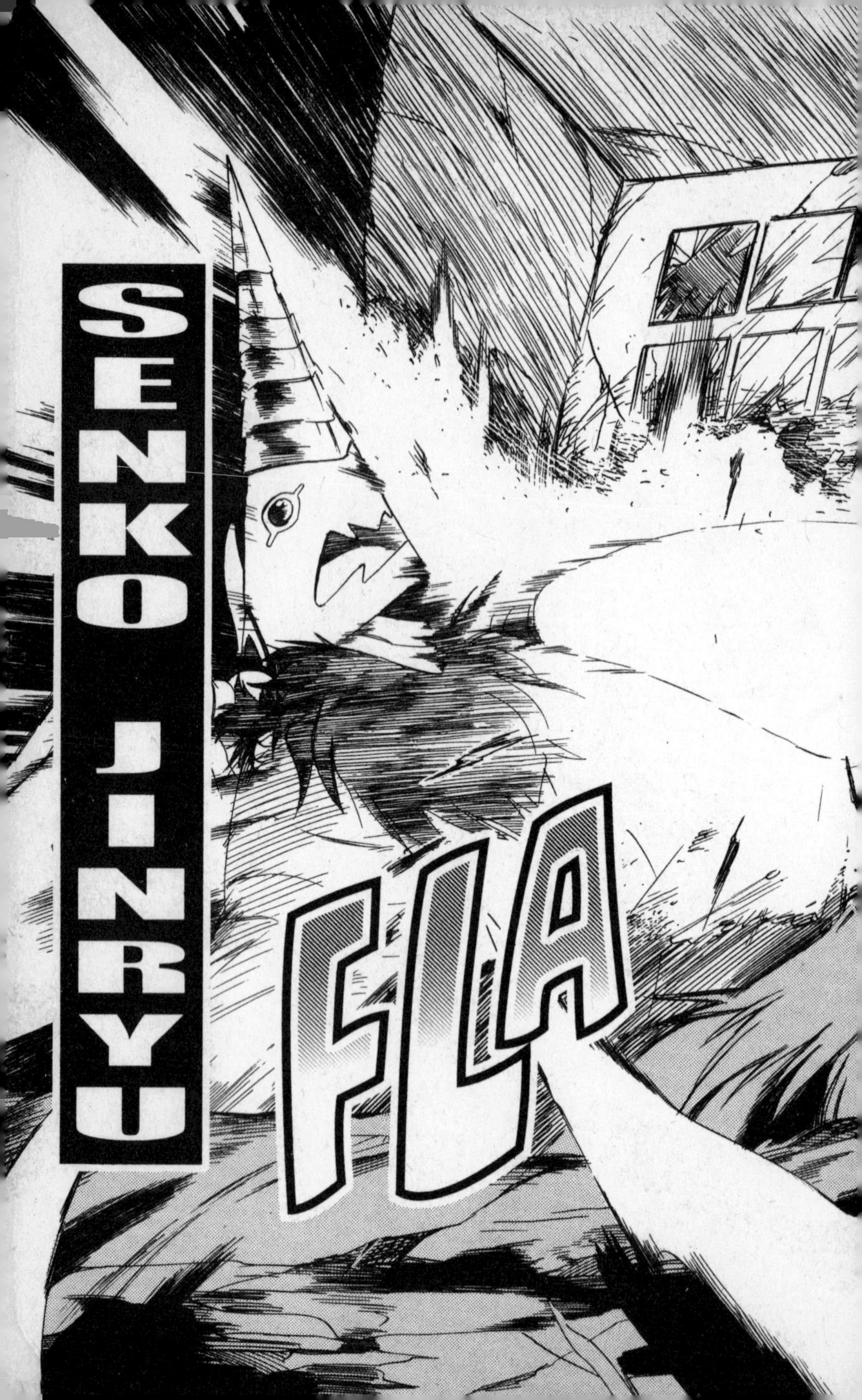
SENKO JINRYU
FLA

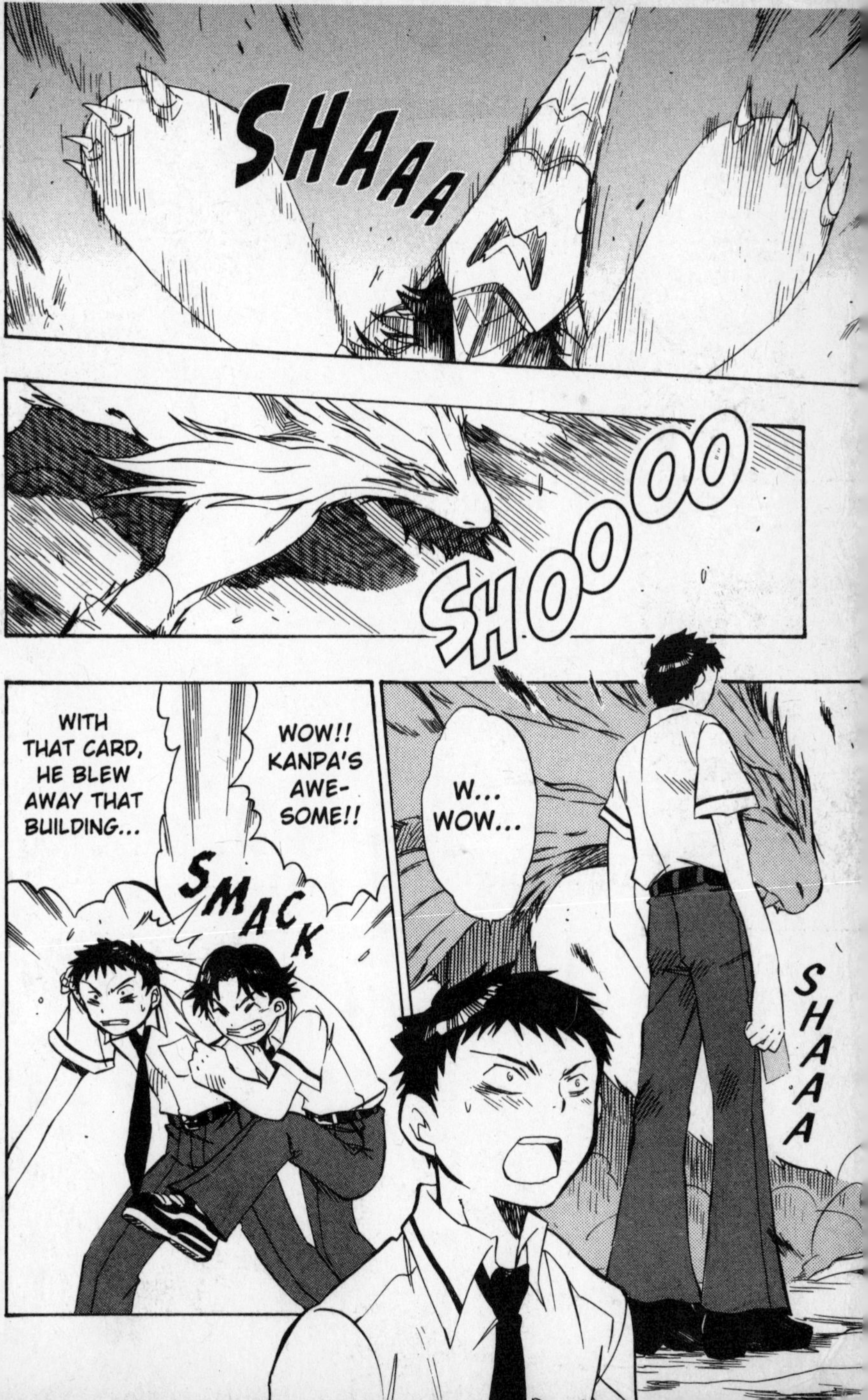
SHAAA
SHOOOO
W... WOW...
SHAAAA
WOW!! KANPA'S AWE-SOME!!
WITH THAT CARD, HE BLEW AWAY THAT BUILDING...
SMACK

READ THIS WAY

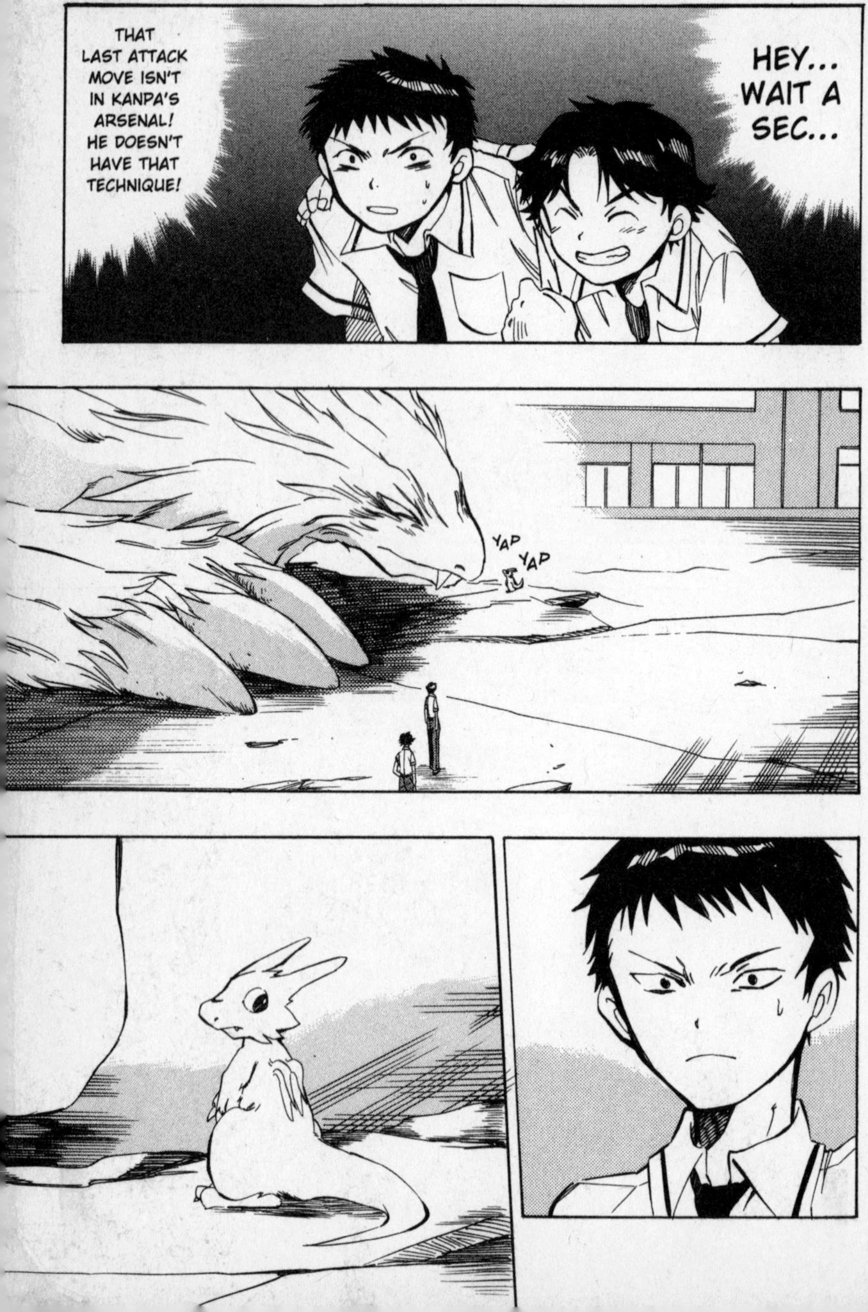
HEY... WAIT A SEC...
THAT LAST ATTACK MOVE ISN'T IN KANPA'S ARSENAL! HE DOESN'T HAVE THAT TECHNIQUE!
YAP YAP

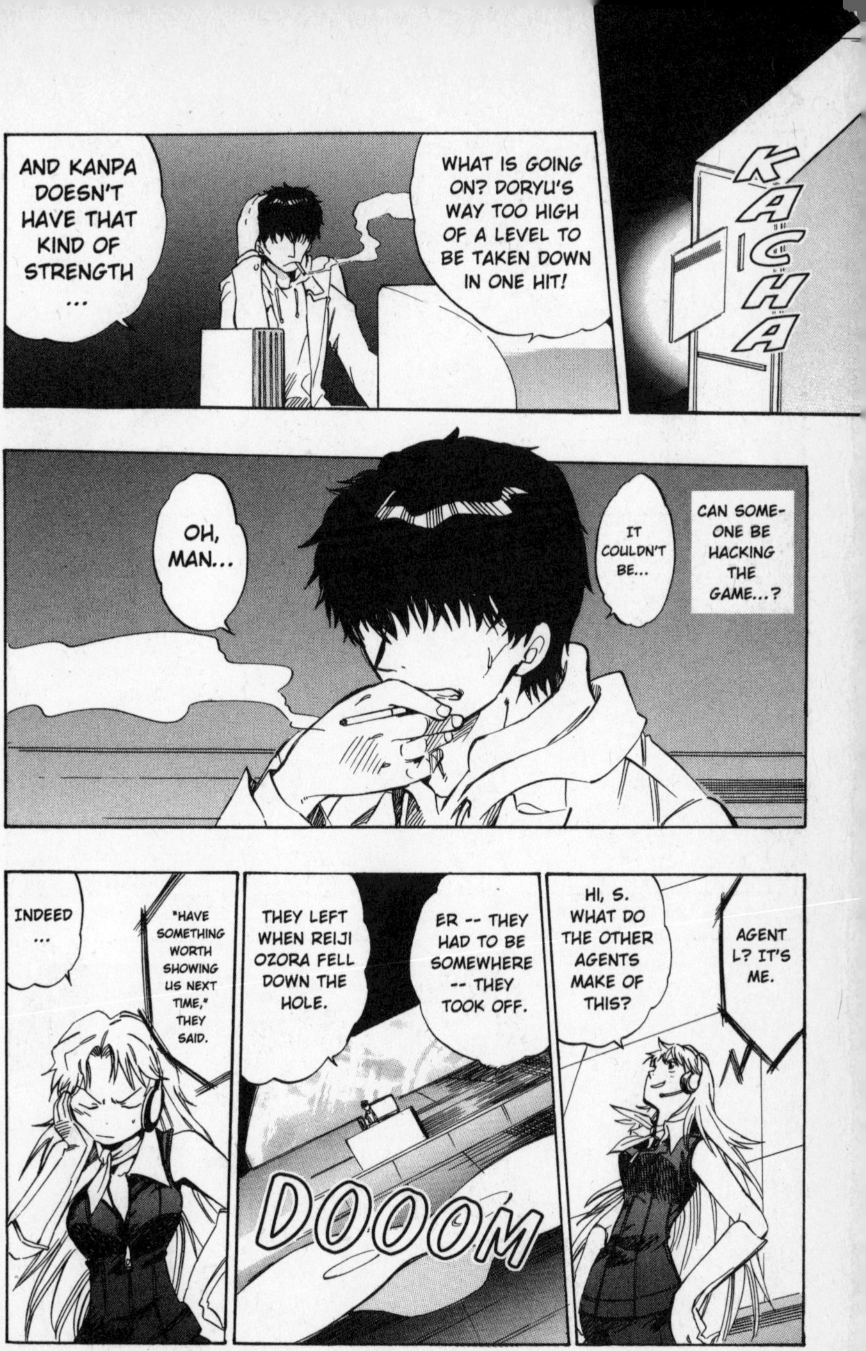
KACHA
WHAT IS GOING ON? DORYU'S WAY TOO HIGH OF A LEVEL TO BE TAKEN DOWN IN ONE HIT!
AND KANPA DOESN'T HAVE THAT KIND OF STRENGTH ...
CAN SOME-ONE BE HACKING THE GAME...?
IT COULDN'T BE...
OH, MAN...
AGENT L? IT'S ME.
HI, S. WHAT DO THE OTHER AGENTS MAKE OF THIS?
ER -- THEY HAD TO BE SOMEWHERE -- THEY TOOK OFF.
THEY LEFT WHEN REIJI OZORA FELL DOWN THE HOLE.
DOOOM
"HAVE SOMETHING WORTH SHOWING US NEXT TIME," THEY SAID.
INDEED ...

READ THIS WAY

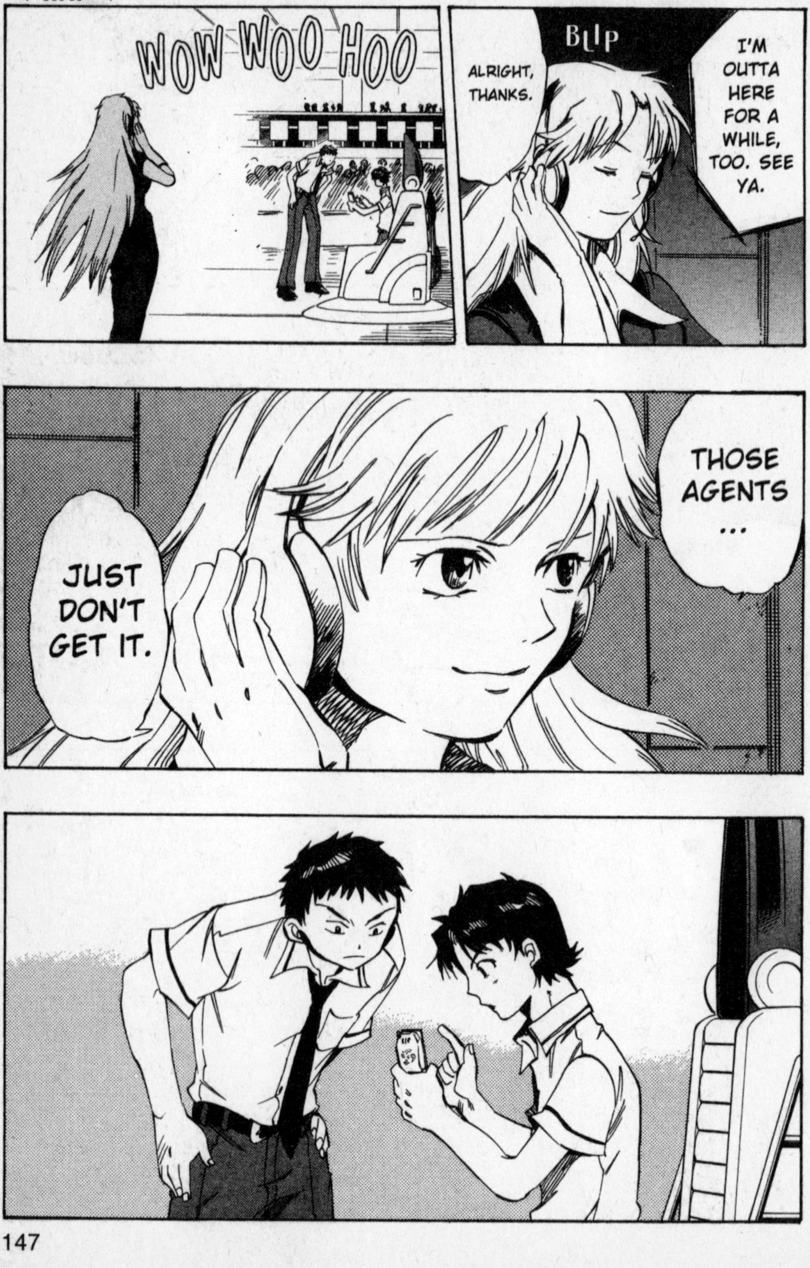
BLIP
I'M OUTTA HERE FOR A WHILE, TOO. SEE YA.
ALRIGHT, THANKS.
WOW WOO HOO
THOSE AGENTS...
JUST DON'T GET IT.

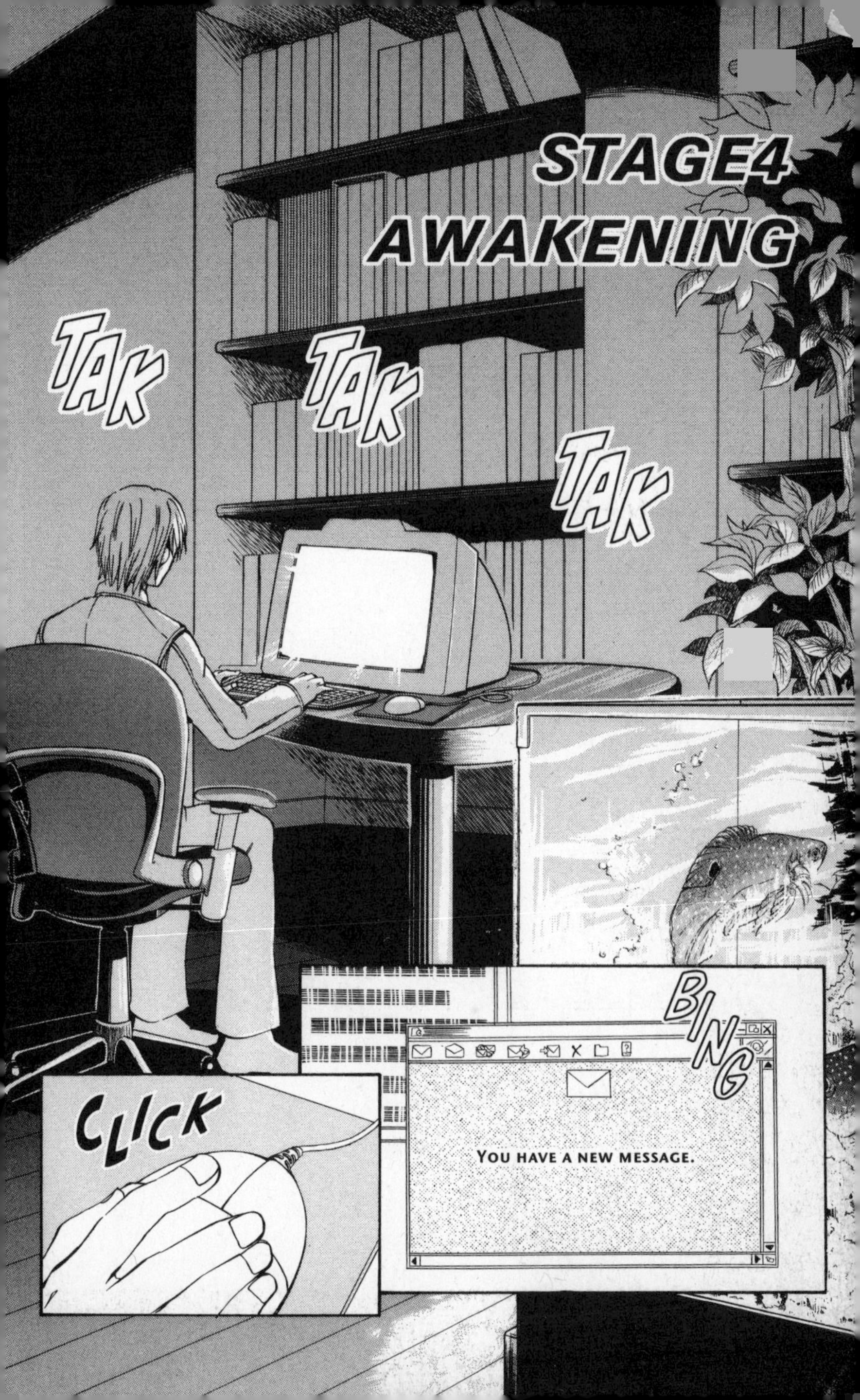
STAGE4
AWAKENING
TAK
TAK
TAK
BING
YOU HAVE A NEW MESSAGE.
CLICK

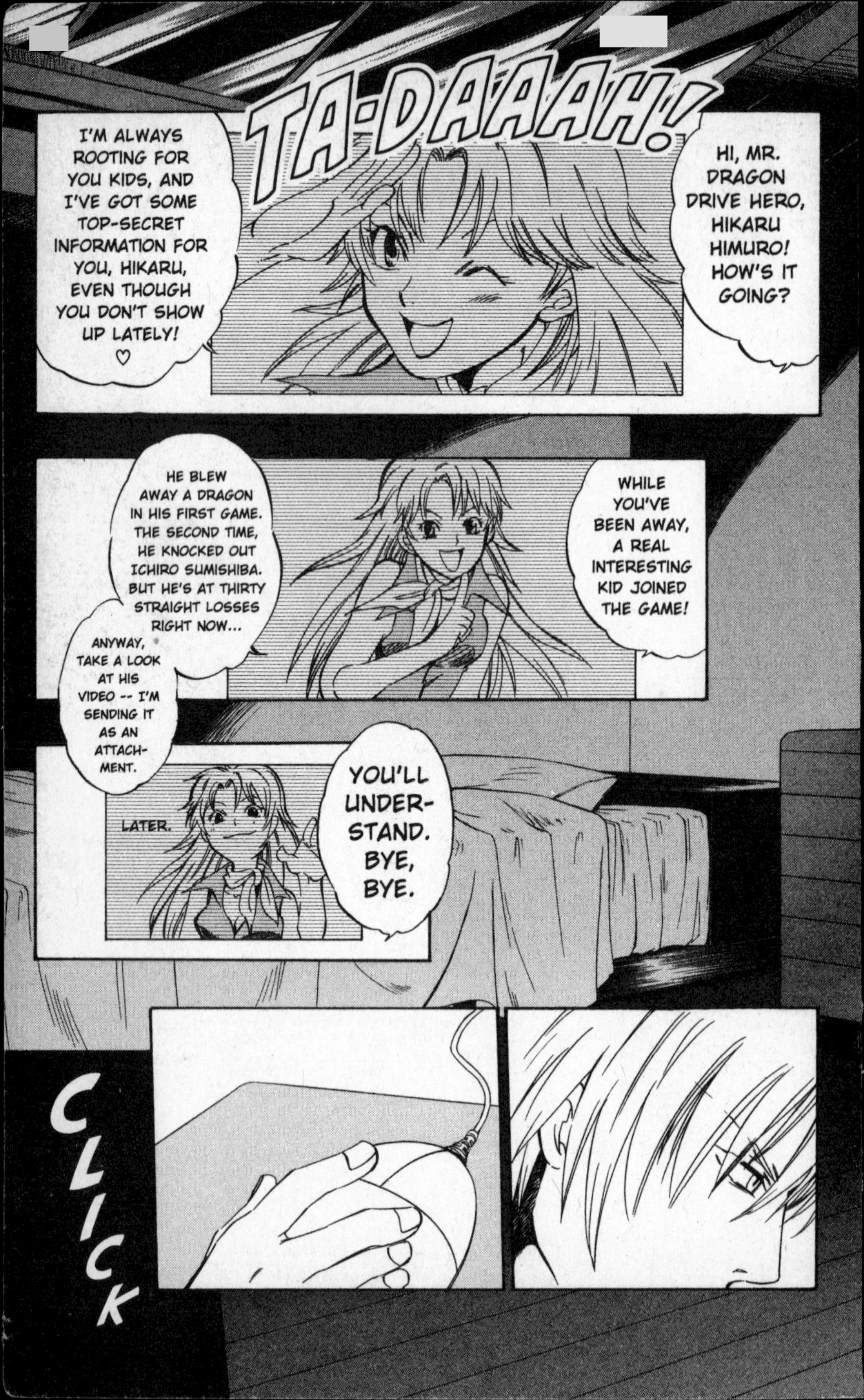
TA-DAAAH!
HI, MR. DRAGON DRIVE HERO, HIKARU HIMURO! HOW'S IT GOING?
I'M ALWAYS ROOTING FOR YOU KIDS, AND I'VE GOT SOME TOP-SECRET INFORMATION FOR YOU, HIKARU, EVEN THOUGH YOU DON'T SHOW UP LATELY! ♡
WHILE YOU'VE BEEN AWAY, A REAL INTERESTING KID JOINED THE GAME!
HE BLEW AWAY A DRAGON IN HIS FIRST GAME. THE SECOND TIME, HE KNOCKED OUT ICHIRO SUMISHIBA. BUT HE'S AT THIRTY STRAIGHT LOSSES RIGHT NOW...
ANYWAY, TAKE A LOOK AT HIS VIDEO -- I'M SENDING IT AS AN ATTACH-MENT.
YOU'LL UNDER-STAND. BYE, BYE.
LATER.
CLICK

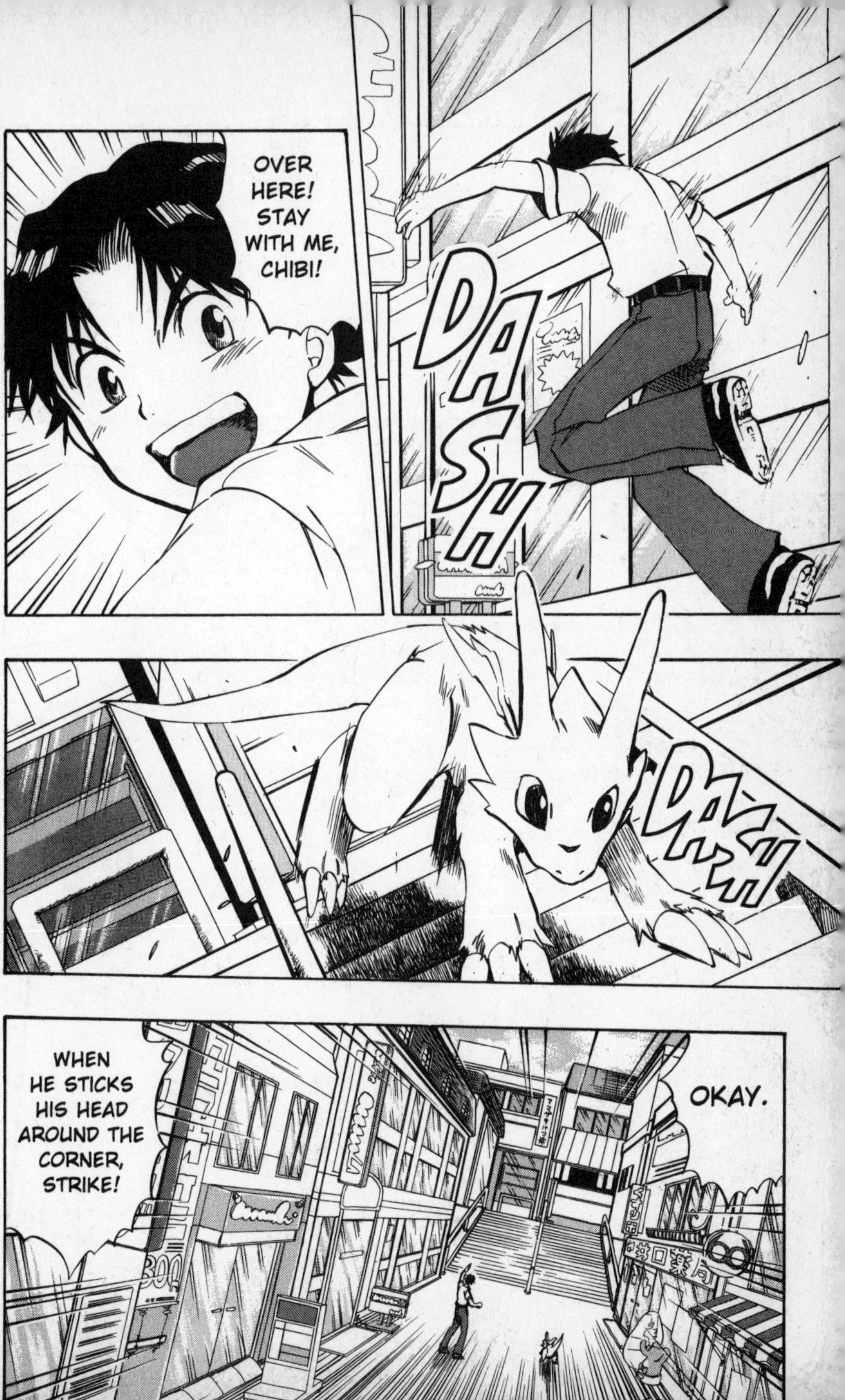
DASH
OVER HERE! STAY WITH ME, CHIBI!
DASH
WHEN HE STICKS HIS HEAD AROUND THE CORNER, STRIKE!
OKAY.

READ THIS WAY

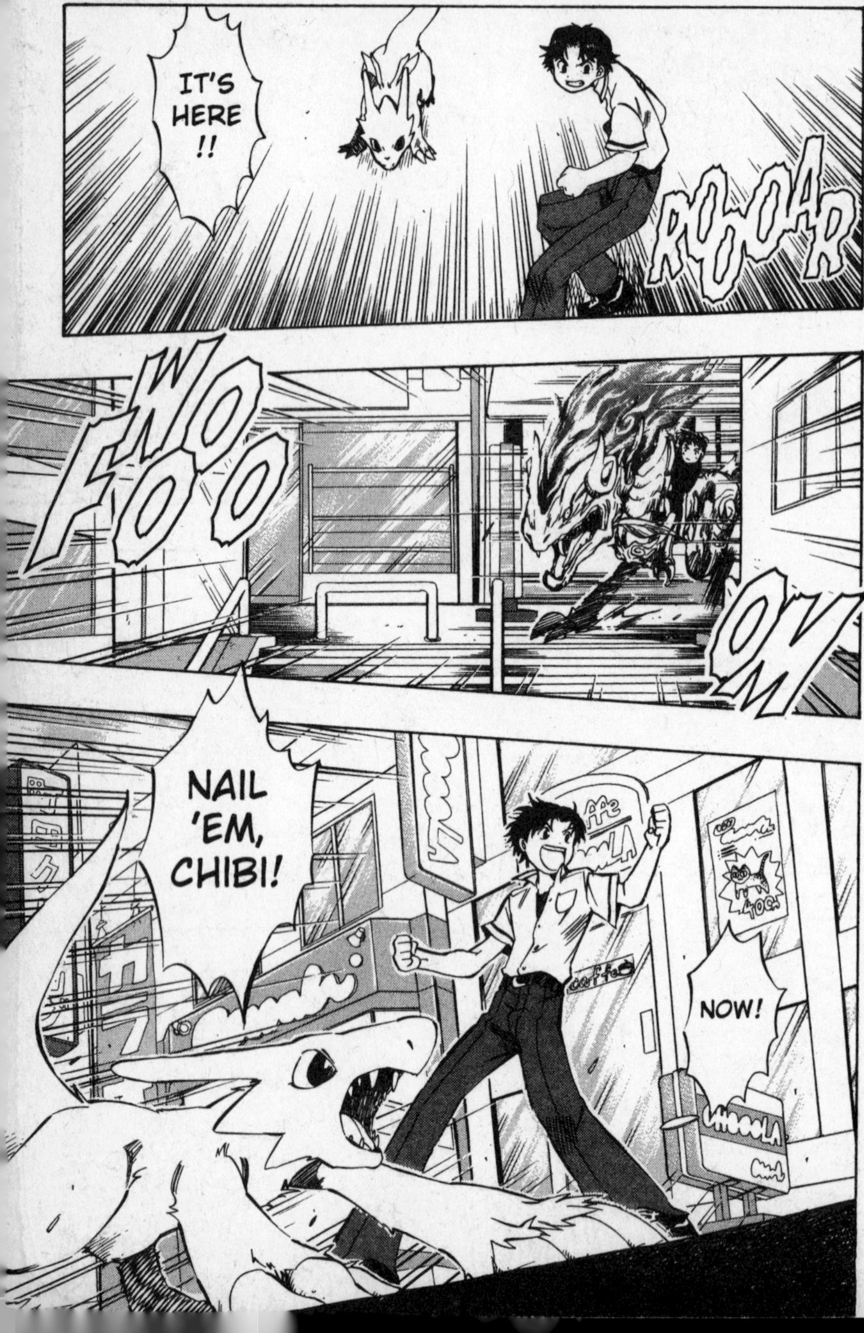
IT'S HERE!!
ROOOAR
FWOOOOOM
NAIL 'EM, CHIBI!
NOW!

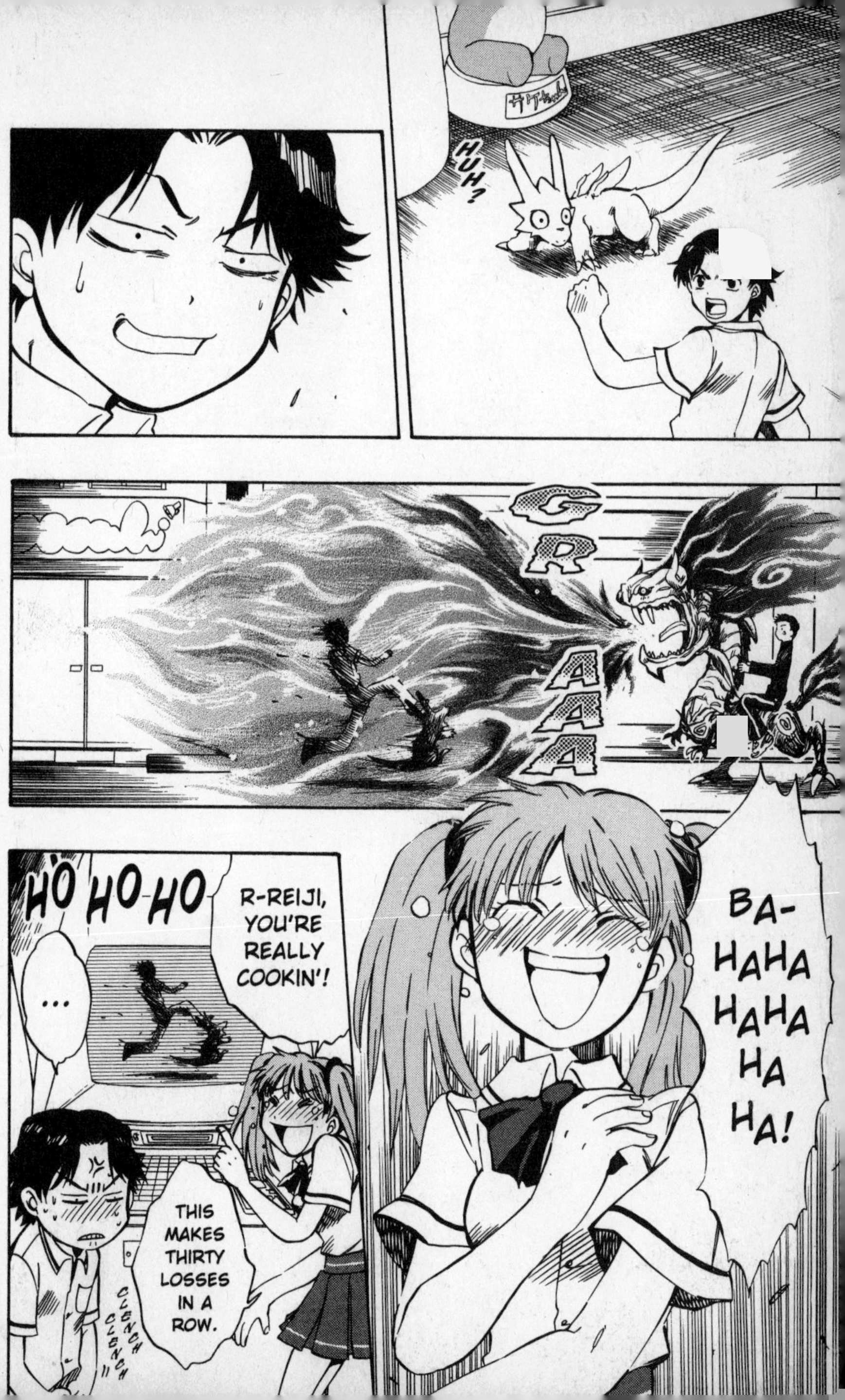
HUH?
GRAAAA
BA-HAHAHAHAHAHAHAHA!
R-REIJI, YOU'RE REALLY COOKIN'!
HO HO-HO
...
THIS MAKES THIRTY LOSSES IN A ROW.
CLENCH CLENCH

READ THIS WAY

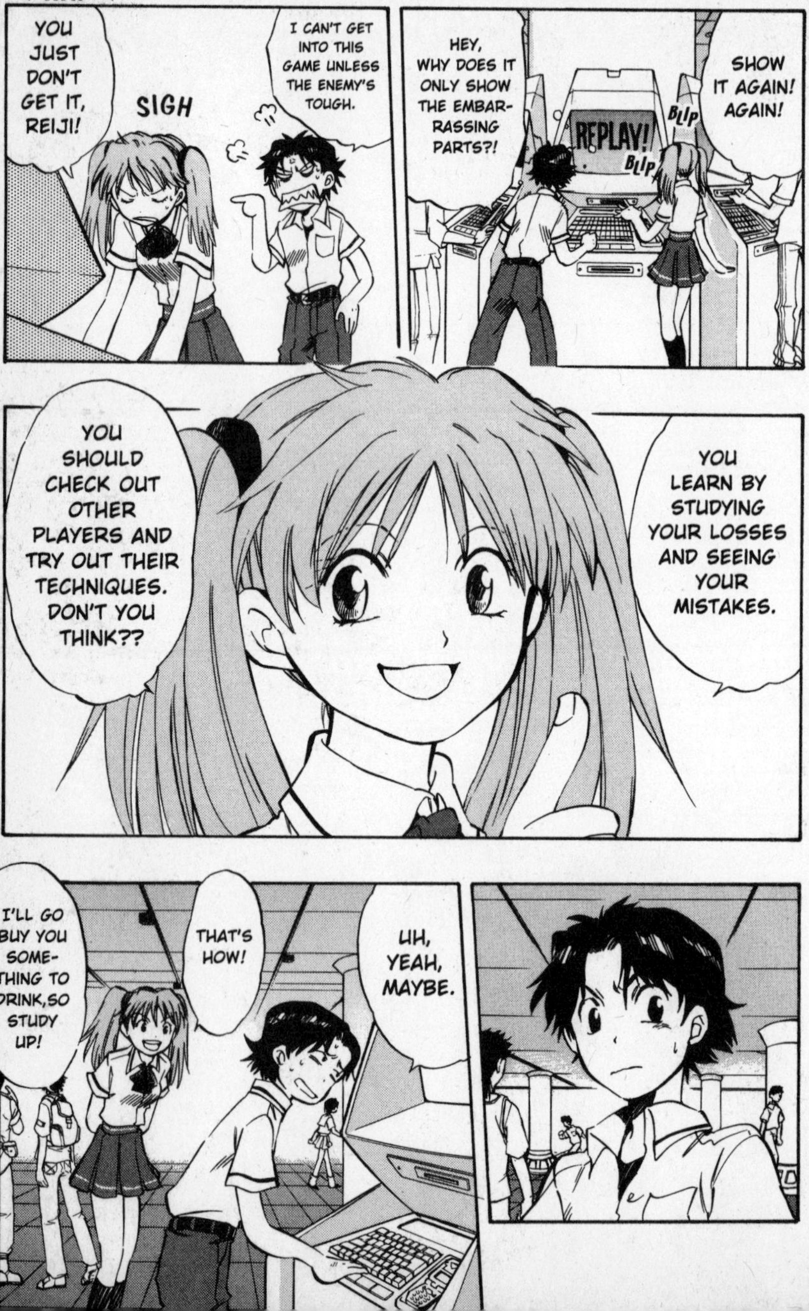
SHOW IT AGAIN! AGAIN!
BLIP
REPLAY!
BLIP
HEY, WHY DOES IT ONLY SHOW THE EMBARRASSING PARTS?!
I CAN'T GET INTO THIS GAME UNLESS THE ENEMY'S TOUGH.
SIGH
YOU JUST DON'T GET IT, REIJI!
YOU LEARN BY STUDYING YOUR LOSSES AND SEEING YOUR MISTAKES.
YOU SHOULD CHECK OUT OTHER PLAYERS AND TRY OUT THEIR TECHNIQUES. DON'T YOU THINK??
UH, YEAH, MAYBE.
THAT'S HOW!
I'LL GO BUY YOU SOMETHING TO DRINK,SO STUDY UP!

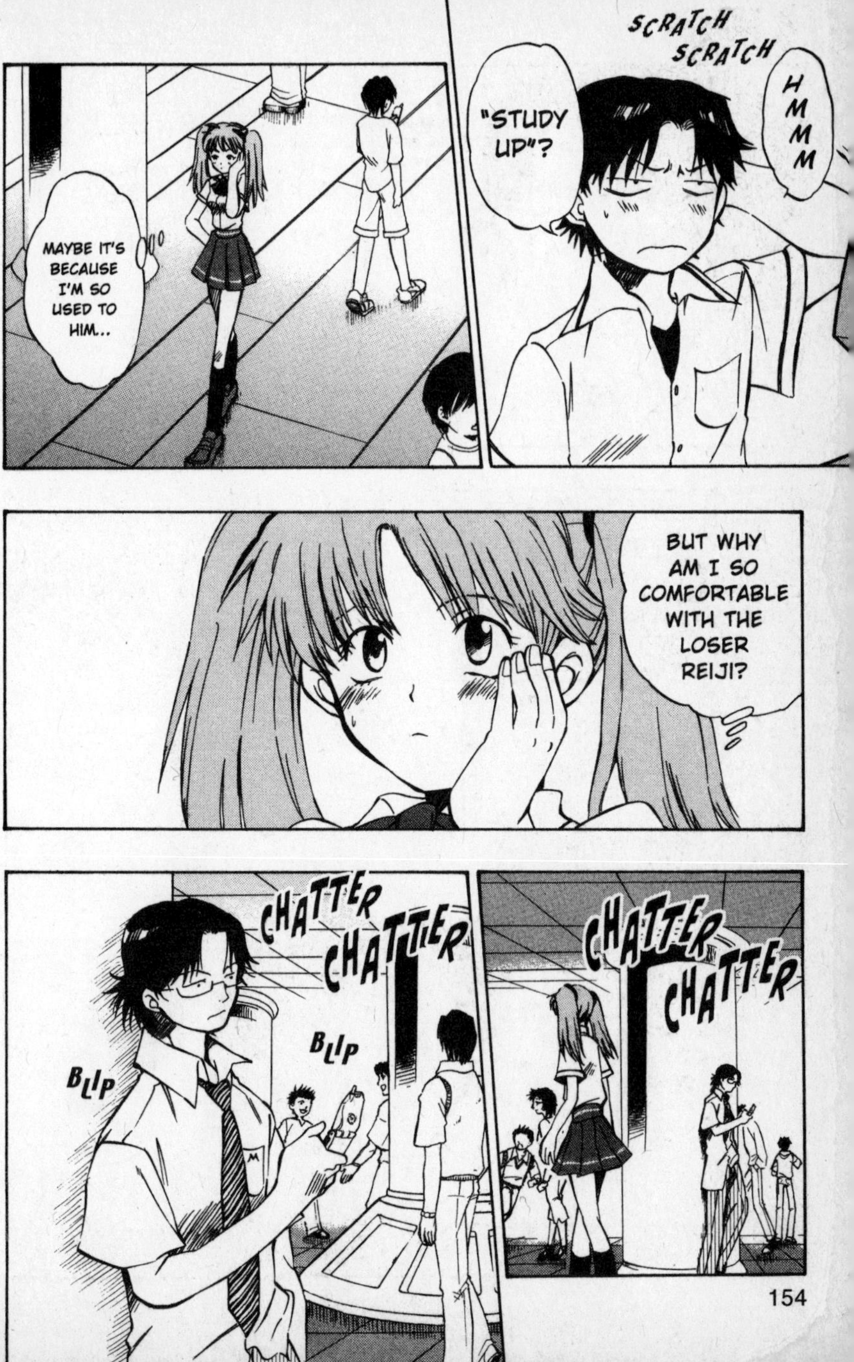
SCRATCH SCRATCH
HMMM
"STUDY UP"?
MAYBE IT'S BECAUSE I'M SO USED TO HIM...
BUT WHY AM I SO COMFORTABLE WITH THE LOSER REIJI?
CHATTER CHATTER
CHATTER CHATTER
BLIP
BLIP

READ THIS WAY

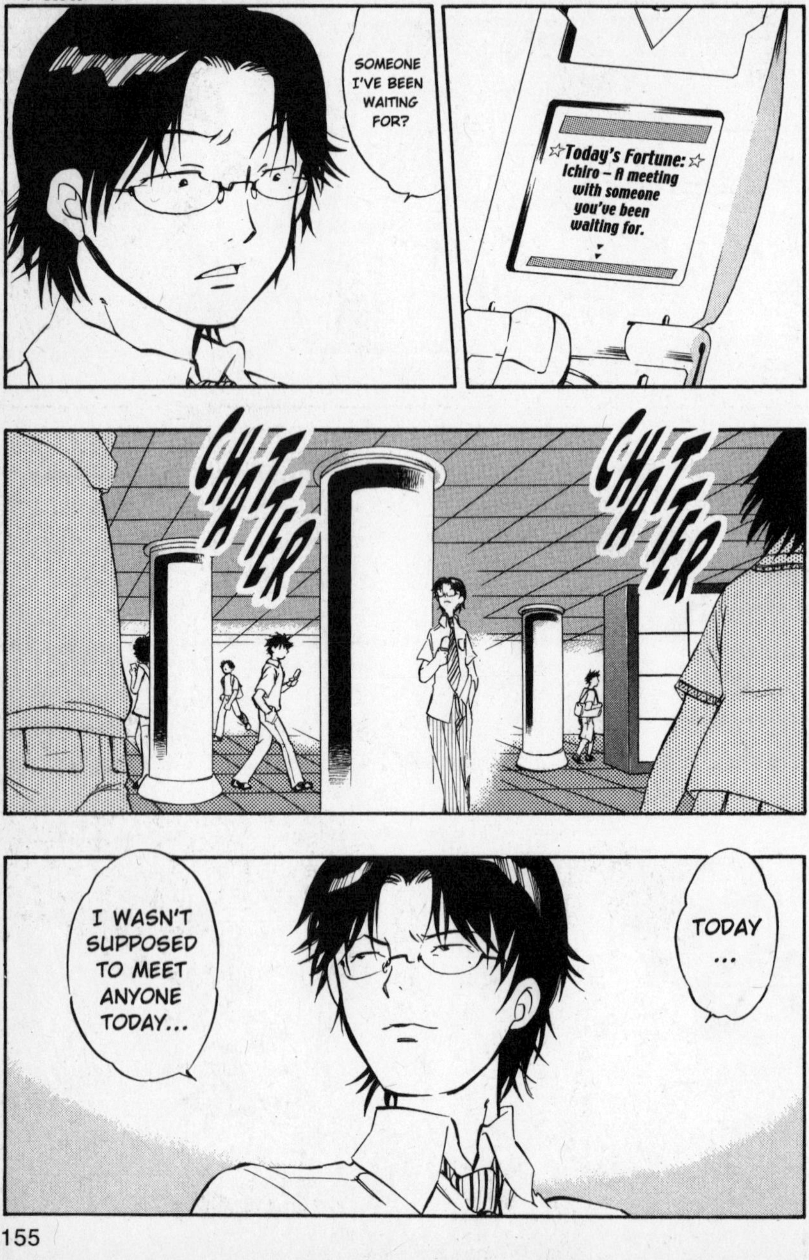
☆Today's Fortune:☆ Ichiro – A meeting with someone you've been waiting for.
SOMEONE I'VE BEEN WAITING FOR?
CHATTER
CHATTER
TODAY ...
I WASN'T SUPPOSED TO MEET ANYONE TODAY...

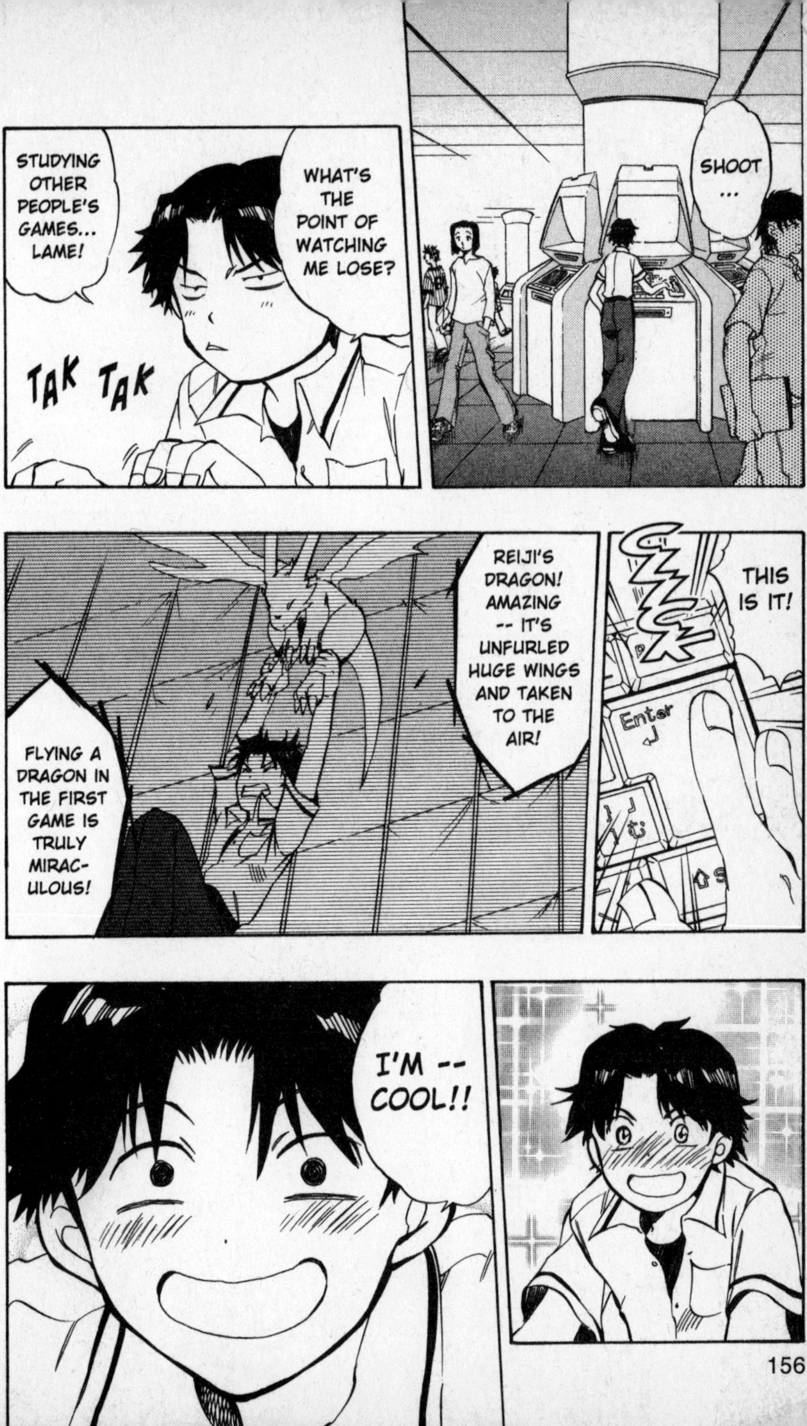
SHOOT ...
WHAT'S THE POINT OF WATCHING ME LOSE?
STUDYING OTHER PEOPLE'S GAMES... LAME!
TAK TAK
THIS IS IT!
REIJI'S DRAGON! AMAZING -- IT'S UNFURLED HUGE WINGS AND TAKEN TO THE AIR!
FLYING A DRAGON IN THE FIRST GAME IS TRULY MIRAC-ULOUS!
I'M -- COOL!!

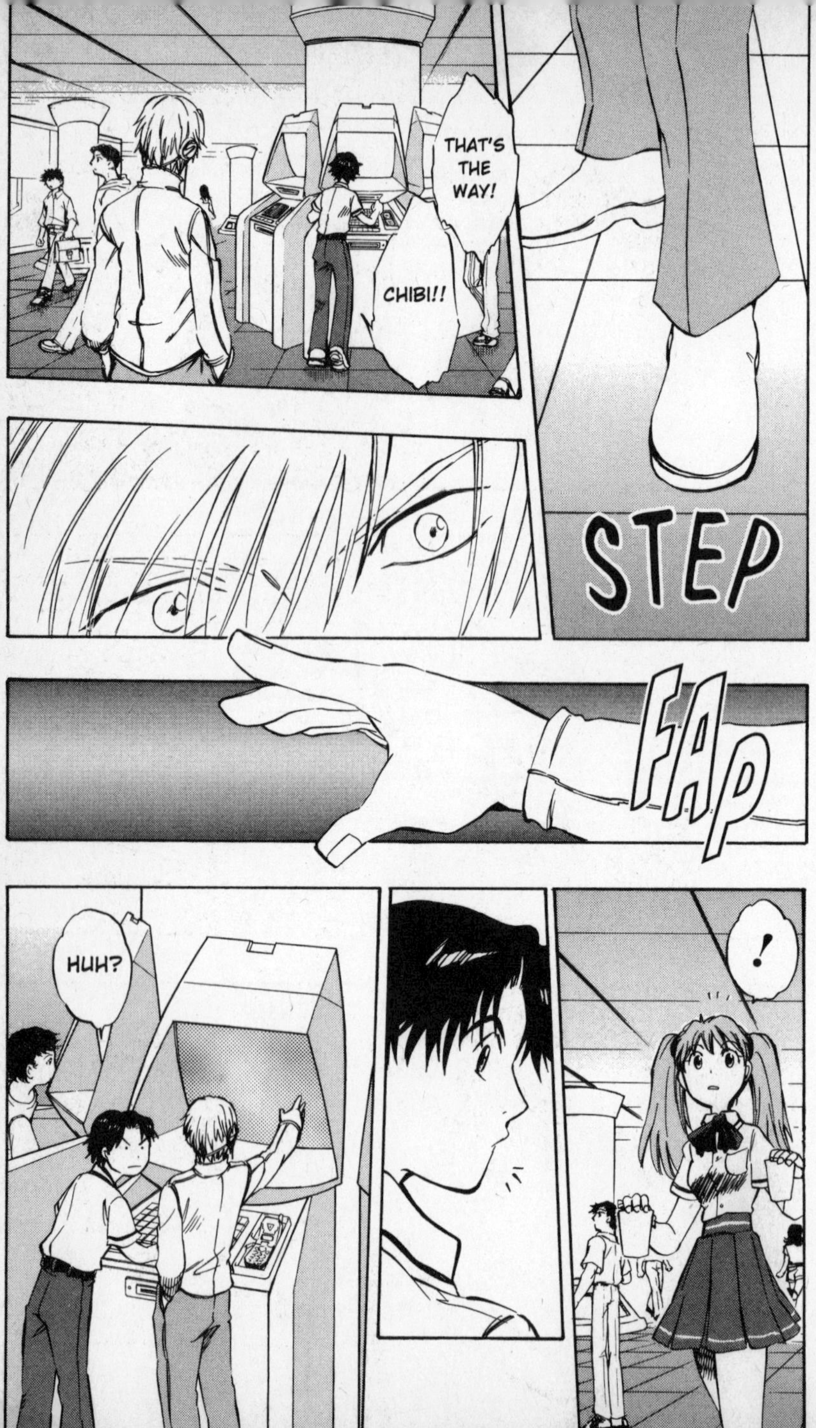
STEP
THAT'S THE WAY!
CHIBI!!
FAP
!
HUH?

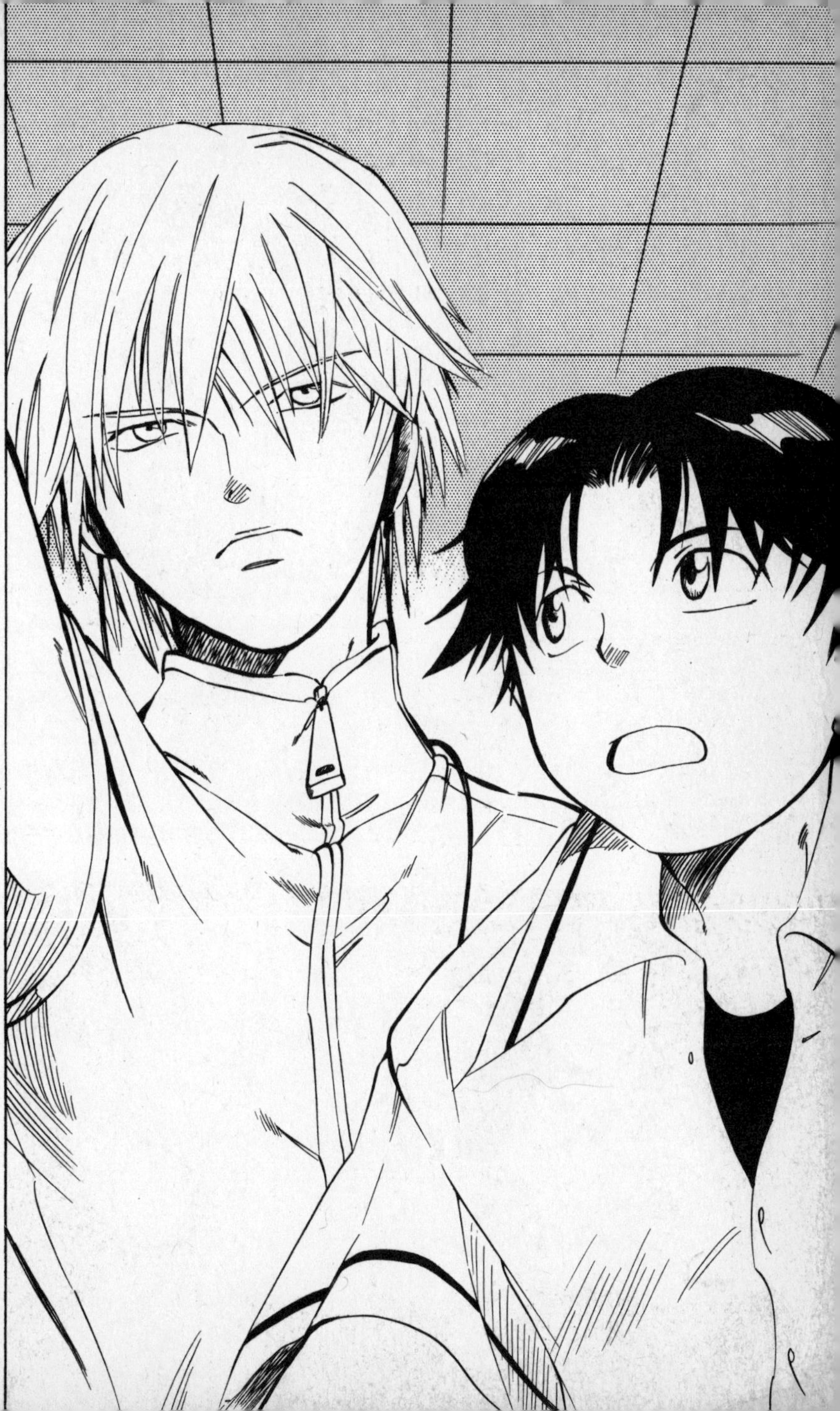

READ THIS WAY

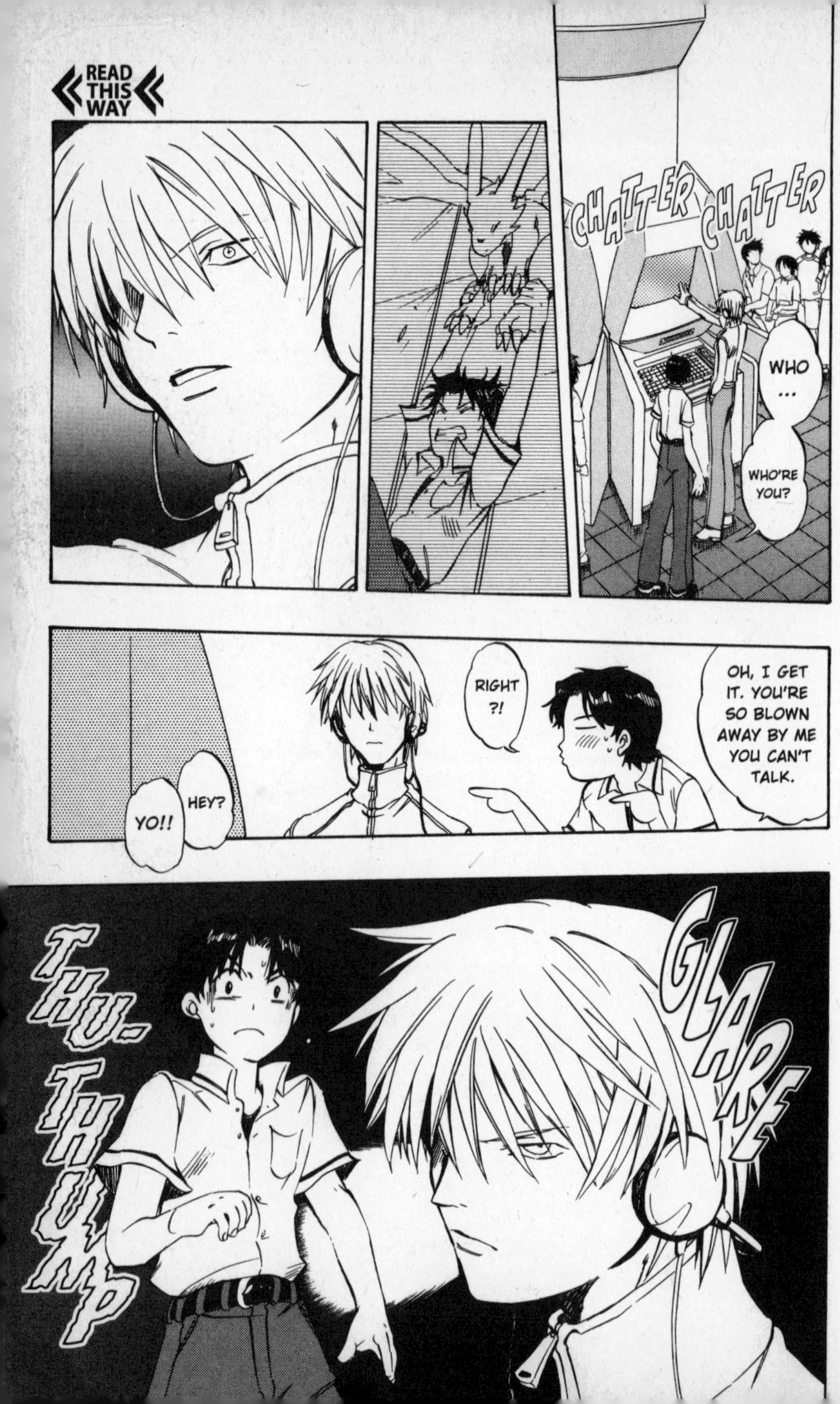
CHATTER CHATTER
WHO ...
WHO'RE YOU?
OH, I GET IT. YOU'RE SO BLOWN AWAY BY ME YOU CAN'T TALK.
RIGHT ?!
HEY?
YO!!
GLARE
THU-THUMP

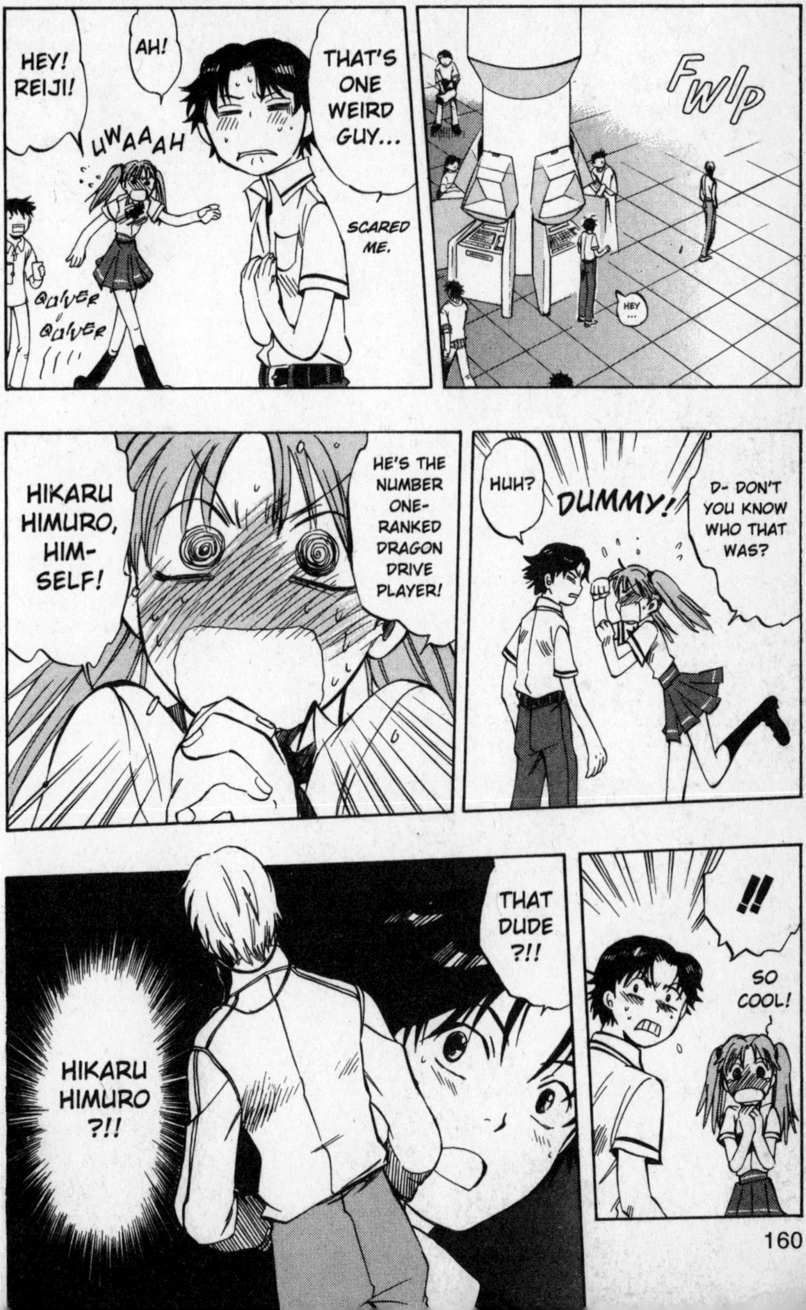

FWIP
HEY...
THAT'S ONE WEIRD GUY...
AH!
HEY! REIJI!
UWAAAH
SCARED ME.
QUIVER QUIVER
D- DON'T YOU KNOW WHO THAT WAS?
DUMMY!
HUH?
HE'S THE NUMBER ONE-RANKED DRAGON DRIVE PLAYER!
HIKARU HIMURO, HIMSELF!
!!
SO COOL!
THAT DUDE ?!!
HIKARU HIMURO ?!!

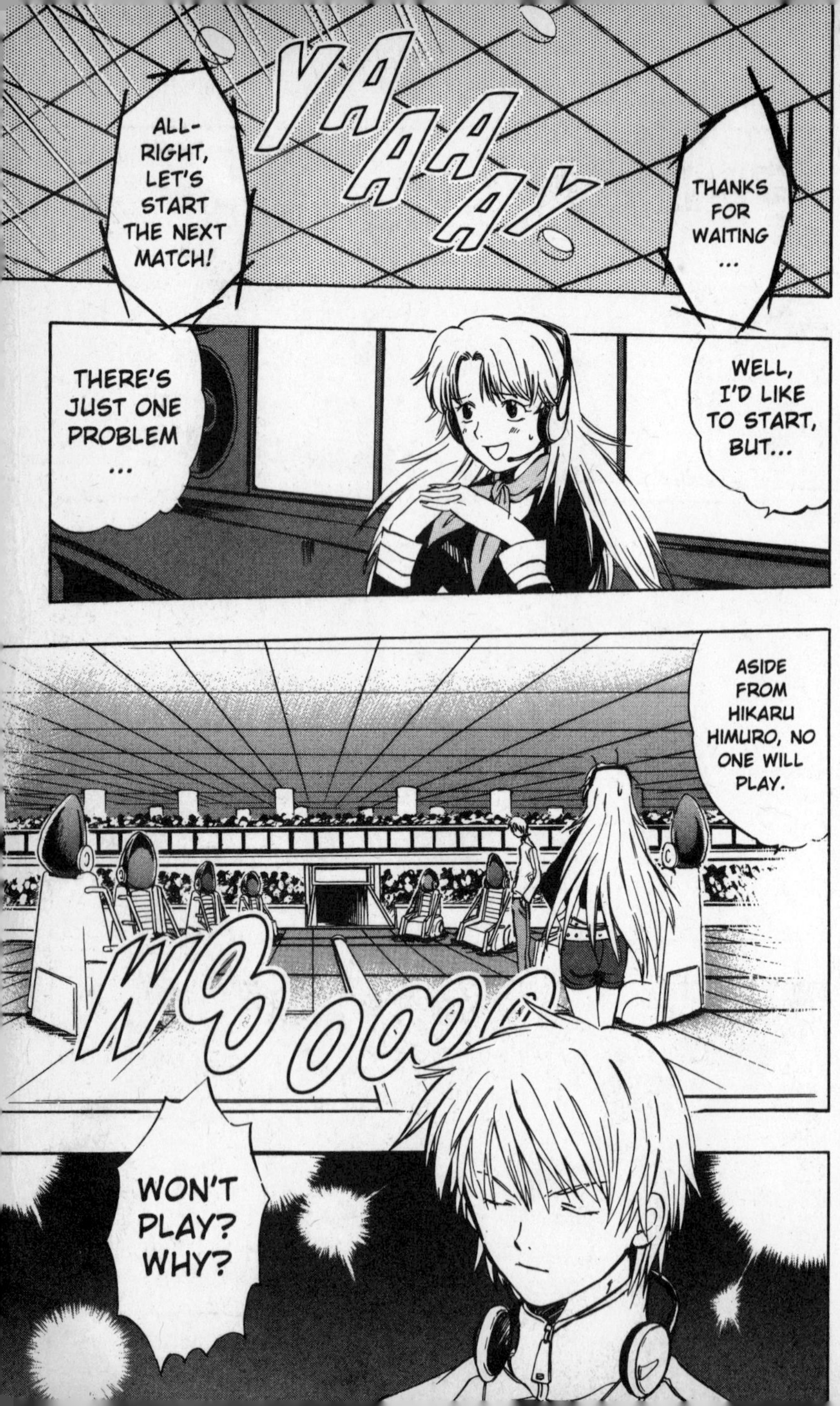
THANKS FOR WAITING...
YAAAAY
ALL-RIGHT, LET'S START THE NEXT MATCH!
WELL, I'D LIKE TO START, BUT...
THERE'S JUST ONE PROBLEM...
ASIDE FROM HIKARU HIMURO, NO ONE WILL PLAY.
WOOOO
WON'T PLAY? WHY?

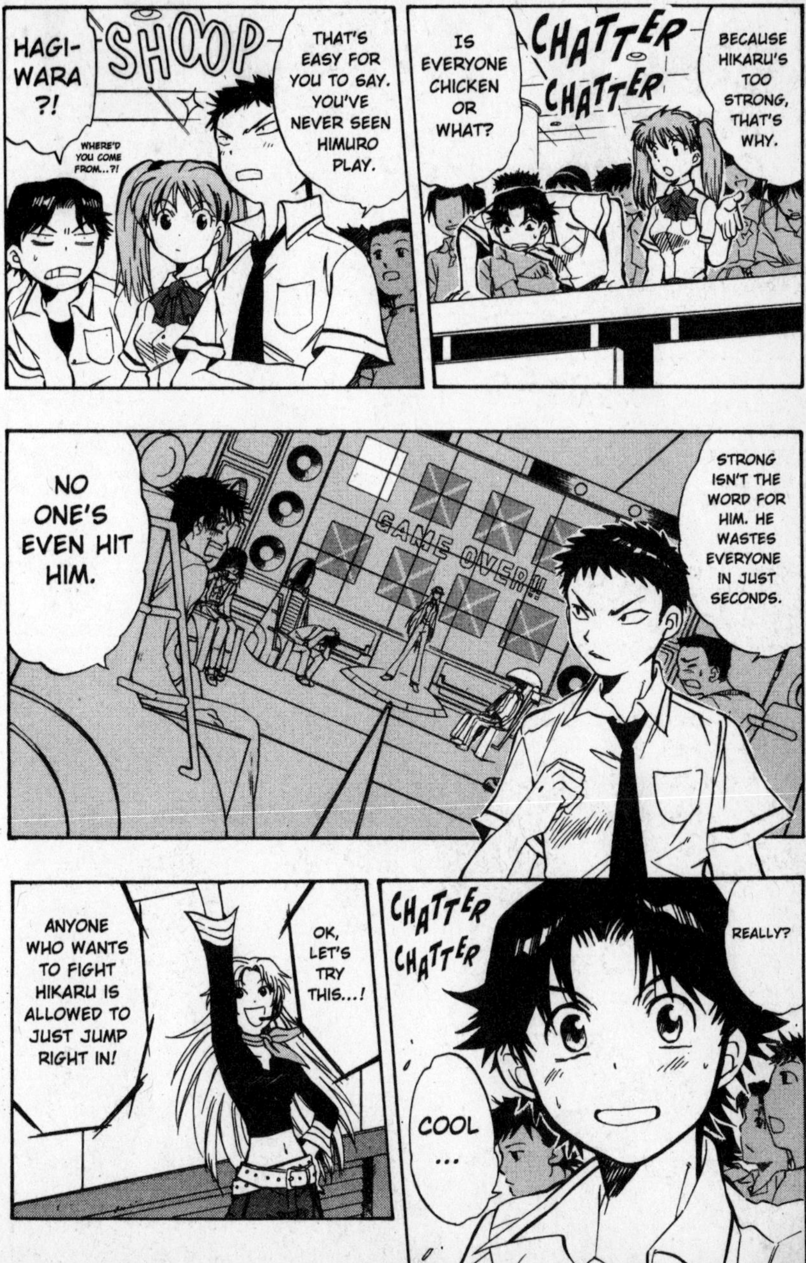
BECAUSE HIKARU'S TOO STRONG, THAT'S WHY.
CHATTER CHATTER
IS EVERYONE CHICKEN OR WHAT?
THAT'S EASY FOR YOU TO SAY. YOU'VE NEVER SEEN HIMURO PLAY.
SHOOP
HAGI-WARA?!
WHERE'D YOU COME FROM...?!
STRONG ISN'T THE WORD FOR HIM. HE WASTES EVERYONE IN JUST SECONDS.
GAME OVER!!
NO ONE'S EVEN HIT HIM.
REALLY?
CHATTER CHATTER
COOL...
OK, LET'S TRY THIS...!
ANYONE WHO WANTS TO FIGHT HIKARU IS ALLOWED TO JUST JUMP RIGHT IN!

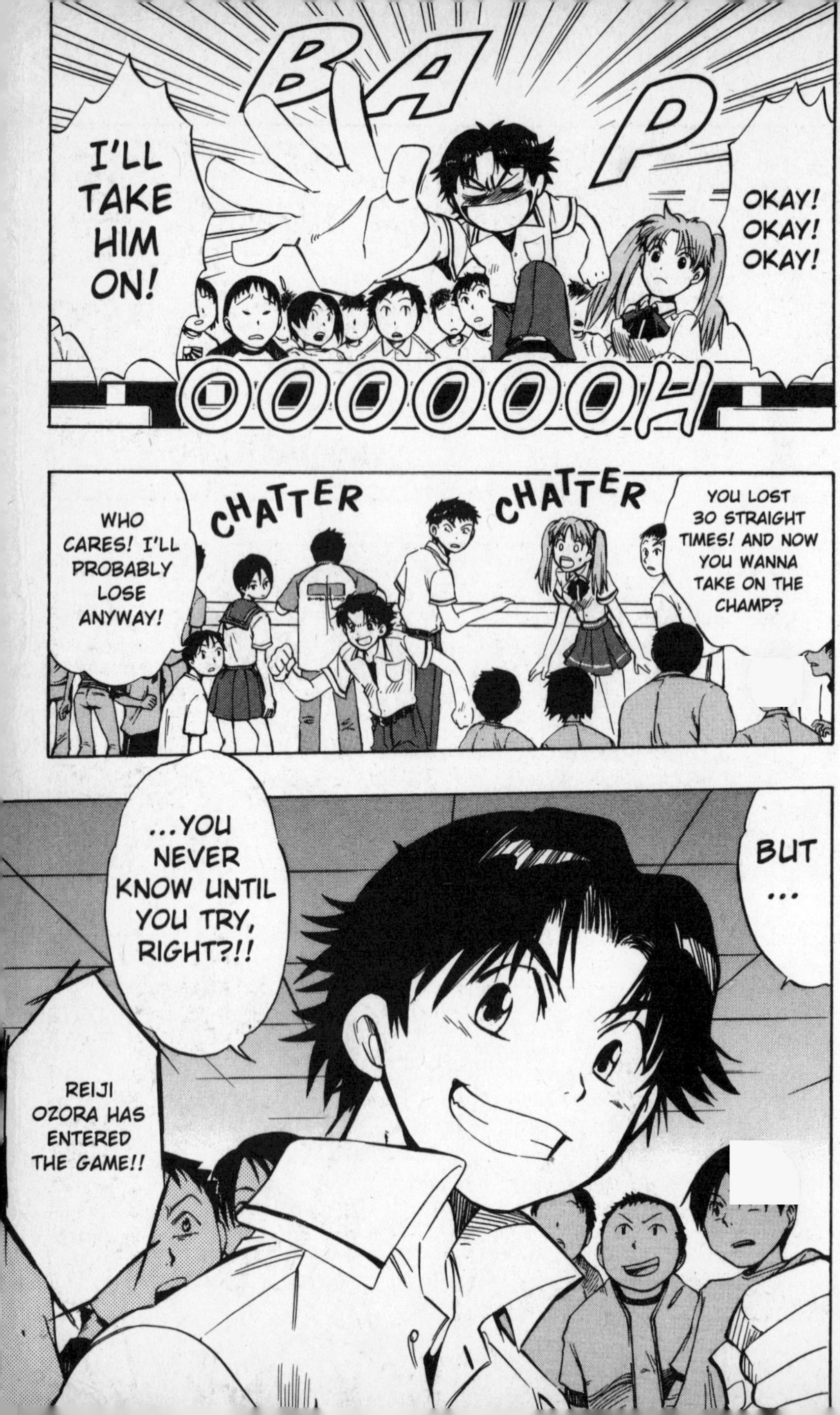
BAP
OKAY! OKAY! OKAY!
I'LL TAKE HIM ON!
OOOOOOH
YOU LOST 30 STRAIGHT TIMES! AND NOW YOU WANNA TAKE ON THE CHAMP?
CHATTER
CHATTER
WHO CARES! I'LL PROBABLY LOSE ANYWAY!
BUT ...
...YOU NEVER KNOW UNTIL YOU TRY, RIGHT?!!
REIJI OZORA HAS ENTERED THE GAME!!

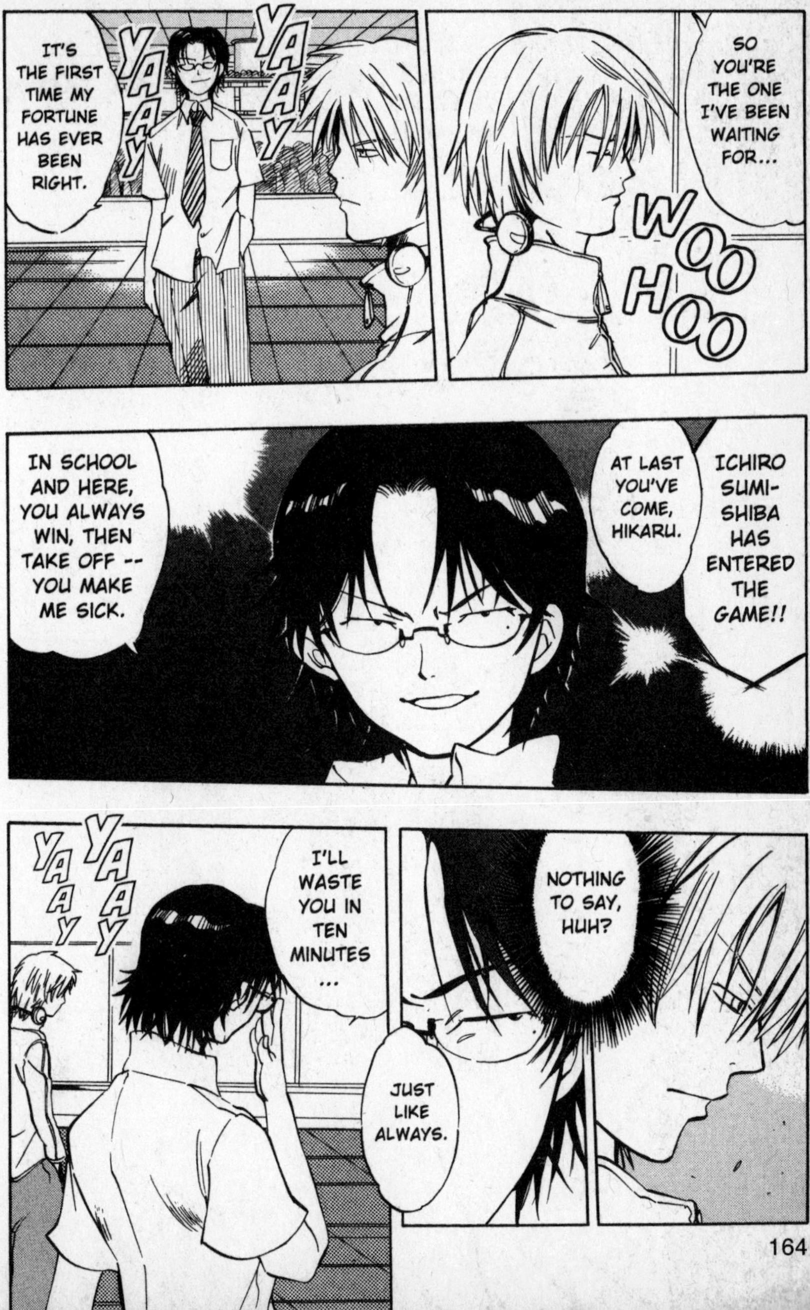
SO YOU'RE THE ONE I'VE BEEN WAITING FOR...
WOO HOO
IT'S THE FIRST TIME MY FORTUNE HAS EVER BEEN RIGHT.
YAAY
YAAY
ICHIRO SUMI-SHIBA HAS ENTERED THE GAME!!
AT LAST YOU'VE COME, HIKARU.
IN SCHOOL AND HERE, YOU ALWAYS WIN, THEN TAKE OFF -- YOU MAKE ME SICK.
NOTHING TO SAY, HUH?
JUST LIKE ALWAYS.
I'LL WASTE YOU IN TEN MINUTES ...
YAAY
YAAY

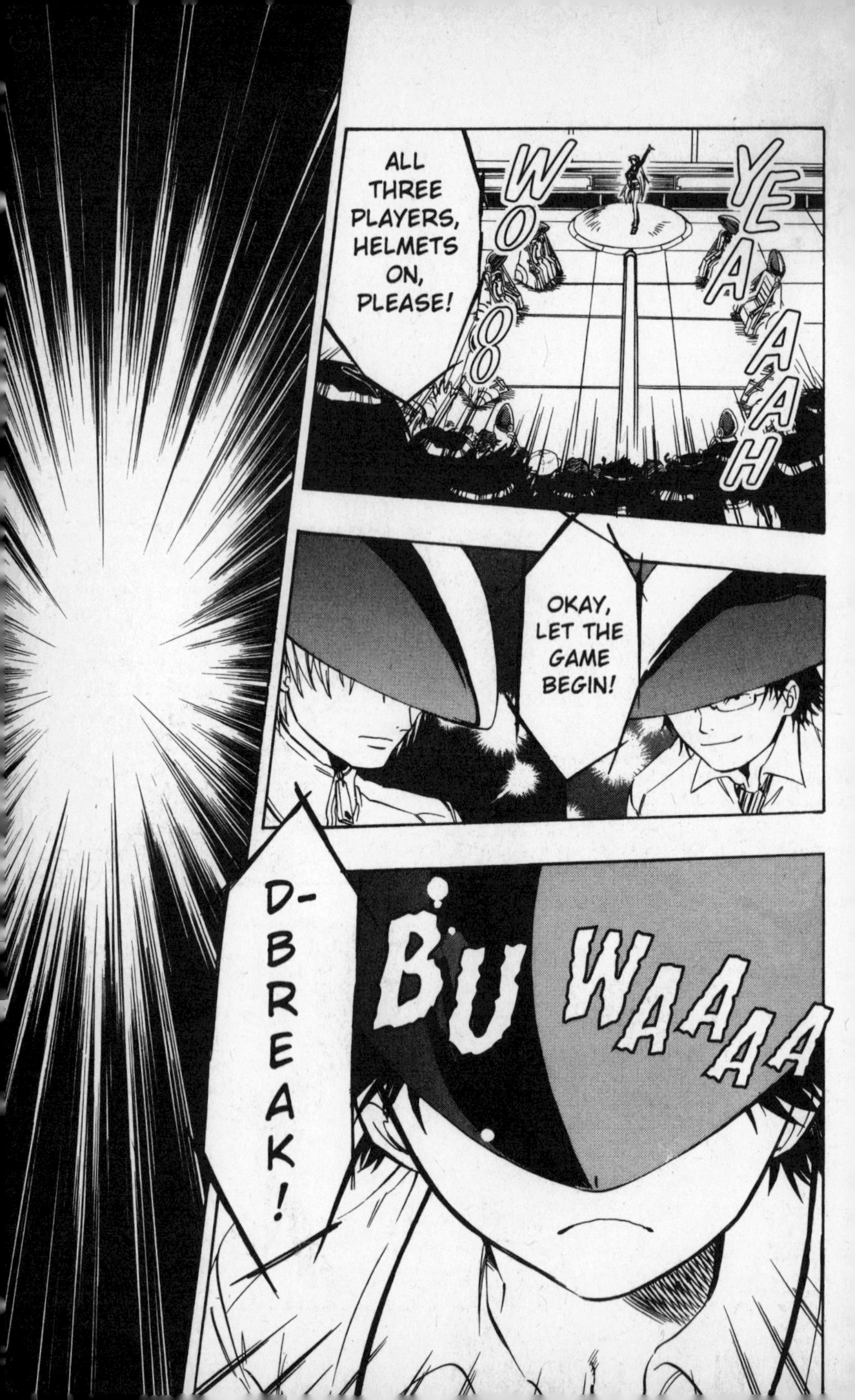
YEAAAAH
WOOO
ALL THREE PLAYERS, HELMETS ON, PLEASE!
OKAY, LET THE GAME BEGIN!
BUWAAAAA
D-BREAK!

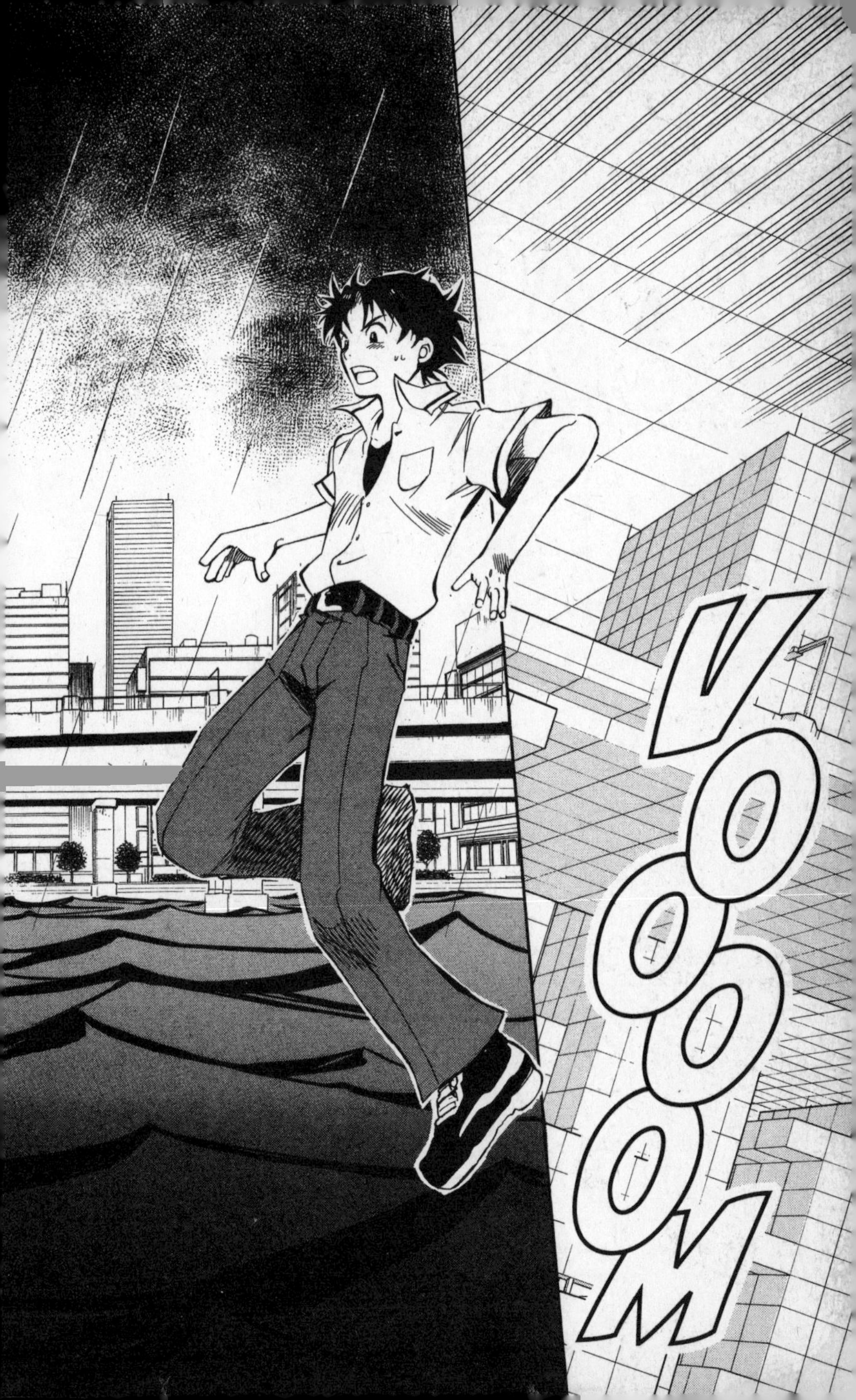
VOOOOOM

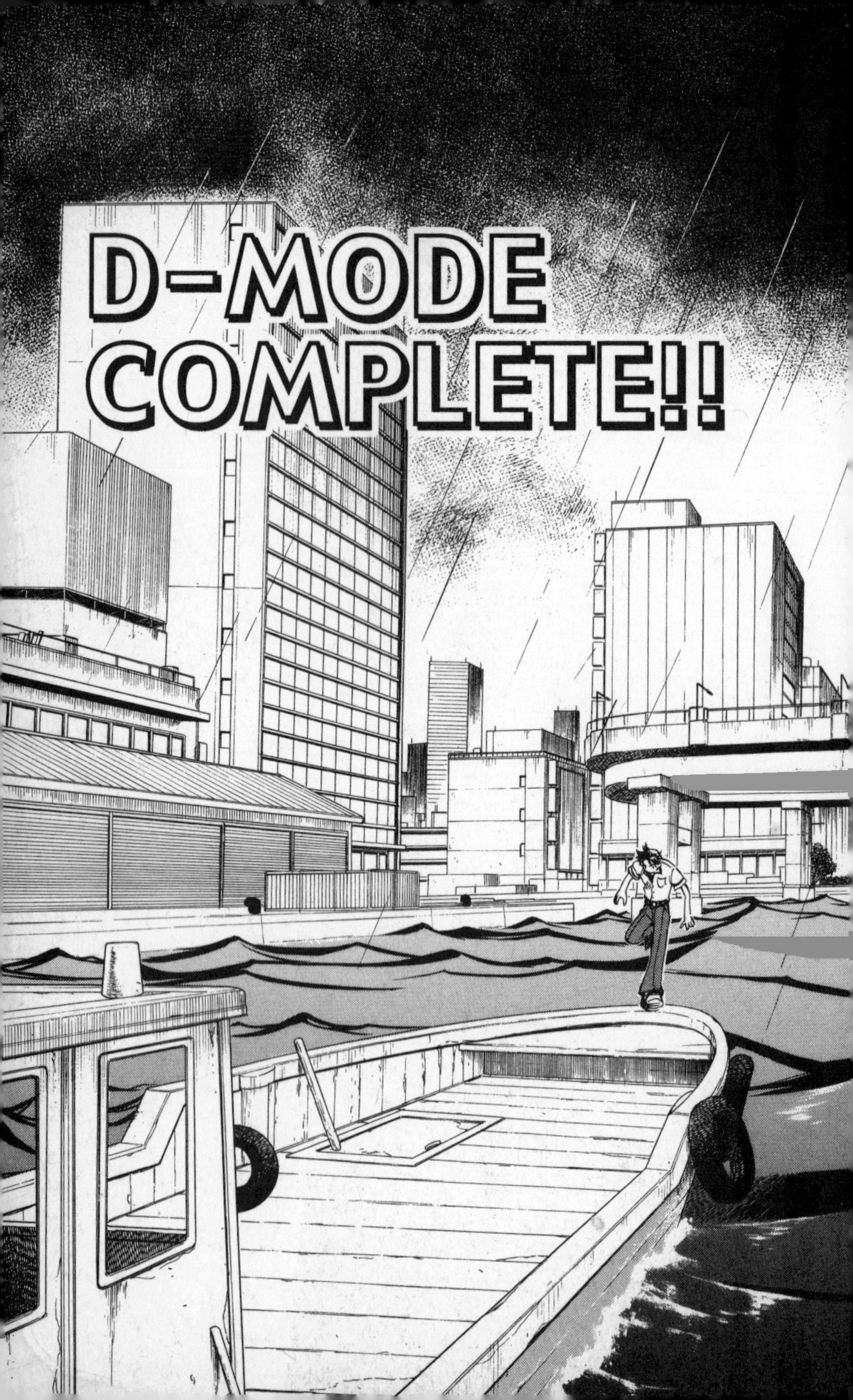
D-MODE
COMPLETE!!

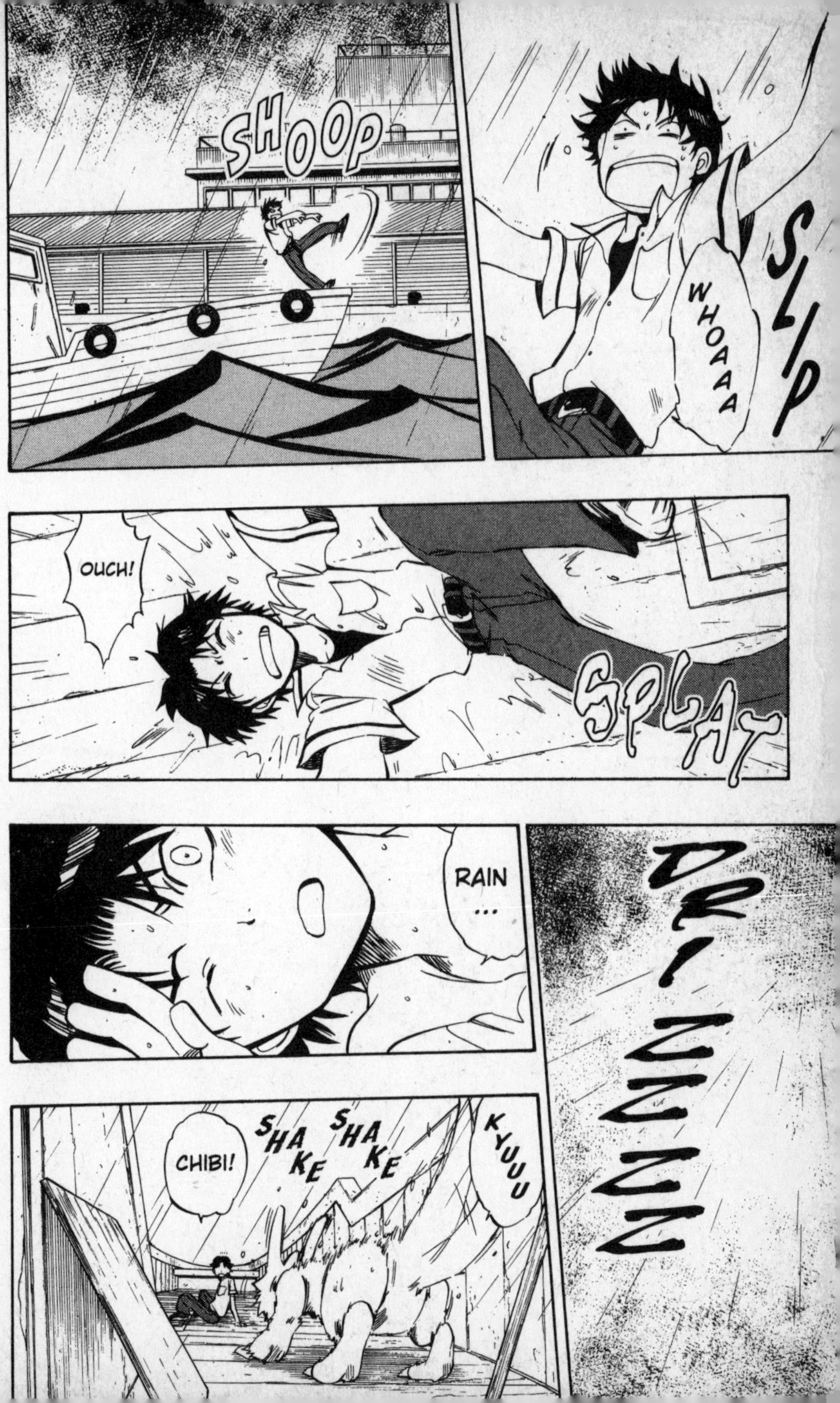
SLIP
WHOAAA
SHOOP
OUCH!
SPLAT
DRIZZZZZ
RAIN ...
KYUUU
SHAKE SHAKE
CHIBI!

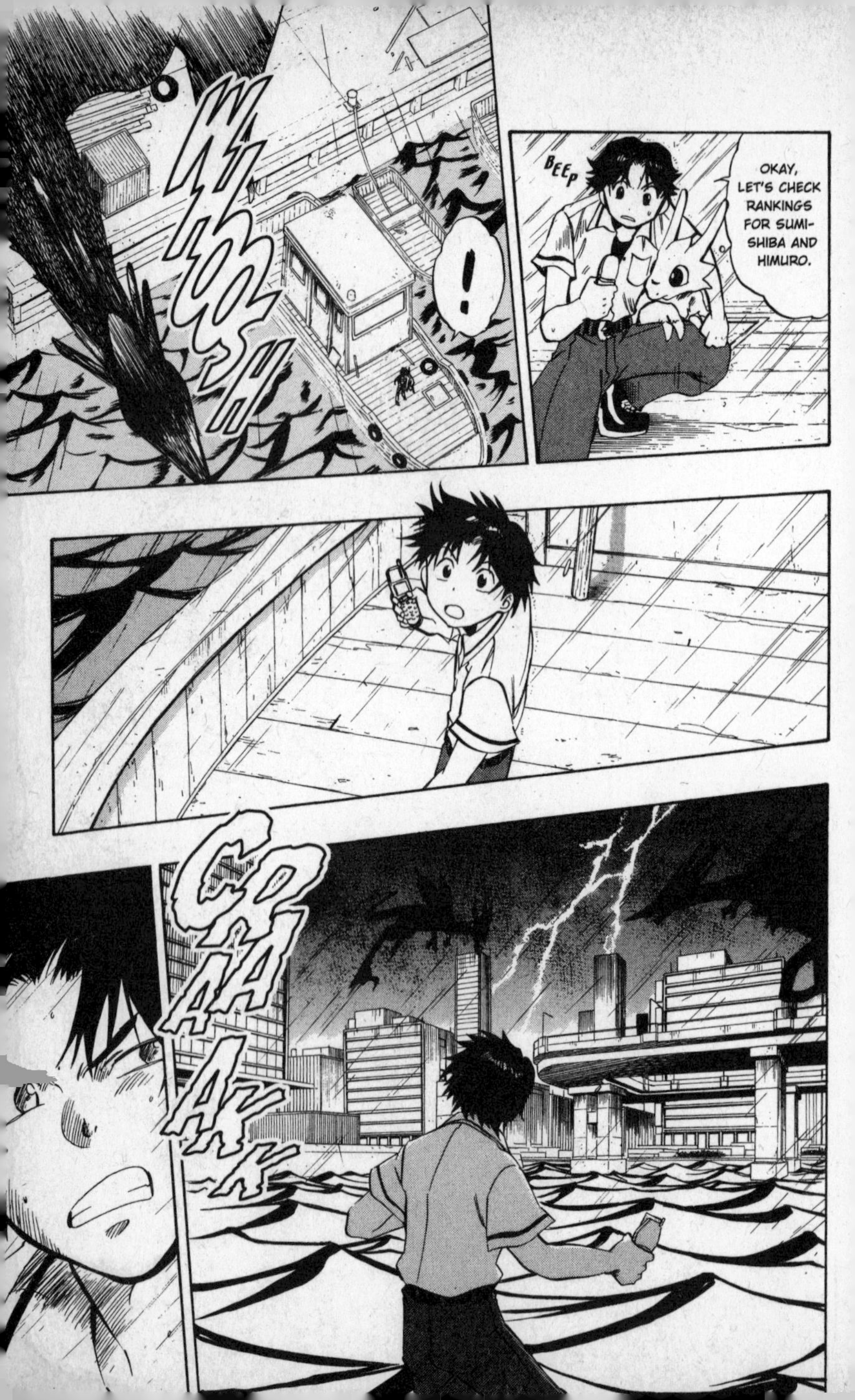
BEEP
OKAY, LET'S CHECK RANKINGS FOR SUMI-SHIBA AND HIMURO.
WHOOSH
!
CRAAAAK

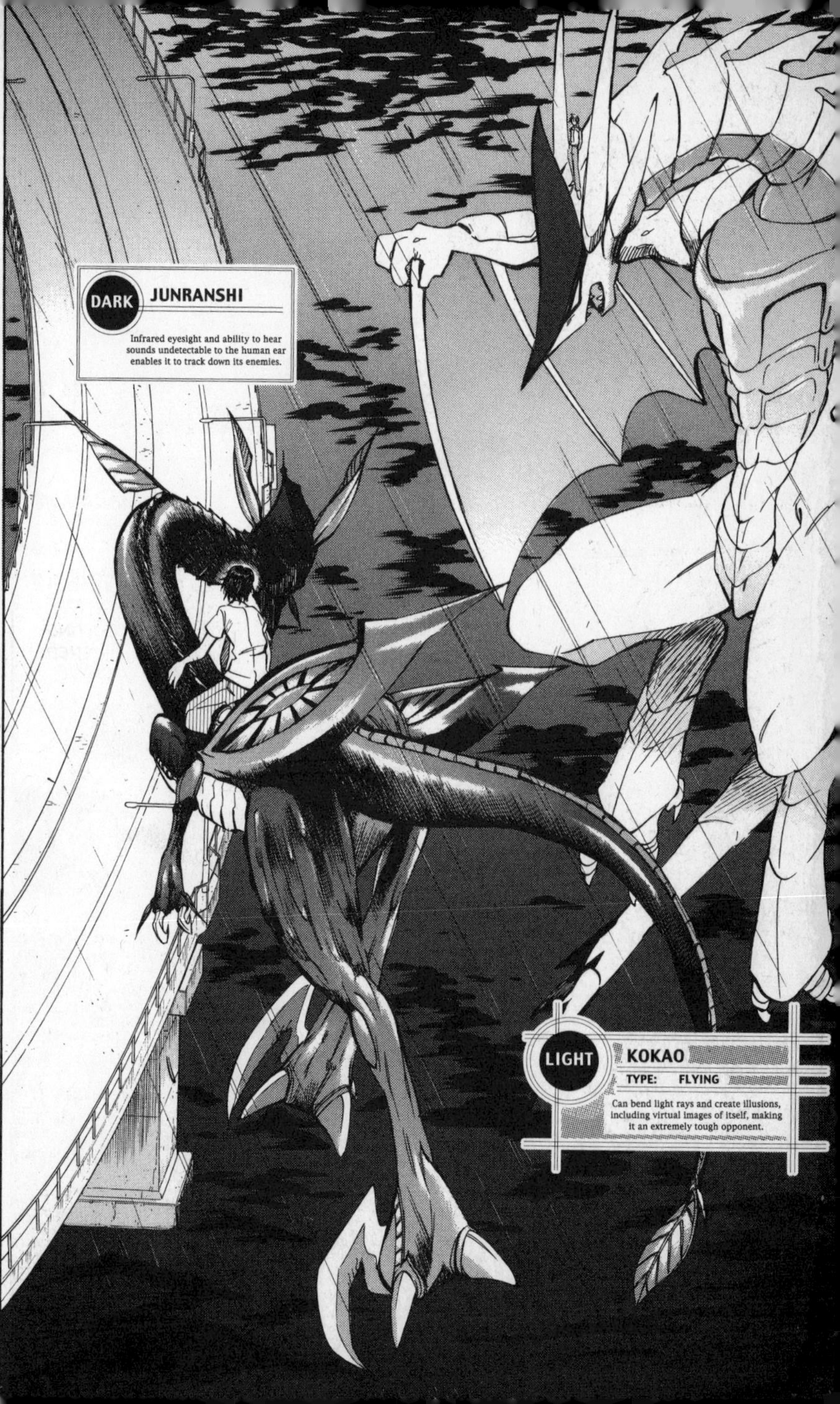
DARK
JUNRANSHI
Infrared eyesight and ability to hear sounds undetectable to the human ear enables it to track down its enemies.
LIGHT
KOKAO
TYPE: FLYING
Can bend light rays and create illusions, including virtual images of itself, making it an extremely tough opponent.

READ THIS WAY

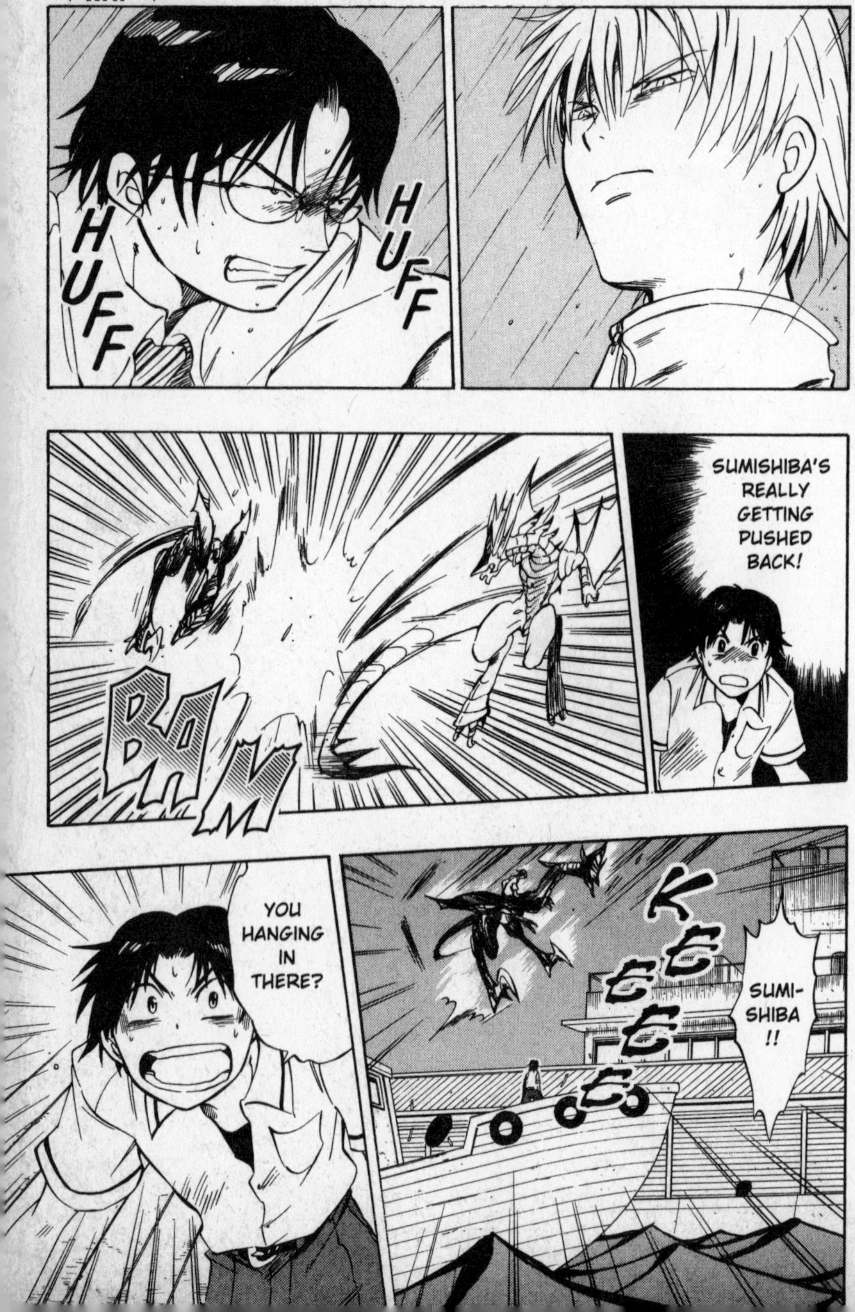
HUFF
HUFF
SUMISHIBA'S REALLY GETTING PUSHED BACK!
BAM
KEEEEE
SUMI-SHIBA!!
YOU HANGING IN THERE?

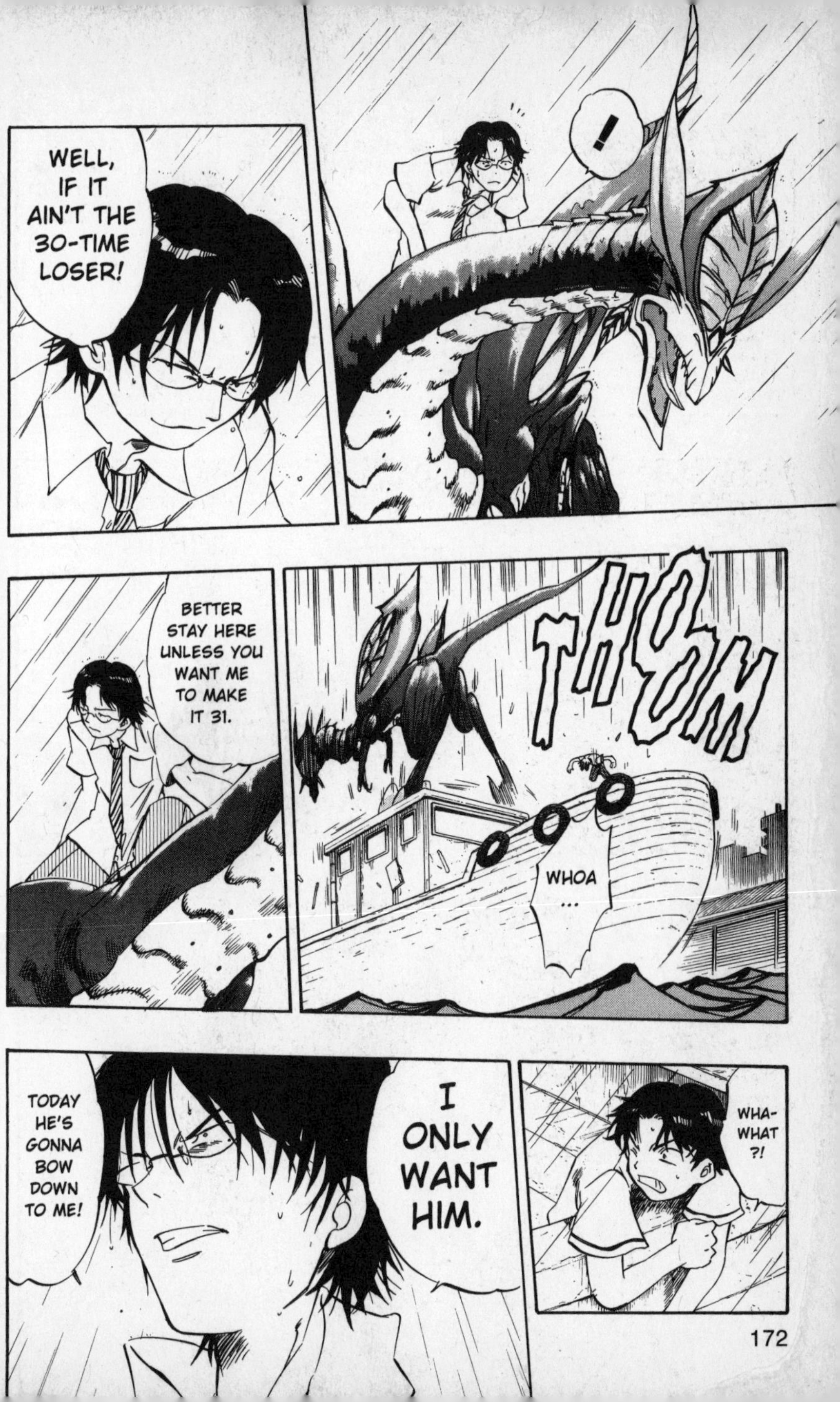
!
WELL, IF IT AIN'T THE 30-TIME LOSER!
THOM
WHOA ...
BETTER STAY HERE UNLESS YOU WANT ME TO MAKE IT 31.
WHA-WHAT?!
I ONLY WANT HIM.
TODAY HE'S GONNA BOW DOWN TO ME!

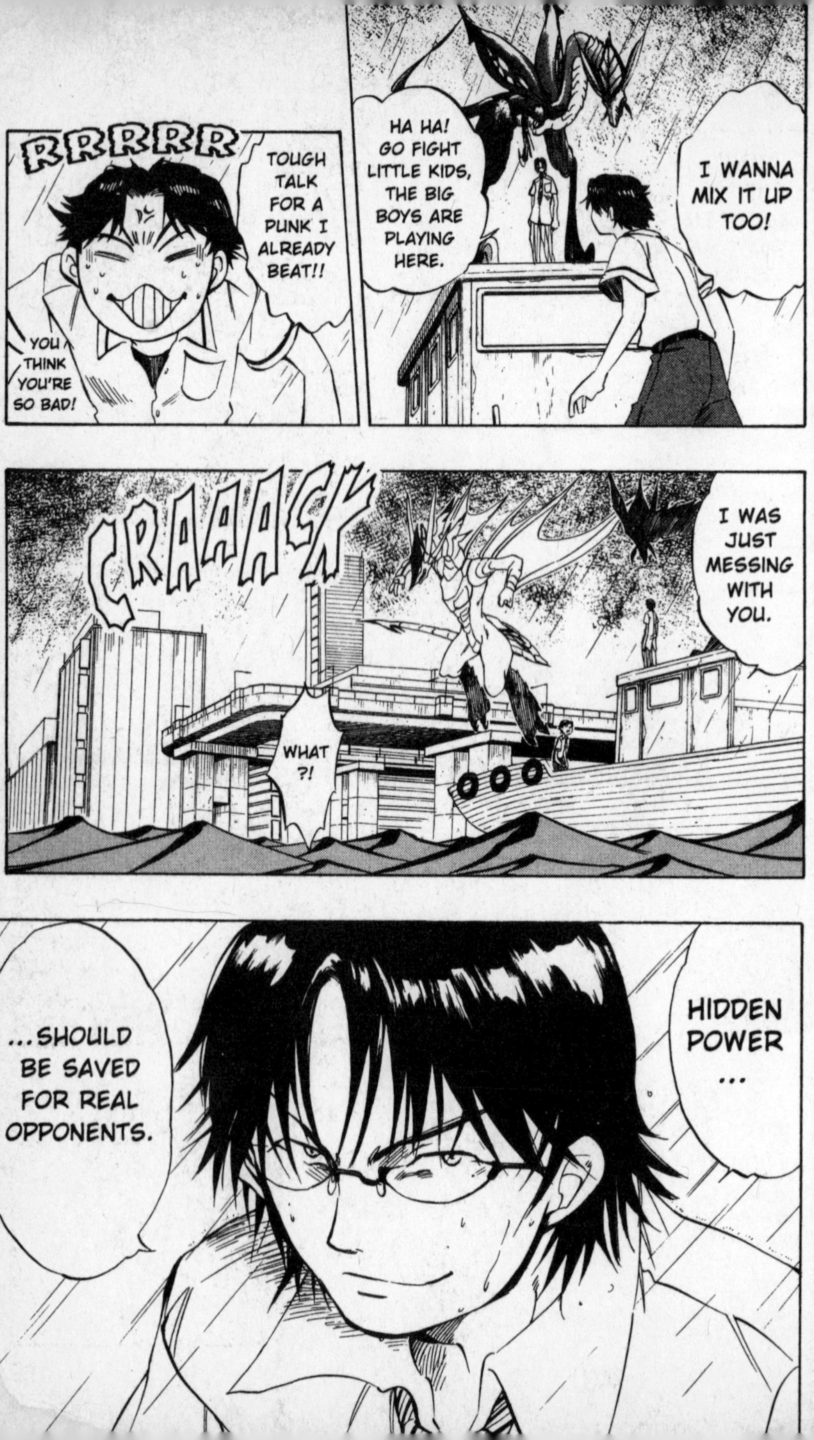
I WANNA MIX IT UP TOO!
HA HA! GO FIGHT LITTLE KIDS, THE BIG BOYS ARE PLAYING HERE.
RRRRR
TOUGH TALK FOR A PUNK I ALREADY BEAT!!
YOU THINK YOU'RE SO BAD!
I WAS JUST MESSING WITH YOU.
CRAAACK
WHAT?!
HIDDEN POWER...
...SHOULD BE SAVED FOR REAL OPPONENTS.

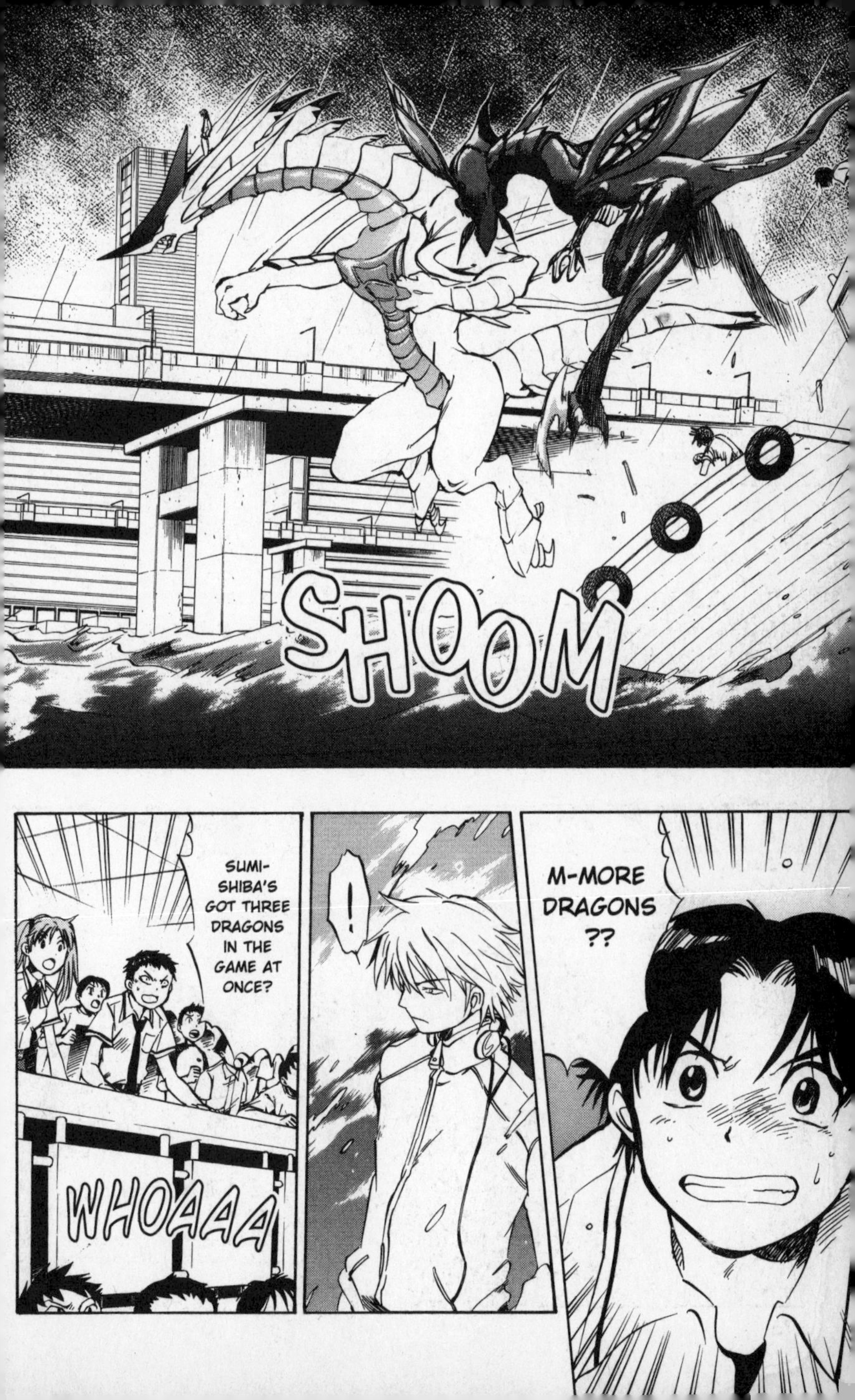
SHOOM
M-MORE DRAGONS ??
!
SUMI-SHIBA'S GOT THREE DRAGONS IN THE GAME AT ONCE?
WHOAAA

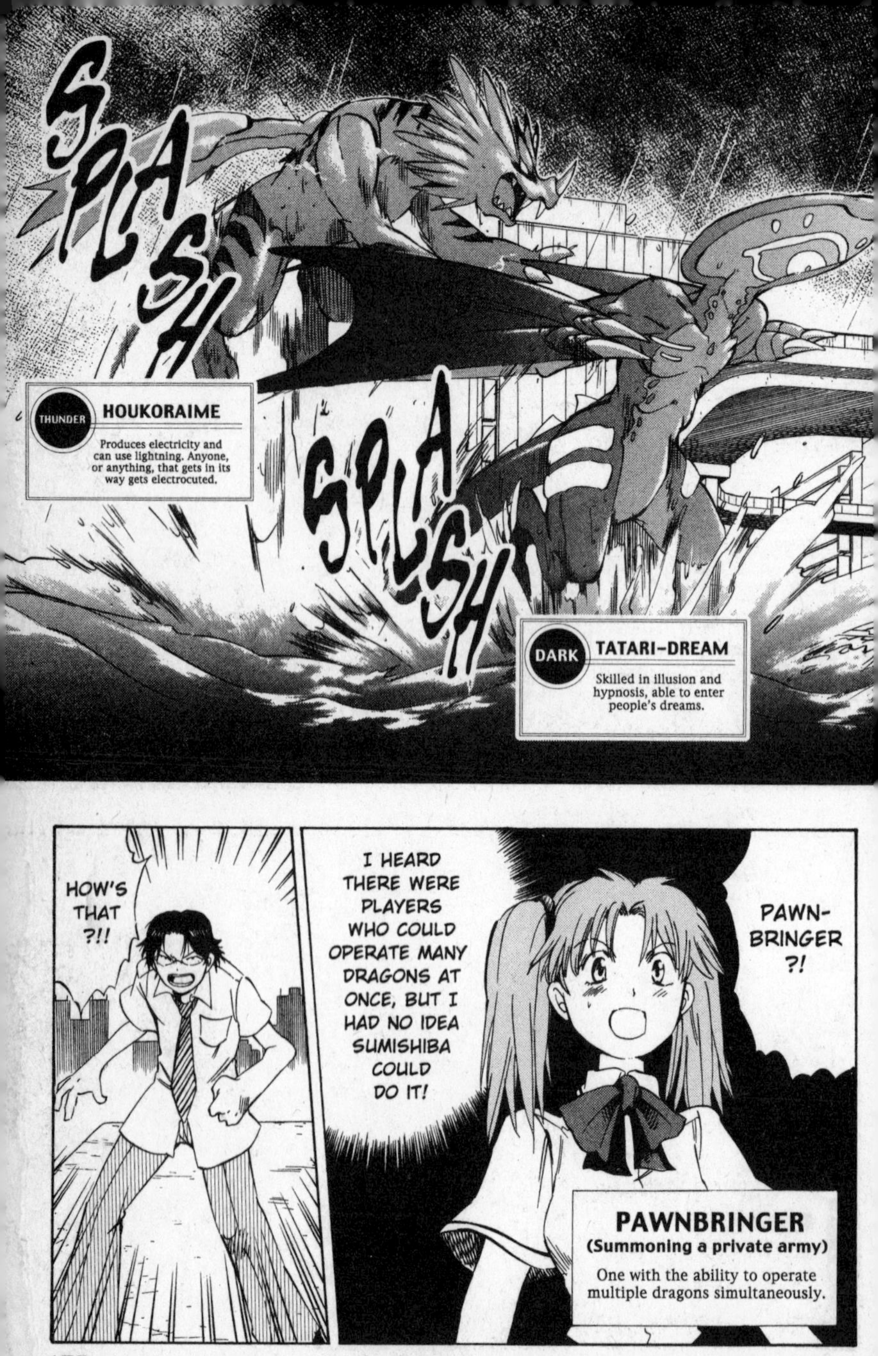
SPLASH
THUNDER HOUKORAIME
Produces electricity and can use lightning. Anyone, or anything, that gets in its way gets electrocuted.
SPLASH
DARK TATARI-DREAM
Skilled in illusion and hypnosis, able to enter people's dreams.
PAWN-BRINGER?!
I HEARD THERE WERE PLAYERS WHO COULD OPERATE MANY DRAGONS AT ONCE, BUT I HAD NO IDEA SUMISHIBA COULD DO IT!
PAWNBRINGER (Summoning a private army)
One with the ability to operate multiple dragons simultaneously.
HOW'S THAT?!!

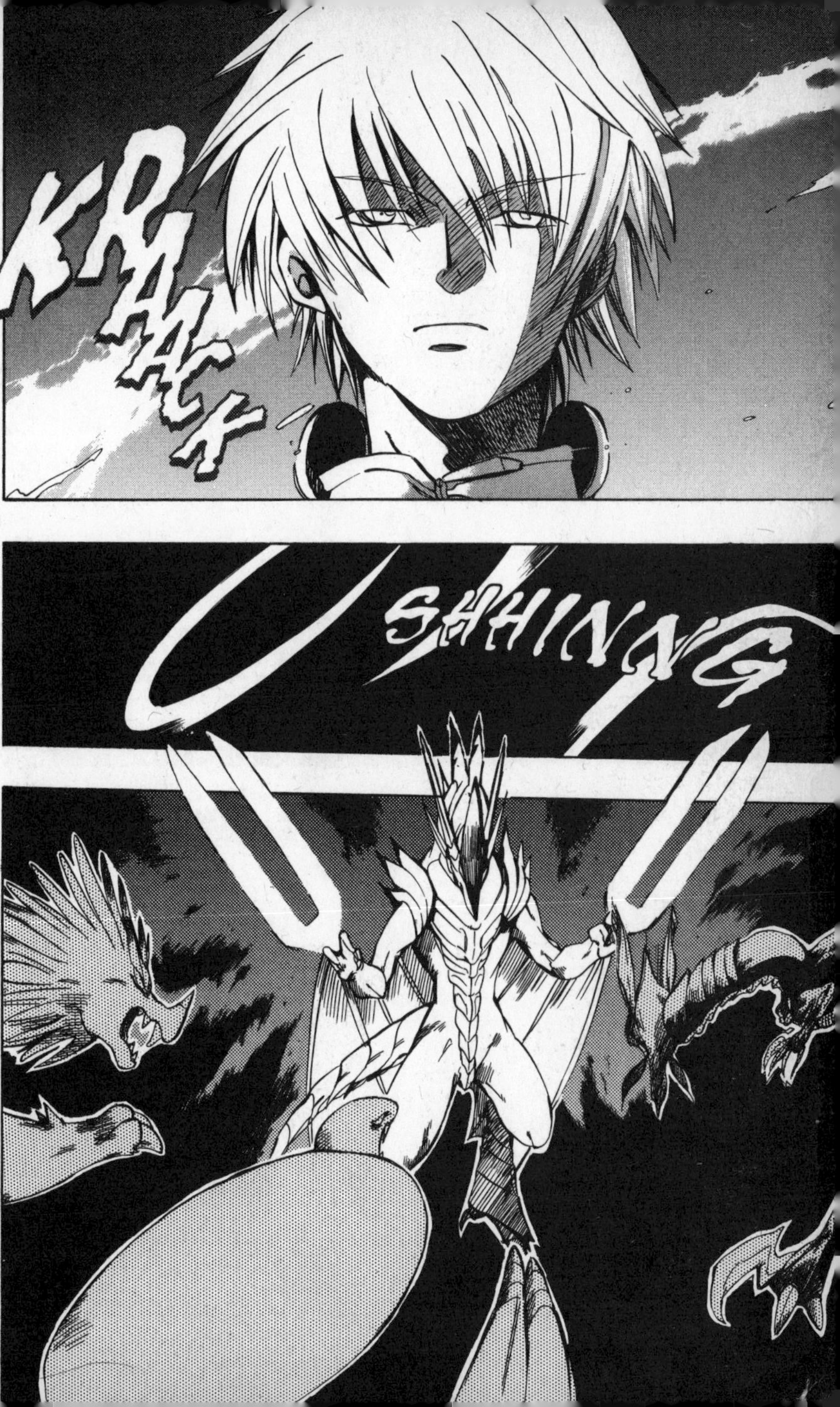
KRACK
SHHINNG

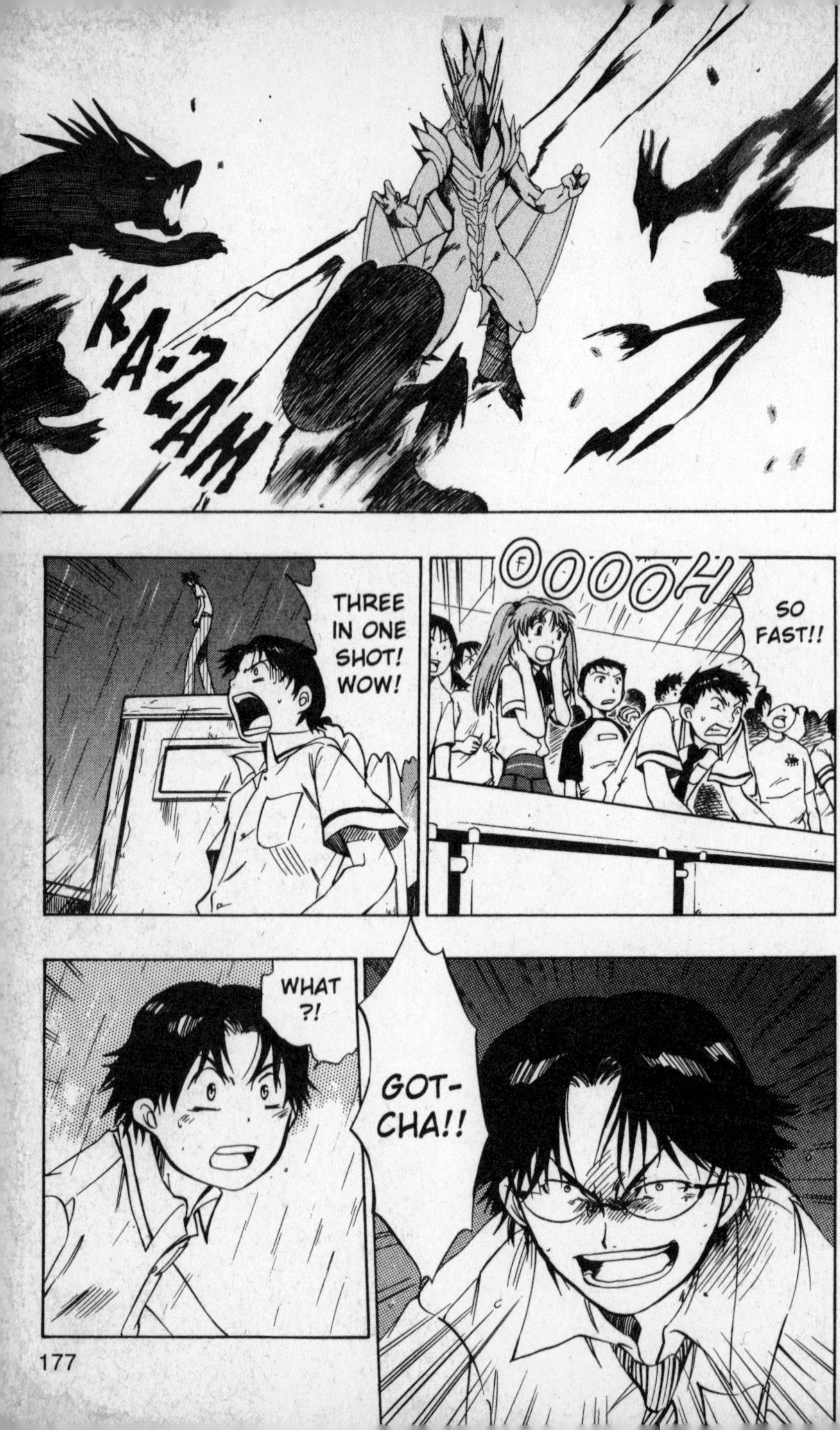
KA-ZAM
OOOOH
SO FAST!!
THREE IN ONE SHOT! WOW!
GOT-CHA!!
WHAT ?!

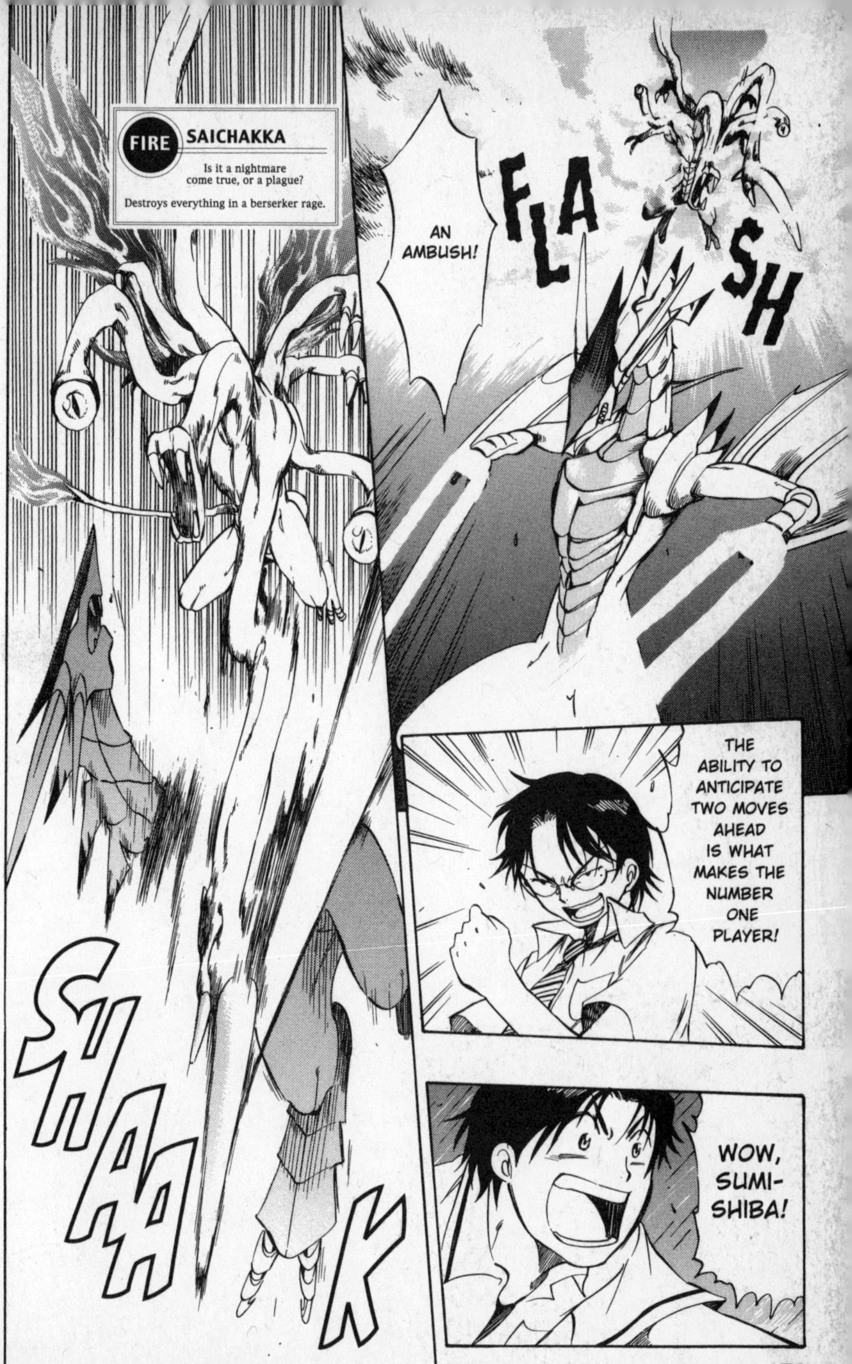
AN AMBUSH!
FLASH
THE ABILITY TO ANTICIPATE TWO MOVES AHEAD IS WHAT MAKES THE NUMBER ONE PLAYER!
WOW, SUMI-SHIBA!
FIRE
SAICHAKKA
Is it a nightmare come true, or a plague?
Destroys everything in a berserker rage.
SHAAK

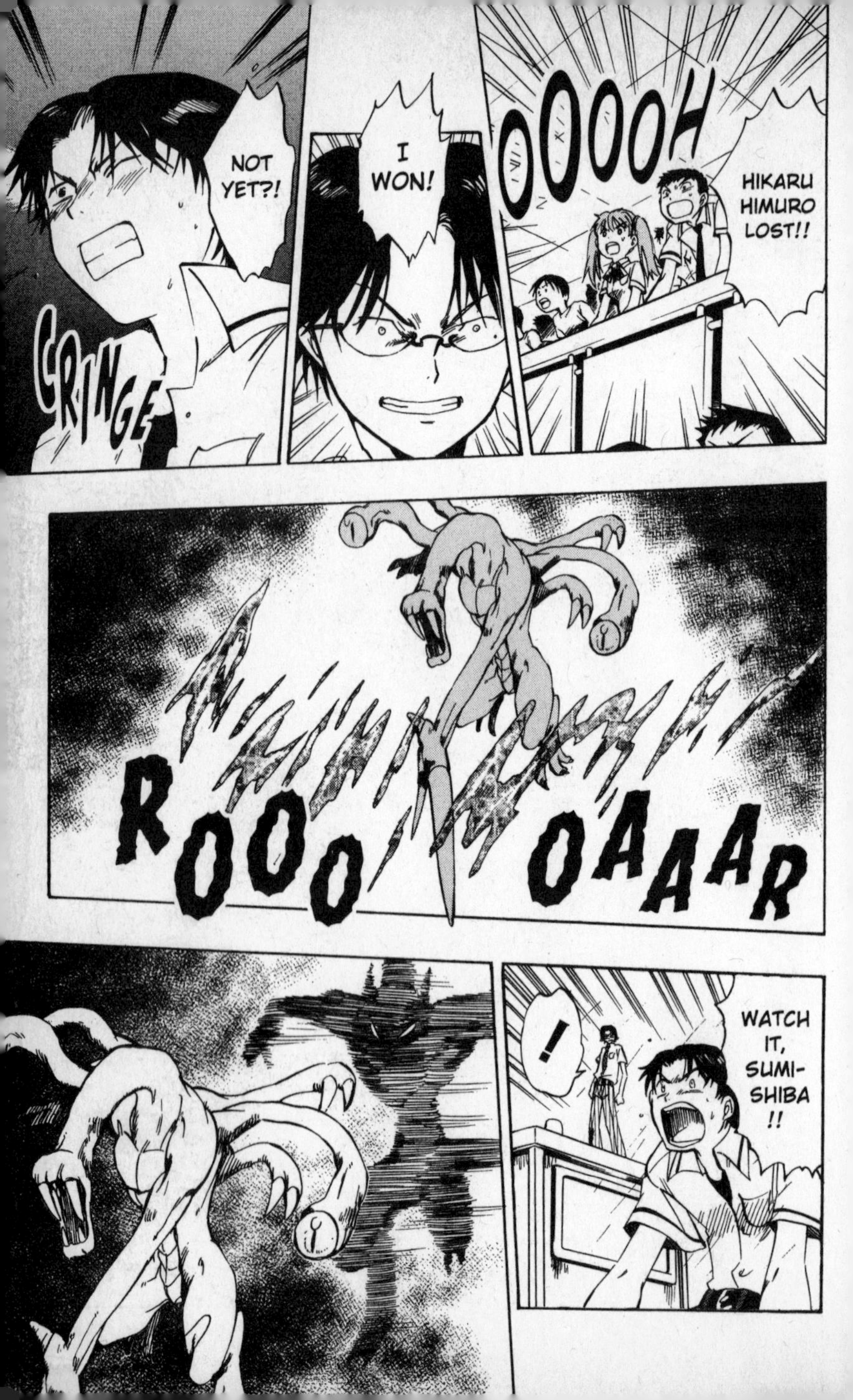
OOOOH
HIKARU HIMURO LOST!!
I WON!
NOT YET?!
CRINGE
ROOO OAAAR
WATCH IT, SUMI-SHIBA!!
!

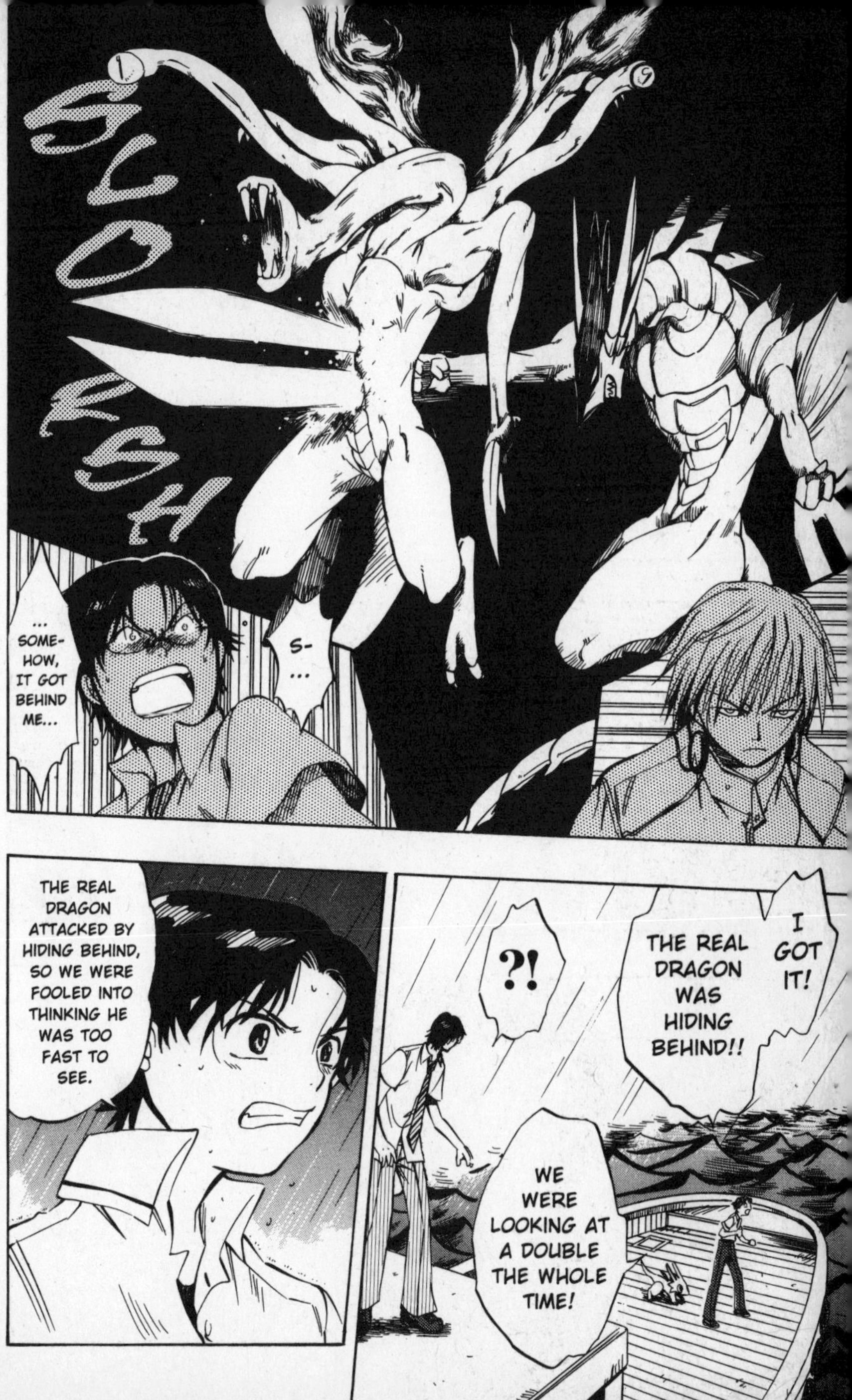
SWOOSH
S-...
...SOMEHOW, IT GOT BEHIND ME...
I GOT IT!
THE REAL DRAGON WAS HIDING BEHIND!!
?!
WE WERE LOOKING AT A DOUBLE THE WHOLE TIME!
THE REAL DRAGON ATTACKED BY HIDING BEHIND, SO WE WERE FOOLED INTO THINKING HE WAS TOO FAST TO SEE.

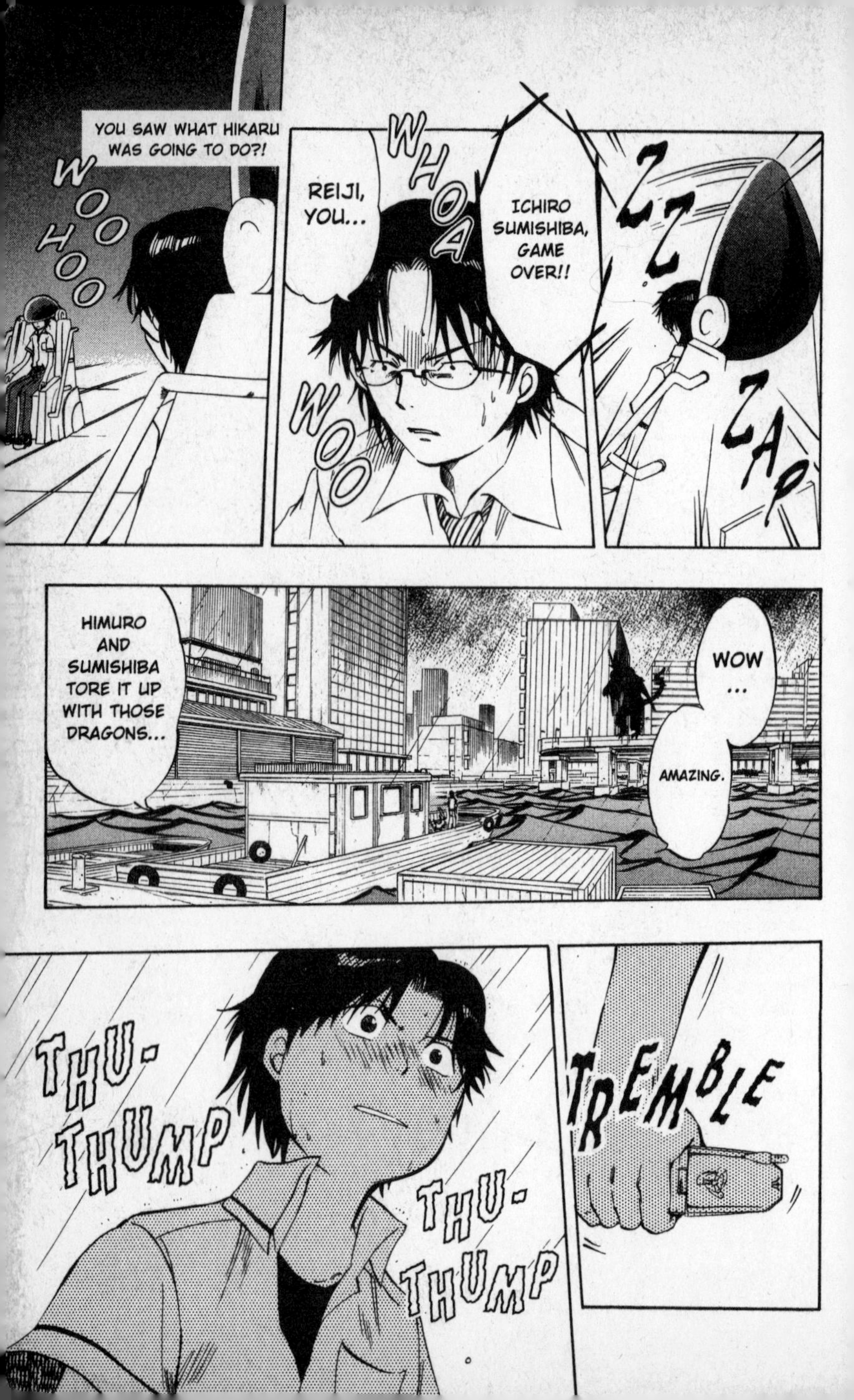
ZZZ
ZAP
ICHIRO SUMISHIBA, GAME OVER!!
WHOA
REIJI, YOU...
WOO
YOU SAW WHAT HIKARU WAS GOING TO DO?!
WOO HOO HOO
WOW...
AMAZING.
HIMURO AND SUMISHIBA TORE IT UP WITH THOSE DRAGONS...
TREMBLE
THU-THUMP
THU-THUMP

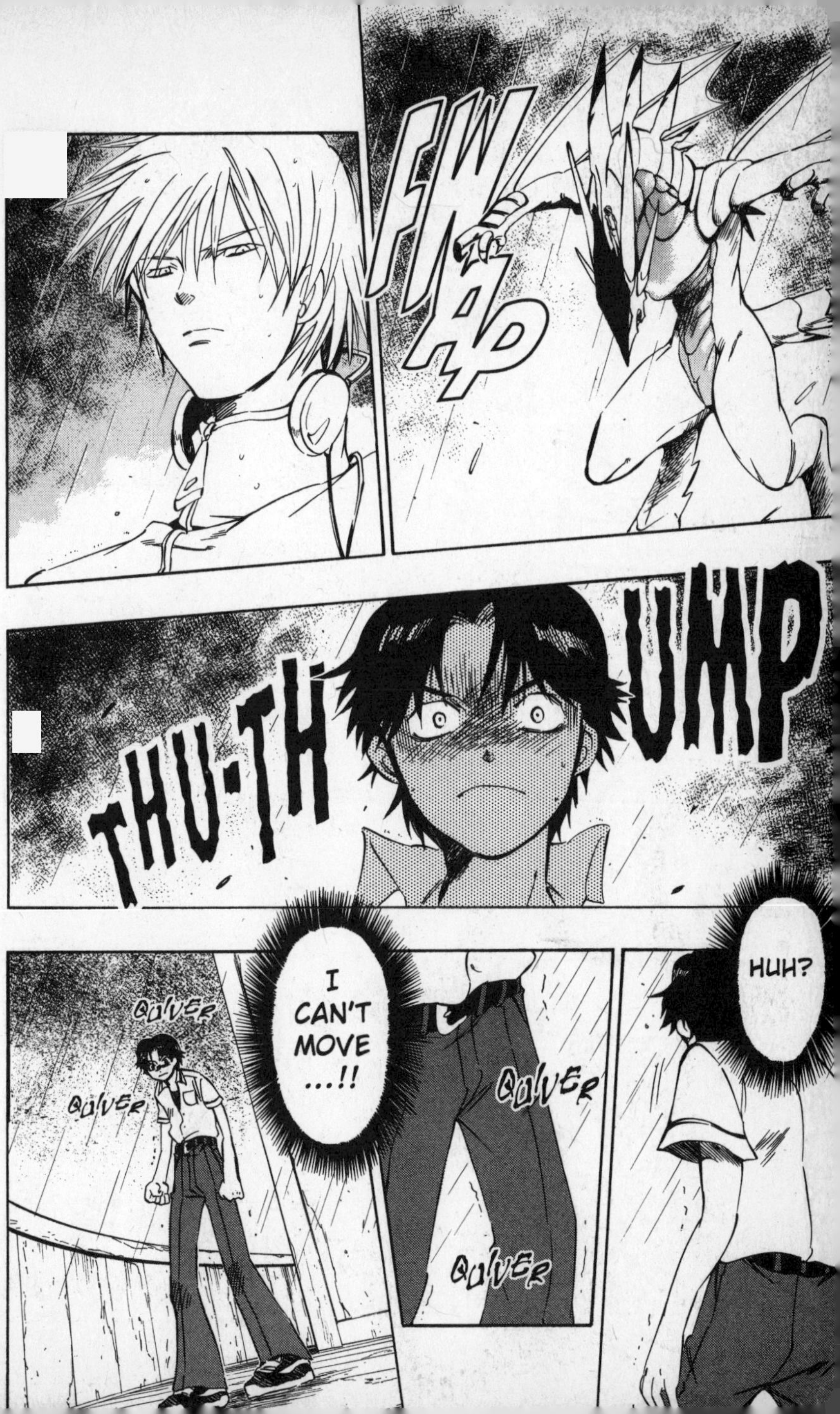
FWAP
THU-THUMP
HUH?
I CAN'T MOVE ...!!
QUIVER
QUIVER
QUIVER
QUIVER

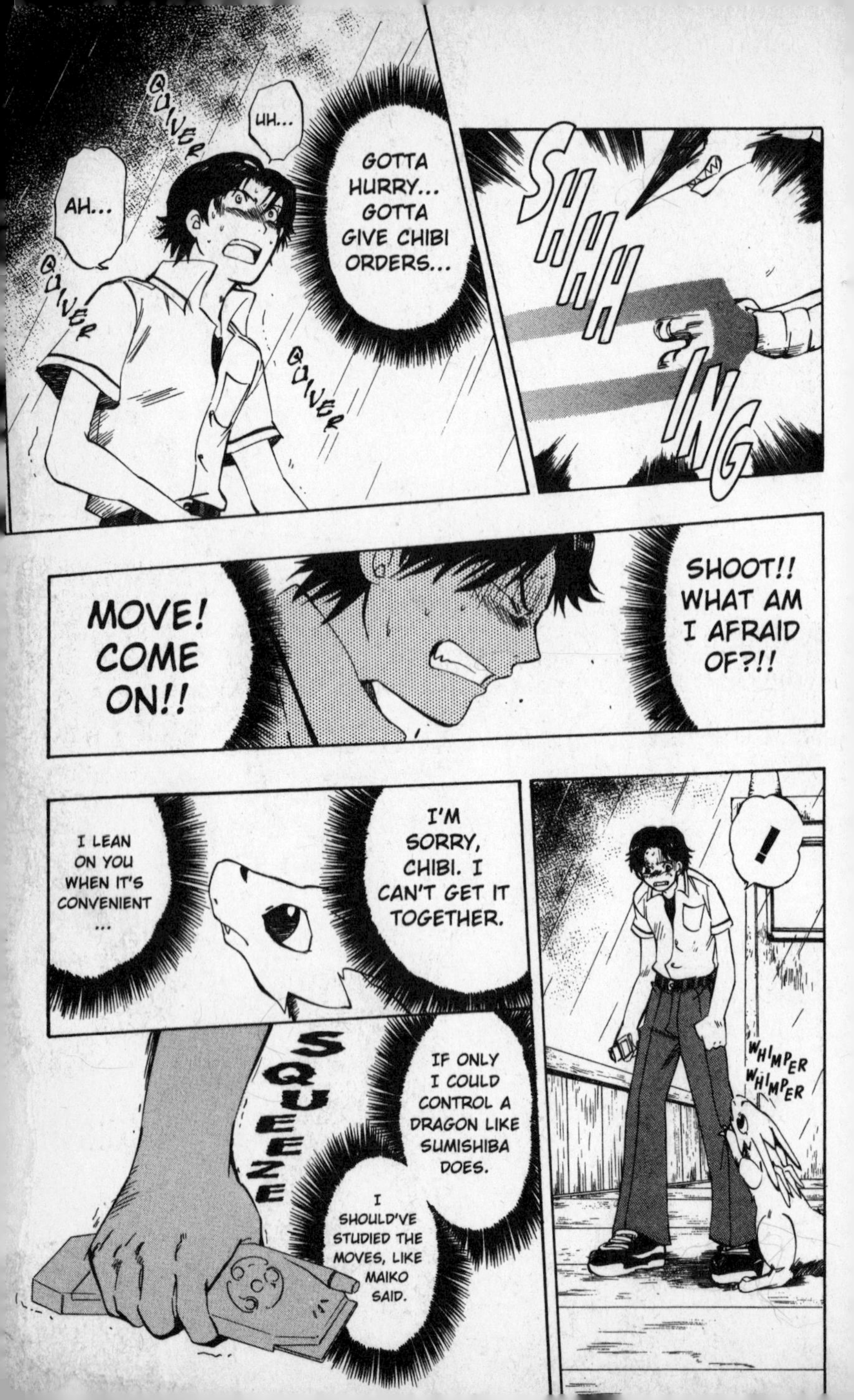
SCHING
UH...
GOTTA HURRY... GOTTA GIVE CHIBI ORDERS...
QUIVER
AH...
QUIVER
QUIVER
SHOOT!! WHAT AM I AFRAID OF?!!
MOVE! COME ON!!
!
WHIMPER WHIMPER
I'M SORRY, CHIBI. I CAN'T GET IT TOGETHER.
I LEAN ON YOU WHEN IT'S CONVENIENT ...
SQUEEZE
IF ONLY I COULD CONTROL A DRAGON LIKE SUMISHIBA DOES.
I SHOULD'VE STUDIED THE MOVES, LIKE MAIKO SAID.

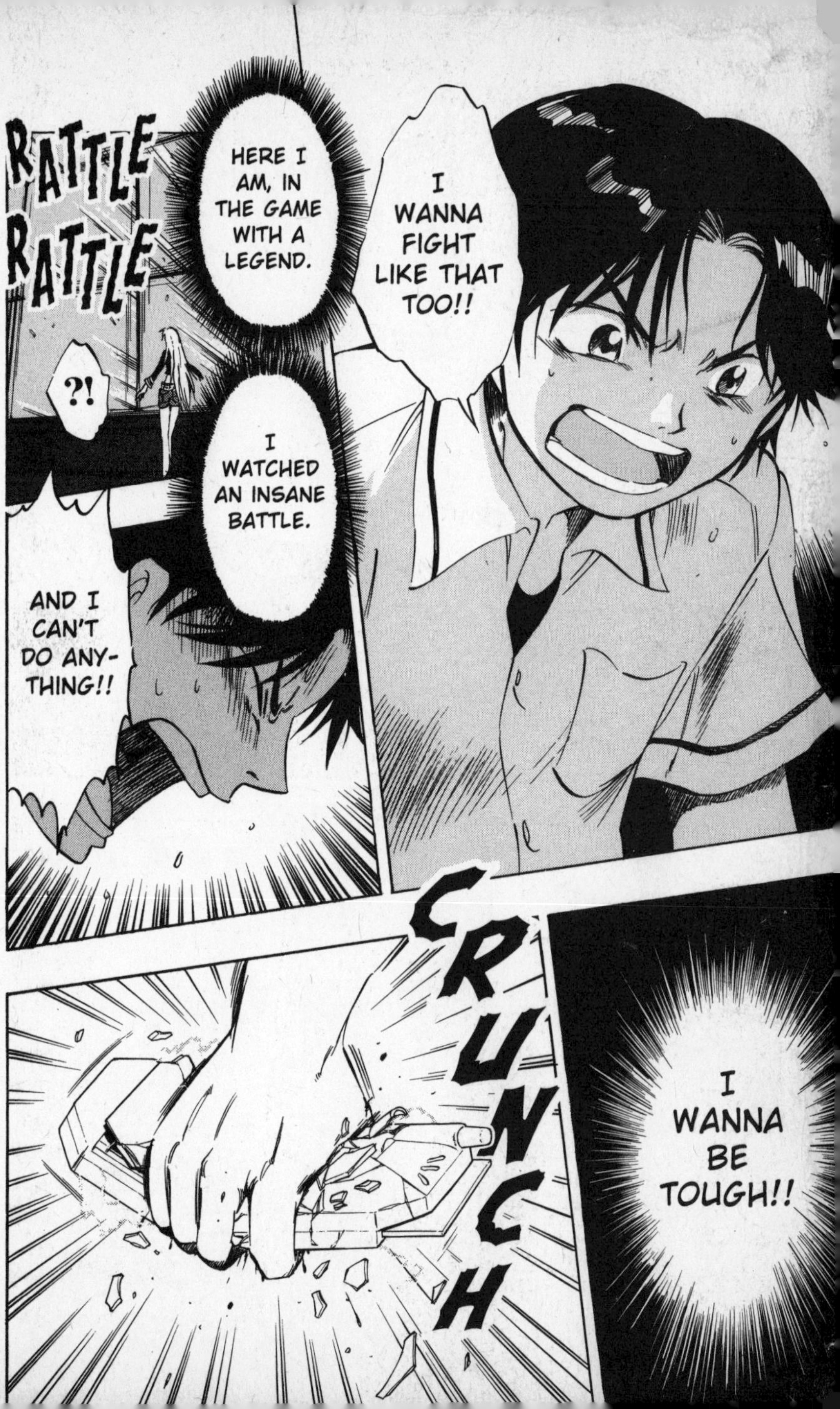
I WANNA FIGHT LIKE THAT TOO!!
HERE I AM, IN THE GAME WITH A LEGEND.
RATTLE RATTLE
?!
I WATCHED AN INSANE BATTLE.
AND I CAN'T DO ANY-THING!!
I WANNA BE TOUGH!!
CRUNCH

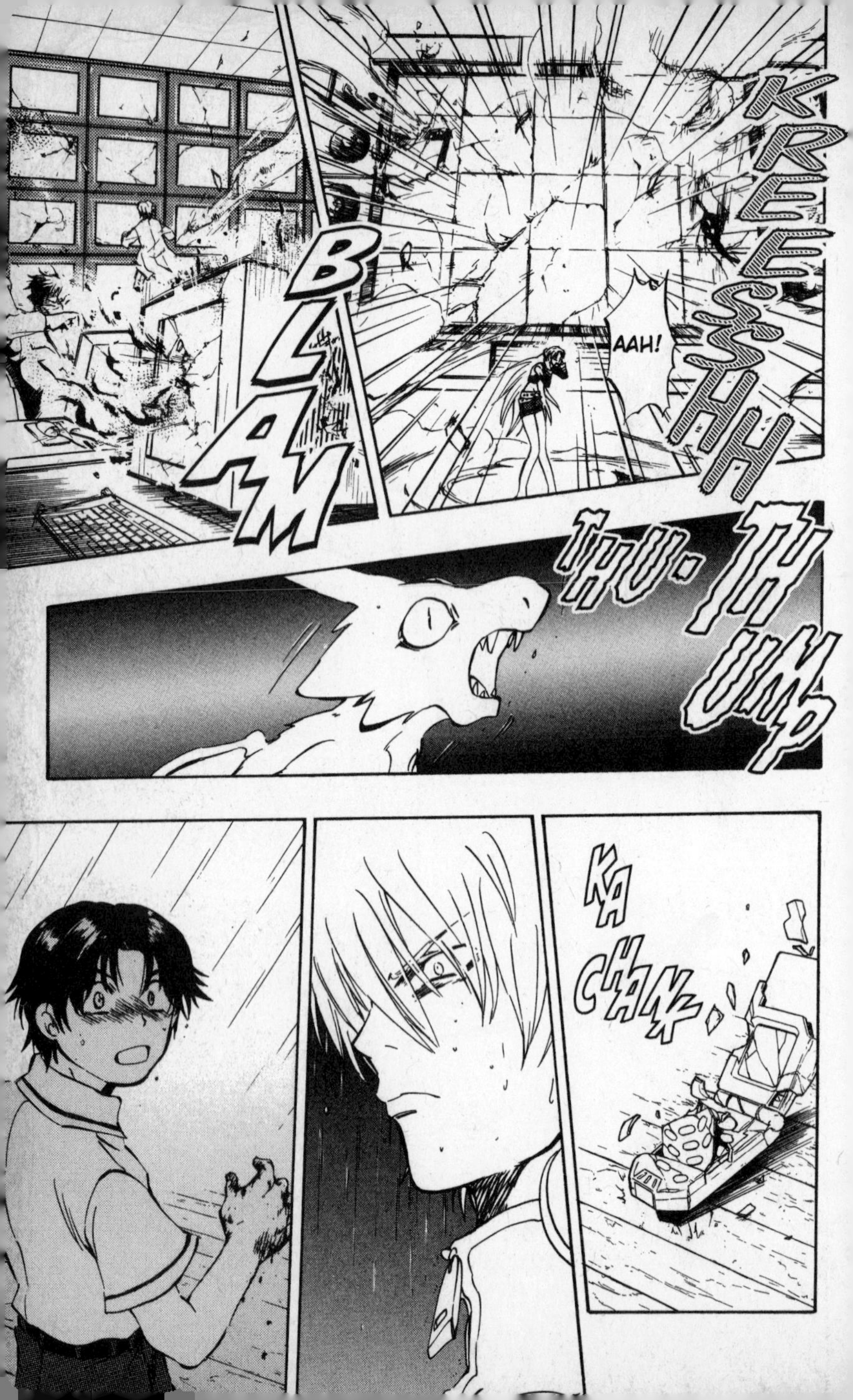
KRESSHH
AAH!
BLAM
THU-THUMP
KA CHANK

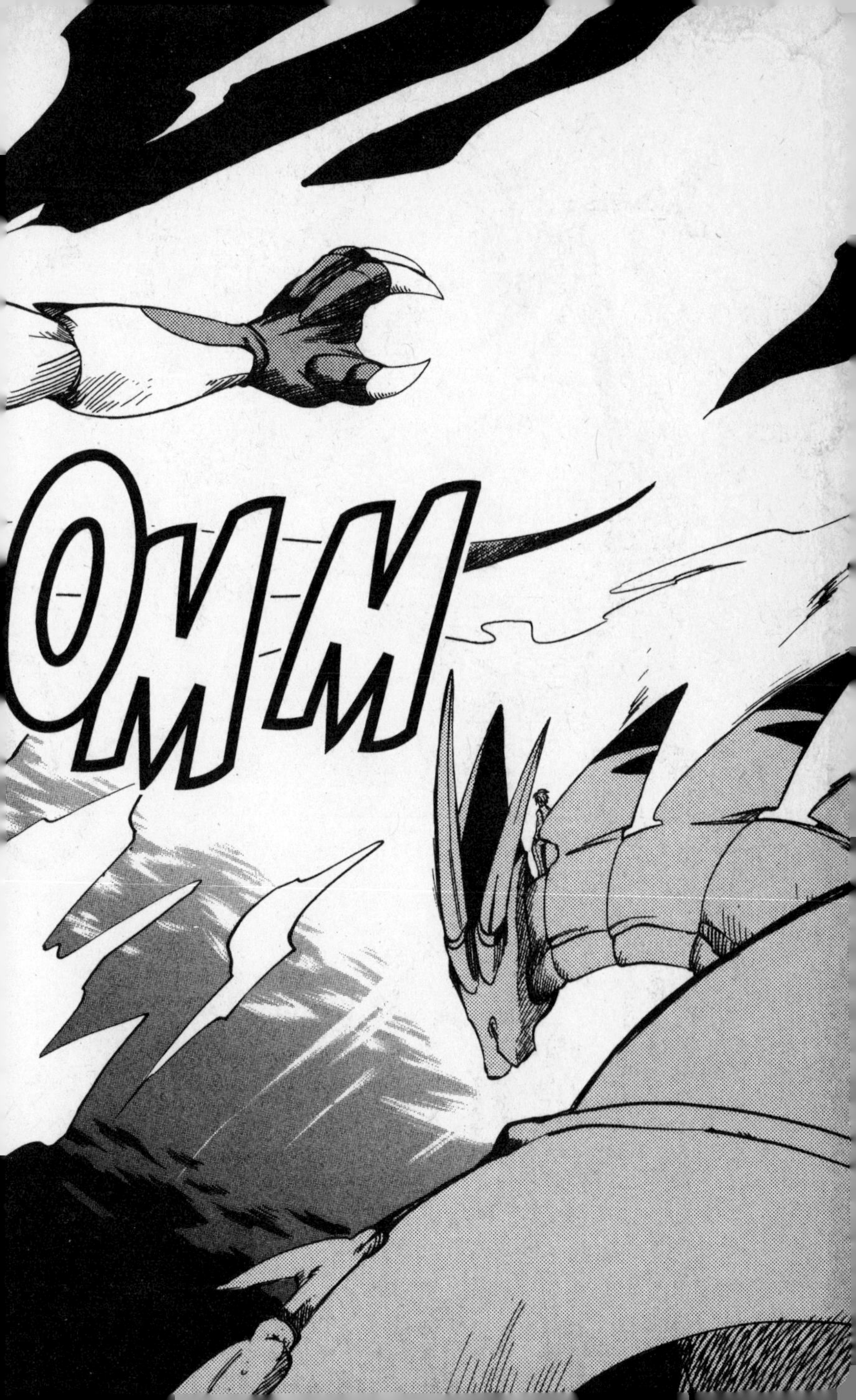
OMMM

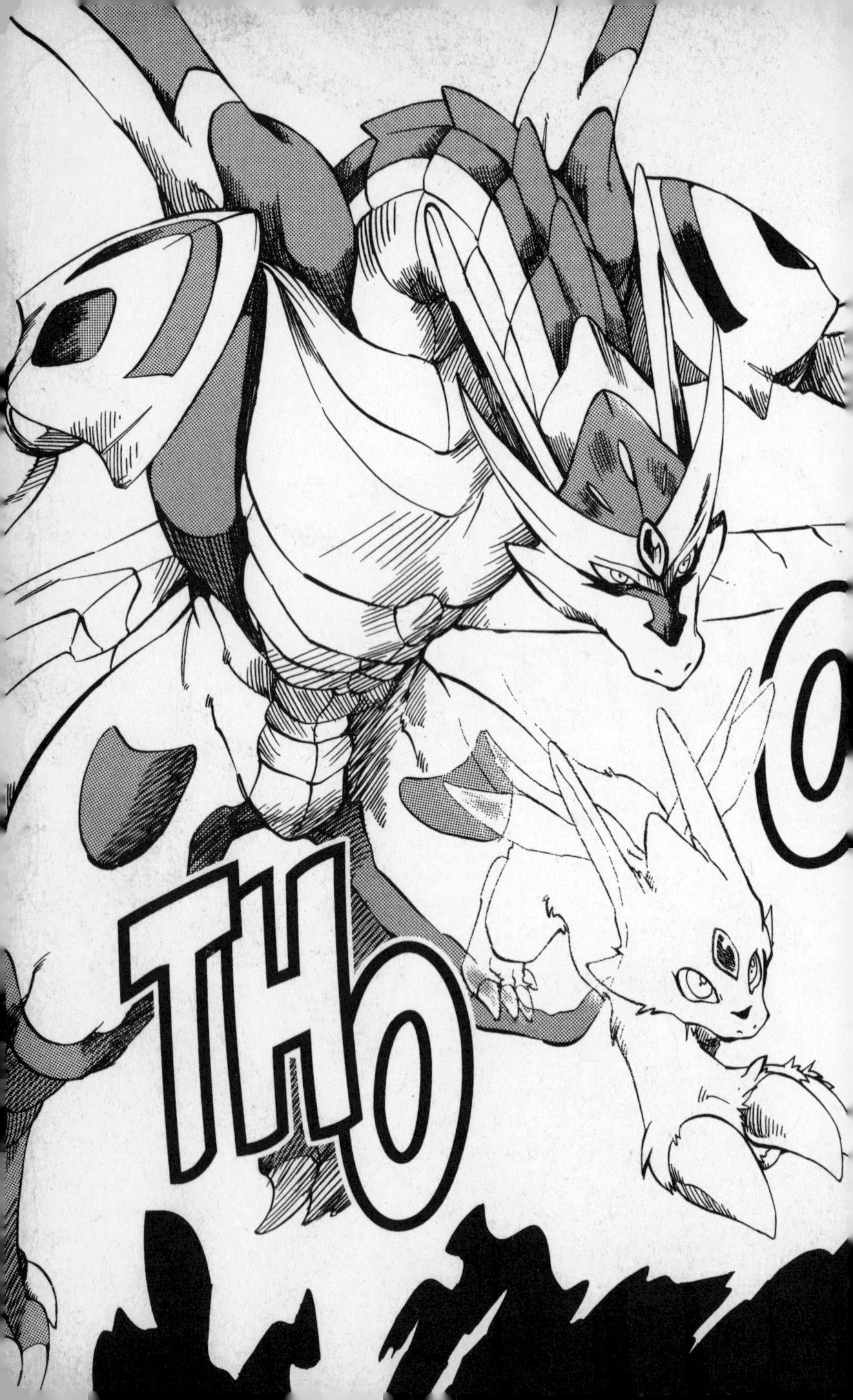
THO

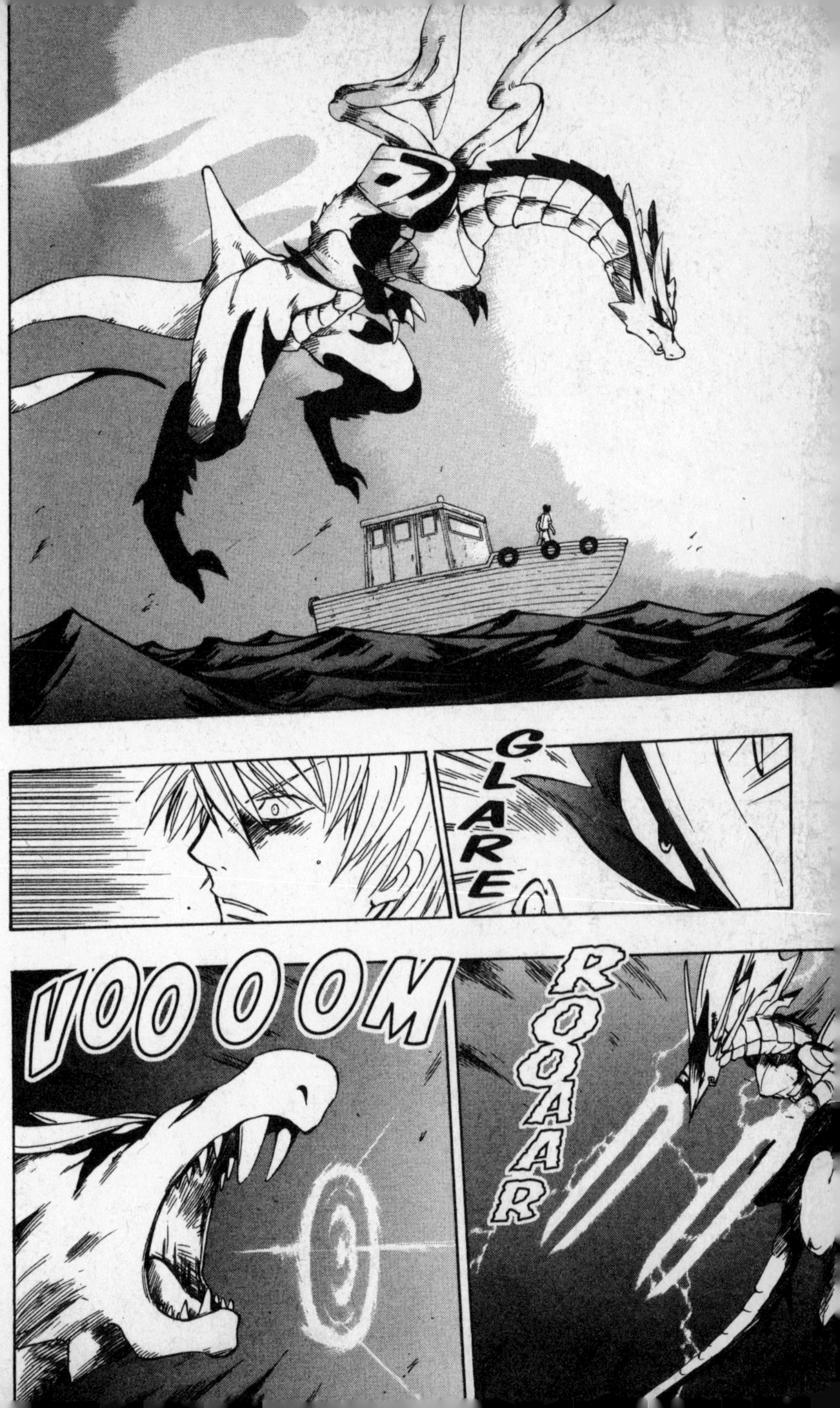
GLARE
ROOAAR
VOOOOM

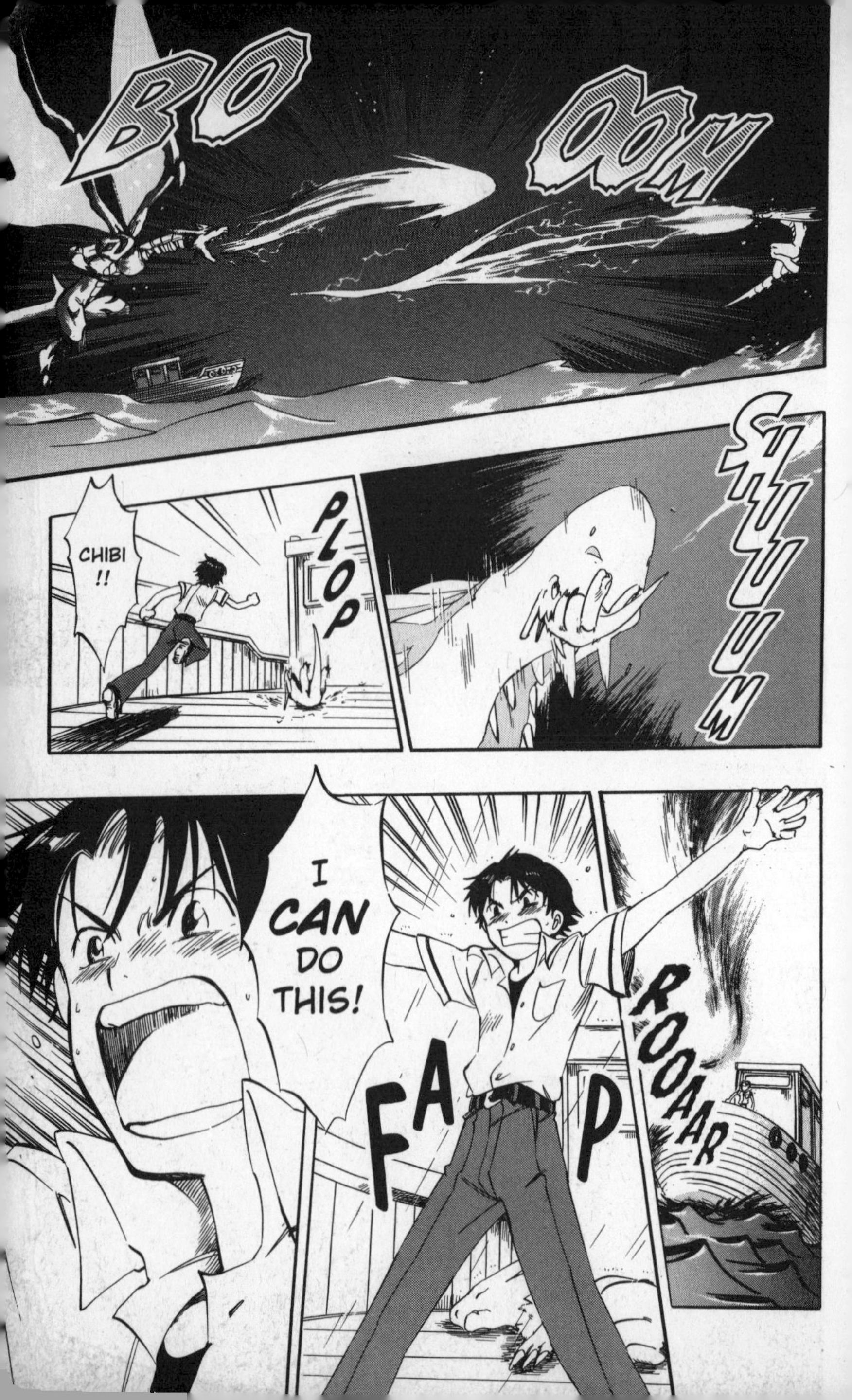
BOOOM
SHUUUM
PLOP
CHIBI!!
ROOOAAR
FAP
I CAN DO THIS!

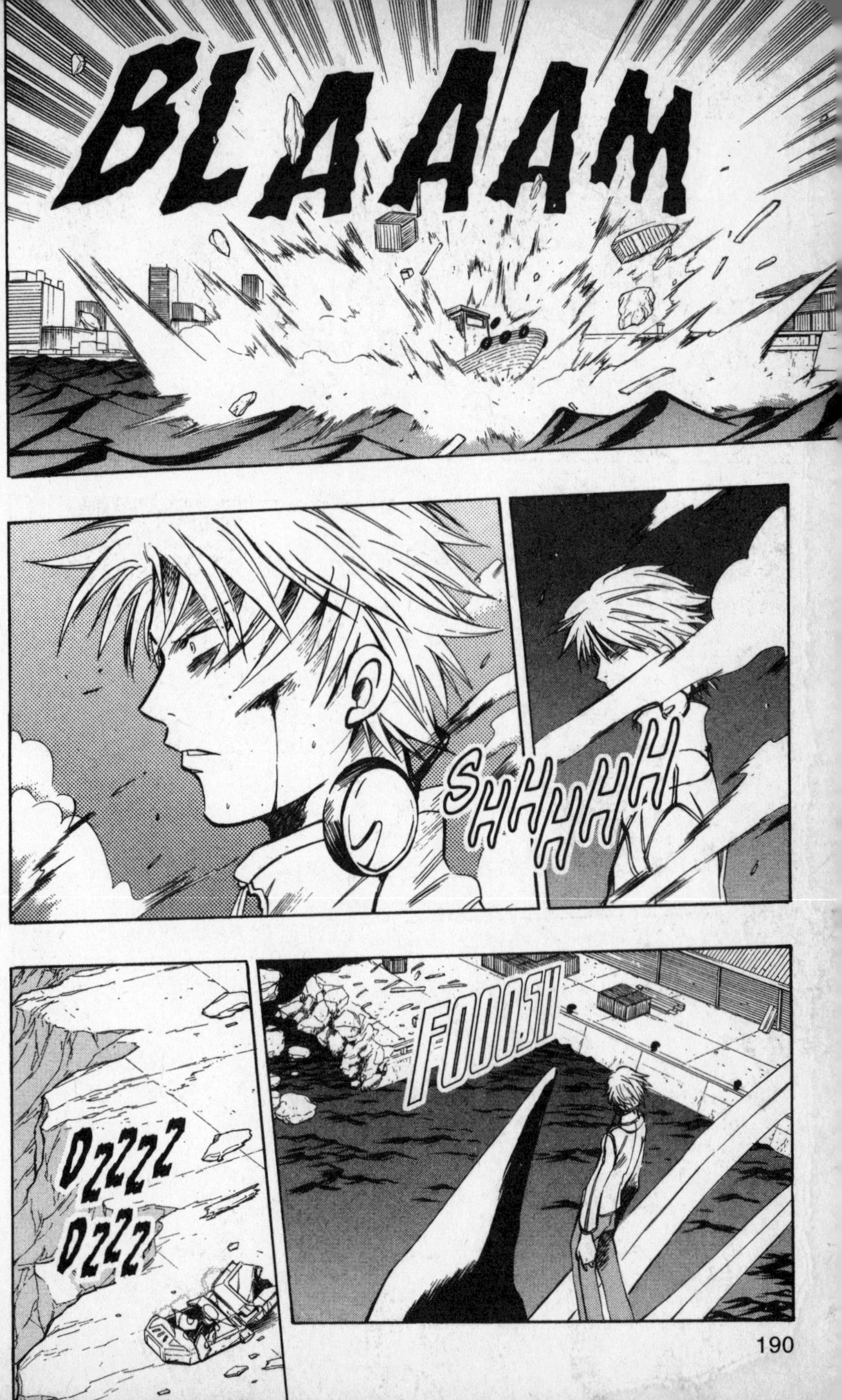
BLAAAM
SHHHHH
FOOOSH
DZZZZ
DZZZ

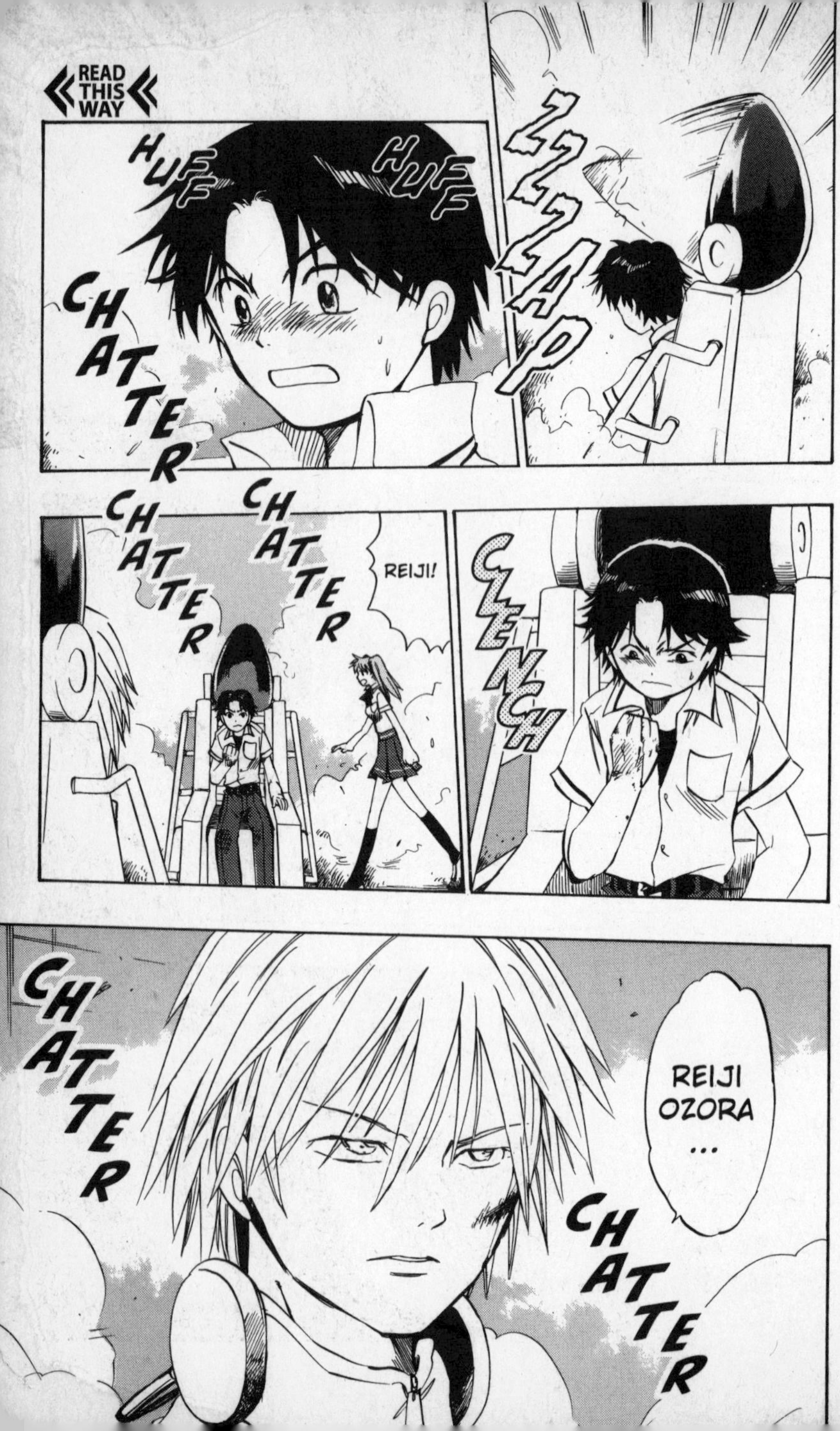
READ THIS WAY
ZZZAP
HUFF HUFF
CHATTER
CLENCH
REIJI!
CHATTER
CHATTER
CHATTER
REIJI OZORA ...
CHATTER

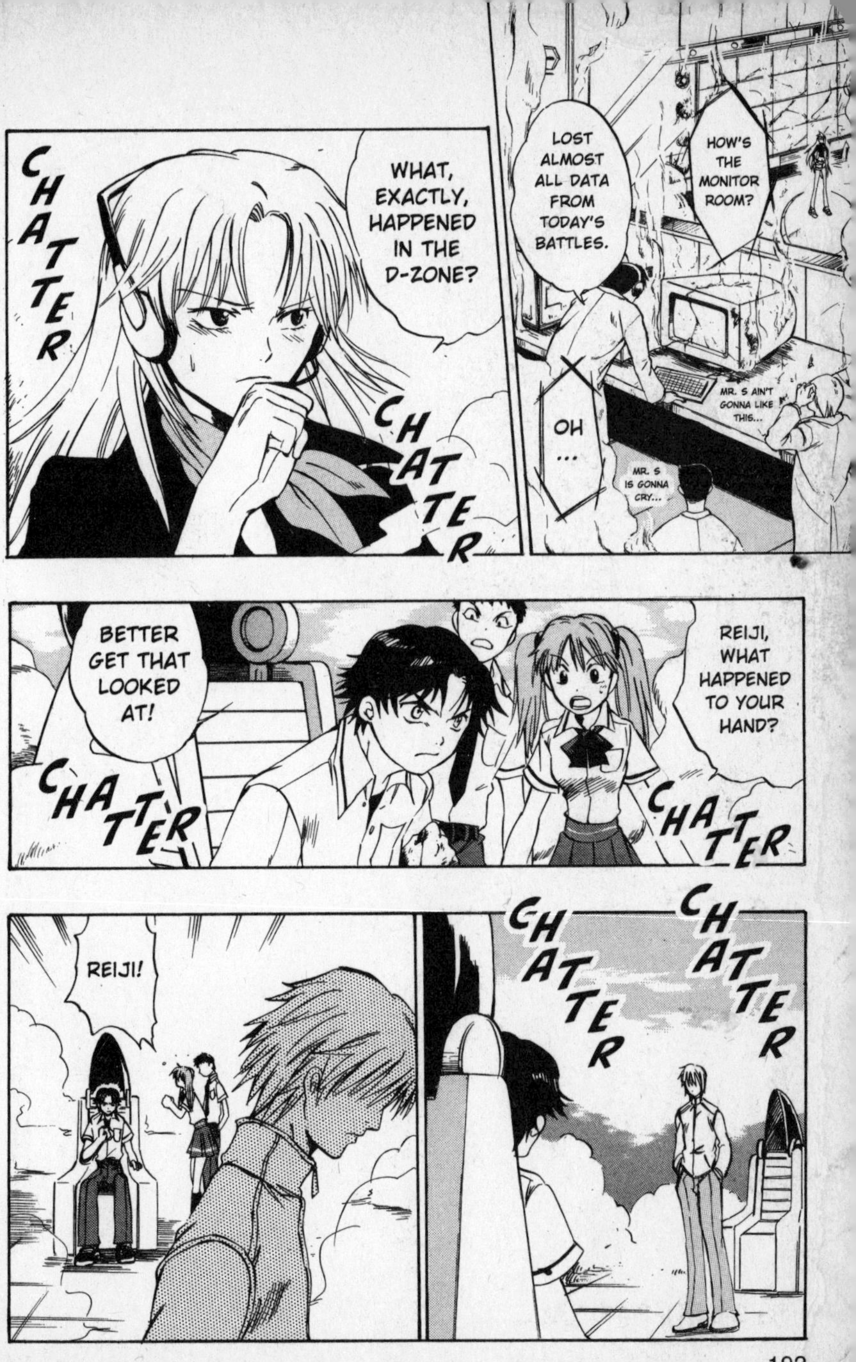
HOW'S THE MONITOR ROOM?
LOST ALMOST ALL DATA FROM TODAY'S BATTLES.
MR. S AIN'T GONNA LIKE THIS...
OH ...
MR. S IS GONNA CRY...
WHAT, EXACTLY, HAPPENED IN THE D-ZONE?
CHATTER
CHATTER
REIJI, WHAT HAPPENED TO YOUR HAND?
CHATTER
BETTER GET THAT LOOKED AT!
CHATTER
CHATTER
CHATTER
REIJI!

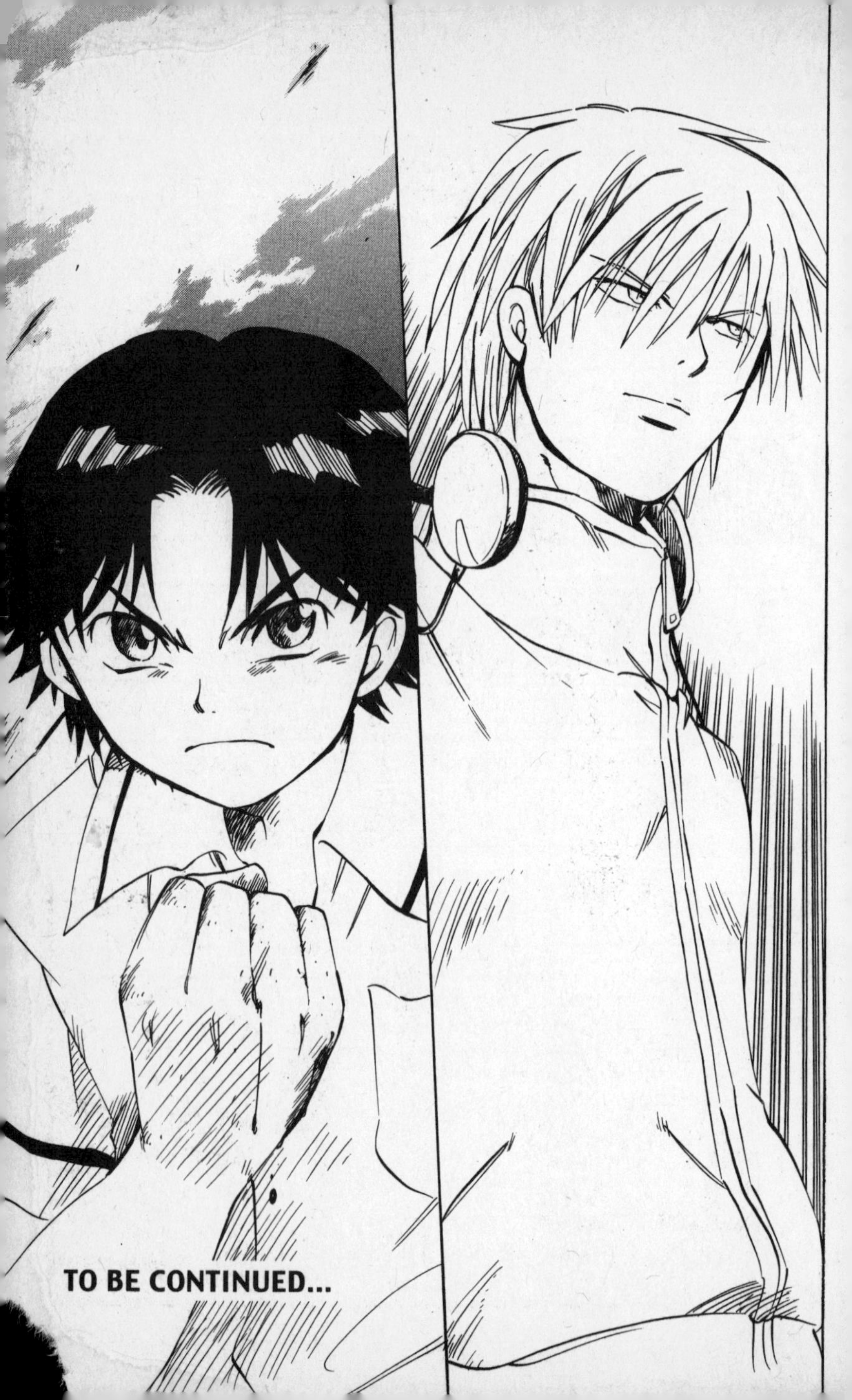
TO BE CONTINUED...

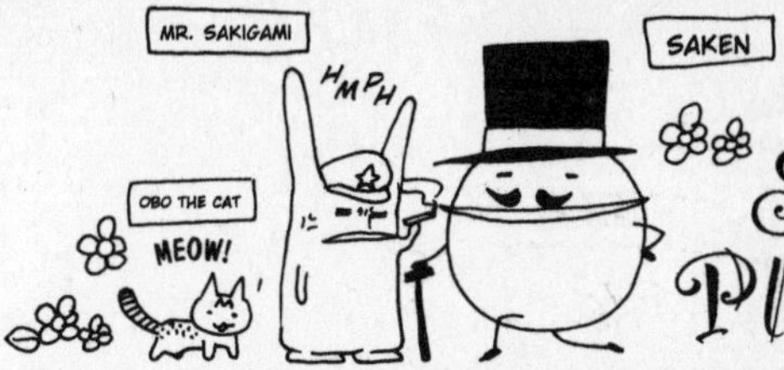
MR. SAKIGAMI
SAKEN
HMPH
OBO THE CAT
MEOW!

Saken Playhouse

BY SAKEN

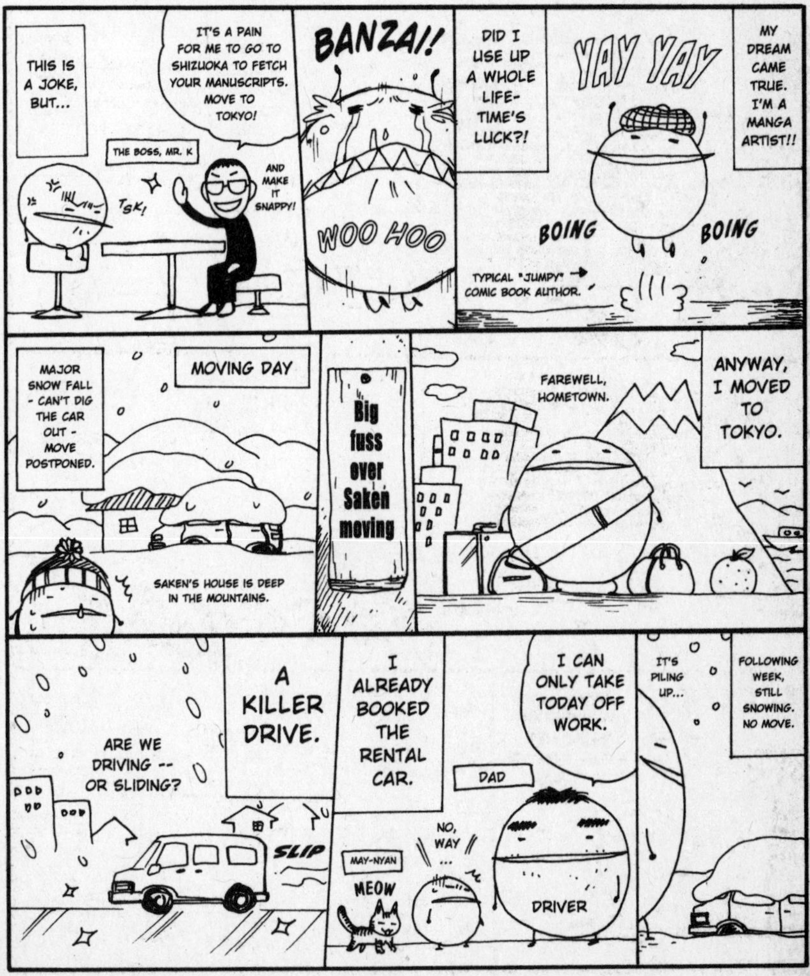
MY DREAM CAME TRUE. I'M A MANGA ARTIST!!
YAY YAY
DID I USE UP A WHOLE LIFE-TIME'S LUCK?!
BOING
BOING
TYPICAL "JUMPY" COMIC BOOK AUTHOR.
BANZAI!
WOO HOO
IT'S A PAIN FOR ME TO GO TO SHIZUOKA TO FETCH YOUR MANUSCRIPTS. MOVE TO TOKYO!
THE BOSS, MR. K
AND MAKE IT SNAPPY!
THIS IS A JOKE, BUT...
TSK!
ANYWAY, I MOVED TO TOKYO.
FAREWELL, HOMETOWN.
Big fuss over Saken moving
MOVING DAY
MAJOR SNOW FALL - CAN'T DIG THE CAR OUT - MOVE POSTPONED.
SAKEN'S HOUSE IS DEEP IN THE MOUNTAINS.
FOLLOWING WEEK, STILL SNOWING. NO MOVE.
IT'S PILING UP...
I CAN ONLY TAKE TODAY OFF WORK.
DAD
DRIVER
I ALREADY BOOKED THE RENTAL CAR.
NO, WAY ...
MAY-NYAN
MEOW
A KILLER DRIVE.
ARE WE DRIVING -- OR SLIDING?
SLIP

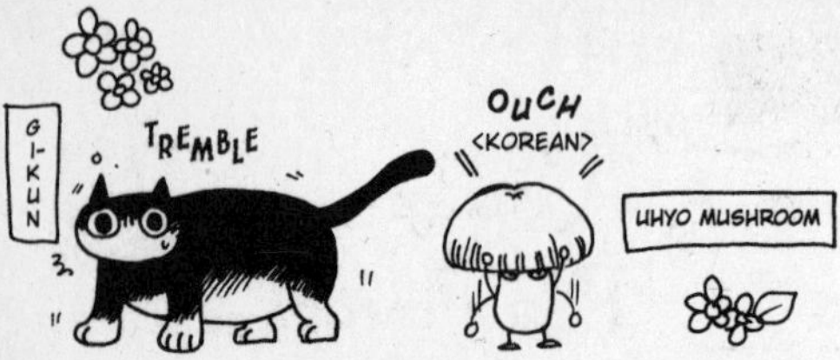
UHYO MUSHROOM
OUCH
<KOREAN>
TREMBLE
GI-KUN

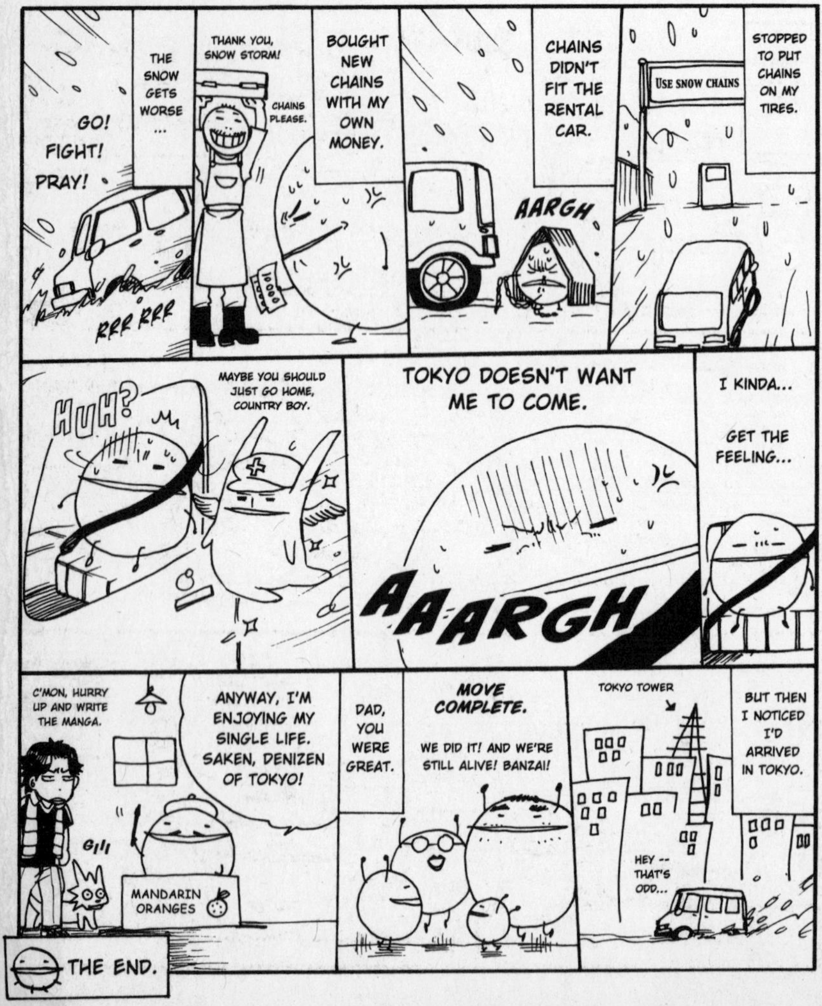
STOPPED TO PUT CHAINS ON MY TIRES.
USE SNOW CHAINS
CHAINS DIDN'T FIT THE RENTAL CAR.
AARGH
BOUGHT NEW CHAINS WITH MY OWN MONEY.
THANK YOU, SNOW STORM!
CHAINS PLEASE.
THE SNOW GETS WORSE...
GO! FIGHT! PRAY!
RRR RRR
I KINDA... GET THE FEELING...
TOKYO DOESN'T WANT ME TO COME.
AAARGH
MAYBE YOU SHOULD JUST GO HOME, COUNTRY BOY.
HUH?
BUT THEN I NOTICED I'D ARRIVED IN TOKYO.
TOKYO TOWER
HEY -- THAT'S ODD...
MOVE COMPLETE.
WE DID IT! AND WE'RE STILL ALIVE! BANZAI!
DAD, YOU WERE GREAT.
ANYWAY, I'M ENJOYING MY SINGLE LIFE. SAKEN, DENIZEN OF TOKYO!
C'MON, HURRY UP AND WRITE THE MANGA.
GI'I
MANDARIN ORANGES
THE END.

COMING NEXT VOLUME...

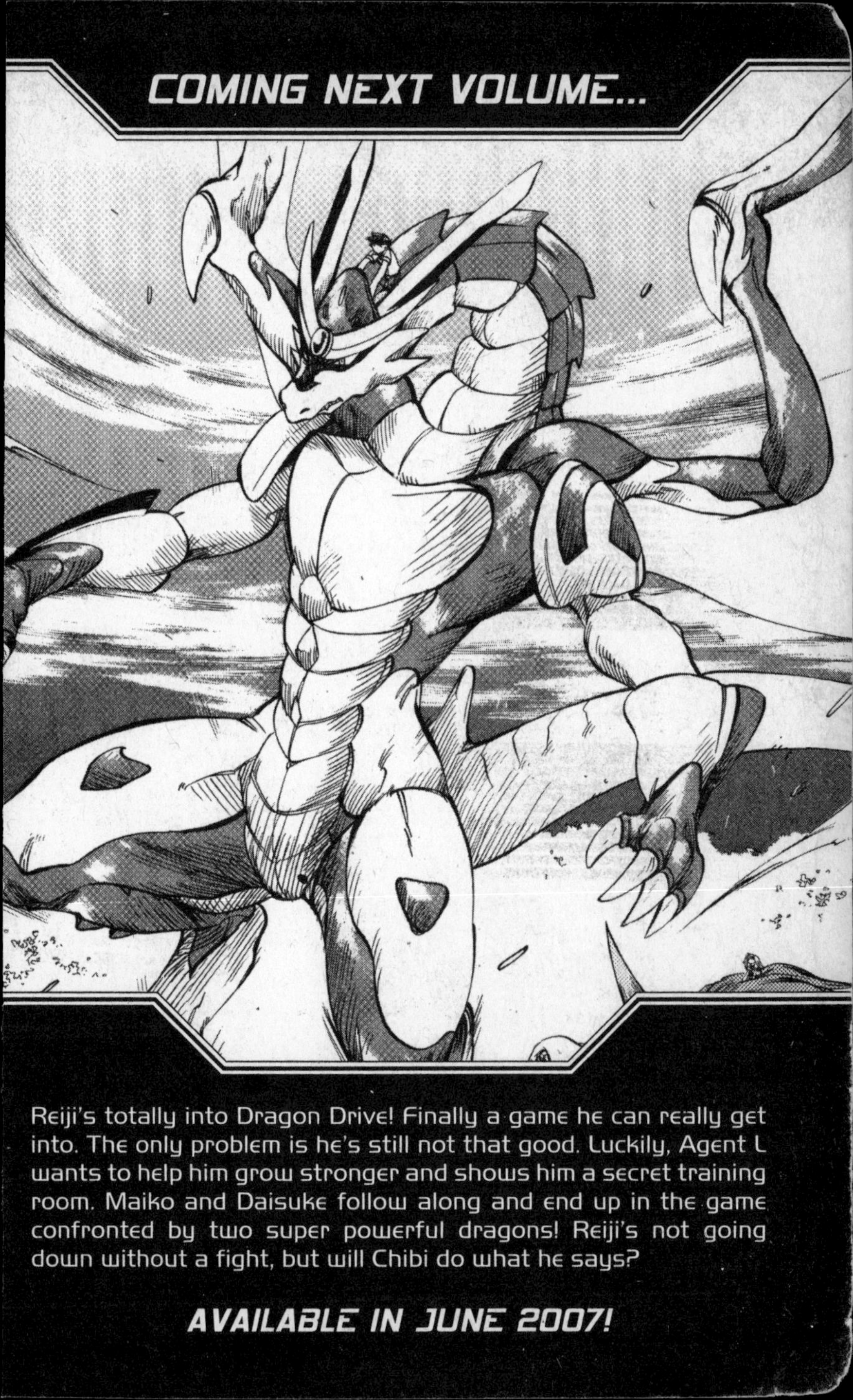

Reiji's totally into Dragon Drive! Finally a game he can really get into. The only problem is he's still not that good. Luckily, Agent L wants to help him grow stronger and shows him a secret training room. Maiko and Daisuke follow along and end up in the game confronted by two super powerful dragons! Reiji's not going down without a fight, but will Chibi do what he says?

AVAILABLE IN JUNE 2007!

NARUTO™

Manga on sale now!

$7.95

NARUTO 1

SHONEN JUMP GRAPHIC NOVEL
Story & Art by Masashi Kishimoto volume 1

Naruto is determined to become the greatest ninja ever!

SHONEN JUMP MANGA

Tell us what you think about SHONEN JUMP manga!

Our survey is now available online.
Go to: www.SHONENJUMP.com/mangasurvey

Help us make our product offering better!

THE REAL ACTION STARTS IN...

SHONEN JUMP
THE WORLD'S MOST POPULAR MANGA
www.shonenjump.com

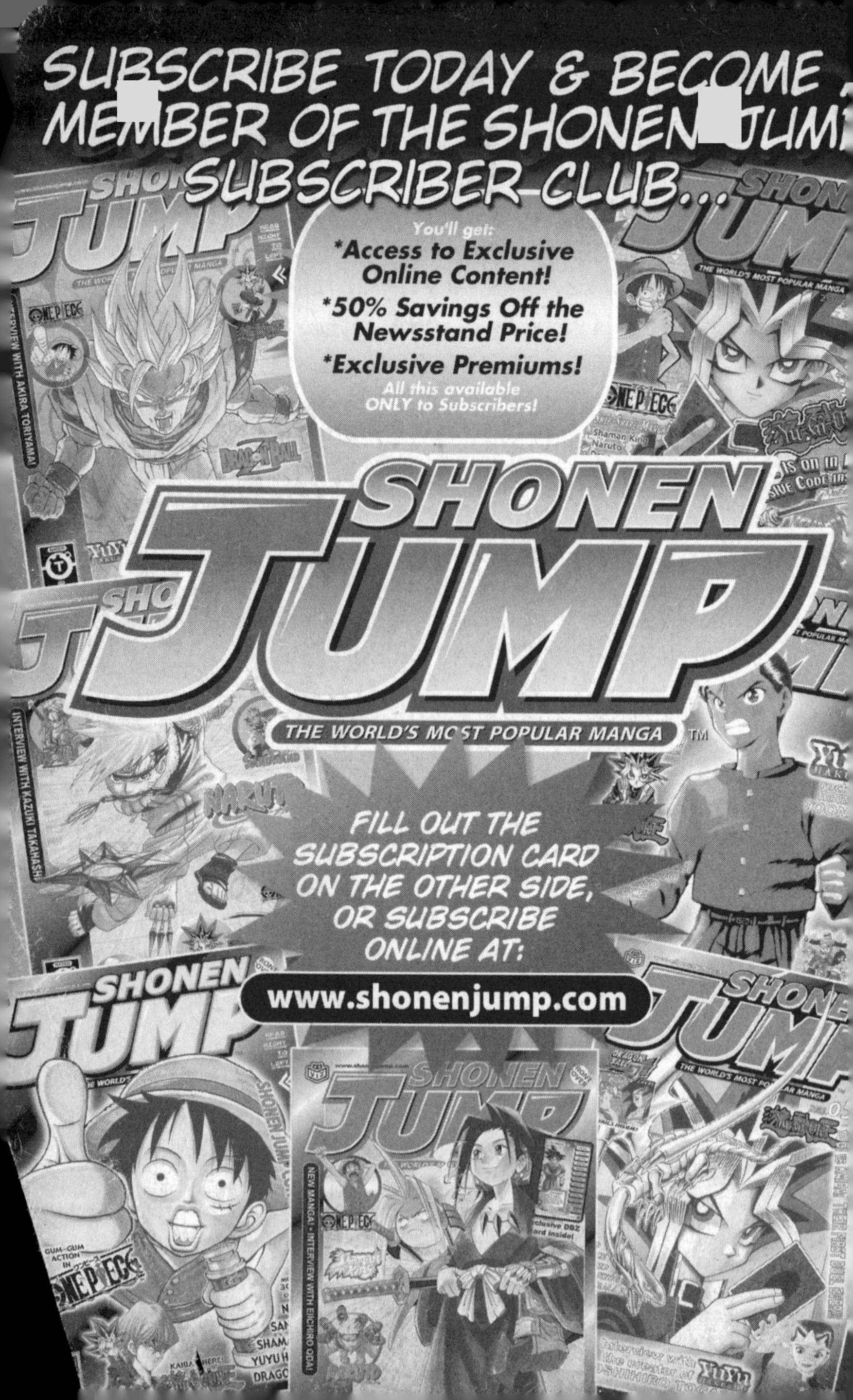
SUBSCRIBE TODAY & BECOME
MEMBER OF THE SHONEN JUM
SUBSCRIBER CLUB...
You'll get:
*Access to Exclusive Online Content!
*50% Savings Off the Newsstand Price!
*Exclusive Premiums!
All this available ONLY to Subscribers!
SHONEN JUMP
THE WORLD'S MOST POPULAR MANGA
TM
FILL OUT THE SUBSCRIPTION CARD ON THE OTHER SIDE, OR SUBSCRIBE ONLINE AT:
www.shonenjump.com